Generative AI's "Creative" Process in the Era of Privatisation of Knowledge

Generative AI's "Creative" Process in the Era of Privatisation of Knowledge

Reflections on the Social Function of Copyright Law and the EU Artificial Intelligence Act

By

Francesca Rotolo

BRILL | NIJHOFF

ISBN 978-90-04-50551-3
ISBN 978-90-04-73073-1 (PDF)
DOI https://doi.org/10.1163/9789004730731

Library of Congress Control Number: 2026935334

Brill Nijhoff and Koninklijke Brill BV are part of De Gruyter Brill.
www.degruyterbrill.com

Questions about General Product Safety Regulation: productsafety@degruyterbrill.com

To E., for enlightening me to always seek a "gentle kind of law"

Contents

SECTION 2
The State of the Art

SECTION 3
At the Core of the Input–Output Debates

Acknowledgments

I began working on the topic of this volume shortly before starting my PhD in Law, Market, and Person at Ca' Foscari University of Venice in late 2020, and just before the publication of the proposal for the EU AI Regulation in 2021. Since then, developments in EU and global AI law and Copyright Law have accompanied my studies day after day, month after month, novelty after novelty (and there have been many). Stitching everything together has been – and continues to be – a work of careful weaving that would not have been possible without the precious support I received from so many directions and from so many people throughout the experiences I was fortunate to encounter.

It certainly would not have been possible without the clear and gentle guidance of Professor Claudia Irti, who welcomed me into the doctoral program in Venice and encouraged me to move forward, allowing me to explore with trust while pursuing the purest form of freedom in the sciences and the arts. Nor would it have been possible without the valuable advice of Professor Barbara Pasa, with whom I first began exploring the subject during my years of professional activity as a lawyer, and on whom I can always rely for sincere words and steadfast support. Knowing this would be the fuel for even the most daunting enterprises.

It would not have been possible without the support of the mentors from my years in the Master's degree program at the Università degli Studi di Bari Aldo Moro, who opened me to the possibility of making research a part of my journey; nor without those at the DReDIS department of the IRJS at Université Paris 1 Panthéon-Sorbonne, who guided me in 2022 at the beginning of this path; and, finally, those at the CREATe Centre in Glasgow, who in 2025 offered me exceptional human support and a sharp, timely perspective on the subject of this manuscript.

Finally, it would not have been possible without the support of my large family, which has always provided me with the best training ground for rich and complex exchanges of viewpoints – "50 million", at least – and without my friends, colleagues and my "thought companions", with whom I am proud to share the longing to seek, always, in the midst of confusion and brutality, that which is bright, and clear, and just.

Introduction

The debate surrounding artificial intelligence (hereinafter also referred to as "AI") and the social, economic, and legal challenges posed by this evolving set of technologies has significantly intensified in recent years. One of the main drivers of this acceleration has been the increasing public awareness of AI's integration into daily life, especially through Internet of Things technologies[1] or the recent rise of generative AI tools such as DALL·E, Midjourney, LlaMA, ChatGPT, Grok, Claude, DeepSeek, etc.

With their capability of generating images, composing complex texts, solving mathematical problems, and creating stories, biographies, and the like, these systems have increasingly dispelled any lingering doubts that AI was not merely "coming" – as long anticipated, echoing the iconic "winter is coming" refrain from Game of Thrones – revealing it to be instead a present and tangible reality already.

What we now refer to with "AI" is the product of a long-standing synergy between the imagination of novelists, the passion of computer scientists, decades of research on algorithms, and the enduring fascination that technology has always held for humankind, in its timeless quest to transcend itself and become something more than human. However, whereas in the past AI innovations were often associated, in the public imagination, with the media-friendly domain of robotics, the true paradigm shift observed in recent years lies in the increasing applicability of AI technologies to everyday life, across recreational, professional, or domestic domains.

With particular regard to the cultural and (re)creative sectors, nearly a decade has passed since scholars, legal experts, and industry stakeholders began acknowledging the strategic relevance and economic significance of integrating AI systems into these domains. A symbolic milestone in this regard can be identified in October 2018, when the auction house Christie's was involved for the first time in the sale of the painting of the imaginary

1 For a comprehensive definition of the concept of the Internet of Things – a term first used by Kevin Ashton in 1999 to describe a set of technologies that enable any kind of object and/or apparatus to be connected to the Internet – see, among other references, Haller S, Karnouskos S and Schroth C, "The Internet of Things in an Enterprise Context" in John Domingue, Dieter Fensel and Paolo Traverso (eds), First Future Internet Symposium – FIS 2008 (LNCS 5468, Springer 2009), 14–28.

Note: This book, with particular reference to Chapter 4, §2 (from p. 69), Chapter 5 (from p. 81), and Chapter 7, §§3.2 and 5 (from pp. 149 and 167), has not been updated after September 2025.

 | HTTPS://DOI.ORG/10.1163/9789004730731-002

Edmond de Belamy,[2] created by an AI program of the French collective Obvious,[3] for US $432,500.00.

From that moment on, a substantial corpus of intellectual works across literature, music, sculpture, painting, and other fields – created more or less automatedly by AI systems – has permeated and influenced academic discourse globally. Such heterogeneous outputs (spanning digital artworks, musical pieces, and textual productions of varying complexity) tend to be appraised less for their artistic or cultural merit than for their commercial value, industrial relevance, and disruptive potential within their respective markets.[4]

The aim of this manuscript is to offer a critical reflection on the increasing use of AI in these domains. It does so by examining the role of law, and of copyright law in particular, in both responding to and shaping the challenges posed by these technologies, while also considering how such technologies are themselves transforming legal discourse. It further adopts a comparative approach across jurisdictions, with specific reference to the EU AI Act.[5]

The premises underlying this exploration are threefold.

First and foremost is the recognition of the geopolitical context in which the phenomenon of AI is unfolding: a world in which the digitalization and

---

2 See "A Collaboration Between Two Artists – One Human, One a Machine" (Christie's, 22 March 2023) <https://www.christies.com/en/stories/a-collaboration-between-two-artists-one-human-one-a-machine-0cd01f4e232f4279a525a446d60d4cd1> accessed 10 June 2025.

3 See the Guidelines of the Study Question "Copyright in artificially generated works" referred to by Jan Bernd Nordemann, "AIPPI: No copyright protection for AI works without human input, but related rights remain" (Kluwer Copyright Blog, 21 November 2019) <https://copyrightblog.kluweriplaw.com/2019/11/21/aippi-no-copyright-protection-for-ai-works-without-human-input-but-related-rights-remain/>, accessed 22 May 2025.

4 The Edmond de Belamy affair is just one example of this phenomenon. In this case, what sparked widespread astonishment was not so much the alleged artistic capability of the AI system, nor the fact that such a work had been sold (other portraits from the fictitious De Belamy family had already been sold, albeit at more modest prices), but rather the art market's ability to present the sale of the first AI-generated painting at auction as a landmark event. The high price achieved by the work primarily reflects the market's fascination with the new "creative" technique attributed to AI. See, on this point Bensamoun B and Farchy J, Intelligence artificielle et culture : mission CSPLA, rapport final (Conseil supérieur de la propriété littéraire et artistique, ministère de la Culture 27 January 2020) (French version), 24.

5 Regulation (EU) 2024/1689 of the European Parliament and of the Council of 13 June 2024 laying down harmonized rules on artificial intelligence and amending Regulations (EC) No 300/2008, (EU) No 167/2013, (EU) No 168/2013, (EU) 2018/858, (EU) 2018/1139 and (EU) 2019/2144 and Directives 2014/90/EU, (EU) 2016/797 and (EU) 2020/1828 (Artificial Intelligence Act) [2024] OJ L 2024/1689, 12.7.2024, see Chapter 5 for a more comprehensive analysis on the AI Act.

datafication[6] of every human interaction – whether political, social, or economic – have changed the rules of the game and acted as facilitators of the broader phenomenon of globalization. This global, digitalized, and datafied environment has given rise to new patterns of inequality, the emergence of "propertarianism" (*propriétarisme*),[7] and a new phase of capitalism characterized by the centrality of information as capital and of information networks as the primary means of production: the so-called knowledge capitalism.[8] At the same time, this is a world increasingly marked by the resurgence of new forms of nationalism,[9] which have emerged as a counterforce to globalization, fueling a deepening sense of crisis within Western democracies, particularly concerning two of their foundational values: freedom and solidarity.[10]

Second is the need to preserve an anthropocentric approach to the challenges posed by information and communication technologies (ICT), in alignment with the increasing centrality of the individual (the "person") in both national and European legal systems since the second half of the twentieth century, as well as with the objectives of the EU Digital Agenda,[11] without, however, disregarding the importance of collective interests, including the promotion of culture and the advancement of society as a whole.

Third and finally is the desirability of reimagining copyright law as a paradigm of an "inclusive" property model – one that not only safeguards the exclusive prerogatives of authors and other (copy)rights holders but also upholds the public's right to access creative works and serves the broader objective of

---

6 "Datafication renders a diverse range of information as machine-readable, quantifiable data for the purpose of aggregation and analysis. Datafication is also used as a term to describe a logic that sees things in the world as sources of data to be 'mined' for correlations or sold, and from which insights can be gained about human behavior and social issues. This term is often employed by scholars seeking to critique such logics and processes". See Southerton, C. (2022). Datafication. In: Schintler, L.A., McNeely, C.L. (eds) Encyclopedia of Big Data. Springer, Cham. <https://doi.org/10.1007/978-3-319-32010-6_332>.

7 Piketty T, Capitale e ideologia (trad Federico Ferrone, La nave di Teseo 2020).

8 Burton-Jones A, "The Transition to Knowledge Capitalism" in Alan Burton-Jones, *Knowledge Capitalism* (1st edn, Oxford University PressOxford 1999) <https://academic.oup.com/book/8553/chapter/154436851> accessed 9 August 2025.

9 See Luiza Jarovsky's newsletter "The New AI Nationalism", 15 July 2025, according to whom "As countries' economic, political, and legal priorities regarding AI become clearer, a new type of AI nationalism is emerging".

10 Harari YN, 21 lezioni per il XXI secolo (Bompiani 2019).

11 For example, the AI Act (n 5) argues for the need to govern the AI phenomenon having regard to the rights and freedoms of individuals; see also, before the AI Act, the European Parliament, *Report on Intellectual Property Rights for the Development of Artificial Intelligence Technologies* (A9-0176/2020, 2 October 2020) 7.

promoting culture, consistent with the ongoing process of the "constitutionalization of Intellectual Property Law".[12]

This discussion will lead to the recognition that the challenges arising from both the input and the output dimensions of the algorithmic creative process cannot be properly addressed without first adopting a clear position on the role and function of copyright – a debate that, it is here acknowledged, substantially predates the emergence of AI – and without a renewed systematization of copyright law, which AI has once again brought into focus, around its social function of promoting culture and fostering a pluralistic cultural environment. An attempt to operationalize the social function of copyright law will be made in the final part of this work, specifically by arguing for a teleological interpretation of core copyright concepts and mechanisms – such as (on the input side) the three-step test, exceptions and limitations, lawful access, and (on the output side) the very notions of "work" and "originality".

The motivations underlying this study are closely linked to the aim of advancing scholarship on the inherent tendency of generative AI – if left unregulated – to produce adverse outcomes in terms of privatization of knowledge, with far-reaching implications for society at large. These include, to put it starkly, a crisis of public discourse, the erosion of cultural pluralism, and the polarization of opinions, all of which have been increasingly emphasized by scholars in recent debates.[13]

In the face of these challenges, the role of law is particularly complex[14] with that of intellectual property law – and, more specifically, copyright law – being even more so. Indeed, legal scholars focusing on ICT have long been con-

12 Geiger C and Izyumenko E, "The Constitutionalization of Intellectual Property Law in the EU and the Funke Medien, Pelham and Spiegel Online Decisions of the CJEU: Progress, But Still Some Way to Go"! (2020) 51(3) International Review of Intellectual Property and Competition Law 282, Centre for International Intellectual Property Studies (CEIPI) Research Paper No 2019 09 <https://ssrn.com/abstract=3472852> or <http://dx.doi.org/10.2139/ssrn.3472852> accessed 9 August 2025.

13 Indeed, these risks, as is well known, have both a direct and indirect impact on the mechanisms underpinning liberal democracy, which, from the 1990s until at least the 2008 financial crisis, largely remained unchallenged as the principal ideological model of the Western world and a core element of its identity. Harari (n 10).

14 Zuboff, in her analysis of surveillance capitalism (Shoshana Zuboff, *The Age of Surveillance Capitalism: The Fight for a Human Future at the New Frontier of Power* (Profile Books 2019)), frequently mentions that it is built on "lawlessness". In her view, markets based on data exist beyond the reach of traditional laws and operate according to their own rules. While this perspective has merit, it overlooks the extent to which these companies rely on the law for their power. Indeed, the role of law in shaping and reinforcing private power in the information age cannot be understated. As Kapczynski

cerned with the adequacy of existing doctrinal and regulatory frameworks for addressing new forms of information, algorithms, technical protocols, and online behavior. They have persistently questioned how the law should respond to the transformations occurring around it.

For some, law operates as an impediment to the development of ICT – conceived as technologies of freedom, capable of addressing humanity's most urgent challenges – rather than as a facilitator of their progress. On this view, the recurring complaint is that the law, unable to move at the speed of human thought, should stop undermining technology's potential and instead "either get with the program or get out of the way".[15] Other scholars take the opposite position, contending that such technologies pose significant threats to the rule of law and therefore require robust regulatory intervention; they stress the need to preserve legal structures in order to avoid a descent into social and political disorder.[16]

This manuscript, however, proceeds from the premise that neither of these positions is entirely satisfactory, since neither technology nor law can be conceived as neutral or monolithic entities. Instead, both must be situated within the broader context from which they emerge, and their evaluation as good or bad tools must be assessed accordingly.[17]

(Kapczynski A, "The Law of Informational Capitalism" (2020) 129 Yale Law Journal 1465) points out, private power in the informational economy has not emerged from a legal vacuum; rather, it has been shaped by a legal system that has prioritized efficiency, market supremacy, and innovation at the expense of public interests. Law has facilitated this transformation by enabling the creation of de facto property regimes in both data and algorithms, despite neither being formally classified as property. In the past, assetless companies like Uber and Airbnb have thrived by exploiting laws that facilitate the accumulation of immaterial capital. Historians of capitalism and neoliberalism have emphasized how legal systems not only enable markets but also protect them from democratic challenges that could alter their trajectory. See Cohen JE, *Between Truth and Power: The Legal Constructions of Informational Capitalism* (Oxford University Press 2019) 44.

15 Cohen (n 14).

16 Ibid.

17 Recognizing that neither law nor technology are monolithic force, but rather embedded within a broader and more complex socioeconomic and political context, is essential to the purpose of this manuscript. It underscores the critical importance of a conscious and deliberate legal regulation in the face of the economic and political structures driving contemporary transformations – while also asserting the inherent complexity of law, and more broadly, of the political, as opposed to the reductive tendencies of New institutional economics, see Klein PG, "New Institutional Economics" (July 1998) <https://ssrn.com/abstract=115811> accessed 9 August 2025. In this regard, see the reflections of Resta G ("La comparazione tra diritto e storia economica: rileggendo Karl Polanyi" in Brutti M and Somma A (eds), Diritto: storia e comparazione. Nuovi propositi per un

First, the critical challenges surrounding the crisis of the rule of law, democracy, and public discourse do exist and are real and pressing; however, they do not stem from the technologies themselves, but from their entanglement with the broader sociopolitical and economic context, including, for instance, the business models they sustain. As recognized in the scholarship on technology and society, technological developments do not follow predetermined or value-neutral trajectories;[18] instead, they evolve in ways that reflect the specific priorities, interests, and worldviews of those who design and deploy them. This is also true of generative AI: this technology encapsulates both constructive and disruptive capacities across multiple domains, including the cultural one, as a result of the business models within which it operates. Much like the Internet – once celebrated as an inevitable servant of truth and a "technology of freedom" promoting political and economic self-determination, yet later revealing a far more complex and ambivalent reality – generative AI manifests a similar duality. While frequently depicted as a democratizing force for creativity, it also entails significant risks, and its impact ultimately depends on how it is integrated into the wider sociopolitical and economic structures that frame its use.

At the same time, law – and, similarly, intellectual property law – cannot be regarded in monolithic terms as either inherently beneficial or detrimental, since it operates as a key locus for the exercise and negotiation of political and economic power.[19] Its role in relation to technology therefore resists generalization. Whether law appears as an enabler of innovation or as an obstacle to it (on the assumption that it cannot keep pace with technological change and the demands of the ICT industry) varies depending on how regulatory responses are articulated in each context: on the rights they establish, the

---

binomio antico (Max Planck Institute for European Legal History 2018) 463), who warns against the uncritical acceptance and generalization of certain pillars of economic neo-institutionalism when interpreting contemporary reality and the role of law within it. Indeed, while the theoretical foundations of neoclassical economics may offer valuable tools for understanding reality – particularly when examining economic systems and institutional frameworks rooted in liberal market economies – they "collapse" (or at the very least demand critical re-evaluation) when analysis shifts, diachronically, to historical periods predating the Industrial Revolution and the advent of modern capitalism (such as when the Magna Carta is interpreted as a Coasian bargain, or feudal serfdom is reconstructed as an "efficient contractual agreement" justified by underlying transaction costs), or, synchronically, to cultural contexts external to the Western.

18 With reference to AI, Crawford notices that "artificial intelligence as we know it depends entirely on a much wider set of political and social structures", see Crawford K, *Atlas of AI: Power, Politics, and the Planetary Costs of Artificial Intelligence* (Yale University Press 2021).

19 Cohen (n 14) 1–2.

scope of protection they confer, and the normative justifications that underpin them.

In light of the foregoing, critically examining both the use of AI in the cultural and creative sectors and the structural forces underpinning their adoption is essential to addressing the core question of this study: what kind of copyright law might mitigate the risks arising from an uncritical acceptance of the (only seemingly) inevitable privatization of knowledge implied by the architecture and use of AI technologies. The ultimate objective is to determine how the use of generative AI in the creative sector can be most effectively regulated so as to foster a democratic and sustainable development of this technology.

SECTION 1

The Technological "Paradigm Shift"

CHAPTER 1

The Era of Knowledge Capitalism

1 The Fourth Industrial Revolution

As Harari observed, we live in an era in which "a plethora of mystery words unstoppably punctuate TED conferences, government think tanks, and forums on new technologies": globalization, blockchain, genetic engineering, artificial intelligence, machine learning – concepts whose actual scope and impact, even in 2018, were assumed to be largely unknown to "most people in Birmingham, Istanbul, St. Petersburg, and Mumbai".[20]

The recent rapid acceleration of technological development has fostered a widespread sense of disorientation, which has become even more pervasive in the face of AI. For over thirty years, intermittent waves of optimism, nihilistic disillusionment, and a persistent sense of impending catastrophe have cyclically shaped the discourse of politicians, legislators, legal practitioners, and other stakeholders confronting the challenges posed by so-called "new" technologies – whose applications have continued to evolve in unprecedented ways, thus still justifying the use of the adjective "new", even if they are no longer new in themselves.

As is well known, early analyses of this phenomenon were often optimistic, and influential voices argued that digital advancements would enable greater freedom and abundance by harnessing the non-rival nature of information, human creativity, and the collective intelligence of people. Digital networks were widely celebrated for fostering collaboration and new forms of creative production, while information technologies were seen as tools that could provide – if not outright guarantee – a more empowering workplace and higher living standards for all.

However, today's perspective on these technological developments has darkened considerably, shaped by a series of recent revelations[21] and by growing fears that the new capabilities of information and communication technologies are reshaping fundamental aspects of everyone's life – including their

20 Harari (n 10), translation by the Author.

21 Such as news related to the fact that Facebook has conducted experiments to manipulate users' emotional states; Cambridge Analytica exploited surreptitiously harvested Facebook data to influence elections; some independent trolls and bots, as well as some state-sponsored ones, deliberately spread misinformation and sow discord on social media, see Kapczynski (n 14) 1462–1463.

 | HTTPS://DOI.ORG/10.1163/9789004730731-003

private sphere and their public participation in a democratic society.[22] Increasing concern has also emerged over the erosion of human relationships, sleep, attention spans, and even the very essence of humanity, driven by compulsive interactions with computers, apps, and social media.[23]

Over time, amidst the disorientation provoked by these changes, it became increasingly important, as has been suggested, "to understand the overall topography" of what has often been described as "a jungle-like" phenomenon – that of AI, – "lest one inadvertently stumble into quicksand or wander over a cliff".[24] Ethical, legal, political, and technological considerations surrounding AI – together with the challenge of identifying the most appropriate regulatory model – have consequently become central to many contemporary discourses around the world.

Yet fully grasping the multifaceted nature of AI – its societal impacts, its legal implications (not least for copyright), the risks it carries, and the motivations behind the European Union's adoption of the AI Act[25] – requires situating it within the geopolitical and economic framework in which it has emerged and thrived.

No account of these dimensions would be complete without acknowledging the broader historical and economic context in which it has evolved.

In this regard, it is worth noting that AI operates within an increasingly globalized and interconnected world – a landscape shaped by an unprecedented web of relationships, marked by the intensified mobility of people, goods, and services, and by the deepening internationalization of economic activity.[26]

As is known, globalization has historically been driven by the commercial, migratory, and financial integration of the world. A process traceable to the sixteenth century, it reached its peak and took on an entirely new dimension during the digital and hyper-capitalist globalization of the 1990s–2020s,[27] ulti-

22 Among other concerns, research suggests that engagement-driven algorithms contribute to political polarization and employers increasingly use digital technologies to monitor and manipulate workers.

23 Kapczynski (n 14) 1462–1463.

24 Cohen (n 14) 1–2.

25 Regulation (EU) 2024/1689 of the European Parliament and of the Council of 13 June 2024 laying down harmonized rules on artificial intelligence and amending Regulations (EC) No 300/2008, (EU) No 167/2013, (EU) No 168/2013, (EU) 2018/858, (EU) 2018/1139 and (EU) 2019/2144 and Directives 2014/90/EU, (EU) 2016/797 and (EU) 2020/1828 (Artificial Intelligence Act) [2024] OJ L 2024/1689, 12.7.2024.

26 Alpa G, Bonell MJ, L Corapi, L Moccia, V Zeno-Zencovich and A Zoppini, Diritto privato comparato (Laterza 2012) 3.

27 Piketty (n 7).

mately becoming one of the defining factors shaping the current challenges of regulating the ICT worldwide.

A crucial factor in the geopolitical, economic, and technological transformation of recent decades of globalization has been the Internet, as the origin and cradle of digital technologies. As the driving force behind the so-called "fourth industrial revolution",[28] the Internet paved the way for the era of AI and, even before that, for the Internet of Things and big data.[29] As has been observed, the unprecedented levels of cultural, socioeconomic, and political-ideological interdependence among different global areas characteristic of this era have been driven by the instantaneous distribution of texts, images, and sounds made possible by the Internet and digital technologies.[30]

This "widespread availability of electronic storage media, specifically mainframe computers, servers, and server farms"[31] has ultimately catalyzed a technological "paradigm shift"[32] that is reshaping our present reality.

Much like the aftermath of the Industrial Revolution in the nineteenth century – when new production processes turned many landowners into entrepreneurs and peasants into factory workers, reshaping consumer behavior and societal structures[33] – the digital revolution has similarly redefined economic and social dynamics on a global scale.

In the new landscape shaped by the digital revolution, the Internet and digital technologies have in fact radically transformed market structures, production organization, and labor relations, progressively introducing new public (international organizations) and private actors (big tech companies) into the social, cultural, and legal fabric.

---

28 Ross P and Maynard K, "Towards a 4th Industrial Revolution" (2021) 13 (3) Intelligent Buildings International 159 <https://doi.org/10.1080/17508975.2021.1873625> accessed 22 May 2025; Floridi L, The Fourth Revolution: On the Impact of Information and Communication Technologies (Oxford University Press 2014); Floridi L, La quarta rivoluzione. Come l'infosfera sta trasformando il mondo (Milano 2017) 185.

29 For a comprehensive analysis of the intersections between big data and law, see, *inter alias* Ghidini G, Olivieri G and Falce V, "Informazione e Big Data tra innovazione e concorrenza" in Quaderni Romani di Diritto Commerciale (Giuffrè 2018); Gambino AM and Prosperetti E, "Proprietà intellettuale nei sistemi di big data e nell'uso delle tecnologie di Intelligenza artificiale" in Giordano R, Panzarola A, Police A, Preziosi S and Proto M (eds), Il diritto nell'era digitale. Persona, Mercato, Amministrazione, Giustizia (Giuffrè 2022).

30 Piketty (n 7) 741–745.

31 Gitelman L (ed), *"Raw Data" Is an Oxymoron* (MIT Press 2013) 8.

32 Harari (n 10).

33 Quarta A, Non-proprietà. Teoria e prassi dell'accesso ai beni (Edizioni Scientifiche Italiane 2016) 54.

As these transformations unfolded, an ongoing discourse involving society, academia, and several stakeholders has emerged, accompanied by growing efforts to identify the "best way" to regulate and govern these technologies. Although the geopolitical landscape is evolving rapidly and continuously, it is striking that the proliferation of such debates has recently crystallized into the recognition of distinct regulatory frameworks emerging across three key global blocs: the United States, China, and the European Union. These range from the fundamental-rights-centered model of the European Union to the market-driven paradigm of the United States and the state-centric approach of China.[34]

A brief reflection on their broader political and economic philosophies suffices to convey the extent of this regulatory divergence. The US model has historically prioritized the free flow of information and emphasized the role of private technology companies as central actors in the digital economy. China, by contrast, advances a model of "cyber sovereignty", characterized by extensive state control over data and digital infrastructure. The European Union occupies an intermediate position between these two approaches, favoring a regulatory framework that places individual rights and data protection at its core.[35]

It is in this context that the development of AI took shape: a process that, far from being solely driven by a "neutral pursuit" of technological progress, has primarily resulted from specific, deliberate economic choices with far-reaching consequences across all socioeconomic sectors. Organizations like OpenAI, with their remarkable transformation – from being initially founded as a nonprofit entity ("an independent charity committed to safety and transparency") to becoming, within just eight years, a multibillion-dollar, market-dominating for-profit corporation[36] – illustrate how the technological development of such tools is frequently and inextricably intertwined with broader economic considerations that extend well beyond the mere idea of providing a service to a community.

---

34 Bradford A, Digital Empires. The Global Battle to Regulate Technology (Oxford University Press, 2023).

35 Musoni M, Karkare P, Teevan C, and Domingo E, Global Approaches to Digital Sovereignty: Competing Definitions and Contrasting Policy (ECDPM Discussion Paper No 344, May 2023) <https://ecdpm.org/work/global-approaches-digital-sovereignty-competing-definitions-and-contrasting-policy> accessed 22 May 2025.

36 *Musk v Altman*, Case No 4:24-cv-04722-YGR (ND Cal, 15 April 2025) Statement of Recent Decision, ECF No 157.

OpenAI's trajectory mirrors that of other digital giants such as Google, Apple, and Facebook, which had emerged long before the rise of the now-renowned ChatGPT company, yet within the same geopolitical, economic, and ideological framework. The business models they designed, as well as the tools they developed to respond to the growing emphasis on individualization – a notion to which we will return shortly, and a defining feature of what sociologists have termed the "second" and "third modernity"[37] – were guided by the explicit intent to respond to economic imperatives. This is a consideration that might appear predictable, yet one that should not be taken for granted, considering how the advocacy-oriented guise that these companies came to assume[38] was often invoked to legitimize early practices operating in legally grey territory.

Notably, the concept of individualization refers to the process by which individuals come to see themselves as unique beings – not merely as the inheritors of preordained life paths or fixed social roles, but as active protagonists in constructing their own identities and futures. It is a model of life that enshrines the right – but also imposes the responsibility – to choose one's own trajectory and personal characteristics.

Individualization was precisely the gateway through which Google – by identifying and exploiting the growing demand for personalized digital experiences – evolved into a dominant market actor and a key player in the development and normalization of "surveillance" practices within the emerging digital paradigm.[39] More specifically, as has been argued, Google based its activities on harnessing online "data exhaust" to transform its well-known search engine into a recursive learning system capable of continuously refining search results. The company recognized that online traces functioned as a "broad sensor of human behavior" which, when aggregated and analyzed, could yield powerful insights. By incorporating data on website links, click-through rates, and user interests into its PageRank algorithm, Google was able to deliver search results increasingly aligned with individual expectations; an approach that was soon extended to other products, including spell-check, translation, and voice recognition services. Apple, too, exploited this cultural shift and the economic advantages deriving from offering a more personalized and less "mass-market" consumer experience to its users, in order to build its empire: its breakthrough with the iPod lay precisely in its ability to satisfy the growing drive for individualization by allowing users for the first time to curate their own music libraries.[40]

---

37 Zuboff (n 14).

38 It is the so-called "advocacy-oriented capitalism", see Kapczynski (n 14) 1462–1463.

39 Zuboff (n 14).

40 Ibid, 38 ff.

As observed above, it is within this broader context that AI emerged – exploiting, in its turn, the growing demand for individualization, which culminated in the development of AI tools such as ChatGPT, Midjourney, and DALL·E. These tools have been heralded – not least by the firms that produce them –[41] as vehicles for the "democratization" of access to creative expression, as well as to cultural and recreational production. Such technologies enable even individuals without technical expertise or artistic training to generate creative content "from the comfort of their own homes".[42] This has reinforced the perception of a more personalized mode of production tailored to individual needs, in line with the broader logic of individualization – an aspect that the companies behind popular generative AI tools have clearly recognized and strategically leveraged to advance both their models and business strategies.

The logic underpinning these innovations closely resembles that of earlier digital giants and suggests that vast domains of knowledge, culture, and information may be progressively privatized under the guise of offering more personalized content. While digital technologies and AI undoubtedly offer significant opportunities, the prevailing narrative should not obscure the underlying economic structures that shape these tools and their applications. If left unexamined, the "unseen" logics embedded in these systems risk producing unintended consequences, including the erosion of foundational principles underpinning contemporary legal systems and democratic societies.

2 Information Society, Data-Driven Economy, and Knowledge Capitalism

The development of AI has often been framed within what has been termed a "data-driven society", "data-driven economy", and "knowledge-driven economy". These concepts have been useful in emphasizing the central role of information, data, and knowledge in contemporary socioeconomic dynamics, especially as digitalization has placed the infosphere at the heart of these

41 Othman A, "Democratizing Creativity: The Rise of Generative AI in Digital Art and Storytelling" (November 2024) <https://www.researchgate.net/publication/385710773_Democratizing_Creativity_The_Rise_of_Generative_AI_in_Digital_Art_and_Storytelling> doi:10.13140/RG.2.2.11126.10563 accessed 10 June 2025.

42 The expression is a reference to the term "Bedroom Producers" as used by Rauh Ortega AA, "Under-the-Radar" Electronic Dance Musicians: Opportunities and Challenges with Digital Communication Technologies (PhD thesis, University of Leeds 2018) <https://etheses.whiterose.ac.uk/21375/> accessed 9 August 2025.

processes. However, they fall short of capturing the full complexity of current debates surrounding AI systems and their broader implications.

Indeed, the notion of an "information society"[43] and that of a "data-driven society"[44] have undoubtedly played a pivotal role in illustrating how the flow of information now permeates virtually every facet of human life. This constant flow functions as a continuous multiplier of the "datafication" of socio-economic relations, marking the transformation of ICT from mere communication tools into a fundamental force reshaping reality[45] – giving rise to a world where "what is real is informational, and what is informational is real".[46]

Yet, while these terms help describe the broader social and geopolitical context in which digital technologies operate, they fail to adequately capture the specific economic structures underpinning this transformation, which are essential to the present analysis.

The term "data-driven economy" may help to bridge this conceptual gap. However, even this term remains insufficient. While contemporary power struggles are indeed centered on data, their implications extend well beyond – into the broader domain of knowledge itself.

A more appropriate framework, therefore, would need to reflect this shift. The concept of a "knowledge-driven economy" may serve as a useful reference point, as it underscores the centrality of knowledge as a key economic asset and driving force behind innovation, productivity, and competitiveness in the digital age. However, it too remains inadequate, as it fails to fully capture a critical dimension of the context in which AI is evolving: its entrenchment not merely within a broad economic structure, but specifically within capitalism.

The development, distribution, and deployment of AI are indeed deeply embedded in an accumulation strategy that both reflects and reinforces the logics of capitalism – concentrating resources and power in the hands of a few dominant market actors.

---

43 Webster F, *Theories of the Information Society* (2nd edn, Routledge 2002).

44 By way of example, Pentland A, "The Data-Driven Society" (2013) 309 *Scientific American* 78, doi:10.1038/scientificamerican1013-78.; Henke N et al, *The Age of Analytics: Competing in a Data-Driven World* (McKinsey & Company 2016) <https://www.mckinsey.com/business-functions/mckinsey-analytics/our-insights/the-age-of-analytics-competing-in-a-data-driven-world> accessed 22 May 2025; Amanda Lee, "Towards Informatic Personhood: Understanding Contemporary Subjects in a Data-Driven Society" (2019) *Information, Communication & Society* 1, doi:10.1080/1369118X.2019.1637446.

45 Sica S and D'Antonio V, "La commodification dei dati personali nella data driven society" in Stanzione P (ed), I "Poteri privati" delle piattaforme e le nuove frontiere della privacy (Giappichelli 2022) 129.

46 Floridi, La quarta rivoluzione (n 28) 185.

In the age of AI, this concentration of power manifests in a specific form of capitalism, characterized by the increasing commodification of knowledge and its consolidation among a small number of powerful entities. This dynamic entails a significant redistribution of power, which is gradually shifting away from individuals and toward corporations and other big market players.

Thus, as further elaborated below, a more precise term for capturing this reality seems to be "knowledge capitalism": an economic system in which control over knowledge has become the primary locus for the exercise of economic and political power.

2.1 Capital Accumulation and Private Ownership of the Means of Production

Capitalism does not constitute a monolithic system. It is indeed inherently unstable and liable to morphological change, yet it remains constrained by some binding factor, be it the available labor force, as in Classical economics, or natural resources. It originated in Western Europe during the modern era, following the enclosure movement and the dissolution of feudalism. However, historical narratives of this transition are often presented through a teleological interpretation, treating capitalism as "the natural realization of ever-present tendencies".[47]

At the risk of oversimplifying a topic that would deserve far more extensive treatment, it is important to acknowledge, before delving into the notion of (knowledge) capitalism, that today, a wide variety of institutional frameworks regulate economic functioning and evolution. In this regard, Screpanti has shown that different property rights regimes and accumulation governance structures can exist, often even coexisting and operating simultaneously within a given economy. The former determines how wealth and surplus value are distributed, while the latter refers to the institutional mechanisms governing the use of surplus value to sustain capital accumulation.[48] Indeed, a property rights regime is a system of normative, transactional, and behavioral institutions that regulate the distribution of wealth and surplus value. Specifically, it defines which social actors are entitled to acquire property rights and establishes the rules governing their transfer.

Three primary types of property rights regimes have been identified: concentrated private property, diffused private property, and state prop-

47 Pre-Marxian accounts frequently described the evolution of capitalism as the emergence of a "commercial society" that was not ordered by the state but rather by a form of natural or divine law, see Kapczynski (n 14) 1481.

48 Screpanti E, "Capitalist Forms and the Essence of Capitalism" (1999) 6 Review of International Political Economy 1, 2.

erty.[49] Among these, concentrated private property regimes concentrate wealth in the hands of a specific class (the bourgeoisie), excluding the working class from property ownership. This system, characteristic of capitalism during the time of Smith and Marx, creates conditions for exploitation by compelling workers to sell their labor under the authority of those who own the means of production.[50] By contrast, diffused private property is more prevalent in contemporary capitalism, particularly in advanced economies. Although capital remains highly concentrated,[51] an increasing number of individuals have gained access to wealth, either directly as shareholders or indirectly through financial instruments such as investment funds and pension funds. This system integrates a broader segment of society into wealth ownership, even though the underlying mechanisms of surplus value extraction remain largely unchanged.

That said, variations in the combinations of property rights regimes and accumulation governance structures account for the differences among the diverse expressions of capitalism. The classical theory has conceptualized a "commonsense view" of it that broadly aligns with the perspectives of classical economists, according to which capitalism is an economic system in which control of production and the allocation of real and financial resources are based on private ownership of the means of production. In line with this view, certain fundamental characteristics are consistent across its different manifestations.[52]

---

49 Screpanti (n 48).

50 Notably, an internal hierarchy is indispensable for surplus value extraction within capitalist production. Not only is this hierarchy present across all capitalist systems, but it also constitutes a fundamental structure of capitalism itself, as it establishes the power dynamics that allow capitalists to direct labor activity and sustain exploitation (Screpanti (n 48) 3–5).

51 Wolff EN, *Top Heavy: The Increasing Inequality of Wealth in America and What Can Be Done About It* (The New Press 1995).

52 One of them is the centrality of exchange relations in structuring economic interactions. Karl Marx and his intellectual successors were the first to describe capitalism as "modern societies in which the majority of the population meets its needs through specialized production in a complex division of labor determined by commercial exchange", see Grewal DS, "The Legal Constitution of Capitalism" in Boushey H, DeLong JB and Steinbaum M (eds), After Piketty: The Agenda for Economics and Inequality (Harvard University Press 2017)) 471, 475. In a capitalist system, all economic relations take the form of exchange transactions between legally recognized individuals who are "free and equal" in their contractual capacity: both workers and producers basically "depend on the market" for access to the means of production. Also, the appropriation of surplus relies primarily on the "purely 'economic' mechanisms of the market" rather than through "extra-economic" means of appropriation – such as direct coercion via military, political,

Among them, particularly relevant to the present analysis is that (i) property rights regimes are grounded in private ownership; and (ii) capitalism is driven by the imperative of capital valorization and accumulation, with the surplus extracted from production directed toward capital accumulation – the prime mover of production[53] – ensuring that investment decisions remain in the hands of those who own and control capital, thereby reinforcing existing power structures and perpetuating systemic inequalities.

Seen from this perspective, capitalism is intrinsically linked to what has been termed "propertarianism":[54] a political ideology that emerged in the eighteenth century, well before the advent of large-scale industry and international finance, and centers on the absolute protection of private property rights, initially conceived as a universal entitlement, independent of traditional, status-based inequalities. Even more. As Piketty has observed, the form of capitalism that emerged in the late twentieth and early twenty-first centuries, which they term "hypercapitalism",[55] can be seen as an evolution of "propertarianism" in the age of digital technologies,[56] increasingly extending the boundaries of private property and wealth accumulation beyond traditional forms of ownership and across national borders.[57]

2.2 Knowledge Capitalism

Following the technological paradigm shift brought about by the fourth digital revolution, the new form of propertarianism has increasingly centered around information, data, and knowledge itself. This shift signals a transition from an industrial capitalist society to a new phase of capitalism in which information constitutes the primary form of capital, and information networks function as

---

or judicial power – which were historically used by feudal lords to extract surplus labor from peasants. Kapczynski (n 14) 1480. Another defining characteristic is the role of the employment contract, which represents the most significant relational contract in capitalist production. In fact, the capitalistic framework excludes forms of hierarchical dependency such as personal bondage, feudal obligations, or marital authority, establishing a system where interactions are only defined by legally enforceable agreements. These contracts only formalize the worker's obligation to obey within the labor process but also establish the legal and social authority of the capitalist firm to govern labor. While this authority is not absolute – being limited by laws, customs, and contractual provisions – it remains essential for the exploitation of labor within production Screpanti (n 48) 24.

53 Ibid, 22–23.

54 Piketty (n 7) 185–187.

55 Ibid.

56 Ibid.

57 Ibid.

the main means of production.[58] The most significant manifestations of this transformation include the well-known phenomena of the increasing privatization of knowledge and consequent patrimonialization of public spaces,[59] as well as the expansion of exclusive rights, including in the sector of intellectual property.[60]

This transformation does not merely represent a variation within the classical conception of capitalism but rather signals the emergence of a distinct new form of it. Indeed, the paradigm shift toward what has been termed "Information Capitalism",[61] "Informational Capitalism",[62] "Cognitive Capitalism",[63] or "Knowledge Capitalism"[64] reflects the increasing centrality of information within capitalist frameworks, particularly in the context of globalization and rapid technological development.

2.2.1 The "Knowledge Society"

The choice to use the term knowledge capitalism in this analysis, rather than other similar expressions, such as those just mentioned, stems from the intention to explicitly refer to a comprehensive notion of knowledge – one that encompasses not only data and information but also the value that can be extracted from them. This understanding aligns with the so-called DIKW hierarchy,[65] which positions knowledge above data and information, and just

58 Tirino M, "Il capitalismo informazionale nella società delle reti. Evoluzione e critica della teoria sociale di Manuel Castells" in Pendenza M, Romania V, Ricotta G, Iannone R and Susca E (eds), Capitalismo e teoria sociologica (FrancoAngeli 2019) 105.

59 Resta G, "La privatizzazione della conoscenza e la promessa dei beni comuni: riflessioni sul caso 'Myriad Genetics'" (2011) Rivista critica del diritto privato 281; Resta G, "La privatizzazione del patrimonio culturale nell'era digitale" (2013) 1 Parolechiave.

60 See also Chapter 9.

61 Ignatow G, "Information Capitalism" in George Ritzer (ed), *The Wiley-Blackwell Encyclopedia of Globalization* (Wiley-Blackwell 2017) <https://doi.org/10.1002/9780470670590.wbeog299.pub2>.

62 Castells M, *The Rise of the Network Society* (2nd edn, Wiley-Blackwell 2010), Kapczynski (n 14), Cohen (n 14).

63 Vercellone C, The Hypothesis of Cognitive Capitalism (Birkbeck College and SOAS 2005) <https://halshs.archives-ouvertes.fr/halshs-00273641> accessed 10 June 2025; Fumagalli A, Bioeconomia e capitalismo cognitivo: verso un nuovo paradigma di accumulazione (4th reprint, first edn 2007, Carocci 2011); Fumagalli A, Giuliani A, Lucarelli S and Vercellone C, Cognitive Capitalism, Welfare and Labor: The Commonfare Hypothesis (1st edn, Routledge 2019).

64 Burton-Jones (n 8).

65 DIKW stands for "data, information, knowledge, and wisdom", Rowley JE, "The Wisdom Hierarchy: Representations of the DIKW Hierarchy" (2007) 33(2) Journal of Information Science 163 <https://doi.org/10.1177/0165551506070706>, 163.

below wisdom. According to it, data and information represent the lower levels of this hierarchy, while knowledge stands on a higher tier of the DIKW scale. Indeed, it constitutes a value in itself, encompassing not only what can be inferred from data but also the broader significance that arises through the interpretation and use of information.

Within semiotic theory, which identifies three dimensions of signs (syntactics, semantics, and pragmatics),[66] knowledge may be mapped onto the lat-

66 Morris CW, cited in Nöth W, *Handbook of Semiotics* (First paperback ed, [4 Dr], Indiana Univ Press 1998). In this framework, data belongs to the syntactic dimension, that is, the most elementary level, which concerns the formal structure of signs – their "corporeal aspects" – without reference to their meaning. Syntactics addresses the question "how does the sign signify?" (Nake F, Data, Information, and Knowledge (Science Direct Working Paper No S1574 034X(04)70128 3, July 2002) (University of Bremen) <https://ssrn.com/abstract=3125391>, 658–659). At this level, the sign is stripped of its interpretative depth, reduced to a mere signal – which is "a sign in a state where the object and the interpretant tend to coincide", a sign whose function is to point to something without conveying any meaning on its own. Data, in this sense, can be viewed as the raw material of information: a set of discrete, objective facts or observations that are recorded but not yet processed, structured, or interpreted, and which "do not convey any specific meaning" (Awad and Ghaziri, 2004, Chaffey and Wood, 2005, Pearlson and Saunders, 2004, Bocij et al., 2003, cited in Baškarada S and Koronios A, "Data, Information, Knowledge, Wisdom (DIKW): A Semiotic Theoretical and Empirical Exploration of the Hierarchy and Its Quality Dimension" (2013) 18(1) Australasian Journal of Information Systems 5 <https://doi.org/10.3127/ajis.v18i1.748> accessed 10 June 2025). Although this view risks oversimplifying the contemporary understanding of data, particularly in the era of big data, where the notion of data as merely objective and neutral entities is itself an illusion (Gitelman (n 31), 2), framing data as syntactic signs nonetheless offers valuable insights into the distinction between data and information. Information, which can be extracted from data, belongs to the semantic dimension of signs, that is, the level at which a conventional meaning begins to emerge. In this dimension, from the semiotic standpoint, the central question is "what does the sign signify?" Information is not simply a collection of facts, but data that have been organized, processed, and shaped into a form that holds significance within a social group, community, or culture. In other words, information is data made meaningful and useful – something that human beings can interpret and use to make sense of the world around them (Laudon and Laudon, 2006, 13, cited in Baškarada and Koronios (n 66)). Another perspective has been used by Herbert Zech to describe the difference among the different dimensions of signs, speaking to syntactic "information" – that is, information represented by a given quantity of signs – and distinguishing it from semantic information (i.e., information with a specific meaning) and structural information (i.e., information represented by the structure of a physical object). As the author explains, each of the three types of information can be found in everyday life: when we speak of news, a story, or the "content" of a book, we refer to the semantic level. The composition of a text or a file pertains to the syntactic level. Finally, when we deal with a CD, a printed book, and so on, we refer to the structural level. Naturally, the three levels are interconnected, as meaning can be embedded in a text, and a text can be printed. Thus, the physical layer carries the syntactic layer,

ter – the most complex and elusive level of signification. At this stage, the key question is no longer simply what a sign means, but why it signifies and for what purpose. Whereas information represents explicit knowledge reduced to its semantic dimension,[67] knowledge itself "gains its full context only within the purpose of its use". It is inherently tied to personal context and application, encompassing discourse around the meaning of words, the significance of artworks, or the impact of films: "Knowledge is a person's lived life. It is total, whole, and inseparable".[68]

Unlike data and information, knowledge is not something that can be fully made explicit or quantified: it is lived rather than merely represented. Also, it is the combination of data and information organized and processed to convey understanding, experience, accumulated learning, and expertise as they apply to a current problem or activity. It possibly results in a valuable asset that can be used to aid decision-making.[69] While data and information provide the raw material, knowledge is what emerges when they are interpreted, structured, and applied.

Haggart[70] outlines eight principles that help describe what knowledge is and how it functions in society. The first principle, in line with what has been just described, distinguishes knowledge from information, data, or

---

and the syntactic layer carries the semantic layer. However, from an economic and legal perspective, each level represents an independent basis for defining a particular quantity of information. In economics, information is most often used in the sense of semantic information. In this view, to know something means to have access to semantic information. Consequently, an invention (understood as applied knowledge) constitutes semantic information (Herbert Zech, "Information as Property" (2015) 6(3) Journal of Intellectual Property, Information Technology and Electronic Commerce Law 192, see Irti C, Consenso "negoziato" e circolazione dei dati personali (Giappichelli, Studi di diritto privato 66, Torino 2021) 19 and De Franceschi A (ed), European Contract Law and the Digital Single Market (Intersentia 2016) 51 ff. Finally, within the Italian legal scholarship, Messinetti had also addressed the semantic scope of the term information, which legitimizes the coincidence of the concepts of information (in the sense of news or factual content) and informational goods (in the sense both of processed information and of the technical procedures used to process it), as suggested to legal scholars by empirical observation (Messinetti D, "Circolazione dei dati personali e dispositivi di regolazione dei poteri individuali" (1998) 16(3) Rivista critica del diritto privato 339 ff., 340). On this aspect, see Irti (n 112) 19.

67 "Information is what is left of knowledge when the subjective context and situation are abstracted away" see Nake (n 113) 660.

68 Ibid.

69 Turban et al., 2005, 38, Chaffey & Wood, 2005, 223, cited in Baškarada and Koronios (n 66).

70 Haggart B and Tusikov N, The New Knowledge: Information, Data and the Remaking of Global Power, vol 1 (Rowman & Littlefield Publishers 2023).

facts, emphasizing that it is more complex and contextual than the other two elements of the DIKW hierarchy and factual events. The second principle highlights that knowledge is inherently governed by rules and norms, positioning it as a social construct. In other words, knowledge doesn't exist in a vacuum: it's shaped by the society and culture in which it is produced and used. Contrary to data that are "property of things, knowledge is a property of people that predisposes them to act in a particular way".[71] This leads to the third principle: those who control the definition, creation, and use of knowledge hold significant power. They can shape the direction and development of knowledge, which in turn can influence society. According to the fourth principle, knowledge is cumulative. New knowledge is built upon existing knowledge, making control over it a critical political issue – one that renders such control not just about holding information but about influencing what is deemed valuable and relevant in shaping future developments. The fifth principle argues that the process itself of knowledge production is deeply influenced by the society in which it occurs. Knowledge creation is a product of human action, and decisions about what counts as knowledge are influenced by social norms and values. A given society decides what knowledge is deemed important and how it should be structured, and these decisions are in turn shaped by the cultural and political context. Principle six, drawing from Polanyi, asserts that in a market society, knowledge becomes what he termed a "fictitious commodity". This means that while knowledge is not something that is created or produced for the market, it is still treated as something that can be bought, sold, and traded within the marketplace. The seventh principle is a reminder of the fact that knowledge is intangible – due to the fact that it cannot be physically touched or seen, though holding an immense value in shaping society and driving economic and cultural development. Finally, the eighth principle warns that a society built on the exploitation of knowledge requires constant surveillance to function efficiently. Polanyi's concept of fictitious commodities becomes especially relevant here: just as treating natural resources as ordinary commodities – without recognising that they are essential to collective survival – risks destroying the very foundations of people's existence, so too unchecked exploitation of knowledge as a mere commodity threatens to undermine the integrity of the social systems that depend on it. Together, these principles offer a framework for understanding knowledge not just as an abstract concept, but as a powerful, politically charged force that shapes and is shaped by society, and, as will be discussed in greater detail below, point to its interconnection with copyright law

71 Boddy et al., 2005, 9 cited in Baškarada and Koronios (n 66).

2.2.2 From Privatization of Data to Privatization of Knowledge

As discussed, the term knowledge capitalism is preferred within the context of this analysis over other concepts that describe similar data-driven forms of capitalism – such as information(al) capitalism, its related notion informationalism, and surveillance capitalism. The term "knowledge capitalism" appears to have been introduced for the first time by Burton-Jones,[72] who, however, did not provide a clear definition of it, but nonetheless emphasized the growing importance of knowledge and skills in the economy, suggesting that the current era is best characterized as "global knowledge capitalism", in which the circulation of knowledge has become more crucial than the movement of physical resources.[73]

This concept is preferred here because this framework is conceived as a broader and more inclusive one than informational capitalism. However, knowledge capitalism shares several points of convergence with this latter, which began to emerge as a distinct phase of capitalist development in the 1970s, when computer technology first entered homes and workplaces in advanced economies[74] and kept on evolving alongside the technological evolution.[75] One of the most comprehensive theorizations of informational capitalism has been offered by Castells in his Information Age trilogy: The Rise of the Network Society (1996), The Power of Identity (1997), and End of Millennium (1998).[76] Castells argued that information technology underpinned a

---

72 Burton Jones (n 8).

73 Stehr N, Knowledge Capitalism (1st edn, Routledge 2022) <https://www.taylorfrancis.com/books/9781003296157> accessed 9 August 2025, note 1.

74 In The Coming of Postindustrial Society (1973), Daniel Bell described the social shifts accompanying the emergence of a new form of capitalism from industrial to informational capitalism, based on services rather than industrial production. He noted that, in this postindustrial society, "a majority of the labor force is no longer engaged in agriculture or manufacturing but in services, which are defined, residually, as trade, finance, transport, health, recreation, research, education, and government" (Bell D, *The Coming of Post-Industrial Society: A Venture in Social Forecasting* (Basic Books 1973) xiii, 507 pp, ISBN 0-465-01281-7).

75 A more decisive turning point for information capitalism occurred in the late 1990s, when large-scale investments in information technology began to drive significant productivity gains, see Dale W Jorgenson, "Information Technology and the US Economy" (2001) 91(1) *The American Economic Review* 1. By that time, informational capitalism had extended beyond a niche of knowledge workers and the high-tech sector, becoming deeply embedded across industries and even within governmental operations.

76 Castells M, *The Rise of the Network Society* (The Information Age: Economy, Society and Culture, vol 1, Blackwell 1996); *The Power of Identity* (vol 2, Blackwell 1997); *End of Millennium* (vol 3, Blackwell 1998).

new network logic of social organization, by accelerating the exchange and accumulation of information and knowledge. This, he claimed, represented the culmination of a historical trend in which the core functions and processes of advanced economies were increasingly organized around networks. These networks constituted, according to his opinion, the new social morphology of contemporary societies, and the diffusion of networking logic substantially modified the operation and outcomes in processes of production, experience, power, and culture.[77]

So far, the concept of informational capitalism has been essential for understanding both the continuities and disruptions in capital accumulation in relation to earlier historical forms of capitalism. In terms of continuity, it can be worth noting that the core economic relationships of information capitalism remain grounded in traditional capitalist structures. The relationship between industrialism and informationalism (understood as a broader mode of development within contemporary political economy[78]) is therefore not one of simple succession, but of cumulative transformation.[79] As for the discontinuities, it is notable that the locus of accumulation has shifted from material to immaterial production – that is, from an economy primarily based on manufacturing to one centered on the generation, accumulation, and processing of information.[80] While classical capitalism prioritizes profit maximization through the private ownership of the means of production and circulation, informational capitalism emphasizes the accumulation of data and information, alongside increasingly sophisticated techniques of data processing.[81] Within this regime, market actors extract and appropriate surplus value –

77 Castells M, *The Rise of the Network Society* (2nd edn, Blackwell 2000) 500. This transformation illustrates how capitalism has evolved from industrial production to informational production, with networks emerging as the defining structure of economic, political, and social organization in the twenty-first century. It is worth noting that the emergence of this new form of capitalism has undoubtedly been enabled by advances in information technology. Besides this, these technologies have also contributed to a significant acceleration in the globalization of capitalism: the flexibility afforded by information technologies has allowed capital to expand more rapidly, providing entrepreneurs with the means to exploit global information networks and access emerging markets. This has generated a cycle of exponential growth that has further reinforced the logic of capitalist accumulation through an essentially self-reinforcing process. See Tirino et al. (n 58).

78 Informationalism, a central concept for Castells, identifies "the action of knowledge upon knowledge itself as the main source of productivity" and signals the rise of both a "new economy" and a "new society", see Castells, 1996 (n 76) 17.

79 Cohen (n 14) 6.

80 Ibid.

81 Ibid.

including consumer surplus – through their control over networked information technologies and the data they produce.

All that said, this analysis finds knowledge capitalism to be a more appropriate conceptual framework than information(al) capitalism because it highlights how accumulation no longer concerns data and information alone, but knowledge itself, with the governance of its circulation becoming a key instrument of societal control. The current socioeconomic context is defined by the systematic generation of new knowledge through the storage, analysis, and automated processing of vast datasets (i.e., big data), rather than merely by the reproduction and transmission of information. This shift has given rise to a new industrial sector in its own right – one that is becoming increasingly pervasive with the advent of AI. In this sense, knowledge capitalism has the merit of transcending the more limited scope of informational capitalism and taking into account all these new challenges of the information society.[82] It does so by accounting for the centrality of knowledge in all its forms, ranging from raw data to embodied experience, as a commodity in its own right; that is, as something possessing intrinsic value beyond its merely instrumental function.

Moreover, knowledge capitalism captures the broader societal transformations driven by the logic of capital accumulation – often at the expense of knowledge's essential cultural, social, and scientific functions[83] – ultimately

82 Notably, knowledge capitalism also offers a distinct perspective from surveillance capitalism, even if in certain respects it also aligns with it. It shifts the focus beyond surveillance and its goals, emphasizing instead the deeper logic of accumulation – namely, the covert appropriation of knowledge itself as a means of control and value extraction. Surveillance capitalism, as defined by Shoshana Zuboff (n 14), refers to the process by which companies "unilaterally claim human experience as free raw material for translation into behavioral data", using such data to "anticipate what you will do now, soon, and later". These companies aim not only to predict but also to shape behavior at scale, possessing a new form of instrumentarian power which is able to shape human behavior toward outcomes aligned with corporate interests, see Kapczynski (n 14) 1464. Zuboff's account – according to which current technologies facilitate a new paradigm of private power that appropriates personal data for profit, and which is concentrated in the hands of a few dominant corporations – has been widely regarded as groundbreaking. However, her emphasis on surveillance and the erosion of individual autonomy may obscure other equally critical dimensions of the information age – such as platform power, winner-take-all market dynamics, and the transformation of labor. Issues like monopoly concentration and socioeconomic inequality receive relatively limited attention in her framework, see Kapczynski (n 14) 1474 ff.

83 Interesting enough, according to Stehr (n 73), "the legal encoding of knowledge through national and international law is the lever that enables the transformation of the knowledge society into knowledge capitalism. It is the TRIPs Agreement [Marrakesh Agreement Establishing the World Trade Organization, Annex 1C: Agreement on Trade-Related Aspects of Intellectual Property Rights (TRIPS Agreement) (signed 15 April 1994,

underscoring the urgent need to recognize that the accumulation of knowledge gives rise to a new form of power, one that increasingly shapes and governs human life itself.[84]

3 Drawing a Line through Knowledge Capitalism, IP Law, and Generative AI

For the purposes of this analysis, acknowledging AI's embeddedness within the capitalist system – more specifically, within the logics of knowledge capitalism – offers critical insights. Not only does this perspective shed light on the strengths and limitations of the EU's legal framwework on this matter, but it also reveals the often-overlooked mutual interdependencies between AI technologies, copyright law – as a specific branch of intellectual property law –, and the broader socioeconomic context in which they operate. Examining these interrelations offers a valuable opportunity to better map the topography of this complex and rapidly evolving phenomenon.

First, the interaction between AI and copyright is now more pronounced than ever. Ongoing debates surrounding the protection of input data and the copyrightability of AI-generated outputs are actively shaping the broader discourse on AI. Conversely, discussions about AI systems – and the attempts to govern them through intellectual property law, and copyright within it – are reshaping the contours of copyright law and its classical categories, if not *de jure*, then certainly *de facto*.

Second, both these fields are deeply entangled with the framework of knowledge capitalism. AI and copyright law both function as central mechanisms in the circulation and control of knowledge. On the one hand, AI is a matter of technical and social practices, institutions and infrastructures, politics, and culture. As Crawford puts it, "AI is fundamentally political": "artificial intelligence as we know it depends entirely on a much wider set of political and social structures. And due to the capital required to build AI at scale, and the ways of seeing that it optimizes, AI systems are ultimately designed to serve existing dominant interests. In this sense, artificial intelligence is a reg-

---

entered into force 1 January 1995) 1869 UNTS 299], negotiated between 1986 and April 15, 1994 as part of the WTO (World Trade Organization), that is the backbone of the modern, legal encircling of knowledge".

84 Capitalism seeks to bend human capacities – including language and the rational ability to generate knowledge – toward the logic of exploitation, primarily through the dynamics of social relations, see Fumagalli (n 63) 10.

istry of power".[85] Moreover, AI systems ingest and generate ever-larger quantities of data and extract value from them.

At the same time, copyright law has long played a central role in regulating the flow of ideas and information. By its very nature, it can function both as a means of enabling access to knowledge and as a tool for restricting it. In recent decades, however, it has increasingly been employed to confer expansive exclusive rights on a wide range of stakeholders across the information production and dissemination value chain, thereby privileging its restrictive function over its access-enabling one.

Indeed, an expansion of copyright law – and, more generally, of the entire field of IP law of which it forms part –, both in terms of subject matter[86] and in the proliferation of rights within its scope,[87] has been central in recent years. This trend, driven by proprietary logics and thus aligned with knowledge capitalism's inherent tendency toward propertarianism,[88] has significantly contributed to the commodification of knowledge – commodification that has been lately further exacerbated by the rise of AI.

With the advent of AI, the mechanisms of knowledge capitalism have become more explicit than ever, as they risk becoming key tools in the extraction of (economic) value from individuals' cognitive and relational capacities.[89] Such extraction is reaching its peak with the widespread accessibility of some generative AI models such as ChatGPT, DeepSeek, and Claude. Thanks to their sophisticated architectures, these systems are capable of extracting and replicating understanding, experience, accumulated learning, and expertise to assist with real-time decision-making processes,[90] becoming pervasive across all forms of human interaction through their user-friendly chatbot interfaces.

---

85 Crawford (n 18) 17.

86 Beckerman-Rodau A, "The Problem with Intellectual Property Rights: Subject Matter Expansion" (2010) 13 Yale Journal of Law & Technology 35, also published as Suffolk University Law School Research Paper No 11-14 <https://ssrn.com/abstract=1754781> accessed 9 August 2025.

87 Geiger C, "The Social Function of Intellectual Property Rights, or How Ethics Can Influence the Shape and Use of IP Law" in Graeme B Dinwoodie (ed), *Intellectual Property Law: Methods and Perspectives* (Edward Elgar 2013) 153–176; also published as Max Planck Institute for Intellectual Property & Competition Law Research Paper No 13-06, <https://ssrn.com/abstract=2228067> accessed 10 June 2025.

88 Propertarianism – the process through which new and diverse forms of ownership, particularly over intangible assets, are codified and legitimized (Piketty (n 7) 185–187) – is one of the defining characteristics of (knowledge) capitalism, which extends proprietary boundaries to areas that were previously considered part of the public domain. This redefinition of private property boundaries, directly driven by the logic of knowledge capitalism, has also increasingly influenced the evolution of intellectual property law over time.

89 Fumagalli (n 63) 10.

90 Turban et al., 2005, 38, Chaffey & Wood, 2005, 223, cited in Baškarada and Koronios (n 66).

In this context, what is at stake is not merely the commodification of data or information, but the commodification of knowledge itself – of the very processes through which knowledge is produced, distributed, and controlled.

Indeed, information and data are increasingly being processed to generate value that now permeates across virtually all forms of human interaction.

What is even more significant – and concerning – about this process is that much of the underlying information and data is often initially sourced from publicly accessible repositories, only to be subsequently privatized through algorithmic transformation.

The knowledge and understanding derived from these processes are thus increasingly appropriated by private entities – both through *de facto* control exercised by dominant economic actors (such as AI providers and the platforms that host them), and through *de jure* legal entitlements, such as those granted by intellectual property law and trade secrets regimes.[91] On the one hand, the fact that OpenAI's generative models were trained in large part on publicly accessible datasets, yet their most advanced iterations are now placed behind a paywall, symbolically illustrates this *de facto* process of privatization, where control over access to resources that once formed part of the public domain is consolidated by private actors. On the other hand, the "proprietarization" of common goods through the expansion of intellectual property law – used to normalize the transfer of entire domains of public knowledge into private ownership – epitomizes the *de jure* dimension of knowledge privatization, whereby resources that arguably belong to humanity are increasingly enclosed within exclusive legal rights.

Seen through this lens, regulating AI and reshaping the boundaries of copyright law can have far-reaching, indirect effects on knowledge – on its production, its protection, and its potential privatization. For this reason, regulatory interventions in this field and, more broadly, debate over these issues must be approached with particular caution.

The control and regulation of knowledge is not a neutral or merely technical matter. Rather, it is a deeply political exercise that inevitably produces winners and losers.[92] Decisions about which data to collect for training algorithms, or which elements of a piece of content should qualify for copyright protection, are never made in a vacuum. These choices inherently favor certain individuals, groups, and interests over others, and function as a primary mechanism for the exertion of economic power. As such, they may benefit some while disadvantaging others – and, at times, may even operate to the detriment of society as a whole.

---

91 Ricolfi M, "Regulating de facto powers: shifting the focus" in *Law 2022* (Elgar 2022) ch 12, 174–84, DOI: 10.4337/9781803922256.00017.

92 Haggart and Tusikov (n 70) 9.

The regulation of knowledge through IP rights represents, in the era of generative AI more than ever, a delicate balancing act between freedom and control.[93] By establishing mechanisms to manage competing interests, IP law – and copyright within it – shapes the outcomes of fundamental decisions such as what kinds of knowledge are eligible for protection, who gets to claim ownership, and under what terms that knowledge can be accessed and used. Ultimately, these mechanisms can contribute to the concentration of creative and informational resources in the hands of a limited number of powerful actors, which, in the case of generative AI applied to cultural domains that are the focus of this work, include, at the very least, the cultural industry, the AI one, and the digital platform one.

From this perspective, the prism of knowledge capitalism brings new nuance to the longstanding debate on the function of intellectual property law, challenging the seemingly "necessary" propertarian and exclusivist approach that has come to dominate the field – an approach that, in practice, can give rise to undesirable consequences with far-reaching societal implications.

This propertarian drift is most visible in the shifting boundary of what qualifies as appropriable in the realm of intellectual and creative works has increasingly been justified by the argument that stronger IP rights foster innovation and creativity. Yet, if not critically examined and carefully regulated, the ongoing reinforcement of IP's utilitarian rationale – particularly through the indiscriminate expansion of protection, for example, in the generative AI domain – risks deepening existing inequalities.

Specifically, this expansion threatens to further tilt the balance of power in favor of major actors – big tech corporations (notably within the AI sector), cultural industries, and digital platforms (AI-driven and otherwise) – at the expense of users, independent creators, artists, and civil society as a whole.[94]

---

93 Ibid, 26.

94 As Piketty (n 7) argues, every human society must justify its inequalities and construct its own narratives to do so. Identifying and scrutinizing these rationales is crucial; otherwise, the entire political and social structure risks collapse. In contemporary societies, proprietarist, entrepreneurial, and meritocratic narratives are commonly used to justify capital accumulation and uphold systemic inequalities. According to this idea, modern inequality is deemed just because it is perceived as the outcome of a freely chosen process in which everyone ostensibly has equal opportunities to access markets and property. Furthermore, it is assumed that all individuals ultimately benefit from the wealth accumulated by the richest, who are regarded as the most enterprising, meritorious, and useful members of society. This perspective positions contemporary inequality in stark contrast to the rigid, arbitrary, and often despotic status-based inequalities of traditional societies; nevertheless, these are still narratives designed to justify and perpetuate inequality.

Against this backdrop, the argument that strong intellectual property rights – particularly in their exclusive form – are inherently just and essential for fostering innovation and AI development must be recognized for what it is: a mere narrative, which moreover risks obscuring the vested interests behind wealth accumulation by major tech corporations, ultimately reinforcing systemic disparities rather than enabling genuine innovation or equitable technological progress.

Propertarianism, the dominance of technology over law, the logic of capitalism, and the power of digital technology itself – including AI – are not inevitable, not even in relation to IP law, but contingent. These forces only gain their strength when supported by a legal framework that enables their expansion.[95]

It is precisely this contingency that the remainder of this work seeks to exploit: if copyright is one of the legal levers through which knowledge capitalism privatises the commons, it can equally be reshaped to resist that enclosure. The concrete battlegrounds on which this contest plays out – the protection of training data on the input side and the copyrightability of AI-based content on the output side – are examined in Chapters 7 and 8, while the present analysis returns, in its final part, to the social function of copyright as the principle capable of re-orienting these mechanisms towards access to knowledge and cultural pluralism rather than their enclosure.

95 Hence the importance of recognizing how different geopolitical blocs approach the regulation of emerging technologies. From the EU's fundamental rights-based framework to the market-centric orientation of the United States and the state-driven model adopted by China, each model reflects a different conception of law's role in mediating technological development. These regulatory paradigms also shape – and are shaped by – the use of copyright law as a key instrument in the control and governance of knowledge. Also, capitalism is necessarily intertwined with the legal frameworks within which it has evolved, being "produced as the outworking of legal rights and duties that offer special protections to asset-holders legitimated through a constitutional order", and "legitimated through constitutional ratification by an ultimate popular sovereign that then rules in theory, without in practice surrendering governmental administration to ongoing popular control", see Grewal (n 95), 485.

CHAPTER 2

The Use of AI in the Cultural and (Re)Creative Context

AI systems are increasingly employed to manage, recommend, or produce cultural and creative content, and they are used not only in creative fields but also in recreational settings. For the purposes of this chapter, such uses will be collectively referred to as the use of AI in the cultural and (re)creative context.

Regardless of the specific segment of the AI value chain in which these systems are deployed, their use in this realm – while offering remarkable opportunities, including more efficient content management and novel forms of expression – can nonetheless have significant adverse effects and raise risks that compound the broader and well-documented concerns generally associated with AI, such as algorithmic biases and system opacity. The latter, in particular, stems not only from the structural complexity of AI systems, which often involve interactions between multiple software and hardware components, but also from the fact that the algorithms themselves are frequently protected as trade secrets.

These risks take on specific forms in the (re)creative and cultural sector where they can be approached at two different levels of analysis. First, in a broad and transversal sense, there is the view that such systems, specifically generative AI and other general-purpose models, pose growing risks to cultural diversity and freedom of expression – risks that, due to the scale of their impact, could rise to the level of systemic concerns. Second, a more granular perspective focuses on specific segments of the AI value chain in cultural production. This includes, on the one hand, copyright management and enforcement mechanisms, such as filtering systems, and on the other hand, the generation of original content itself.

1 Systemic Risk for Cultural Diversity and Freedom of Expression

Within the EU context, recitals 99 and 105 of the AI Act explicitly classify large generative AI models as "general-purpose AI models", noting that they "allow for flexible generation of content, such as in the form of text, audio, images, or video, that can readily accommodate a wide range of distinctive tasks" (Recital 99). While these technologies are expected to deliver significant societal and economic benefits, they are also raising increasing concerns about their effects on society, particularly within the cultural sector, including potential threats to cultural diversity and freedom of artistic expression.[96]

As for their architecture – referring to the type and nature of the model, the number of parameters, computing capacity, and input data format – the main concern is that it may reinforce dominant market and cultural trends.[97] A clear illustration is the use of training datasets and prompts that can reproduce cultural biases, often reflecting the dominant culture of generative AI developers or the platforms hosting these models and systems.

Among the many risks posed by AI systems to the cultural and (re)creative sector, one particularly significant concern relates to their impact on cultural diversity – a dimension that resonates with long-standing debates on cultural dominance and imperialism driven by the Global North and Western countries.

As Klein warned in a 2023 article for The Guardian, in a context of hyper-concentrated power and wealth, AI is likely to become "a fearsome tool of further dispossession and devastation".[98] Indeed, these concerns have been explored through the lens of digital colonialism[99] and are set to gain renewed urgency with the rapid proliferation of generative AI models, which increasingly act as vectors of the dominant cultures of the countries where their developers or over-the-top platform hosts are based.[100]

Such concerns resonate particularly in the Global South, where there is growing apprehension that AI may serve not as a tool for inclusive development, but rather as a new mechanism for the expropriation of resources, disguised as technological aid and progress. This sentiment was powerfully articulated by Brazil's Foreign Minister Mauro Vieira during a high-level insti-

96 Wachowicz M, "The Role of Artificial Intelligence on the Promotion of Cultural Diversity and Intellectual Property Rights" (2024) 55(8) *IIC – International Review of Intellectual Property and Competition Law* 1221; See also the EU Commission's commissioned study on "Opportunities and Challenges of Artificial Intelligence (AI) Technologies for the Cultural and Creative Sectors", 2024, available online.

97 Bensamoun and Farchy (n 4).

98 <https://www.theguardian.com/commentisfree/2023/may/08/ai-machines-hallucinating-naomi-klein>.

99 Kwet M, "US Empire and the New Imperialism in the Global South" (2019) 60(4) *Race & Class* 3.

100 Shakespeare D, Porcaro L, Gómez E, and Castillo C, "Exploring Artist Gender Bias in Music Recommendation" (25 September 2020) Proceedings of the 2nd Workshop on the Impact of Recommender Systems (ImpactRS, ACM RecSys 2020).

tutional event held in Paris in February 2025 (Artificial Intelligence Action Summit), where he warned that, unless AI is governed in a fair and inclusive manner, it risks becoming yet another instrument of exploitation and oppression by the Global North against the Global South.[101]

Beyond these concerns, other risks associated with AI systems in the cultural and (re)creative sectors include phenomena such as the potential displacement of the market for human literary and artistic works, i.e., the displacement of entire segments of creators from the labor market, as AI systems are able to perform tasks that were previously considered the exclusive domain of human activity.[102]

As early as 2018, it was observed that the technological revolution could, in a short period, displace billions of people from the workforce, "causing social and political upheavals for which there is no ideology capable of controlling the consequences".[103] Even earlier, the European Parliament had noted in its 2017 Resolution on Robotics that the economic changes and employment consequences of robotics and machine learning needed to be carefully assessed, as, despite the undeniable benefits brought by robotics, it may lead to a transformation of the labor market and consequently necessitate reflection on the future of education, employment, and social policies.[104]

These considerations are even more pressing when applied to the labor market in the creative sector, where the implications of automation and AI-driven systems touch upon not "only" employment but also, ultimately, the cultural production as a whole. If, even prior to the emergence of generative AI, this field already suffered from issues related to the lack of recognition and legitimization of its professional workforce, the advent of AI systems capable of generating original outputs has compounded these challenges. Today, they are exacerbated by a sharp decline in both opportunities and working conditions within the creative industry.

---

101 Del Monte D, "L'altra faccia dell'AI Summit di Parigi: i timori del Sud globale, che vede nell'intelligenza artificiale 'l'ennesimo strumento di oppressione'" (*Guerre di Rete*, 19 February 2025) <https://www.guerredirete.it/laltra-faccia-dellai-summit-di-parigi/?utm_source=substack&utm_medium=email> accessed 10 June 2025.

102 As Erickson has observed, it is not always a matter of job losses, but rather of job displacement – often to other segments of the AI production value chain, see Erickson K, "AI and Work in the Creative Industries: Digital Continuity or Discontinuity?" (28 October 2024) Creative Industries Journal (online early version, forthcoming 2024) <https://ssrn.com/abstract=5006065> accessed 10 June 2025.

103 Harari (n 10) 42.

104 European Parliament, *European Parliament Resolution with Recommendations to the Commission on Civil Law Rules on Robotics* (2015/2103(INL), 16 February 2017).

The protests by US film and television workers, which lasted an impressive 148 days,[105] and the simultaneous strike by screenwriters, both part of the two landmark labor actions of summer 2023, will be remembered as the first major union demonstrations against AI. These actions were aimed at raising awareness of the risks posed by the unchecked use of AI. Both ended with the adoption of agreements – between the actors' and screenwriters' unions and film and television producers, respectively – focused specifically on concerns about the excessive use of AI to "minimizing the costs of business while mortifying the role and wages of human beings".[106]

When viewed more closely, this expressed concern is not only relevant to economic issues. It reveals instead a broader set of stakes that may have a profound impact on cultural diversity and artistic expression, by potentially and indirectly weakening the foundations of professional artistry. In particular, it may contribute to the inhibition of independent production, as the possibility of sustaining a livelihood through creative work appears increasingly limited to a small number of high-profile creators.[107] As independent and emerging voices risk being pushed to the margins, the overall diversity of artistic expression could gradually be reduced.

How to address, from a legal perspective, these potential "systematic" harms that generative AI systems may pose to cultural diversity and freedom of artistic expression, both of which are fundamental rights protected under international human rights instruments,[108] is currently a matter of debate. One line of reasoning suggests that these harms could be conceptualized as "systemic" risks.

In EU, existing digital frameworks, such as the AI Act and the Digital Services Act, have introduced the concept of "systemic risk" to address the "risk that is specific to the high-impact capabilities of general-purpose AI models, having a significant impact on the Union market due to their reach, or due to actual or reasonably foreseeable negative effects on public health, safety, pub-

---

105 Dalton A and Fauria K, "Hollywood's Strikes Are Both Now Over as Actors Reach Deal with Studios and Return to Work with Writers" (AP News, 9 November 2023) <https://apnews.com/article/actors-strike-ends-hollywood-5769ab584bca99fe708c67d00d2ec241> accessed 10 June 2025.

106 Belisario E and Riccio GM, "Spoiler alert: quello di Hollywood non sarà l'ultimo sciopero contro l'IA" (Legge Zero newsletter #1, 25 November 2023) <https://leggezero.substack.com/p/legge-zero-1-spoiler-alert-quello>.

107 <https://www.project-syndicate.org/onpoint/how-ai-profits-can-help-fund-cultural-production-by-mariana-mazzucato-and-fausto-gernone-2025-07>.

108 International Covenant on Economic, Social and Cultural Rights (adopted 16 December 1966, entered into force 3 January 1976) 993 UNTS 3, arts 13 and 15; see also UNESCO, *Universal Declaration on Cultural Diversity* (2 November 2001).

lic security, fundamental rights, or the society as a whole, that can be propagated at scale across the value chain".[109]

However, the precise scope of this notion remains unclear. In particular, it is uncertain whether the impacts on such human rights are adequately recognized as "systemic risks" according to these two pieces of legislation.

While the answer appears to be increasingly affirmative, also due to recent developments in academic discourse,[110] it still remains unclear what the practical implications of such a framing would be. For instance, it is unclear how such risks, if recognized as systemic, could be effectively addressed when regulatory obligations are placed solely on general-purpose AI model providers, who are the exclusive addressees of such provisions. Also, it remains debatable whether specific principles and tools (including those derived from other legal frameworks, such as intellectual property law) are already available to address these concerns from a systemic risk perspective.

This study takes that very question as one of its threads: it argues that copyright law, read through the lens of its social function, is not merely a passive bystander to these systemic risks but one of the instruments through which they may be mitigated. How that re-reading operates in practice – on lawful access and the exceptions on the input side, and on the notions of "work" and "originality" on the output side – is developed in Chapters 7 and 8 and systematised in the concluding part.

2 Copyright Management and Recommendation Tools

The intersections between artificial and the cultural and (re)creative context can occur at various stages along the intellectual production value chain: not only during the creation of content in the strict sense (such as texts, images, and multimedia works of varying complexity) but also later, in the stage of

109 Regulation (EU) 2024/1689 of the European Parliament and of the Council of 13 June 2024 laying down harmonized rules on artificial intelligence (Artificial Intelligence Act – AI Act) (OJ L 1689, 12 July 2024), art 3(65).

110 See Loi M, Making sense of the Digital Services Act. How to define platforms' systemic risks to democracy, AlgorithmWatch, 2023. The Author refers to systemic risks of digital platforms to freedom of speech and media pluralism, according to the DSA (n 285); see also Palumbo A, Enabling a sociotechnical approach to AI risk management: what are systemic risks to social systems?, 2025, in <https://www.law.kuleuven.be/citip/blog/enabling-a-sociotechnical-approach-to-ai-risk-management-what-are-systemic-risks-to-social-systems/>.

technological protection of such content, or, more transversally, in user profiling.

As highlighted during the ALAI conference held in Paris on June 22–23, 2023, on the topic "*Droit d'auteur, droits voisins et intelligence artificielle*",[111] AI systems can surely serve as tools for generating creative outputs, but also as instruments for copyright management and enforcement (see, for instance, the *Glaze* project[112]), as well as recommendation tools.

Firstly, copyright management and filtering tools, in line with the well-known motto "the answer to the machine is in the machine",[113] typically operate by providing copyright and related rights holders with systems that match protected works and materials to metadata available online.[114] These tools are designed to identify such works or materials and assess the extent of their economic exploitation, to filter and limit unauthorized uses (through take-down and stay-down procedures), and ultimately to ensure content monetization.

Secondly, recommendation tools function by selecting content – such as playlists – based on users' prior choices. In doing so, they profile users with the aim of identifying preferences and behavioral patterns.[115]

When AI systems are deployed in the cultural and (re)creative field, a number of critical concerns emerge, due both to the operational mechanisms of these technologies and the socioeconomic structure in which they function. These concerns primarily relate to the potential of AI to undermine cultural pluralism and freedom of artistic expression, which may also indirectly affect the formation of an informed public debate. Additionally, they raise questions about the circulation of informational resources in digital environments.

With regard to AI technologies used for copyright management and enforcement, serious concerns have been raised about the potential for content filtering tools – for example, implemented pursuant to Article 17 of the Copyright in the Digital Single Market Directive (CDSM Directive), in the EU context – to lead to over-blocking and, consequently, to more or less inten-

111 ALAI, "Questionnaire: Authorship and Artificial Intelligence" (ALAI Paris Congress 2023) <https://alai-paris2023.org/questionnaire/> accessed 10 June 2023.

112 See the response to the ALAI questionnaire by the US, "which attempts to use AI technology to protect works of visual art posted on the internet from being used as training data by visual arts AI platforms", <https://glaze.cs.uchicago.edu/aboutus.html> accessed 10 June 2025.

113 Hugenholtz PB (ed), The Future of Copyright in a Digital Environment (Kluwer Law International 1996) 139 ff. For an overview on EU Copyright Law, see also Pasa B, Industrial Design and Artistic Expression. The Challenge of Legal Protection (Brill 2020).

114 See the response to the ALAI questionnaire by the Italian group, point 3.1, <https://alai-paris2023.org/questionnaire/> accessed 10 June 2023.

115 "The user's *attitude profiled by the service and/or the user's genre requests*". See the response to the ALAI questionnaire by the Italian group, point 3.3 (Ibid).

tional forms of censorship. In addition, such systems risk altering the proper functioning of the mechanism of copyright exceptions and limitations: less sophisticated AI may block content that is, in fact, lawfully permitted under existing exceptions.[116]

A potentially undesirable implication of AI systems used as recommendation tools, instead, stems from the broader dynamics of the "platformization" of culture, whereby cultural content is increasingly accessed and consumed through digital platforms. In this context, the creation and consumption of content is shaped not only by the personal choices of authors and the freely formed preferences of users but also by the logic of what might be described as a "turbo-mainstream", which poses a threat to cultural pluralism and freedom of artistic expression.

Profiling mechanisms employed by major streaming platforms – such as Spotify, Netflix, Prime Video, Disney+, among others – play a central role in shaping users' cultural consumption. A notable example is the introduction of features like "discovery mode", which offers algorithmic promotion in exchange for a 30% reduction in royalties on selected tracks.[117] This model has been criticized for reinforcing market concentration and disadvantaging independent artists, potentially leading to distortions in revenue distribution.

As a result, by weakening the economic position of independent and emerging artists, such mechanisms ultimately narrow the diversity of available cultural content, thereby feeding back into the very threat to cultural pluralism noted above.

Recommendation tools also tend to favor mainstream content: algorithmic curation typically prioritizes what is already popular, marginalizing less conventional or niche productions. Additionally, risks of discrimination may arise from algorithmic biases, which can undermine the fairness and inclusivity of content recommendations delivered to users.

However, risks to the cultural sector arising from these recommendation systems can also materialize indirectly. These systems facilitate the polarization of user preferences through the creation of filter bubbles, which may undermine users' critical engagement with culture. Moreover, given their

---

116 Directive (EU) 2019/790 of the European Parliament and of the Council of 17 April 2019 on copyright and related rights in the Digital Single Market and amending Directives 96/9/EC and 2001/29/EC [2019] OJ L130/92. For critical analysis on the risks raised by filtering tools, see Rotolo F, "Diritto d'autore e intelligenza artificiale: il controllo dei contenuti online tramite sistemi di automatic filtering" in Camardi C (ed), La via europea per l'intelligenza artificiale. Atti del Convegno del Progetto Dottorale di Alta Formazione in Scienze Giuridiche – Ca' Foscari Venezia, 25–26 novembre 2021 (CEDAM 2023).

117 Alberto Puliafito, "Internazionale" newsletter (28 February 2025).

access to vast amounts of data on cultural consumption, intermediaries in the creative industries may – now more than ever – further narrow the production and distribution of content that deviates from dominant market logics or is perceived as commercially less viable.[118]

In light of the above, these tools show that the cultural risks of AI can arise when machines select and distribute cultural content. They are, in this sense, an early instance of the broader pattern this book traces: the way the architecture and deployment of AI, embedded in specific business models, can quietly tilt the cultural sphere toward concentration and homogenization. Against this backdrop, whether copyright law amplifies this drift or works against it – the question that animates the remainder of this study – depends on how its core categories and mechanisms are interpreted, a problem to which the analysis will return in its final part.

3 The Use of AI for Creating Original Content

3.1 The Deepfakes

A particular type of original output that can be generated by AI systems used as creative tools is the AI-generated or manipulated "image, audio, or video content that resembles existing persons, objects, places, entities, or events and would falsely appear to a person to be authentic or truthful".[119]

Under EU law, such content is defined as "deepfake" and is considered to raise significant ethical considerations.

One particularly problematic concern from this standpoint, for example, is the possibility of artificially "bringing back to life" deceased artists through projects that exploit their creative style and/or their vocal, physiognomic, or other personal features. A notable reference in this regard is the position expressed by the Japanese group in their response to the questionnaire prepared for the ALAI Annual Congress held in Paris in June 2023.[120]

However, beyond the ethical concerns they raise, deepfakes also pose a number of legal questions, including those related to the infringement of rights to one's name, image, privacy, and personal data, as well as exposure to fake news

118 See on this point Bensamoun and Farchy (n 4).

119 Article 3(60) of the AI Act (n 5).

120 <https://alai-paris2023.org/wp-content/uploads/2023/06/20230603ALAI_Paris_Questionnaire_Japon_En.pdf>.

or unfair political propaganda.[121] These concerns affect both public figures and private individuals who may be depicted in AI-generated content without their consent. The legal scholarship has identified two key areas of particular concern in this regard: image-based sexual abuse and disinformation.[122]

From a legislative perspective, it is worth noting that the EU legislator has made explicit reference to deepfakes, including them within the scope of the AI Act. In particular, the Act introduces transparency obligations regarding their dissemination (see Article 3(60), Recital 134, and Chapter 4).[123] It remains to be seen whether these obligations, imposed on the providers of such systems, will prove enforceable in practice.

However, the most significant and intensely debated effects of AI-generated content in creative contexts – potentially including deepfakes – on copyright law lie in their potential to disrupt, whether *de facto* or *de jure*, traditional legal categories such as the "addressees" of protection (authors, copyright holders), the subject matter (intellectual works), and the creative process itself (including the distinction between idea and expression, and the requirement of fixation).

3.2 Examples of AI-Generated Content

AI has found creative applications across a wide range of fields over several decades.

In the field of music, for instance, the relationship between AI and creative production has deep historical roots. As early as the 1980s, American composer and scientist David Cope developed EMI (Experiments in Musical Intelligence), a system capable of generating hundreds of compositions in the style of Bach, Mozart, and Rachmaninoff.[124] Some scholars trace the phenomenon

---

121 <https://www.turing.ac.uk/news/9-10-concerned-about-deepfakes-affecting-election-results>.

122 Regarding the risks of creating *deep fakes*, it has been noted that "regulators are increasingly concerned by the developments and applications of this technology in two main areas: image-based sexual abuse and disinformation". (see Fernandez A, "Regulating Deep Fakes in the Proposed AI Act" (2022) MediaLaws).

123 It is notable that such systems have long been classified as posing only a "limited risk" (see <https://digital-strategy.ec.europa.eu/en/policies/regulatory-framework-ai>). However, the potentially pervasive nature of their use, particularly in the dissemination of fake news and the erosion of democratic processes – has increasingly called this classification into question.

124 Da Silva P, *David Cope and Experiments in Musical Intelligence* (University of Athens, Department of Music Studies, undated) <https://eclass.uoa.gr/modules/document/file.php/MUSIC124/%CE%94%CE%B9%CE%B1%CE%BB%CE%AD%CE%BE%CE%B5%CE%B9%CF%82/da-silva-david-cope-and-emi.pdf> accessed 10 June 2025.

back even further,[125] identifying early forms of technological-musical interaction in the late 1960s, when musical works began to be produced based on compositional rules expressed in algorithmic language.[126] By the 1990s, neural network architectures were already being applied to music composition, including for real-time improvisation of rhythms and melodies within jazz ensembles.[127]

Today, most AI systems in the field of music composition operate through deep learning networks, which are capable of identifying rhythmic and melodic patterns by processing vast amounts of musical data.[128]

Some commercial applications in this field allow users to create songs by selecting from a limited set of predefined parameters – such as a specific emotion or musical genre – effectively translating those inputs into music. Others are intended for expert users (musicians, composers, programmers), offering a wider range of variables to control and thereby enabling a higher degree of complexity and customization in the resulting work.[129] In both cases, how-

---

125 Burkholder JP, Grout DJ, and Palisca CV, A History of Western Music (5th edn, WW Norton & Company 1996).

126 The Illiac suite, composed in 1957, (Lejaren Hiller and Leornard Isaacson, Experimental Music: Composition With an Electronic Computer. McGraw-Hill (1959)) or Iannis Xenakis' "Morsima-Amorsima" (1962) are but a few of these experiments, ses Deltorn JM and Macrez F, "Authorship in the Age of Machine Learning and Artificial Intelligence" in O'Connor (ed), The Oxford Handbook of Music Law and Policy (Oxford University Press 2019) Centre for International Intellectual Property Studies (CEIPI) Research Paper No 2018-10, 3.

127 Nishijima M and Watanabe K, "Interactive Music Composer Based on Neural Networks" (1993) 29(2) Fujitsu Scientific and Technical Journal 189.

128 Bensamoun and Farchy (n 4) 23. Among the many examples of recent AI-generated musical works, one notable case is a song composed by AI software that, in December 2017, was featured on several New Music Friday playlists on Spotify – with the full endorsement of the platform's executives (https://www.billboard.com/articles/business/8333911/artificial-intelligence-music-reshaping-destroying-industry/). The following year , in 2018, news circulated of the first album said to be "entirely composed and produced by an AI": I AM AI, by US singer and actress Taryn Southern (https://www.digitaltrends.com/music/artificial-intelligence-taryn-southern-album-interview/). The project made use of no fewer than four different AI systems: Amper Music, IBM's Watson Beat, Google's Magenta, and AIVA (https://developer.nvidia.com/blog/ai-composer-creates-music-for-films-and-games/). Further examples of AI-generated music have emerged through public initiatives such as the AI Song Contest, an international competition organized by the Dutch public broadcaster VPRO (https://www.vprobroadcast.com/titles/ai-songcontest.html) which showcases songs created with the assistance of AI. The growing relevance of this phenomenon is illustrated by the fact that similar events have recently been supported by major players in the creative music industry, including companies affiliated with the Sony group (https://www.aisongcontest.com/ai-creation-day-2022).

129 Bensamoun and Farchy (n 4) 24.

ever, the artistic or cultural value of the output is not the primary focus. Instead, the significance of these productions seems to lie in their potential for profitable commercial exploitation.[130]

AIVA Technologies – one of the leading startups in AI music composition – has been particularly pioneering in this field. AIVA is considered the first non-human entity to be officially recognized as a "composer", having been registered with the copyright collecting societies of France and Luxembourg (SACEM).[131] Moreover, confirming the predominantly commercial orientation of such technologies, at the time of their release, AIVA's music tracks were expected to be used by advertising agencies, filmmakers, and game studios. Sony has also played a pioneering role in this area.[132] In 2012, as part of the Flow Machines project, a team led by François Pachet – then Director of the Sony Computer Science Laboratories in Paris – developed an AI system intended to support and enhance musical composition. The project gained broader public visibility in 2016, with the release of two AI-generated songs: DeepBach, composed in the style of J.S. Bach, and Daddy's Car, in the style of The Beatles.[133] Notably, the objective was not merely to replicate a musical style, but to explore the creative potential of collaboration between humans and machines.[134]

As for figurative art, the advent of generative AI models such as ChatGPT, DALL·E, DALL·E 2, Midjourney, and others has led to a proliferation of examples of visual artworks created by – or with the assistance of – AI. Among these, several cases stand out for the public and institutional debates they have provoked. Notably, "A Recent Entrance to Paradise",[135] generated by Stephen Thaler's "Creativity Machine" software, sparked controversy before the US Copyright Office; the graphic novel "Zarya of the Dawn"[136] (see Chapter 8) also raised questions regarding authorship and protection; and "Pseudomne-

130 Keith Nelson Jr, "Taryn Southern's New Album Is Produced Entirely by AI" (*Digital Trends*, 19 February 2018) <https://www.digitaltrends.com/music/artificial-intelligence-taryn-southern-album-interview/> accessed 10 June 2025.

131 Bensamoun and Farchy (n 4) 23.

132 <https://www.aisongcontest.com/ai-creation-day-2022>.

133 To listen to the song, access <https://www.youtube.com/watch?v=LSHZ_b05W70>.

134 Bensamoun and Farchy (n 4) 25.

135 <https://upload.wikimedia.org/wikipedia/commons/2/2f/A_Recent_Entrance_to_Paradise.jpg>; US Copyright Office, Letter of 12 August 2019, No 1-3ZPC6C3 (A Recent Entrance to Paradise) <https://www.copyright.gov/rulings-filings/review-board/docs/a-recent-entrance-to-paradise.pdf>.

136 US Copyright Office, Letter of 21 February 2023, Registration No VAu001480196 (Zarya of the Dawn), see <https://www.copyright.gov/docs/zarya-of-the-dawn.pdf>.

sia – The Electrician",[137] by German photographer Boris Eldagsen, drew international attention when the artist, having been awarded first place at the Sony World Photography Awards 2023, publicly refused the prize. He revealed – only after the announcement – that the image had been created using AI and stated that his intention was to "test the competition".[138] These works are generally produced using natural language prompts, often synthesized in under a minute,[139] highlighting the remarkable capabilities of current AI systems. Their operation relies increasingly on developments in the field of so-called prompt engineering, which involves applying communication and linguistic strategies to guide the outputs of deep learning systems.[140]

Taken together, these examples make a point that matters for the argument of this book: the use of AI in the (re)creative domain is not, in itself, a historical novelty. What is new is its scale, its accessibility, and its entanglement with the concentrated economic power described in Chapter 1 – and it is this that turns the question into one about the privatisation of knowledge and the social function of copyright, the theme to which the final part of this study is devoted. Before reaching it, however, the next chapter sets out the methodological lens through which these phenomena will be read.

---

137 Paul Glynn, "Sony World Photography Award 2023: Winner Refuses Award after Revealing AI Creation" (*BBC News*, 18 April 2023) <https://www.bbc.com/news/entertainment-arts-65296763> accessed 10 June 2025.

138 "AI images and photography should not compete with each other in an award like this. They are different entities. Artificial intelligence is not photography. Therefore, I will not accept the award", said the German artist; cf. Giaume G, "Vince il concorso fotografico con lo scatto fatto dall'Intelligenza Artificiale. Ma tutti sapevano" (*Artribune*, 20 April 2023) <https://www.artribune.com/arti-visive/fotografia/2023/04/vince-concorso-fotografico-scatto-intelligenza-artificiale-tutti-sapevano/> accessed 10 June 2025.

139 Borji A, "Generated Faces in the Wild: Quantitative Comparison of Stable Diffusion, Midjourney and DALL-E 2" (2022) arXiv preprint <https://doi.org/10.48550/arXiv.2210.00586> accessed 10 June 2025.

140 Ibid.

CHAPTER 3

Insights on the Methodology: Reading the Phenomenon Through…

Before delving into the core of this chapter, the methodology adopted for this research warrants closer consideration. As can also be seen from the discussion above, an interdisciplinary, pluralistic, and multilayered methodological approach was deemed necessary to address the central question of this study, that is, to explore how the phenomenon of AI used in the creative sector might be more effectively and desirably regulated through the prism of intellectual property (IP) law.

The key aspects of this exploration, indeed, have included the recognition that, as noted, both technology and law are in practice shaped by the broader political, economic, and cultural contexts in which the former is developed, and the latter implemented. This recognition has underscored the need to situate the governance of AI[141] within an analysis that accounts for these contextual influences, as well as the wider socioeconomic landscape of the Fourth Industrial Revolution and the dynamics of knowledge capitalism in which AI technologies have emerged…and ultimately within a global framework.[142]

Moreover, as AI systems are increasingly developed and deployed across borders, the legal, ethical, and political challenges they raise must likewise be addressed through the lens of "global governance", an umbrella term that encompasses various organized attempts to manage problems that are deemed global and efforts to achieve coordinated measures to accomplish global objec-

141 United Nations, *Governing AI for Humanity* (United Nations 2024) <https://doi.org/10.18356/9789211067873> accessed 22 May 2025, 7, which states "The development, deployment, and use of such a technology cannot be left to the whims of markets alone".

142 IBM, "What is AI Governance?" (IBM, 2023) <https://www.ibm.com/think/topics/ai-governance> accessed 22 May 2025. According to IBM, AI governance refers to the set of processes, standards, and regulatory frameworks designed to ensure that AI systems are developed and deployed in ways that are safe, ethical, and aligned with fundamental human rights. Effective AI governance frameworks steer the research, design, and implementation of AI technologies by embedding principles such as fairness, transparency, and accountability, while also addressing systemic risks, including bias, surveillance, privacy violations, and misuse. On this view, AI governance also calls for inclusive and participatory solutions, involving a diverse range of stakeholders – developers, users, policymakers, ethicists, and representatives of civil society – to ensure that AI systems reflect and uphold shared societal values.

 | HTTPS://DOI.ORG/10.1163/9789004730731-005

tives.[143] As the United Nations has pointed out, while national governments and regional bodies will have an essential part to play, the inherently cross-border nature of the technology – both in how it is built and how it is used – makes international cooperation indispensable.[144]

Viewed from this perspective, the analysis of the globalization of socioeconomic relations and the parallel emergence of legal globalization were considered, for the purposes of this manuscript, a necessary step toward identifying the most appropriate form of global AI governance framework – one that necessarily requires taking into account the rise of a "transnational law", if not even a nascent form of global law.[145]

Two perspectives were considered particularly significant for the legal analysis of AI governance in a globalized world.

On the one hand is the perspective of comparative law, as an autonomous field of legal inquiry and a functional toolkit[146] equipped with its own methodologies and analytical instruments – increasingly called upon to confront the emerging challenges posed by legal globalization.

On the other hand, there is the perspective of IP law – as a form of property over intangible goods – which emerges as a particularly suitable domain for addressing the governance of AI, especially in relation to its applications within the cultural and creative sectors.

1 Comparative Law

1.1 Comparative Law in a Globalized World

As Gambaro observed, "the legal world that we wish to know, understand, and compare is complex and in a state of continuous transformation".[147]

It is from this premise that contemporary legal research must begin.

143 Husa J, Advanced Introduction to Law and Globalization (Edward Elgar Publishing 2018), 37. One illustrative example of the cross-border challenges raised by AI can be found in the ongoing debates surrounding the protection of AI-generated outputs, as well as in discussions over the regulation of input data used for AI training. These issues pose transnational challenges that call into question the adequacy of traditional, territorially bound legal and copyright frameworks.

144 United Nations, *Governing AI for Humanity* (n 141).

145 Husa (n 143).

146 "Methodik ist handwerkzeug. Nicht mehr", cited in Patti S, Saggi di diritto privato comparato (Giappichelli 1986), 61, recalling Wolfgang Fikentscher, Methoden des Rechts in vergleichender Darstellung, vols I–V (JCB Mohr [Paul Siebeck] 1975–1977).

147 Gambaro 2004, 19, as cited in Husa (n 143) 47.

In the era of AI, the emerging global legal framework is undeniably undergoing such a transformation, posing a significant challenge to classical understandings of comparative law and its interrelations with the transnational challenges at stake.

Indeed, even when viewed through the lens of socio-legal pluralism, the plurality of this nascent "global law" manifests as a transnational socio-legal reality, detached from its original legal frameworks.[148] Hence, it differs indeed significantly from comparative law as classically understood,[149] which has traditionally presupposed state-based positive law and distinct legal systems to compare.[150]

---

148 Husa (n 143) 35. In this sense, global law can be meaningfully understood as independent from positive law, and ultimately autonomous from both international and domestic legal orders.

149 However the original conception of comparative law shares with global law the implicit notion of universalism. This is not without ambiguity. As Husa notes, global law may be defined as "the law that regulates actions or events that transcend national borders", or alternatively, "as a particularly qualified subset of transnational law" (Husa (n 143) 33 ff.; Scarciglia R, Methods and Legal Comparison: Challenges for Methodological Pluralism (Edward Elgar Publishing 2023) 159). Such law may emerge through formal processes within international fora – such as multilateral deliberations at the United Nations – or through more informal mechanisms, evolving from the shared practices of professional communities (Husa (n 143) 33 ff.). Concerning comparative law, Saleilles and Lambert originally envisioned comparative law as a means to establish a droit *commun de l'humanité* – a common law of humanity – aimed at overcoming national legal barriers (Varano V and Barsotti V, La tradizione giuridica occidentale: Testo e materiali per un confronto civil law common law (8th edn, Giappichelli 2024)). However, this ambition eventually revealed its limitations, as it became apparent that the creation of a universal legal order risked masking an imperialistic vision of comparative law. As Husa warns, such a universalist approach carries the danger of "universalizing over other legal cultures" (Husa (n 143) 167), a critique echoed by Berman, who emphasizes that "universalism inevitably erases diversity". See Schiff Berman P, "The Evolution of Global Legal Pluralism" in Roger Cotterrell and Maksymilian Del Mar (eds), *Authority in Transnational Legal Theory: Theorizing Across Disciplines* (Edward Elgar Publishing 2016) 151, 171. Concerning global law, it may indeed carry a universalist dimension, as it often appears to be concerned with protecting the common interests of humanity (Morgera E, "Global Environmental Law and the Comparative Legal Method(s)" (2015) 24(3) *Review of European Community and International Environmental Law* 254, cited in Husa (n 143) 43). On these aspects, see also Nicola FG, "Mis-uses of Comparative Law in International Development" (Max Planck Lecture in Legal History and Legal Theory, Max Planck Institute for Legal History and Legal Theory, Frankfurt, 2 July 2025) <https://www.lhlt.mpg.de/events/41707/2670740>, accessed 22 May 2025.

150 As is known, classical comparative law is grounded in state-based positive legal systems and often mediated through private international law, see Varano and Barsotti (n 148).

As a result, the defining features of global law have led some scholars to question whether the comparative method remains applicable in this renewed transnational context.

Contrary to these views, however, the development of global law does not diminish the relevance of comparative legal analysis – quite the opposite, instead. While it is true that classical comparison, as developed in the past, may no longer be well-suited to the realities of legal globalization,[151] comparative law retains nonetheless a vital role in navigating the pluralist and evolving nature of global legal interactions. First and foremost, it possesses intrinsic value as a precondition for the understanding of law itself, and it serves as a powerful tool for the renewal and advancement of legal scholarship. Also, it has increasingly become a necessary – or at least highly beneficial – component across all branches of positive legal disciplines.[152] Moreover, comparative law has long engaged with challenges of a global scale, challenges that, although planetary in dimension, produce tangible local effects – issues that affect individuals directly while simultaneously compelling them to look beyond their immediate environments.[153]

In this light, even in the age of global law, comparison can be envisioned as a compass – both in the sense of a navigational instrument that offers direction, and as a tool that measures distance and traces pathways through complex legal landscapes.[154]

Moreover, in recent decades, comparative law has progressively aligned itself with the dynamics of legal globalization, moving beyond its traditional state-centric conception of law and embracing a pluralist, socio-legal understanding of globalization processes.[155]

Within this new transnational framework, its focus has necessarily evolved. Increasingly, it has shifted from identifying differences between legal systems to examining their similarities and their functions within a more complex and

151 Ibid, 38.

152 Moccia L, "La comparaison juridique comme « global compass » pour l'étude du droit" (2024) 76(2) *Revue internationale de droit comparé* 7, 10; Marini G, "Diritto e politica. La costruzione delle tradizioni giuridiche nell'epoca della globalizzazione" (2010) 1 *Pòlemos* 31, p. 31.

153 Moccia (n 152) 11.

154 Moccia (n 152) 11.

155 Husa (n 143) 46.

contested geopolitical landscape.[156] A telling example of this shift is the gradual blurring[157] of the classic dichotomy between common law and civil law.[158]

In this light, the comparative method is by no means excluded from the context of legal globalization. Yet significant challenges remain: the real issue is not whether comparative law retains its relevance, but how it can be effectively deployed within this transformed legal and geopolitical environment.

When faced with globally relevant issues such as the governance of AI, a number of critical challenges arise, the first being the identification of the "appropriate stage" of comparative law research,[159] the specific interests to be pursued through the comparative method, and the very nature of these interests – whether they aim at integration or at highlighting tensions between the objects of comparison.[160]

---

156 Marini (n 152) 33.

157 Mattei U and Pes LG, "Civil Law and Common Law: Toward Convergence"? in Whittington KE, Kelemen RD and Caldeira GA (eds), The Oxford Handbook of Law and Politics (Oxford University Press 2008) 267.

158 This distinction is often reframed as a contrast between a European system (where French and German legal models are integrated with others) and an American system. Common law itself is becoming a contested field, interpreted as aligning with one or the other depending on the analytical perspective. Also, within this framework, legal systems that had long been marginalized – such as Chinese, Indian, Latin American, and African legal traditions, previously relegated to the status of "third world", "developing", or "transitional" systems – have regained prominence, see Marini (n 152) 34.

159 With regard to the different stages of comparative legal research, Husa offers a nuanced framework that reflects the diversity of comparative engagements in the context of global legal dynamics (Husa (n 143) 41 ff.). The first stage involves the use of comparison in the drafting of legislation, where foreign models are consulted for the purposes of developing or critiquing one's own legal system. This stage is primarily instrumental and not yet systemic in nature. The second stage concerns the harmonization of legal rules and represents an integrative approach aimed at finding optimal or economically efficient solutions to shared legal problems. This stage has gained particular relevance in Europe and serves broader goals of legal convergence and global governance (Husa (n 143) 41). The third stage introduces a more systematic comparison within specific legal domains, relying on an external conceptual framework rather than internal legal categories – though, in practice, it often overlaps with the second stage. The fourth stage delves into explanations for legal similarities and differences, drawing on socio-legal studies, legal history, and legal anthropology, thereby moving toward more theoretical and epistemological inquiry. Finally, the fifth stage sees comparative law converge with theoretical global law discourse, entering a meta-comparative phase that reflects on the development of comparative legal theory and methodology itself.

160 Diverse are the interests that may guide the use of comparative methodology. From a functional perspective, comparative law may serve as a tool of legal policy, as a research instrument in legal history, or as a structural approach to understanding legal systems. These interests can be further distinguished by their integrative or contrastive character: the former aims to identify and complement similarities across legal systems, while the

Second, there is the challenge of choosing between functional, structural, critical, or systematic approaches, etc., depending on the aims and context of the inquiry.[161] In this regard, interestingly, contemporary comparative law no longer requires adherence to a single methodology. On the contrary, methodological pluralism has emerged as a defining feature of the field. This principle acknowledges the legitimacy of employing multiple comparative methods in proportion to the objectives of the research. In other words, the contemporary comparative law scholar is increasingly confronted with a combination of these methodologies that coexist and complement one another, insofar as they remain aligned with the objectives of the specific comparative inquiry at hand.[162]

Finally, there is the challenge of choosing the disciplinary lenses through which to frame the inquiry. In this respect, the connection between comparative law and interdisciplinarity is especially noteworthy,[163] as it is demanded by the very nature of comparative analysis, and even more so within a globalized legal landscape. It is legal globalization itself that requires an interdisciplinary approach.[164] Interdisciplinarity here is understood as "a network of complementary, integrating, and interacting relationships whereby different disciplines converge on common principles in both research methods and theoretical construction".[165] This dimension becomes particularly relevant

latter seeks to explore their differences (Scarciglia, "Methods and Legal Comparison" (n 148) 47 ff.). Interestingly, as Marini (n 152) observes, over the years there has been a "progressive shift away from a comparative approach focused on differences – which traditionally aimed to affirm national identity and, at times, the superiority of one legal system over another – toward a comparison of similarities, oriented instead toward bringing legal systems closer together". However, today the pendulum appears to be swinging back once more towards opposition. Yet this renewed antagonism no longer serves the reaffirmation of national identity, but rather reflects a form of competition between legal systems within the new transnational framework" ("progressivo superamento della comparazione delle 'differenze', il cui obiettivo era valorizzare l'identità nazionale e magari la superiorità di un sistema sull'altro, a favore della comparazione delle 'somiglianze', che si proponeva invece il riavvicinamento degli ordinamenti. Oggi il pendolo sembra essere tornato di nuovo verso la contrapposizione, l'antagonismo però non è più funzionale alla riaffermazione di un'identità nazionale, quanto piuttosto a mettere in competizione fra loro ordinamenti diversi nel nuovo quadro transnazionale"), see Marini (n 152) 33–34.

161 Scarciglia, "Methods and Legal Comparison" (n 148).

162 Ibid, 30, 103.

163 Engel C, "Challenges in the Interdisciplinary Use of Comparative Law" (MPI Collective Goods Discussion Paper No 2020/29, 30 November 2020) <https://ssrn.com/abstract=3739754> accessed 22 May 2025.

164 Scarciglia, "Methods and Legal Comparison" (n 148) 160.

165 Ibid, 122.

when comparative law engages with critical legal analysis,[166] where legal systems are examined not only for their internal coherence, but also in relation to their broader social, cultural, and historical contexts.

The relationship between comparative law and the social sciences, in particular, has long been regarded, together with economic sciences,[167] as essential in the analysis of different legal traditions.[168] According to Marini, it is precisely the so-called "cultural approach"[169] – shifting the focus toward the social, socioeconomic, or cultural contexts in which legal norms are understood and operate[170] – that constitutes one of the most enriching aspects of the comparative method.

1.2 Methodological Choices within This Manuscript

As previously noted, the ultimate objective of this manuscript is to provide an interpretive framework, grounded in law and sociological and policy considerations, that may serve as a foundation for developing a common strategy for the governance of AI, primarily from a European Union perspective. More specifically, it seeks to offer a legal interpretive lens for AI governance, with particular attention to the potential role of law, and particularly IP law, as both part of the problem and part of the solution to the excessive privatization of knowledge that looms in the current knowledge capitalism. This analysis begins with the core questions at the center of current debates – namely, the discussion above the protection of the input data and the outputs of the algorithmic creative process, as well as the responses given and those missed by the AI Act in this context – and aims to examine existing gaps in copyright law, as part of IP law, in relation to these issues, adopting a comparative perspective of the different jurisdictions affected by this phenomenon.

Ultimately, this manuscript argues that a holistic analysis of the phenomenon – including its economic, social, and political dimensions – makes clear

---

166 Ibid, 47 ff.

167 Marini (n 152) 36.

168 However, it must be emphasized that such integration should be both theoretically grounded and methodologically controlled, so as to avoid superficial or uncritical borrowings from other disciplines, see Scarciglia, "Methods and Legal Comparison" (n 148) 47 ff.

169 Marini (n 152) 33.

170 Interestingly, "i riferimenti della comparazione (...) non sono più costituiti (solo) dalle scienze sociali ed economiche; entrano in gioco infatti le scienze umane ed in particolare la critica letteraria e gli studi culturali. L'importazione dei loro schemi analitici permette di considerare il diritto come un prodotto culturale, una pratica culturale", see Marini (n 152) 36.

the need to rethink copyright law, it being a fundamental actor, depending on how it is shaped, of knowledge capitalism or, *viceversa*, access to knowledge.

The attempt to reconstruct a more "inclusive" copyright framework as a "landing concept" of the analysis is by no means intended to impose uniformity on the diverse legal systems affected by the phenomenon. Instead, the aim is rather to identify a fil rouge, a shared analytical path that may serve as common ground for addressing the complex issues at stake.

That said, in pursuit of this goal, this manuscript will adopt a multilayered and methodologically pluralist approach – one particularly well-suited to addressing "complex problems"[171] such as the governance of digital technologies. As with most issues related to law and globalization,[172] the (global) governance of AI is inherently controversial, ambiguous, and multifaceted.

Multiple comparative methods and perspectives will be adopted, with the aim to align with the idea of "going somewhat beyond disciplinary boundaries",[173] embracing a vision that is dynamic, context-sensitive, and attuned to the multifaceted nature of global legal phenomena.

As said, law is a fundamental dimension of the analysis, not least because it actively contributes to shaping the very phenomena arising from this context.[174] In line with the multilayered approach, the legal analysis will draw on IP law, on the one hand, and certain elements of legal theory and property law, on the other, as these are essential to understanding the foundations of IP – and by extension, of copyright law. These reflections will be further supported by references to both hard and soft law instruments, and they take into account the local, regional, national, and international dimensions of legal regulation, as required by the dynamics of globalization.[175]

As for the legal systems considered, the sources examined are essentially transnational in nature. Particular focus is given to European Union ones, complemented by references to the international dimension and, unavoidably, to national legislation. Specifically, the EU dimension has been analyzed with reference to its legal framework on AI (notably the AI Act), as well as to policy statements concerning AI, digital assets and IP, to landmark decisions that have helped define key components of copyright law, and to scholarly contributions advocating for a rethinking of copyright in light of its social function. The international dimension has primarily been addressed in rela-

171 Scarciglia, "Methods and Legal Comparison" (n 148) 126.
172 Husa (n 143) 11.
173 Scarciglia, "Methods and Legal Comparison" (n 148) 124.
174 Provided it is understood not merely as a cultural product, but also as a cultural practice, see Marini (n 152) 36.
175 Scarciglia, "Methods and Legal Comparison" (n 148) 160.

tion to the broader framework of IP law. As for the national dimension, case law and academic contributions from certain EU Member States – most notably Italy and France – have been considered in relation to both the ongoing debate on generative AI and the practical functioning and scope of copyright frameworks. A peculiar reference has been made to the US legal framework, doctrinal debates, and case law – including decisions by administrative authorities – concerning both the input and output sides of the generative AI process (see Chapters 7 and 8). In addition, a reference was made to the UK legal system as the first country to have expressly recognized protection for computer-generated works decades ago.

Within this framework, the functionalist comparative methodology has been prioritized, which aims to analytically identify the interests at stake and to understand their significance.[176] This approach was chosen not only for its inherent flexibility in addressing legal phenomena[177] but also because it enables an exploration of the role of AI in contemporary society and the social risks it poses to the very interests it engages. Crucially, it allows for a broader inquiry into how existing legal frameworks – such as copyright law at the national, EU, and international levels – and emerging regulatory instruments (e.g., the AI Act and other EU digital regulations) respond to the complex challenges raised by AI. Moreover, the functionalist lens has proven essential in reconstructing the rationale and philosophical justifications underlying IP.

To fully understand the significance of the interests at stake, the law has been considered as only one of the many components that constitute legal systems themselves. Indeed, to shed light on the breadth and complexity of the issues at stake, this manuscript has drawn on insights from other disciplines, primarily sociology. In particular, it has situated the legal analysis of generative AI within the current socioeconomic context, which constitutes the framework of "problems of an extra-large nature".[178]

176 Functionalism can be described as the tendency to prioritize function over structure. This analytical orientation enables a problem to be examined through the lens of its functionality, placing emphasis on performance and practical operation rather than on the formal, conceptual, or structural characteristics of the object under study (Britannica Online, cited in Scarciglia, "Methods and Legal Comparison" (n 148) 99).

177 Scarciglia, "Methods and Legal Comparison" (n 148) 98.

178 As Scarciglia notes ("Methods and Legal Comparison" (n 148) 125), sociological inquiry is one of the three hypotheses of advanced interdisciplinary research, referred to by Mathias Siems in "The Taxonomy of Interdisciplinary Legal Research: Finding the Way Out of the Desert" (2009), where he outlines a framework for navigating interdisciplinary legal inquiry (Mathias Siems, "The Taxonomy of Interdisciplinary Legal Research: Finding the Way Out of the Desert" (2009) 7(1) *Journal of Commonwealth Law and Legal Education* 5, 7).

Of course, this manuscript does not claim to undertake a sociological inquiry in the strict sense; such an attempt would risk falling into what Scarciglia refers to as a "pseudo-comparative sociology".[179] Nevertheless, a sociological perspective – drawing on thinkers such as Zuboff, Crawford, Stehr, and Castells, as already referenced to in Chapter 1 – has provided the conceptual foundation for the analyses.

More specifically, as seen, the phenomenon under consideration has been situated within the framework of knowledge capitalism – an analytical lens that will provide a coherent interpretive key for understanding interconnected issues such as EU copyright law and the AI Act.

Moreover, the exploration has necessarily engaged with disciplines such as computer science, art, and philosophy – an interdisciplinary approach prompted by the very nature of the subject matter. Indeed, the questions raised by generative AI demand not only a basic understanding of how algorithms operate, or legal reasoning based on classical copyright categories but also philosophical reflection and aesthetic inquiry into the meaning of creativity, authorship, and art in a digital context.

2 Intellectual Property Law

This manuscript aims to use the lens of IP and, more specifically, copyright law to provide an interpretation of the phenomenon of generative AI and its impacts in the context of knowledge capitalism. Conversely, the decision was made not to delegate the governance of the phenomenon exclusively to other branches of law, such as commercial law, data protection law, consumer protection, or competition law.

It is worth clarifying, in this regard, that while the analysis acknowledges the fact that IP encompasses a variety of regulatory regimes[180] – protecting trademarks, inventions, creative works, trade secrets, and more – which differ significantly in nature, scope, and objectives, the term IP will be used, in this

---

179 Scarciglia, "Methods and Legal Comparison" (n 148) 123.

180 It is also acknowledged hereto the variety of possible regulatory approaches outlined by the recent UNESCO, *Consultation Paper on AI Regulation: Emerging Approaches Across the World* (2024) <https://unesdoc.unesco.org/ark:/48223/pf0000390979> accessed 22 May 2025, which distinguishes between "Principles-based Approach; Standards-based Approach; Agile and Experimentalist Approach; Facilitating and Enabling Approach; Adapting Existing Laws Approach; Access to Information and Transparency Mandates Approach; Risks-based Approach; Rights-based Approach; Liability Approach".

context, as a unified concept. Such a unitary reference[181] is justified whenever it serves to highlight the common ultimate function of this subset of regulations: the protection of intangible assets derived from human creative and inventive activity in the artistic, scientific, and industrial fields.[182]

The decision to analyze the phenomenon through the lens of IP law – and more specifically, copyright law – is only seemingly self-evident. It is grounded in multiple motivations.

From a phenomenological standpoint, this choice is justified by the observation that the inputs of generative AI systems often consist of in-copyright works, while their outputs frequently fall within domains traditionally governed by copyright, such as music, literature, and the visual arts. Moreover, AI-generated works tend to be "objectively" – indeed, "externally" – indistinguishable from those produced by human authors.

Further reinforcing the relevance of a copyright-based perspective is the increasing emergence of new forms of exclusivity – affecting both input data and outputs – that echo the proprietary prerogatives typically associated with copyright holders.

From a more systemic perspective, the analysis of generative AI and its regulation through the prism of copyright is supported by the normative desirability of this legal domain assuming responsibility for the challenges posed by such technologies – particularly in light of the historical role copyright has played in governing and facilitating the circulation of information and

---

181 The category understood in a unitary sense finds its unequivocal source in various international regulations. For example, in the Convention signed in Stockholm in 1967, establishing the World Intellectual Property Organization (WIPO), it is defined as the totality of related rights (see Art. 2): "literary, artistic, and scientific works; performances of performing artists, phonograms, and broadcasts; inventions in all fields of human endeavor; scientific discoveries; industrial designs; trademarks, service marks, and commercial names and designations; protection against unfair competition, and all other rights resulting from intellectual activity in the industrial, scientific, literary or artistic fields". A not too dissimilar list of legal fields that can be ascribed to intellectual property is also offered by the TRIPs Agreement (n 83). With regard to the definition of "intellectual property", it has been noted that the imperfect coincidence of the definitions of intellectual property contained in the WIPO Convention and in the TRIPs Agreement gives the impression of a matter that, as has been well pointed out by our doctrine, presents itself to the observer with a very variable geometry, with uncertain and, at least to some extent, elastic boundaries, cf. Giorgio Spedicato, *Principi di diritto d'autore* (Mulino 2020) 12.

182 Ministero degli Affari Esteri e della Cooperazione Internazionale, "Cos'è la proprietà intellettuale" (MAECI) <https://www.esteri.it/it/diplomazia-economica-e-politica-commerciale/diplomaziaeconomica/tutela-e-promozione-della-proprieta/cos-e-la-proprieta-intellettuale/> accessed 22 May 2025.

ideas.[183] So far, one of the primary legal frameworks used to govern and control knowledge has been IP law – and copyright law within it. IP law operates at the intersection between the circulation and restriction of information, mediating between the dissemination and the privatization of knowledge.

If copyright were to shy away from the challenges posed by generative AI – relegating the governance of the phenomenon to remedial tools and corrective measures found in other areas of law,[184] and thus avoiding engagement with the core issues it raises, this would entail the wholesale exclusion of this phenomenon from the scope of investigation and application of copyright law. Other legal instruments would then be left to bear, alone, the burden of addressing the risks associated with the growing dominance of the powerful actors in this market.

Such a retreat would effectively oust copyright from entire areas of intervention it has traditionally governed, potentially leading to an irreversible marginalization of its role in the circulation of information within the creative and cultural digital environment[185] – while, paradoxically, it would continue to operate within the underlying logics of knowledge capitalism. In doing so, it would further confirm the ongoing crisis of public legitimacy that copyright has been facing for some time.[186]

Under these premises, this manuscript advances the view that copyright law should assume the role of an active player in the governance – or, more precisely, in one of the levels of governance[187] – of generative AI. It should not be excluded from the set of essential legal tools needed to rebalance the competing interests at stake in the age of knowledge capitalism.

---

183 In fact, copyright has always played a fundamental role in this, even at the cost of sometimes constituting an instrument of political control of ideas and, on occasion, of censorship. see Ardizzone A, Benussi L, Blengino C, Glorioso A, Ramello GB, Ruffo G and Travostino M, Copyright digitale. L'impatto delle nuove tecnologie tra economia e diritto (Giappichelli 2009) 6.

184 For example, competition law and civil law, with their remedies against abuse of a dominant position and the contract-related remedies.

185 Ardizzone et al. (n 183) 6.

186 Geiger, "The Social Function of Intellectual Property Rights" (n 87); Ginsburg JC, "How Copyright Got a Bad Name for Itself" (2002) 26(1) Columbia Journal of Law and the Arts 61; Dusollier S, "Open Source and Copyleft: Authorship Reconsidered?" (2003) 26 Columbia Journal of Law and the Arts 281 <https://ssrn.com/abstract=2186190> accessed 22 May 2025.

187 On the multilevel nature of IA *governance*, see Orlando S, "Intervista al Prof. Salvatore Orlando. Diritto privato e nuove tecnologie: i contenuti degli insegnamenti sul diritto dei dati" (Diritto Mercato Tecnologia, 2023) <https://www.dimt.it/news/intervista-al-prof-salvatore-orlando-diritto-privato-e-nuove-tecnologie-i-contenuti-degli-insegnamenti-sul-diritto-dei-dati/> accessed 22 May 2025.

The chosen field of investigation encompasses both the analysis of the usability of input data for training AI – where such data may consist of elements of protected works – and the assessment of whether the outputs of an AI system's algorithmic process should, or should not, be eligible for copyright protection.

The rationale for this dual focus lies in the fact that both inputs and outputs – representing the initial and final expressions of an algorithmic "creative" process – offer a privileged lens through which to reflect on the meaning of creation in the context of knowledge capitalism.

Accordingly, the inquiry into AI governance serves as a starting point for a broader assessment – not only of the EU's regulatory choices in addressing this phenomenon, but also – of the systemic resilience of copyright law. This prompts two fundamental questions: (i) at what stage in its elaboration can "information" be considered subject to legal appropriation under copyright law? and, upstream, (ii) within the context of generative AI, how should we reinterpret the notion of "free ideas" versus "protected expressions of those ideas"?

As one might ask: "E*t, si l'intelligence artificielle était l'occasion* (…) *de tenter de mieux décrypter ce qu'est véritablement créer?*".[188] Or, from another angle: what if the growing adoption of AI systems within the creative and cultural sectors served as an opportunity for a systematic renewal of the entire field of copyright law?

188 Vivant M, "Intelligence artificielle et propriété intellectuelle" (2018) No 11 *Communication – Commerce électronique* 4, 4.

SECTION 2

The State of the Art

CHAPTER 4

The Rise of Artificial Intelligence

Artificial intelligence has often been welcomed as one of the most advanced examples of the technological evolution that characterized the decades after World War II to the present day.[189]

As is well known, the debate around this new technology – *rectius*, set of technologies – is important insofar as they have the ability to collect, cross-reference, and reprocess vast amounts of data and are able to perform tasks that had always been thought to be the exclusive prerogative of human intelligence.[190]

As the advent of technologies such as Google's PaLM 2, Meta's LLaMA 2, Amazon's Titan, OpenAI's ChatGPT, Butterfly Effect's Manus, and – last but not least – High-Flyer's DeepSeek has now made clear, these systems are capable of engaging in dialogue, writing newspaper articles, novels, jingles, and more complex musical compositions, as well as, more broadly, producing genuine works of art and design that can rival human creations.[191]

The idea that the scenario imagined and described in science-fiction films of all time was just around the corner has, for some time now, led to increasing media attention on everything revolving around the world of artificial intelligence.

To date, the significance of artificial intelligence within the "thematic areas" or "polarities" of the data economy identified by knowledge capitalism – namely, knowledge, circulation, languages, and artificial intelligence[192] – is widely acknowledged and no longer seriously contested.

What remains contested, however, is its very definition and the appropriate means for its regulation.

189 Guizzardi S, "La protezione d'autore dell'opera dell'ingegno creata dall'Intelligenza Artificiale" (2018) XXVII AIDA – Annali Italiani del Diritto d'Autore, della Cultura e dello Spettacolo 1, 43.

190 See, inter alia, Mozur P, Google's AlphaGo Defeats Chinese Go Master in Win for A.I., in The New York Times, 23 May 2017, <https://www.nytimes.com/2017/05/23/business/google-deepmind-alphago-go-champion-defeat.html>.

191 The story of the German photographer Boris Eldagsen, who, with his work *Pseudomnesia – The Electrician*, was awarded first place at the *Sony World Photography Awards 2023*, is well known. See Giaume (n 138).

192 Orlando (n 187).

 | HTTPS://DOI.ORG/10.1163/9789004730731-006

1 Defining Artificial Intelligence

In recent decades, artificial intelligence has experienced alternating phases of intense media attention and periods of stagnation.[193] The earliest reflections on the subject date back to the 1950s, an era in which stories of robots and "intelligent" machines flourished in science fiction, capturing the public imagination.

The term "artificial intelligence" appears to have been first introduced by American computer scientist and cognitive theorist John McCarthy in 1956, on the occasion of the Dartmouth Summer Research Project.[194] As will be demonstrated by the multiplicity of definitions assigned to AI, its applications are so heterogeneous that referring to it as a singular concept has become increasingly problematic – albeit not without a certain degree of necessary approximation.

Interest in artificial intelligence has evolved over time in response to technological and social developments.

The most recent decisive breakthrough occurred in the 2010s,[195] following roughly sixty years marked by alternating progress and setbacks, with the "revolution of deep learning"[196] – where the term "deep" refers to the multilayered structure of the artificial neural networks[197] that are at the core functioning of these models and distinguish them from the simpler models proposed in the 1960s. Deep learning systems are a subset of "machine learning", which can be defined as "a field of artificial intelligence focused on designing computer systems that can automatically learn and improve based on data or experience, without relying on explicitly programmed rules".[198] Its core technique involves building a statistical model based on examples of inputs and corresponding expected outputs, known as "training data", along with a metric for evaluating the model's performance.

---

193 Bensamoun and Farchy (n 4) 7.

194 Scarciglia, "Methods and Legal Comparison" (n 148) 175.

195 Bensamoun and Farchy (n 4).

196 Sejnowski TJ, *The Deep Learning Revolution* (MIT Press 2018).

197 Ibid. USCO states: "Neural networks are mathematical functions that map, or transform, input data to output data.16 These functions are described by a general structure and large collections of numbers, called parameters, which define the mapping of inputs to outputs.17 With billions of parameters, collectively referred to as the network's 'weights'".

198 US Copyright Office, Copyright and Artificial Intelligence: Part 3 – Generative AI Training prepublication version: A Report of the Register of Copyrights (July 2024) <https://www.copyright.gov/ai/Copyright-and-Artificial-Intelligence-Part-3-Generative-AI-Training-Report-Pre-Publication-Version.pdf>.

A key driver of the latest resurgence of AI, the so-called "AI spring"[199], has been not only the enhancement of computing power and advancements in scientific research – particularly in the area of convolutional neural networks[200] – but, above all, the commercialization of distributed computing networks through platforms such as Amazon Web Services, Google Cloud, and Microsoft Azure, which enabled smaller firms to access such processing power and data storage capacities that were previously limited to large corporations, academic institutions, or government agencies,[201] along with the rise of the big data phenomenon and the consequent increasing availability of vast datasets on which algorithms can be trained and optimized. This phenomenon is closely linked to what has been termed the "datafication"[202] of reality, as well as the broader trend of "the massive and ongoing digitization of human knowledge over the past few decades, partly the result of the steady encroachment of technologies of digital surveillance and data capture into every corner of people's everyday lives".[203]

Interestingly, Pachet emphasized that the growing interest in AI over the past decades is more attributable to the availability of data than to technological advances alone, by observing that "twenty years ago computer science was driven by the creation of algorithms, to which you used to feed data for it to [be] processed in a specific way" and that, by contrast, nowadays "you start with a massive amount of data, for which you create a very general algorithm that looks for patterns".[204]

---

199 Bommasani R, "AI Spring? Four Takeaways from Major Releases in Foundation Models" (Stanford Institute for Human-Centered Artificial Intelligence, 17 March 2023) <https://hai.stanford.edu/news/ai-spring-four-takeaways-major-releases-foundation-models>, accessed 10 June 2025.

200 The area of convolutional neural networks, in fact, had already been developed since the 1980s, but has sparked a new wave of interest since 2012, thanks to a number of practical applications that have recently enjoyed renewed success. See Bensamoun and Farchy (n 4) 8.

201 Drott E, "Copyright, Compensation, and Commons in the Music AI Industry" (2021) 14 (2) *Creative Industries Journal* 190, 191 <https://doi.org/10.1080/17510694.2020.1839702>, accessed 10 June 2025.

202 Southerton C, "Datafication" in Laurie A Schintler and Connie L McNeely (eds), *Encyclopedia of Big Data* (Springer, Cham 2022) <https://doi.org/10.1007/978-3-319-32010-6_332>, accessed 10 June 2025, who states "Datafication renders a diverse range of information as machine-readable, quantifiable data for the purpose of aggregation and analysis. Datafication is also used as a term to describe a logic that sees things in the world as sources of data to be 'mined' for correlations or sold, and from which insights can be gained about human behavior and social issues. This term is often employed by scholars seeking to critique such logics and processes".

203 Drott (n 201) 191.

204 European Commission, "Computer Science in Music: Interview with François Pachet, Director of the Spotify Creator Technology Research Lab" (28 August 2018) <https://ec.

That said, one of the most controversial aspects of the AI debate lies in the difficulty – if not the impossibility – of establishing a clear and universally accepted definition of such a concept from a legal viewpoint. Indeed, there is currently no broadly agreed-upon understanding of what constitutes artificial intelligence, nor is there consensus on how to draw the boundaries between artificial intelligence as such, artificial intelligence systems, and – more recently – artificial intelligence models, a distinction that has acquired particular relevance with the rise of general-purpose and foundation models.[205]

Nevertheless, several attempts at classification and definition have been made so far.

As early as 1978, while discussing expert systems, Michie characterized AI as a process of refining knowledge, suggesting that it can achieve levels of accuracy and competence in codifying information that far exceed what even the most skilled human expert could reach – perhaps ever. Similarly, in one of the field's most influential textbooks, Russell and Norvig defined AI as the effort to understand and create intelligent agents. They associated intelligence primarily with rational behavior, noting that, ideally, an intelligent agent is one that selects the optimal action in any given situation.[206]

Underlying both these definitions is a first relatively uncontroversial element in the otherwise complex task of defining artificial intelligence, i.e. that the term generally refers both to the capability of a system – its "intelligence" in the strict sense – to solve problems, perform actions, and make decisions with varying degrees of autonomy, and the body of technologies or scientific knowledge underlying such systems.[207] A second widely accepted aspect is that AI systems are often combinations of hardware and software capable of carrying out tasks and activities that were traditionally considered exclusive to human cognition and abilities.

Building on these premises, some other scholars have sought to define the scope of AI by distinguishing between systems based on strong AI – those designed to simulate human intelligence – and weak AI systems, which are

europa.eu/digital-single-market/en/news/computer-science-music-interview-francois-pachet-director-spotify-creator-technology-research>, accessed 10 June 2025.

205 Ebers M and others, "The European Commission's Proposal for an Artificial Intelligence Act – A Critical Assessment by Members of the Robotics and AI Law Society (RAILS)" (2021) 4(4) J 589.

206 Crawford (n 18).

207 CNIL (Commission nationale de l'informatique et des libertés), *Comment permettre à l'homme de garder la main ? Rapport sur les enjeux éthiques des algorithmes et de l'intelligence artificielle* (Paris, 15 December 2017) 14, citing Marvin Minsky and John McCarthy's definition of "artificial intelligence" as « the science of making machines do what humans would do with a certain intelligence ».

limited to solving specific tasks for which they have been explicitly programmed and trained.[208]

Others have drawn a distinction between deductive, rule-based systems (formerly known as "expert systems"), which solve well-defined problems using predefined facts and rules, and inductive systems, which rely on probabilistic models and machine learning algorithms trained on datasets. The former are considered deterministic in nature, as their outputs can be precisely inferred from input data and embedded rules; the latter are capable of autonomous learning, extracting patterns and information from contextual data.[209]

However, these classifications have somewhat lost their relevance in light of more recent developments – most notably the rise of generative AI – , as they do not fully capture the challenges that have been thoroughly highlighted by the now extensive body of literature on the subject.

What has proven particularly relevant for current policy and legislative documents, instead, are the efforts made by some organizations – both at the policy and legislative levels – to identify the distinctive features of this technology.

Some key features were identified as early as 2019 by the High-Level Expert Group on Artificial Intelligence, appointed by the European Commission. In its attempt to provide an initial operational definition of AI systems, the group described them as "software (and possibly also hardware) systems designed by humans that, given a complex goal, act in the physical or digital dimension by perceiving their environment through data acquisition, interpreting the collected structured or unstructured data, reasoning on the knowledge, or processing the information, derived from this data and deciding the best action(s) to take to achieve the given goal. AI systems can either use symbolic rules or learn a numeric model, and they can also adapt their behavior by analyzing how the environment is affected by their previous actions".[210]

According to this definition, AIs would be systems capable of perceiving their surroundings through the acquisition, interpretation, and processing of structured or unstructured data collected and of deciding on the best actions to take in order to achieve a given goal.[211]

A similarly articulated definition of AI was then provided by AI Watch, i.e., the European Commission's service aimed at "monitoring the development, uptake, and impact of artificial intelligence for Europe", which identified the

208 Deltorn and Macrez (n 44) 4.

209 Bensamoun and Farchy (n 4) 8.

210 High-Level Expert Group on Artificial Intelligence, *Ethical Guidelines for Trustworthy AI* (8 April 2019) 9 <https://digital-strategy.ec.europa.eu/en/node/1950/printable/pdf>, accessed 10 June 2025.

211 Ibid.

following four characteristics as common to all artificial intelligence systems the ability "(i) to perceive its environment and its complexity; (ii) to process information, through the collection and interpretation of input; (iii) to enact decision-making, including reasoning, learning and the execution of actions; and (iv) to achieve predefined goals".[212]

At the regulatory level, Article 3(1) of the AI Act represents the first formal attempt to provide an explicit definition of an "artificial intelligence system", specifying that "'AI system' means a machine-based system that is designed to operate with varying levels of autonomy and that may exhibit adaptiveness after deployment, and that, for explicit or implicit objectives, infers, from the input it receives, how to generate outputs such as predictions, content, recommendations, or decisions that can influence physical or virtual environments". This definition is paired with the European Commission's Guidelines on the Application of the Definition of "artificial intelligence system"[213], which provide further clarification of the definition introduced in the AI Act, identifying a set of seven key characteristics, echoing those identified by the Expert Group and the AI Watch. According to the document, an AI system is described as (i) a machine-based system; (ii) designed to operate with varying levels of autonomy; (iii) that may exhibit adaptiveness after deployment; (iv) operating with explicit or implicit objectives; (v) capable of inferring, from the input it receives, how to generate outputs; (vi) such as predictions, content, recommendations, or decisions; (vii) that can influence physical or virtual

---

212 Samoili S, Lopez Cobo M, Gomez Gutierrez E, De Prato G, Martinez-Plumed F, and Delipetrev B, AI Watch. Defining Artificial Intelligence, EUR 30117 EN (Publications Office of the European Union 2020) 8–9 <https://doi.org/10.2760/382730>, accessed 10 June 2025, setting out four dimensions of AI: "i) perception of the environment and real-world complexity; ii) information processing: collecting and interpreting inputs; iii) decision making, including reasoning, learning and taking actions; and iv) achievement of pre-defined goals". Riccio GM and Rotolo F, "La tutela in Italia delle opere dell'ingegno create dall'intelligenza artificiale: la necessità di un'analisi in chiave prospettica" in Pasa B (ed), Design e innovazione digitale: dialogo interdisciplinare per un ripensamento delle tutele (ESI Napoli 2021) 199–230, 205–206, who identify the following characteristics:(i) support the execution of tasks that normally require the intervention of human intelligence; (ii) interact with the outside world, mimicking human behavior; (iii) reprocess huge amounts of data in a tendentially autonomous and self-sufficient manner; and (iv) understand information about the surrounding environment and adapt to the context of reference.

213 European Commission, "Commission Guidelines on the Definition of an Artificial Intelligence System Established by Regulation (EU) 2024/1689 (AI Act)" C(2025) 5053 final (Brussels, 29 July 2025) <https://digital-strategy.ec.europa.eu/library/commission-publishes-guidelines-ai-system-definition-facilitate-first-ai-acts-rules-application>, accessed 10 June 2025.

environments. Importantly, as specified in the Guidelines, the definition of an AI system adopts a lifecycle-based perspective encompassing two main phases: the pre-deployment or "building" phase of the system and the post-deployment or "use" phase of the system.

Notably, in the initial version of the text (April 21, 2021),[214] the concretization of the definition of AI was relegated to Annex I.[215] However, in response to calls for greater flexibility in the definition of such systems – and with the aim of adopting a formulation that is uniform, aligned with those of other international organizations,[216] and technology-neutral, "so that it can apply to the AI systems of today and tomorrow"[217] – it was ultimately decided to repeal this annex.

It is arguable that, in the actual definition, the EU act adopts a perspective that has been described as "inclusive",[218] as it counts predictive analyses, such as Bayesian estimators and deterministic expert systems, among the AI systems covered by the legislation. This is a broader definition than the traditional ones, which often only cover machine learning based on supervised, unsupervised, and reinforcement learning methods[219] and which, conversely,

---

214 In the version of the AI Act of 21 April 2021, an AI system was defined as "software that is developed with one or more of the techniques and approaches listed in Annex I and can, for a given set of human-defined objectives, generate outputs such as content, predictions, recommendations, or decisions influencing the environments they interact with".

215 Annex I of the AI Act proposal included, in particular, the following technologies: "(a) Machine learning approaches, including supervised, unsupervised, and reinforcement learning, using a wide variety of methods including deep learning; (b) Logic- and knowledge-based approaches, including knowledge representation, inductive (logic) programming, knowledge bases, inference and deductive engines, (symbolic) reasoning and expert systems; (c) statistical approaches, Bayesian estimation, search, and optimization methods".

216 Recital 12 of the AI Act (n 5) recalls the need for the notion of "AI system" to be aligned "with the work of international organizations working on AI to ensure legal certainty, facilitate international convergence and wide acceptance, while providing the flexibility to accommodate the rapid technological developments in this field".

217 European Parliament Press Release of 11 May 2023, <https://www.europarl.europa.eu/news/it/press-room/20230505IPR84904/ai-act-a-step-closer-to-the-first-rules-on-artificial-intelligence>, accessed 10 June 2025.

218 Floridi L and others, "capAI – A Procedure for Conducting Conformity Assessment of AI Systems in Line with the EU Artificial Intelligence Act" (2022) <https://ssrn.com/abstract=4064091>, accessed 9 August 2025.

219 Ibid. Also, many associate the term "artificial intelligence" primarily with machine learning, and not with simple automation processes in which preprogrammed rules are executed according to logic-based reasoning (see Ebers et al (n 205)). The reason for this trend is that it is undeniable that advances in machine learning have rendered systems based on predefined rules obsolete in many areas, and that machine learning is therefore

"comes to cover almost all software".[220] The rationale for adopting such a broad definition lies in the emphasis placed by the AI Act on the use case rather than the underlying technology of the system, in line with the principle of the risk-based approach adopted by the act.[221]

Such a broad definition could, however, be problematic and lead to great uncertainty for developers, operators, and users of AI systems.[222]

Thus, as suggested in the past by the EU Council,[223] the notion of AI should at least be based on specific characteristics of AI, such as its ability to learn, reason, or build models ("modeling"), so that it can be distinguished from software based on simpler programming techniques.[224]

As valuable as these definitional efforts may be, they risk becoming obsolete when faced with the complexity of current challenges. This has led Floridi to

today the main avenue of study of AI and marks the transition from programming logic to self-configuring logic (see Bensamoun and Farchy (n 4) 8).

220 Ebers et al (n 205).

221 Floridi et al, capAI (n 218).

222 Ebers et al (n 205).

223 Council of the European Union, "General approach: Proposal for a Regulation of the European Parliament and of the Council laying down harmonized rules on artificial intelligence (Artificial Intelligence Act)" (LIMITE, 14954/22, OR EN, Brussels, 25 November 2022).

224 Underlying the qualitative distinction between AI systems and the simpler software in use to date, "characteristics of AI systems which make them qualitatively different from previous technological advancements [are]: (i) Complexity and interconnectivity: Many AI systems consist of a multiplicity of different components and processes which are interlinked. This complexity and interconnectivity make it difficult to monitor, identify, and prove possible breaches of laws. (ii) Correlation instead of causation: Most data mining techniques are used to spot patterns and statistical correlations instead of searching for causation between the relevant parameters. The inference of these correlations from data input can reinforce systemic biases and errors. This aggravates concerns of autonomy and algorithmic discrimination. (iii) Continuous adaptation: The ability of some AI systems to continuously "learn" and "adapt" over time can lead to unpredictable outcomes and give rise to new risks that are not adequately addressed by the existing legislation. (iv) Autonomous behavior: The ability of some AI systems to generate outputs with limited or no human intervention might violate safety rules and human rights that may not even be noticed. (v) Opacity: The lack of transparency of AI systems (black box problem) makes it difficult to monitor, identify, and prove possible breaches of laws, including legal provisions that protect fundamental rights of humans". Ebers M, "Standardizing AI – The Case of the European Commission's Proposal for an Artificial Intelligence Act" (6 August 2021) The Cambridge Handbook of Artificial Intelligence: Global Perspectives on Law and Ethics, available at SSRN <https://ssrn.com/abstract=3900378> or <http://dx.doi.org/10.2139/ssrn.3900378>.

provocatively claim that "artificial intelligence does not exist".[225] According to his view, what exists instead are extraordinarily powerful technologies that, when placed in the hands of capable human intelligence, can be used to achieve remarkable outcomes – but if mismanaged, could lead to harmful consequences.

In this perspective, artificial intelligence is neither truly "artificial" nor genuinely "intelligent"; it is just a means of power.[226] It is an infrastructure, able to recommend, create, and persuade.

2 First Attempts to Regulate AI

2.1 AI Policies across the World

The governance of artificial intelligence has become a pressing and contentious global issue. A central concern in this debate emerged during a high-level institutional event held in Paris at the beginning of 2025 – the AI Summit in Paris – where it became evident that control over AI development is a delicate matter that must be addressed in a coordinated and collaborative manner.

In recent years, numerous regulatory initiatives have emerged worldwide at the regional, international, and national levels. A comprehensive enumeration of these efforts would be beyond the scope of this discussion; instead, this section highlights the most significant trends and frameworks shaping the current landscape.

The centrality of AI in political and societal agendas is evident across both global and local contexts. Among the various initiatives, the most prominent legislative development to date is the EU's AI Act, which remains, thus far, the only regional regulatory framework to have been formally adopted.

However, at the international level, a particularly significant development is the Council of Europe's Framework Convention on Artificial Intelligence. From a legal standpoint, this represents a major milestone as the first binding international instrument aimed at governing the development and deploy-

225 Floridi L, "L'intelligenza artificiale non esiste" (DiMT, 17 February 2025) <https://www.dimt.it/news/floridi-lintelligenza-artificiale-non-esiste/>, accessed 11 June 2025.

226 Instead, AI is fundamentally embodied and material – it is constructed from natural resources, powered by energy, dependent on human labor, and sustained through infrastructures, logistical networks, historical contexts, and classification systems. AI systems are not inherently autonomous or rational; they are incapable of making sense of the world without extensive, computation-heavy training on large datasets or reliance on predefined rules and reward structures. In reality, AI as it exists today is deeply embedded within broader political and social frameworks, see Crawford (n 18).

ment of AI in line with fundamental values such as human rights, democracy, and the rule of law.[227] Opened for signature on September 5, 2024, the Convention seeks to ensure that all activities throughout the AI system lifecycle are consistent with these core principles, while also fostering innovation and technological advancement.

In the realm of soft law, initiatives have also proliferated. In recent years, sector-specific associations, political organizations, and academic institutions have established dedicated working groups to examine AI technologies and to assess their ethical and legal implications.[228] An institutional perspective has been offered as well by international bodies such as the United Nations, WIPO, WTO, EUIPO, and the OECD, which have made substantial contributions to the global debate on artificial intelligence.[229] Their initiatives include the commissioning of studies aimed at clarifying the normative challenges

227 Council of Europe, *Framework Convention on Artificial Intelligence and Human Rights, Democracy and the Rule of Law* (opened for signature 5 September 2024, Vilnius) CETS No 225.

228 Notable reflections have emerged, for instance, within the work of UNESCO, the European Copyright Society, ALAI, and AIPPI, as well as from academic research centres such as IViR (Institute for Information Law, University of Amsterdam), CREATe (University of Glasgow), CiTiP (KU Leuven), and the Max Planck Institute for Innovation and Competition. Some of these institutions have often generally focused on the interactions between AI and ethics, as well as the broader cultural and societal impacts of information and communication technologies (ICTs), particularly with respect to access to knowledge and the protection of cultural diversity. See, for example, the UNESCO, Recommendation on the Ethics of Artificial Intelligence (adopted 23 November 2021); UNESCO, Consultation Paper on AI Regulation: Emerging Approaches across the World (2024); yet, some others have specifically addressed the intersections between AI and copyright law. See, just to name a few, AIPPI, *Copyright in Artificially Generated Works* (2019); Hartmann C, Allan JEM, Hugenholtz PB, Quintais JP and Gervais D, Trends and Developments in Artificial Intelligence: Challenges to Copyright (Institute for Information Law (IViR) and The Joint Institute for Innovation Policy (JIIP) 2020) <https://www.ivir.nl/publicaties/download/Trends_and_Developments_in_Artificial_Intelligence-1.pdf>, accessed 9 August 2025; Drexl J, Hilty R and others, "Artificial Intelligence and Intellectual Property Law – Position Statement of the Max Planck Institute for Innovation and Competition of 9 April 2021 on the Current Debate" (2021) Max Planck Institute for Innovation & Competition Research Paper No 21-10 <https://ssrn.com/abstract=3822924> or <http://dx.doi.org/10.2139/ssrn.3822924>; ECS, Opinion on the Copyright Implications of Artificial Intelligence (2021); ALAI Paris Congress, Droit d'auteur, droits voisins et intelligence artificielle (2023); more recently, see CREATe Research Centre, Copyright and AI: Response by the CREATe Centre to the UK Government's Consultation (2025).

229 See, for example, United Nations, *Governing AI for Humanity* (n 141); WTO, *ChatWTO: An Analysis of Generative Artificial Intelligence and International Trade* (2024); WIPO, *Generative AI: Navigating Intellectual Property* (2024); OECD, *Initial Policy Considerations for Generative Artificial Intelligence* (2023); EUIPO, *The Development of Generative Artificial Intelligence from a Copyright Perspective* (2025).

and opportunities posed by AI, which have served as a benchmark for policy formulation in many jurisdictions.

In parallel with these supranational efforts, several national governments have also launched important political and legal initiatives to address the challenges posed by artificial intelligence. Within the framework of the European approach to AI governance,[230] numerous EU member states have adopted national strategies and legal instruments aligned with the European values.

Spain, for instance, took a pioneering step in 2023 by establishing the *Agencia Española de Supervisión de la Inteligencia Artificial* (AESIA),[231] becoming the first EU member state to establish a dedicated national AI supervisory authority.[232] The agency has since played an active role in Spain's national approach to AI, and the 2024 National Strategy for Artificial Intelligence[233] has referred to it as "a fundamental anchor of this strategy", dedicating an entire pillar to its mission: "Pillar 3 – Develop transparent, responsible, and humanistic AI".

Although it did not establish a dedicated AI authority,[234] the Italian government too has advanced its AI governance framework in 2023 by creating the *Commissione sull'Intelligenza Artificiale per l'Informazione* to assess the impact of artificial intelligence on copyright law, as well as on the production and dissemination of informational content.[235] Further components of the Italian approach include the *Piano coordinato sull'intelligenza artificiale* [Coo-

---

230 European Commission, *European Approach to Artificial Intelligence* <https://digital-strategy.ec.europa.eu/en/policies/european-approach-artificial-intelligence>, accessed 11 June 2025; for an overview on each EU Member State's AI policy strategy, see <https://ai-watch.ec.europa.eu/countries_en>.

231 AESIA, *Garantizando una IA ética y responsable: Liderando y coordinando la supervisión del desarrollo de la IA* <https://aesia.digital.gob.es/es?utm_source=chatgpt.com>, accessed 11 June 2025.

232 Federico Guerrini, "European Countries Race To Set The AI Regulatory Pace" (Forbes, 4 September 2023) <https://www.forbes.com/sites/federicoguerrini/2023/09/04/european-countries-race-to-set-the-ai-regulatory-pace/>, accessed 11 June 2025.

233 Government of Spain, *2024 National Strategy for Artificial Intelligence* (2024) <https://digital.gob.es/content/dam/portal-mtdfp/comunicacion/comunicacion_sedia/2024/05/2024-05-14/20240514_NdP_EstrategiaIA_2024.pdf>, accessed 11 June 2024.

234 In Italy, the governance of the AI Act has been assigned to AGID (Agenzia per l'Italia Digitale) and ACN (National Cybersecurity Agency), as the lead authorities for technical and cybersecurity matters, respectively. See Law no. 132 of 23 September 2025, entitled "Disposizioni e deleghe al Governo in materia di intelligenza artificiale", delegating to the Government the power to regulate AI and outlining a national legal framework for AI governance.

235 *Commissione Intelligenza Artificiale per l'Informazione*, available at: <https://www.informazioneeditoria.gov.it/it/commissione-ia-per-linformazione/la-commissione-intelligenza-artificiale-per-linformazione/>, accessed 11 June 2025.

rdinated Plan on Artificial Intelligence], as reviewed in 2021,[236] and the *Strategia Italiana per l'Intelligenza Artificiale 2024–2026* [Italian Strategy for Artificial Intelligence 2024–2026].[237] Also of particular interest is the legislative initiative that resulted in Law no. 132 of 23 September 2025, entitled "Disposizioni e deleghe al Governo in materia di intelligenza artificiale", delegating to the Government the power to regulate AI and outlining a national legal framework for AI governance.[238]

The year 2023 also marked a significant period for AI-related developments in France, including the establishment of a Generative AI Committee.[239] This initiative builds on earlier efforts, notably the launch of the *Stratégie Nationale pour l'Intelligence Artificielle* in 2018. The French national strategy has since progressed to its third phase, the most recent of which was released in February 2025, with a focus on research, innovation, and ethical governance.[240] Also noteworthy among France's efforts are two legislative attempts

236 <https://digital-strategy.ec.europa.eu/it/policies/plan-a>, accessed March 2025.

237 Italian Government, *Strategia italiana per l'intelligenza artificiale 2024–2026* (2024) <https://www.agid.gov.it/sites/agid/files/2024-07/Strategia_italiana_per_l_Intelligenza_artificiale_2024-2026.pdf>, accessed 11 June 2025.

238 Law 132/2025 (n 234). Through this Act, the government intends to establish a coherent national legal framework to regulate the development and use of artificial intelligence throughout Italy. Central to the Act is the creation of a governance system for AI at the national level. Specifically, the Act identifies AGID (Agenzia per l'Italia Digitale) and ACN (National Cybersecurity Agency) as the lead authorities for technical and cybersecurity aspects, respectively, and allocates oversight responsibilities to a specially established Coordination Committee, "*Comitato di coordinamento delle attività di indirizzo su enti,organismi e fondazioni che operano nelcampo dell'innovazione digitale e dell'intelligenza artificiale*" (Coordination Committee for guidance activities concerning entities, bodies and foundations operating in the field of digital innovation and artificial intelligence". Moreover, the proposal grants the government the authority to adopt legislative decrees, including decrees aimed at facilitating the implementation of the EU AI Act (n 5) and defining tailored domestic regulations for sectors particularly sensitive to AI-related transformations. Lastly, the Act includes provisions addressing copyright, security, national defence and healthcare, see Resta G, Riccio GM, Il ddl AI è legge: primi spunti di riflessione (Il Quotidiano Giuridico, 18 September 2025) <https://www.altalex.com/documents/2025/09/18/ddl-legge-primi-spunti-riflessione>, accessed 24 September 2025.

239 <https://www.dataia.eu/index.php/en/news/creation-french-generative-artificial-intelligence-committee#:~:text=The%20aim%20of%20this%20Committee,of%20the%20artificial%20intelligence%20revolution>.

240 French Ministry for the Economy and Finance, Stratégie nationale pour l'intelligence artificielle – Phase 3 (February 2025) <https://www.economie.gouv.fr/actualites/strategie-nationale-intelligence-artificielle>, accessed 29 April 2025.

to regulate artificial intelligence in recent years.[241] The first, *Proposition de loi No. 1630, visant à encadrer l'intelligence artificielle par le droit d'auteur*, was submitted on September 12, 2023, and sought to regulate AI through the lens of copyright law.[242] The second, *Proposition de loi No. 675, visant à identifier les images générées par intelligence artificielle publiées sur les réseaux sociaux*, was introduced on December 3, 2024,[243] aimed to introduce mandatory labeling for AI-generated images published on social media platforms.

In Germany, 2023 saw the adoption of a new AI Action Plan issued by the Federal Ministry of Education and Research (BMBF), which builds upon and updates the national AI strategies introduced in 2018 and 2020,[244] and has outlined several overarching objectives, such as reinforcing the foundational pillars of AI development – data availability, computing capacity, skilled professionals, and research – and strengthening the interconnections among them. Notably, in terms of AI governance, six AI competence centers form the backbone of Germany's AI research infrastructure.[245]

Equally noteworthy, in today's rapidly evolving geopolitical landscape, are the AI policies developed by countries outside the European Union.

In the United Kingdom, for example, in addition to the 2021 National Strategy for AI – presented as a "10-year plan to make Britain a global AI superpower"[246] – a major initiative was the establishment of the *Foundation Model Taskforce* (later, Frontier AI Taskforce) in April 2023, tasked with driving the development and deployment of next-generation safe AI systems. In the same year, the UK hosted the inaugural AI Safety Summit at Bletchley Park (November 2023), signaling its ambition to reinforce its leadership in global AI safety. The summit brought together international stakeholders to address AI-related risks and reg-

---

241 Both bills were referred to a permanent committee of the French National Assembly – respectively the Committee on Cultural and Educational Affairs and the Committee on Economic Affairs – but neither has been adopted yet: <https://www.assemblee-nationale.fr/dyn/16/dossiers/encadrer_ia_droit_auteur>; <https://www.assemblee-nationale.fr/dyn/17/dossiers/identification_images_IA_reseaux_sociaux>.

242 <https://www.assemblee-nationale.fr/dyn/16/textes/l16b1630_proposition-loi>.

243 <https://www.assemblee-nationale.fr/dyn/17/textes/l17b0675_proposition-loi>.

244 <https://www.bmbf.de/EN/Research/EmergingTechnologies/ArtificialIntelligence/artificialintelligence_node.html#:~:text=New%20impetus%20for%20AI%20in%20Germany,-Germany%20launched%20its&text=The%20updated%20AI%20Strategy%20was,in%20the%20current%20legislative%20period>.

245 This includes the BIFOLD – Berlin Institute for the Foundations of Learning and Data; DFKI – German Research Center for Artificial Intelligence (Deutsches Forschungszentrum für Künstliche Intelligenz); Lamarr Institute for Machine Learning and Artificial Intelligence; MCML – Munich Center for Machine Learning.

246 <https://www.gov.uk/government/publications/national-ai-strategy/national-ai-strategy-html-version>.

ulatory challenges, culminating in the Bletchley Declaration, which underscored the need for global cooperation in managing AI risks.[247] Building on this momentum, the UK introduced additional initiatives aimed at strengthening its AI governance framework. Notably, the 2023 white paper titled "A Pro-Innovation Approach to AI Regulation" outlined the government's proposals for a proportionate, future-proof, and innovation-friendly AI regulatory framework.[248] Other significant measures include the AI Opportunities Action Plan,[249] which highlighted how the government can harness AI to improve productivity and public service delivery, and the Artificial Intelligence Playbook for the UK Government.[250] The AI Playbook – an evolution of the earlier "Generative AI Framework for HMG"[251] – has been expanded to encompass all current forms of AI. It provides a general overview, primers on various AI domains, links to educational resources, and addresses key areas such as user-centered AI research and emerging cyber threats. It also sets out ten core principles to guide the safe, responsible, and effective use of AI across government institutions. Finally, as part of its broader approach to AI regulation, the UK has also addressed copyright-related concerns, launching a number of public consultations on this subject matter, such as in 2021–2022 on "Artificial Intelligence and IP: copyright and patents",[252] and in 2024–2025 on "Copyright and Artificial Intelligence", which received input from various stakeholders.[253]

China's approach to artificial intelligence is anchored in a long-term strategic vision set out in the New Generation Artificial Intelligence Development Plan, released by the State Council in July 2017. The plan outlines China's ambition to become the global leader in AI by 2030, to transform AI into a trillion-yuan industry, and to shape the ethical norms and standards governing AI development. This strategy is supported by a regulatory framework that seeks to balance risk management with continued technological advancement. Notable recent

---

247 <https://www.gov.uk/government/publications/ai-safety-summit-2023-the-bletchley-declaration/the-bletchley-declaration-by-countries-attending-the-ai-safety-summit-1-2-november-2023>.

248 <https://www.gov.uk/government/publications/ai-regulation-a-pro-innovation-approach/white-paper>.

249 <https://www.gov.uk/government/publications/ai-opportunities-action-plan/ai-opportunities-action-plan>.

250 <https://www.gov.uk/government/publications/ai-playbook-for-the-uk-government/artificial-intelligence-playbook-for-the-uk-government-html>.

251 <https://www.gov.uk/government/publications/generative-ai-framework-for-hmg>.

252 <https://www.gov.uk/government/consultations/artificial-intelligence-and-ip-copyright-and-patents>.

253 The 2024 consultation closed on 25 February 2025. At the time of writing (September 2025), no legislative solution on AI and copyright had yet been adopted. https://www.gov.uk/government/consultations/copyright-and-artificial-intelligence.

examples include the Interim Measures for the Management of Generative AI Services, the Measures for the Labeling of AI-Generated and Synthesized Content and the AI Safety Governance Framework, intended to ensure safety and ethical alignment as AI technologies evolve.[254] China's primary strategic priorities in AI investment include boosting international competitiveness, driving economic growth, and enhancing social governance. Ethical considerations also occupy a prominent position in the country's AI agenda. For example, ongoing analysis of China's evolving approach – particularly in areas such as privacy and medical ethics – is offering insights into the types of governance frameworks that may eventually take shape. However, progress in developing ethical norms and standards remains in its early stages, with current efforts largely confined to broad, high-level principles that lack detailed implementation.[255]

A final and distinct consideration concerns the United States' approach to AI governance, which has undergone notable shifts over the years. In particular, the change in administration at the beginning of 2025 brought significant transformations to the national AI policy landscape. One of the key pillars of the previous US approach to AI was Executive Order 14110, signed by President Biden on October 30, 2023, titled "Safe, Secure, and Trustworthy Development and Use of Artificial Intelligence".[256] The idea was to establish new standards for safe, secure, and trustworthy AI. This Executive Order was built on the principles of the "Blueprint for an AI Bill of Rights: Making Automated Systems Work for the American People", a white paper published in October 2022 by the White House Office of Science and Technology Policy during the Biden administration.[257] The Blueprint aimed to guide the development of policies and practices that would protect civil rights and promote democratic values in the design, deployment, and governance of automated systems. It outlined five core principles and associated practices intended to ensure that such systems were aligned with democratic ideals and upheld civil rights, civil liberties, and privacy. Developed through extensive public consultation, the Blue-

254 <https://www.weforum.org/stories/2025/01/transforming-industries-with-ai-lessons-from-china/#:~:text=China's%20trajectory%20in%20AI%20is,for%20AI%20innovation%20by%202030>.

255 Huw Roberts, Josh Cowls, Jessica Morley, Mariarosaria Taddeo, Vincent Wang, and Luciano Floridi, "The Chinese Approach to Artificial Intelligence: An Analysis of Policy, Ethics, and Regulation" (2021) 36 *AI & Society* 59 <https://doi.org/10.1007/s00146-020-00992-2>.

256 <https://www.federalregister.gov/documents/2023/11/01/2023-24283/safe-secure-and-trustworthy-development-and-use-of-artificial-intelligence>.

257 Executive Order 14110 of October 30, 2023, Safe, Secure, and Trustworthy Development and Use of Artificial Intelligence, Section 2, lett (d). See also <https://bidenwhitehouse.archives.gov/ostp/ai-bill-of-rights/>.

print was considered a foundational effort to shape AI use in ways that served the public interest.[258]

However, this trajectory shifted in January 2025. A clear illustration of this change is the revocation of several Executive Orders, including the "Safe, Secure, and Trustworthy Development and Use of Artificial Intelligence", and the issuance of a new directive aimed at dismantling regulatory barriers to reinforce American leadership in AI.[259] One of the most recent and noteworthy developments in this regard, however, occurred on July 23, 2025, when the new administration published the AI Action Plan, Winning the Race: America's AI Action Plan, built upon three pillars: Pillar I – Accelerate AI Innovation; Pillar II – Build American AI Infrastructure; Pillar III – Lead in International AI Diplomacy and Security.

What is particularly noteworthy in the US context, however, is the central role played by the US Copyright Office (USCO) regarding the intersections between AI, particularly generative AI models, and copyright law. As the federal agency responsible for registering creative works, the USCO occupies a unique institutional position. In fact, its legal and policy interpretations carry substantial influence, both at the national and supernational levels, to the extent that numerous legal systems around the world are closely monitoring its actions in anticipation of future regulatory developments. Among the most impactful initiatives undertaken by the USCO in this regard is its exploration of legal and policy challenges posed by artificial intelligence. Since the launch of this effort in early 2023, the Office has been assessing questions such as the extent to which copyright protection applies to AI-generated content and the legality of using copyrighted materials in the training of AI systems. Following a series of public listening sessions and webinars, the Office published a Notice of Inquiry in the Federal Register in August 2023, which prompted

---

258 This initiative appeared to influence several federal agencies in formulating their own frameworks for the responsible use of AI. By the end of 2023, 12 US government agencies – including the Department of Commerce (DOC) and the National Institute of Standards and Technology (NIST) – had adopted AI-related requirements spanning legal, policy, and national security dimensions. At the state level, there were also signs of alignment with the Blueprint. In 2021, for example, New York enacted legislation requiring employers to notify applicants when AI technologies were used in the hiring process. Several other states introduced regulations concerning the use of facial recognition technologies by law enforcement. More recently, the California Civil Rights Council proposed amendments to the Fair Employment and Housing Act (FEHA) to bring it into closer alignment with the principles of the AI Bill of Rights, see <https://www.ibm.com/think/topics/ai-bill-of-rights>.

259 White House, Initial Rescissions of Harmful Executive Orders and Actions, January 2025, <https://www.whitehouse.gov/presidential-actions/2025/01/initial-rescissions-of-harmful-executive-orders-and-actions/>.

over 10,000 responses by the end of that year. The findings are being compiled in a multipart report, with each section to be released upon completion.[260]

These recent shifts in the US approach suggest a broader pivot toward a more deregulated, market-driven model of AI development. Nevertheless, the long-term implications of this shift remain uncertain, and it is difficult to predict how the US approach to AI will evolve in the near future.

These developments, however, point to an increasingly fragmented and complex global landscape, with major powers – most notably the United States, China, and the European Union – in open competition for leadership in the field of artificial intelligence.

2.2 The EU Strategy on AI

In 2025, the European Union marked the 10-year anniversary of its 2015 digital single market strategy.[261] Originally adopted to ensure that Europe's economy, industry, and society could fully seize the opportunities of the digital age, the strategy also aimed to position the EU as a global leader in shaping the regulatory landscape for the digital sector, including artificial intelligence and other strategic technologies[262] – aligning this ambition with the broader vision of extending the so-called "Brussels Effect" to the evolving digital domain.[263]

Among the key themes addressed in EU within the current digital framework are, on the one hand, the promotion of emerging technologies, digital services, and content as engines of EU competitiveness "on a global scale and in the world", and, on the other hand, the commitment to a human-centered digital transition,[264] along with the development and implementation of mechanisms for the collective[265] and procedural[266] protection of rights.

---

260 US Copyright Office, *Copyright and Artificial Intelligence* <https://www.copyright.gov/ai/>, accessed 11 June 2025.

261 European Commission, "Communication to the European Parliament, the Council, the European Economic and Social Committee and the Committee of the Regions 'A Strategy for a Digital Single Market in Europe'" (6 May 2015) COM(2015) 192 final.

262 European Parliament, Shaping the Digital Transformation: EU Strategy Explained <https://www.europarl.europa.eu/news/en/headlines/society/20210414STO02010/shaping-the-digital-transformation-eu-strategy-explained>, accessed 11 June 2025.

263 Bradford A, "The Brussels Effect" (2013) 107 *Northwestern University Law Review* 1.

264 Significant in this respect are the digital principles formulated by the European Commission (European Commission, "Establishing a European Declaration on Digital Rights and Principles for the Digital Decade" COM(2022) 27 final, 26 January 2022) such as "internet access for all; a safe online space; the right to acquire digital skills; people-friendly algorithms; protection of children online".

265 Ricolfi M, "Regulating de facto powers" (n 91).

266 Bernes A, "Data and Genetic Research. From Individual Protection to Procedural Management" (2022) Special Issue 1 *BioLaw Journal – Journal of BioLaw*.

Against this backdrop, and in line with its broader digital strategy, the European Union has recently turned its attention to the field of artificial intelligence, expressing its ambition to position itself as a global hub through what it has termed the "European approach to artificial intelligence".[267] This is a journey that has faced multiple stages[268] and culminated in the European Commission's publication of the White Paper on Artificial Intelligence,[269] the Proposal for a Directive on Artificial Intelligence Liability,[270] and, most recently, the adoption of the so-called AI Pact.[271]

The latter was defined by the European Commission as a "scheme that will foster early implementation of the measures foreseen by the AI Act", aimed, therefore, at encouraging companies to apply, on a voluntary basis, the measures set out in the AI Act, before its (full) entry into force. It should be noted, in this regard, that certain provisions of the AI Act become applicable in stages: while some applied almost immediately, others – e.g., those concerning general-purpose AI models – are subject to a transitional period before becoming applicable. The AI Pact, therefore, sought to encourage the early, voluntary application of these obligations ahead of those deadlines, thereby

---

267 <https://digital-strategy.ec.europa.eu/en/policies/european-approach-artificial-intelligence>.

268 Besides the AI act, there have been many milestones along this path so far, the first of which is represented by the EU Commission press release of 9 March 2018: "Artificial Intelligence: Commission Kicks Off Work on Marrying Cutting-Edge Technology and Ethical Standards" <https://ec.europa.eu/commission/presscorner/detail/en/IP_18_1381>. Other significant milestones are represented by the publication of the JRC's Flagship report on AI: Annoni A, Benczur P, Bertoldi P and others, "Artificial Intelligence: A European Perspective" in Craglia M (ed), EUR 29425 EN (Publications Office of the European Union 2018); and the communications of the European Commission: *Artificial Intelligence for Europe* (Communication) COM(2018) 237 final, 25 April 2018; *Coordinated Plan on Artificial Intelligence* (Communication) COM(2018) 795 final, 7 December 2018; and *Building Trust in Anthropocentric Artificial Intelligence* (Communication) COM (2019) 168 final, 8 April 2019.

269 European Commission, *White Paper on Artificial Intelligence – A European Approach to Excellence and Trust*, 19 February 2020, COM (2020) 65 final.

270 European Commission, "Proposal for a Directive of the European Parliament and of the Council on the Adaptation of the Rules on Noncontractual Liability to Artificial Intelligence (Artificial Intelligence Liability Directive)" COM(2022) 496 final, 28 September 2022. Notably, the proposal was withdrawn from consideration in February 2025: "No foreseeable agreement – the Commission will assess whether another proposal should be tabled or another type of approach should be chosen", see <https://iapp.org/news/a/european-commission-withdraws-ai-liability-directive-from-consideration>.

271 European Commission, *AI Pact* <https://digital-strategy.ec.europa.eu/en/node/12158/printable/pdf>, accessed 11 June 2025.

addressing concerns related to the rapid evolution of generative and general-purpose AI models.

The objectives of the European AI strategy are diverse, all of them to some extent already anticipated by the High-level Expert Group on artificial intelligence in its Ethical Guidelines for Trustworthy AI.[272] These include the need to promote AI that is lawful (that complies with applicable legislation), ethical (that is in line with ethical principles and values), trustworthy and human-centered, and that creates a safe and innovation-friendly environment for its developers and users.

These intentions translate, among other things, into the need to make artificial intelligence robust, transparent, traceable, supervisable by a human being, nondiscriminatory, and ecologically sustainable.

At the heart of this vision lies the promotion of EU digital sovereignty – an objective that the EU has reaffirmed with the adoption of the new Digital Europe Program (DIGITAL) for the 2025–2027 period.[273] As part of this program, the European Commission has announced a €1.3 billion investment with the declared aim to accelerate the deployment of strategic technologies deemed essential for Europe's future and its autonomy in the digital sphere. The initiative focuses on key sectors that are fundamental to the EU's digital transformation, with particular emphasis on artificial intelligence, seeking to enhance the availability and accessibility of generative AI applications, especially in areas such as healthcare and social care.

Within this context, the spring of 2025 marked the launch of the AI Continent Action Plan,[274] which continues to emphasize the development of trustworthy AI technologies – which not only enhance Europe's global competitiveness but also safeguard and promote its democratic values. Its overarching goal is to ensure that the benefits of AI are widely distributed across critical sectors, including healthcare, education, industry, and environmental sustainability. To this end, the strategy sets out measures to build large-scale AI computing and data infrastructures, increase access to high-quality datasets, and foster AI adoption in key areas of the economy.

---

272 High-Level Expert Group on Artificial Intelligence (n 217).

273 European Commission, *Work Programme 2025–2027 of the Digital Europe Program me (DIGITAL)* <https://digital-strategy.ec.europa.eu/en/library/work-programme-2025-2027-digital-europe-programme-digital>, accessed 11 June 2025.

274 European Commission, "AI Continent Action Plan" (Communication to the European Parliament, the Council, the European Economic and Social Committee and the Committee of the Regions, 9 April 2025) COM(2025) 165 final <https://digital-strategy.ec.europa.eu/en/library/ai-continent-action-plan>.

It is within this context that the AI Act was first conceived, then proposed (in April 2021), and ultimately adopted – hailed as the world's first comprehensive legislation on artificial intelligence, with the aim of providing a regulatory framework for AI ensuring the best conditions for the development and use of this technology.[275]

275 The package with which the proposal was presented included: (i) its "*Communication on Fostering a European approach to Artificial Intelligence*", <https://digital-strategy.ec.europa.eu/en/library/communication-fostering-european-approach-artificial-intelligence>; (ii) a review of the *Coordinated Plan on Artificial Intelligence*, <https://digital-strategy.ec.europa.eu/en/policies/plan-ai>; (iii) and an *Impact Assessment of the Regulation on Artificial Intelligence*, <https://digital-strategy.ec.europa.eu/en/library/impact-assessment-regulation-artificial-intelligence>.

CHAPTER 5

The EU AI Act

1 Preliminary Remarks

The Artificial Intelligence Act (AI Act) is a highly complex and extensive piece of legislation, comprising 180 recitals, 113 articles, and 13 annexes. Among its 13 Chapters, the most relevant for the purposes of this study is Chapter 5, which addresses general-purpose AI (GPAI) models and sets out the obligations applicable to their providers – including those relevant to copyright.

The path to the adoption of the Act has been far from straightforward. The proposal for the AI Regulation, along with its annexes, was officially submitted on April 21, 2021.[276] The Commission presented it as a "horizontal regulatory approach to AI that is limited to the minimum necessary requirements to address the risks and problems linked to AI, without unduly constraining or hindering technological development or otherwise disproportionately increasing the cost of placing AI solutions on the market".[277]

The European Commission played a key role in supporting the co-legislators during the interinstitutional negotiations (hence, the expression "the trilogues")[278] aimed at reaching consensus on the final legislative text. However, the adoption of the Act appeared to be at serious risk during the final months of 2023, almost jeopardizing the initial expectations that an agreement would be reached by the end of that year.[279] This slowdown was attributed to opposition from France, Germany, and Italy against the adoption of a tiered approach in

---

276 <https://eur-lex.europa.eu/legal-content/EN/TXT/?uri=celex%3A52021PC0206>.

277 Proposal for a Regulation Laying Down Harmonized Rules on Artificial Intelligence (Artificial Intelligence Act) and Amending Certain Union Legislative Acts, 21.4.2021, COM/2021/206 final, p. 3.

278 See <https://www.kaizenner.eu/post/aiact-part3>.

279 <https://www.euractiv.com/section/artificial-intelligence/news/eus-ai-act-negotiations-hit-the-brakes-over-foundation-models/> <https://www.euractiv.com/section/artificial-intelligence/news/france-germany-italy-push-for-mandatory-self-regulation-for-founda tion-models-in-eus-ai-law/>, <https://www.euractiv.com/section/artificial-intelligence/news/ai-act-eu-commission-attempts-to-revive-tiered-approach-shifting-to-general-pur pose-ai/>; <https://www.euractiv.com/section/artificial-intelligence/news/ai-act-meps-close-ranks-in-asking-for-tighter-rules-for-powerful-ai-models/?utm_source=substack&utm_medium=email>.

the legislative act,[280] which would introduce general horizontal obligations for all foundation models – the core technology behind generative AI[281] – alongside additional, more stringent requirements for those considered to pose a systemic risk to society.[282] The rationale behind this approach – which mirrors the regulatory logic seen in the General Data Protection Regulation,[283] and, more recently, in the Digital Markets Act[284] and the Digital Services Act[285] – is to place greater responsibility on large-scale AI providers, while ensuring that smaller companies are subject to proportionately lighter obligations, and is intended to foster innovation within the EU without compromising societal safeguards.[286] Some sources

---

280 Power grab by France, Germany, and Italy threatens to kill EU's AI bill, 20.11.2023, <https://www.politico.eu/article/france-germany-power-grab-kill-eu-blockbuster-ai-artificial-intelligence-bill/>.

281 "The most prominent example of a foundation model/GPAIM is OpenAI's series of generative pre-trained transformers (GPT), which are large language models that learn statistical relationships from text documents, and which form the basis for generative AI chatbots like ChatGPT", see Peukert A, "Copyright in the Artificial Intelligence Act – A Primer" (2024) 73(6) *GRUR International* 7 <https://ssrn.com/abstract=4771976> or <http://dx.doi.org/10.2139/ssrn.4771976>.

282 In particular, despite the fact that on 24 October 2023 it appeared that a possible consensus had been reached on the text of the regulation to be adopted, the three countries circulated a non-paper on 19 November 2023 in which they argued that the horizontal rules on foundation models go against the AI act's (n 27) technology-neutral and risk-based approach, which aims to preserve innovation and security, and that the risks of artificial intelligence lie in the application of AI systems, rather than in the technology itself.

283 For a broader analysis of the risk-based approach, see Raphaël Gellert, *The Risk-Based Approach to Data Protection* (Oxford University Press 2020); Emilio Tosi, *Civil Liability for Unlawful Processing of Personal Data and Non-Pecuniary Damage. Objectification of Risk and Re-Emergence of Moral Damage with a Deterrent-Sanctioning Function in the Light of Article 82 GDPR* (Milan 2019), Alessandro Mantelero, "Liability and Risk in EU Regulation 2016/679" (2017) *Nuove Leggi Civili Commentate* 144 ff.

284 Regulation (EU) 2022/1925 of the European Parliament and of the Council of 14 September 2022 on fair and contestable markets in the digital sector and amending Directives (EU) 2019/1937 and (EU) 2020/1828 (Digital Markets Act).

285 Regulation (EU) 2022/2065 of the European Parliament and of the Council of 19 October 2022 on a single market for digital services and amending Directive 2000/31/EC (Digital Services Act).

286 The informal document submitted by the three countries opposing the risk-based approach proposed instead a "self-regulatory" model, based on the development of codes of conduct and model cards – technical documentation summarizing information on the capabilities and limitations of models trained for general public use – as well as the establishment of an AI governance body to contribute to the development of guidelines and to carry out appropriate compliance checks. In response to the informal document signed by the three European powers, the European Commission circulated a

suggest that the primary reasons behind this opposition were essentially driven by lobbying interests.[287]

However, a political agreement on the final version of the Act was eventually achieved on December 8, 2023,[288] leading to the formal signing of the AI Act on June 13, 2024.

In its final version, the AI Act has removed the explicit references to foundation models and the definition of generative systems.[289] Instead, Recitals 99 and 105 contain nonbinding mentions of "large generative AI models" as a "typical example of a general-purpose AI model" (which may or may not integrated into an "AI system"),[290] highlighting their ability to enable "flexible generation of content, such as in the form of text, audio, images, or video, that can readily accommodate a wide range of distinctive tasks". As such, these models are regulated under Chapter 5 (Articles 51 and following) of the AI Act.

Interestingly, Chapter 5 was not included in the original proposal of the Regulation in April 2021. Instead, it was introduced during the negotiation

---

possible compromise text on 19 November 2023 which, in an attempt to break the deadlock caused by the opposition of Italy, France and Germany, reintroduced the tiered approach but provided for mitigated transparency obligations for general-purpose AI systems and the adoption of codes of practice for systemic risk models. It appears that most Member States considered the Commission's text a step in the right direction, although some reservations remained concerning the definitions and the broad wording envisaged for secondary legislation. Conversely, greater resistance came from the European Parliament, which had already regarded the tiered approach as a compromise and argued for the adoption of clear, albeit potentially limited, obligations for developers of the most powerful models. However, the majority of MEPs appeared to agree that an approach based solely on voluntary commitments would be unacceptable.

287 Indeed, the pause in negotiations appears to have followed meetings between officials from France, Germany, and Italy, and representatives of the AI industry. See Social Europe, *Big Tech lobbying is derailing the AI Act* <https://www.socialeurope.eu/big-tech-lobbying-is-derailing-the-ai-act?utm_source=substack&utm_medium=email>.

288 See the Joint statement from European creators and rightsholders, 1.2.2024, <https://urheber.info/diskurs/uber-200-europaische-organisationen-fur-ki-verordnung>.

289 The challenge of trying to introduce a regulatory definition of "generative AI" was first taken up by the compromise text of 14 June 2023, which defined these models as "foundation models used in AI systems specifically designed to generate, with varying degrees of autonomy, content such as complex text, images, audio, or video", See Art. 28b of the compromise text of 14 June 2023.

290 See "Annex to the Communication to the Commission Approval of the content of the draft Communication from the Commission – Guidelines on the scope of the obligations for general-purpose AI models established by Regulation (EU) 2024/1689 (AI Act)", p. 17.

process in response to the rapid emergence of generative AI following the launch of ChatGPT in November 2022.[291]

Even though the final version of the Act formally maintains the product-safety perspective underlying the initial proposal, this late-stage insertion of such provisions reflects a logic that does not fully align with it.[292]

Indeed, the original approach was based on the classification of AI systems into four categories of risk, each associated with a corresponding operational regime: (i) unacceptable risk (Chapter 2 – Art. 5),[293] (ii) high risk (Chapter 3 – Art. 6 et seq.),[294] (iii) transparency risk (Art. 50),[295] and (iv) minimal or no

291 Council of the European Union, General approach in legislative procedure 2021/0106 (COD), council document 15698/22, 6 December 2022, recital 12c, art. 3(1b), arts. 4a-4c.

292 Peukert, "Copyright in the Artificial Intelligence Act" (n 281) 2.

293 Systems that present an unacceptable risk, and are therefore prohibited (Art. 5), the AI act (n 5) identifies some significant examples in "real-time" remote biometric identification systems in publicly accessible spaces (e.g., those allowing facial recognition). However, the Act provides for some exceptions in this respect, such as, for instance, remote biometric identification systems not in real time, in cases where the identification may be useful for the prosecution of serious crimes, but only with the approval of the court. Other prohibited models are those that use "subliminal techniques beyond a person's consciousness or purposefully manipulative or deceptive techniques, with the objective, or the effect of materially distorting the behavior of a person or a group of persons by appreciably impairing their ability to make an informed decision (...) in a manner that causes or is reasonably likely to cause that person, another person or group of persons significant harm" and those used for "the evaluation or classification of natural persons or groups of persons over a certain period of time based on their social behavior or known, inferred or predicted personal or personality characteristics" (so-called social scoring – See art. 5, par. 1 of the AI act (n 5)).

294 The use of high-risk models is permitted only if they meet specific requirements (such as, for instance, the adoption of an appropriate risk management system, logging capacity and human supervision), fulfill their obligations (such as, for example, implementing a quality management system, conducting conformity assessments and drafting technical documentation), and undergo a rigorous conformity assessment (See art. 6, art. 16 and art. 43 of the AI act (n 5)) prior to its being placed on the market or put into service. According to Art. 6, these models can be divided into two categories: (i) AI systems intended for use as products or as safety components of products covered by Annex I of the Act and subject to ex-ante conformity assessment by third parties. These systems are used in products (e.g. toys, cars, medical devices, lifts, etc.) falling under the scope of EU product safety legislation; (ii) other AI systems that have implications for fundamental rights, as explicitly listed in Annex III, which must be registered in a specific database (Art. 49 and art. 71 of the AI act (n 5)). Examples of high-risk systems include models related to the management and operation of critical infrastructures, systems used in the recruitment or evaluation of employees, and AI models impacting the application and interpretation of the law, etc.

295 Minimum transparency requirements apply to "AI systems with specific transparency obligations" (Art. 50 dedicated to "Transparency obligations for providers and deployers

risk – category that include systems used, for example, in video games or spam filters, which can be used freely. When it presented the proposal, the Commission noted that the vast majority of AI systems currently used in the EU fall into this latter category.[296]

Yet, following the introduction of Chapter 5 and the introduction of the partially different concept of "general-purpose AI models",[297] this risk-based, preventive approach has started to show some limitations, as it does not align well with the nature of generative AI and GPAI models. By their very nature, such models are not designed for specific, predetermined purposes, making it difficult for their providers to classify them in advance within one of the risk categories proposed by the Act. They are in fact defined as "AI model[s], including where such (...) AI model[s are] trained with a large amount of data using self-supervision at scale, that display(...) significant generality and [are] capable of competently performing a wide range of distinct tasks regardless of the way the model[s are] placed on the market and that can be integrated into a variety of downstream systems or applications, except AI models that are used for research, development or prototyping activities before they are placed on the market".[298]

The uncertainty on how to preventively frame the risk these models may pose has been acknowledged by the EU legislator, who recognized that they

of certain AI systems"). These are intended to ensure that users are informed, for example, when they are interacting with an AI system rather than a human, or when they are exposed to multimedia content that has been automatically generated by AI. Examples of such systems include chatbots, emotion recognition or biometric categorization tools, and systems that generate or manipulate images, audio, or video in a way that closely resembles real people, objects, places, or events – potentially appearing falsely authentic or true to users (commonly referred to as "deepfakes"). For the sake of completeness, it should be noted that while the requirements outlined in Chapter 3, Section 2 apply mandatorily only to high-risk systems, Article 95 encourages operators of all other AI systems to voluntarily comply with these provisions. This may be achieved, for example, by adhering to codes of conduct to be developed by the Commission or Member States and potentially incorporated into national practices.

296 <https://digital-strategy.ec.europa.eu/en/policies/regulatory-framework-ai>.

297 Recital 97 AI act (n 5) provides that "although AI models are essential components of AI systems, they do not constitute AI systems on their own" because "AI models require the addition of further components, such as, for example, a user interface, to become AI systems".

298 Art. 3(63) of the AI Act (n 5). In this context, interestingly, the term "model" refers to an algorithm based on a (nonlinear) mathematical function that produces outputs by identifying patterns learned from training data during the training process. When such a model – specifically a general-purpose AI model (GPAIM) – is integrated into an AI system that can perform a wide range of functions, either through direct use or by being embedded into other AI systems, the resulting system is referred to as a "general-purpose AI system" (GPAIS), see Peukert, "Copyright in the Artificial Intelligence Act" (n 281) 7.

may give rise to a form of "systemic risk"[299] – a concept deliberately[300] broad and flexible, reflecting the difficulty in anticipating the types of risks they may entail. Depending on the circumstances, their specific use downstream may indeed fall into other risk categories, but providers of the models upstream are not in a position to determine this in advance.

Whether this flexible notion of systemic risk can capture the specific dangers that generative AI poses in the cultural domain – the very dangers that run through this study – remains an open question. It is in the field of copyright, however, that the limits of this framework become most visible: a domain governed by an altogether different set of obligations – introduced in the following section, though their substantive implications, especially on the input side, are reserved for Chapter 7.

2 Copyright in the AI Act

2.1 "Two Different Types of Laws"

Chapter 5 of the AI Act, entirely dedicated to the regulation of GPAI models, introduces a set of obligations specifically tailored to developers of large-scale generative AI systems, and represents the primary interface between the AI Act and the EU's copyright framework.

Although the interrelation between copyright and AI has a long history – notably, copyright issues related to AI have been discussed for decades, as evidenced by the organization of the "WIPO Worldwide Symposium on the Intellectual Property Aspects of Artificial Intelligence" at Stanford University in 1991[301] – the Commission in its initial proposal for the AI Act of April 21, 2021, moved away from the historical approach of considering copyright a key element in AI regulation. Consistent with its focus on product safety,[302] in fact, the proposal did not view copyright as a significant concern requiring dedicated regulatory measures and omitted any reference to it.

---

299 Systemic risk is broadly defined as the "risk that is specific to the high-impact capabilities of general-purpose AI models, having a significant impact on the Union market due to their reach, or due to actual or reasonably foreseeable negative effects on public health, safety, public security, fundamental rights, or the society as a whole, that can be propagated at scale across the value chain", see Article 3(65) of the AI act (n 5).

300 It is because of the complex and unpredictable challenges posed by general-purpose AI models.

301 <https://tind.wipo.int/record/19473?ln=en&v=pdf>.

302 Peukert, "Copyright in the Artificial Intelligence Act" (n 281) 2.

Despite the EU Council's introduction of provisions on GPAI already in December 2022, rules concerning copyright were only proposed later, in May 2023, by the European Parliament.[303] In the end, anyway, they have been incorporated into the final version of the Act, which now requires that providers of GPAI models, including those with generative functionalities, comply with a range of legal and technical obligations.[304]

Among these, Article 53(1)(c) and (d) of the AI Act articulate two key copyright-related obligations that apply exclusively to GPAI model providers. As will be better illustrated in Chapter 7, subparagraph (c) requires providers to implement policies aimed at ensuring compliance with Union copyright law, including the explicit recognition of reservations of rights made under Article 4(3) of the CDSM Directive, by means of advanced technological tools. Subparagraph (d) imposes a transparency obligation, mandating the public disclosure of a detailed summary of the data used to train the model, based on a template provided by the AI Office.[305]

The rationale underlying these obligations appears to reflect the deliberate policy choice to promote a structured form of cooperation between developers of generative AI and copyright holders, especially in light of the novel modes of exploitation of creative content that such technologies enable.[306]

Notwithstanding this noble purpose, it has been observed that, by introducing the copyright-relevant rules of Chapter 5 within the framework of this product-safety legislation, the AI Act has undertaken a delicate operation, as it has combined "two different types of law": copyright law, which traditionally

303 European Parliament Draft Compromise Amendments on the Draft Report, 16.5.2023, C9 0146/2021, recital 60h in fine, art. 28b(4)(c).

304 Noteworthy is that the definition of provider in art. 3(3) implies that "model development and release are controlled by the same person or body. It is unclear who qualifies as the "provider" if separate legal entities are responsible for development and release", see Peukert, "Copyright in the Artificial Intelligence Act" (n 281) 9.

305 <https://digital-strategy.ec.europa.eu/en/library/explanatory-notice-and-template-public-summary-training-content-general-purpose-ai-models>. Notably, excluded from the obligation to put in place copyright policy and training content summary are "AI systems and models specifically developed and put into service for the sole purpose of scientific research and development" (see Art. 2(6) and recital 25 AI act (n 5)). Recital 109 AI act (n 5) justifies this exemption by stating that obligations should be commensurate and proportionate to the type of model provider. The recital adds, however, that persons who develop or use models for nonprofessional or scientific research purposes "should nevertheless be encouraged to voluntarily comply with statutory requirements", see Peukert, "Copyright in the Artificial Intelligence Act" (n 281) 9.

306 see Geiger C and Iaia V, "The Forgotten Creator: Toward a Statutory Remuneration Right for Machine Learning of Generative AI" (2023) Computer Law & Security Review <https://papers.ssrn.com/sol3/papers.cfm?abstract_id=4594873> accessed 9 August 2025.

belongs to the realm of private law, and the product safety model, which focuses on setting requirements for products before and during their placement on the market.[307] This combination has led to certain contradictions, if analyzed in coordination with the existing IP legal framework.

First, the risk-based, preventive approach of the AI Act is a well-established feature of product safety, cybersecurity, and platform regulation laws, but it is alien to copyright law. The contradiction in this regard stands in the fact that "while EU law on IP enforcement also includes precautionary measures intended to prevent any imminent infringement of an IP right, the content and limits of IP rights are fixed and not subject to a risk analysis in view of the principle of proportionality".[308]

Second, the AI Act regulates the initial placing on the market, putting into service, and subsequent use of AI systems and models within the Union. However, it does not apply to activities related to research, testing, and development that occur prior to their release. This limited scope stands in sharp contrast to copyright law, which also covers nonpublic acts of (re)production.[309]

Third, the principle of territoriality that underpins (EU) copyright law, according to which protection is granted on a territory-by-territory basis, is in contrast to the territorial scope of the AI Act.[310] The latter indeed, applies to "(a) providers placing on the market or putting into service AI systems or placing on the market GPAI models in the Union, irrespective of whether those providers are established or located within the Union or in a third country; (b) deployers of AI systems that have their place of establishment or are located within the Union; (c) providers and deployers of AI systems that have their place of establishment or are located in a third country, where the output produced by the AI system is used in the Union (...)(g) affected persons that are located in the Union".[311] The contradiction becomes apparent when Article 53, which contains no reference to territorial scope, is read alongside Recital 106, which states that the obligation for providers of GPAI models to implement copyright-compliant policies and respect opt-outs under Article 4(3) of the CDSM Directive should also apply where text and data mining takes place outside the EU. The Recital explicitly affirms that this applies "regardless of the jurisdiction in which the copyright-relevant acts underpin-

307 Peukert, "Copyright in the Artificial Intelligence Act" (n 281) 5.
308 Ibid.
309 Peukert, "Copyright in the Artificial Intelligence Act" (n 281) 5.
310 Quintais JP, "Generative AI, Copyright and the AI Act" (2025) 56 Computer Law & Security Review 106107 <https://doi.org/10.1016/j.clsr.2025.106107> or <https://ssrn.com/abstract=4912701>.
311 Art. 2 AI act (n 5).

ning the training of those general-purpose AI models take place". This wording has prompted some commentators to explore whether the AI Act is attempting to extend the extraterritorial effect of its copyright-related obligations.[312]

How these contradictions will ultimately be resolved remains a matter of intense debate.[313] Nevertheless, the EU's regulatory approach can, overall, be regarded positively, as a first attempt to establish a prescriptive framework to address the specific risks posed by these technological innovations. At the same time, the tensions between copyright and the AI Act reveal the limitations of treating this legislation as a standalone instrument for comprehensive AI governance. Therefore, despite the commendable progress represented by the AI Act in acknowledging the need to address the copyright-related risks of GPAI models, a more holistic approach will likely be required to tackle the broader challenges at stake, particularly in the governance of the models used in the creative context.

2.2 Codes of Practice as Tools for Voluntary Compliance

A pivotal role in ensuring compliance with the AI Act's requirements related to copyright – albeit not only to it – is played by the Codes of Practice set out in Article 56. These are intended to set forth nonbinding guidelines aimed at supporting the implementation of the Regulation throughout the transitional period between the Act's adoption and the development of harmonized standards.

By engaging both public and private stakeholders, the mechanism of the Codes of Practice is intended to offer a more flexible and innovation-friendly approach to risk management compared to traditional regulatory frameworks. Indeed, they are designed to be voluntarily adopted by GPAI model providers to demonstrate compliance with – at least – the obligations set out in Articles 53 and 55 of the Regulation, with the consequence that, in the absence of such adherence, providers will be required to demonstrate compliance through alternative, and potentially more burdensome, means.

The first Code of Practice within the framework of the AI Act was released on July 10, 2025,[314] following a long multi-stakeholder process involving aca-

312 Quintais, Generative AI (n 310).

313 Peukert A, "Regulating IP Exclusion/Inclusion on a Global Scale: The Example of Copyright vs. AI Training" (Faculty of Law of Goethe University Frankfurt/M 2024) Research Paper of the Faculty of Law of Goethe University Frankfurt/M 3/2024 <https://papers.ssrn.com/abstract=4905400> accessed January 27, 2025.

314 European Commission, "Commission Opinion on the Assessment of the General-Purpose AI Code of Practice within the Meaning of Article 56 of Regulation (EU) 2024/

demic and independent experts, GPAI model providers, downstream deployers, civil society representatives, and other relevant actors. Its publication was accompanied by the AI Office's guidelines "on the scope of the rules for general-purpose AI models", published on July 18.[315]

Before its adoption, initially scheduled for early May, the drafting process, launched in October 2024, went through three lengthy and successive rounds, and as many drafts of the Code were published before the final version. Like its predecessors, the final text is structured into three main chapters: Transparency, Copyright, and Safety and Security. The first two apply to all GPAI model providers, while the third concerns only those models that exceed the systemic-risk threshold. However, unlike the previous drafts, the final version is significantly more concise.

Regarding the chapter on Transparency, providers who sign the Code are required to complete a standardized Model Documentation Form, which must be made available to downstream providers and to regulatory authorities upon request, while ensuring that commercially sensitive information remains confidential. The document must include technical details such as the model's architecture, the sources of data used, intended use cases, licensing information, energy consumption, known limitations, and the procedures adopted to manage them.

As for the Safety and Security chapter, it applies, as noted, exclusively to GPAI models that meet the systemic-risk threshold. Signatory providers are required to implement a comprehensive Safety and Security Framework, which includes independent oversight, rigorous evaluations conducted by external experts, and advanced cybersecurity measures such as encryption, access controls, and insider-threat protection. The framework must also ensure that serious incidents are reported promptly to the competent authorities. In addition, providers are expected to implement dedicated corporate governance mechanisms, whistleblowing channels, and regular audits of the security framework, including an annual assessment conducted by third-party experts.

The chapter dedicated to Copyright (Art. 53(c)) requires providers to "draw up, keep up-to-date, and implement" an internal copyright policy that complies with EU law, with an express reference to Article 4(3) of the CDSM Directive. This obligation entails, among other things, that providers assign clear

---

1689" C(2025) 5361 final (Brussels, 1 August 2025), <https://digital-strategy.ec.europa.eu/en/policies/contents-code-gpai>.

315 <https://digital-strategy.ec.europa.eu/en/news/learn-more-about-guidelines-providers-general-purpose-ai-models>.

responsibilities within their organizations for the implementation and oversight of the policy, and encourage them to make a summary of their copyright policy publicly available and regularly updated.

In practice, the implementation of a "copyright policy" involves conducting due diligence on all datasets used, employing web crawlers that respect protocols such as robots.txt to ensure that only lawfully accessible copyright-protected content is reproduced and extracted, explicitly excluding pirate websites, and implementing technical filters to prevent the generation of infringing outputs based on protected content. Particularly noteworthy is the explicit requirement that providers refrain from circumventing technological protection measures, such as paywalls. This non-circumvention obligation has been welcomed as an improvement over earlier drafts, which merely required providers to "ensure" lawful access, a formulation widely considered vague and difficult to enforce.[316]

Additionally, providers are required to designate a clear contact point for rightsholders, establish mechanisms for the submission of notices and complaints, and include clauses in their terms of use prohibiting downstream users from generating infringing material.

Interestingly, this chapter clarifies that signatories who adhere to the Code of Practice and implement the measures it prescribes will be able to demonstrate compliance with Article 53(1)(c) of the AI Act. However, adherence to the Code does not in itself constitute compliance with EU copyright law, underscoring once again the distinct nature of these two legal frameworks.

That said, while the effort behind the Code of Practice is certainly commendable, the measures it contains in the "Copyright" Chapter remain relatively high-level. For instance, they do not include the key performance indicators required under Article 56(4) – which were, by contrast, present in the Second Draft – nor are they tailored to address sector-specific challenges. It has also been noted that the Code leaves several critical issues unresolved, including the operational handling of datasets containing infringing content, the labeling of deepfakes, and the development of strategies to compensate creators for the use of their intellectual property.[317]

The decision to maintain a high-level approach can be attributed partly to the deregulatory stance promoted by several major actors – precisely the GPAI providers to whom the Code is primarily addressed – some of whom were

316 On the concept of "lawful access" and its overlaps with other apparently similar concepts, see Synodinou TE, "Lawfulness for Users in European Copyright Law: Acquis and Perspectives" (2019) 10 JIPITEC 20.

317 <https://copyrightblog.kluweriplaw.com/2025/04/04/second-and-third-drafts-of-the-general-purpose-ai-code-of-practice-have-been-released/>.

quick to state that they would not sign it.[318] It also reflects the broader context of the Code's development: a process that may have been premature, given the ongoing regulatory uncertainties, including those surrounding the very notion of lawful access.[319]

Moreover, the practical effectiveness of the Code remains uncertain. It is explicitly stated that "the commitments in this chapter that require proportionate measures should be commensurate and proportionate to the size of providers, taking due account of the interests of SMEs, including startups". While this approach is understandable, it could create a significant loophole, particularly given the increasingly prominent role of AI start-ups on the global stage.[320]

Nevertheless, the symbolic importance of this instrument should not be underestimated, representing a step toward aligning with emerging international standards and enhancing legal certainty in the governance of GPAI.

---

318 <https://www.politico.eu/article/meta-wont-sign-eu-ai-code/>.

319 <https://copyrightblog.kluweriplaw.com/2025/04/04/second-and-third-drafts-of-the-general-purpose-ai-code-of-practice-have-been-released/>.

320 <https://copyrightblog.kluweriplaw.com/2025/04/04/second-and-third-drafts-of-the-general-purpose-ai-code-of-practice-have-been-released/>.

CHAPTER 6

The Classic Categories of Copyright Law in the Age of AI

1 The *De Facto* or *De Jure* Redefinition of Classic Categories of Copyright Law

Much has been written on generative AI and its interactions with copyright law[321] and not without reason.

With their ability to generate images, complex texts, audio content, videos, and more within the cultural and (re)creative sphere, these technologies have emerged at a particularly critical juncture in the history of intellectual property – one that has, for several decades now, been marked by at least two forms of systemic crisis.

On the one hand, there is a crisis concerning the effectiveness of the very mechanisms of "appropriation" that form the basis of copyright. This crisis stems from the ease with which any user can make "infinite, perfect, and costless copies" of a digital work, as well as from the relative disintermediation between creators and their audiences – where the former can now reach the latter without relying on traditional creative industry intermediaries, and may even coincide with them, as is the case on user-generated content platforms. This crisis has often served as one of the main justifications, or pretexts, for the

321 Bensamoun and Farchy (n 4); Drexl, Hilty et al (n 228); Hartmann et al (n 228); Geiger C, "Elaborating a Human Rights Friendly Copyright Framework for Generative AI" (2024) 7 *International Review for Intellectual Property and Competition Law* <https://ssrn.com/abstract=4634992> or <http://dx.doi.org/10.2139/ssrn.4634992>; Edwards L, Szpotakowski I, Cifrodelli G, Sangaré J and Stewart J, "Private Ordering and Generative AI: What Can We Learn From Model Terms and Conditions?" (2024) CREATe <https://doi.org/10.5281/zenodo.11276105>; Lorenz P, Perset K and Berryhill J, "Initial Policy Considerations for Generative Artificial Intelligence" (2023) 1 OECD Artificial Intelligence Papers; Abbott R and Rothman E, "Disrupting Creativity: Copyright Law in the Age of Generative Artificial Intelligence" (2023) 75 Fla L Rev 1141 <https://ssrn.com/abstract=4185327> accessed 9 August 2025; Ajani G, "Contemporary Artificial Art and the Law. Searching for an Author" (2020) Brill Research Perspectives: Art and Law; Margoni T, "Artificial Intelligence, Machine Learning and EU Copyright Law: Who Owns AI?" (2018) 1(XXVII) AIDA; Ginsburg JC, "People Not Machines: Authorship and What It Means in the Berne Convention" (2018) 49 IIC 131.

progressive expansion of intellectual property rights, a hallmark of contemporary knowledge capitalism.[322]

On the other hand, as in other areas of intellectual property, copyright is experiencing a crisis of public legitimacy.[323] An "anti-copyright sentiment"[324] is emerging indeed, stemming from the fact that the function of this legal framework is not (better, it has not always been) clearly defined, partly due to a lack of transparency regarding the true beneficiaries of its protection,[325] and partly because of the frequent instrumentalization of its normative-political justifications. These factors have, at times, led to its portrayal as "a restriction on access to information, an abusive cultural despot, an obstacle to the freedom of cultural appropriation, and a monopolist of semiotics"[326] rather than as a societal instrument for cultural development, as proclaimed in various international charters.

With the rise of generative AI, these two crises are likely to assume new, and possibly unprecedented, forms, introducing fresh uncertainties into the current and future trajectory of intellectual property law.

General-purpose AI models, including generative ones, may interfere with copyright law both during their development and training and at the stage of their implementation in downstream generative AI systems. This distinction is well established in copyright scholarship and is often framed through reflections on the two key dimensions of the decision-making algorithmic process: the input – referring to the data used to train the AI system and prompts by its users – and the output – namely, the predictions, content, recommendations, or decisions generated by it.[327]

Section 3 will explore in more detail the main copyright issues arising at these two stages of the AI lifecycle, namely, the debates surrounding the possibility of lawfully carrying out text and data mining activities and those around the protectability of AI-generated output. What seems urgent at this

322 The expansion of IP rights has often been presented as a solution to the difficulties in appropriating digital works.

323 "As intellectual property rights have gained importance, they have lost in transparency. This loss is two first of all to their number, with the classical intellectual property rights (such as copyright, patents, trademarks) having been gradually joined by neighboring rights, sui generis rights and indeed intellectual property rights that do not reveal their name (like the right to one's own image or the rights of sports events organizers), in some cases relating to the same object", see Geiger, "The Social Function of Intellectual Property Rights" (n 87) 2.

324 Dusollier, "Open Source and Copyleft: Authorship Reconsidered?" (n 186).

325 Geiger, "The Social Function of Intellectual Property Rights" (n 87) 3.

326 Dusollier, "Open Source and Copyleft: Authorship Reconsidered?" (n 186).

327 Peukert, "Copyright in the Artificial Intelligence Act" (n 281) 11.

point, however, is to provide an overview of how the use of such systems risks reshaping the copyright landscape, potentially leading to a reinterpretation, if not *de jure*, then at least *de facto*, of its traditional categories.

In fact, the use of generative AI is likely to have a significant impact on copyright law and its core concepts. This impact may be direct, should legislative or judicial reinterpretations of the relevant categories occur; or it may be indirect, through a gradual *de facto* shift resulting from (contractual) practices or evolving industry standards that reshape the notions of "creative process", "author", "rightsholder", and "intellectual work".

First of all, generative AI's algorithmic process, when it involves the creation of texts, images, audio, video, and any other similar content, may impact the concept of "creative process" and challenge the well-established idea/expression dichotomy, which is at the core of copyright law. Indeed, it calls into question what has long been regarded as both a prerequisite for, and the normative foundation of, copyright protection: the very moment of transforming "free ideas" (arguably including information and data, such as those used for training/using AI on the input side) into "expressed ideas" (possibly becoming intellectual works on the output side) through the intellectual and expressive activity of a human individual. It does so by challenging the traditional understanding of the stages through which the creative process has historically been understood to unfold: the conception of an idea, the expression of that idea, and the fixation of that expression in a (tangible) medium.

Moreover, the algorithmic nature of the generative AI process may also affect the legal category of "authors/rightsholders" (i.e., the addressees of copyright legislation), potentially leading to a growing divergence between the historical concept of the (human) author and the legal qualification as copyright owners of individuals or entities involved at various stages of the creative process, often in roles that differ significantly from the ones of "traditional" creators.

Finally, generative AI may as well call into question the category of "intellectual works", potentially challenging the very nature and substance of the concept of originality, and possibly prompting a reevaluation of it in more objective terms.

However, the extent of these impacts, particularly those on the subject matter of copyright law, depends on whether, in the end, copyright will be deemed applicable to AI-based outputs – particularly to AI-assisted outputs, and possibly to some AI-generated ones.

2 The Algorithmic "Creative" Process

The potentially disruptive force of generative AI affects the very concept of the creative process as traditionally understood.

While the aforementioned distinction between the input and output phases of the AI-based process remains analytically useful – as also reflected in the structure of this work, particularly Chapters 7 and 8, which are devoted to the respective phases – it ultimately fails to capture the full extent of the transformation brought about by generative AI.

Indeed, the changes at stake affect the very conception of the creative process as a whole. In the era of AI, it merges with the algorithmic decision-making process – hence the conceptual fusion encapsulated in the notion of the "algorithmic creative process", understood as a continuum extending from upstream to downstream stages – and this threatens to disrupt the continuity of human-led production.

The input and output dimensions are, in fact, inextricably linked. This interdependence is evident in one of the most contentious aspects of the debate around AI training activities: the fact that the outputs of generative AI may infringe the rights of those whose works were used on the input side. The New York Times case[328] is emblematic in this regard. By raising concerns about the degree of similarity between AI-generated content and existing New York Times articles available online, the case illustrates how (unlawfully accessed) intellectual works, or parts thereof, circulating on the Internet may resurface in the generated output. Moreover, this reciprocal relationship between the input and output phases of the creative process is exemplified in Article 53(1)(d) of the EU AI Act, which requires providers of general-purpose AI models to "document and make publicly available a sufficiently detailed summary of the use of training data protected under copyright law". Although this provision explicitly refers to the input phase (i.e., training data), it is based on the "assumption that generative AI systems raise significant questions related to the generation of content in breach of ... copyright rules – i.e., an AI output problem".[329]

When generative AI is used to create potentially original content, key questions arise: Is there a break in the chain of authorship between the newly generated content and the works used to train the models? What constitutes an idea, and what qualifies as the protected expression of that idea? On whom does the creation ultimately depend?

---

328 See note 531.

329 Peukert, "Copyright in the Artificial Intelligence Act" (n 281) 3.

Moreover, the introduction of an automated agent into the creative process (an agent capable of altering both the nature and degree of human involvement and control over that process) risks fundamentally challenging the very notion of originality/creativity itself. Specifically, it calls into question the process that leads to the creation of intellectual works, which may no longer be considered fully "creative" in the traditional sense.

2.1 The Expression of the Idea in the Algorithmic Creative Process: The Functioning of Generative AI and…

It is well-known that AI only mimics human creativity.[330] Even the most sophisticated and dynamic machine learning models, such as artificial neural networks, ultimately reduce to sets of mathematical functions that transform input values (upstream weights) into output values (downstream weights).[331]

AI algorithms learn by using pre-existing works and engaging in what is often described as a form of reverse engineering. In particular, AI employs a form of deductive reasoning that emerges from the deconstruction of the works it is trained on, with the aim of identifying the creative methods employed and reassembling them to generate an "artificial work, derived from an equally artificial creativity, which itself originates from preexisting works and from the functioning mechanisms of the minds of the authors of those works".[332] These works are broken down, deconstructed, and then reconstructed and reassembled to develop a new creative model.[333]

To outline the general functioning of major AI systems, recalling generative processes behind tools such as Midjourney, DALL·E, and Imagen[334] can be

---

330 Senftleben M, "Generative AI and Author Remuneration" (2023) 54 IIC 1535.

331 Drexl, Hilty et al (n 228).

332 https://dirittomodaearti.it/intelligenza-artificiale-e-diritto-dautore-quale-tutela-per-il-robot-creatore/#footnote-ref-46.

333 https://dirittomodaearti.it/intelligenza-artificiale-e-diritto-dautore-quale-tutela-per-il-robot-creatore/#footnote-ref-46.

334 Vox, AI art, explained, 1 June 2022, in <https://youtu.be/SVcsDDABEkM>, as well as the sources cited by it: <https://arxiv.org/abs/1511.02793>, <https://arnicas.substack.com/p/titaa-28-visual-poetry-humans-and?s=r>, <https://tedunderwood.com/2021/10/21/latent-spaces-of-culture/>, <https://va2rosa.medium.com/copyright-storm-authorship-in-the-age-of-ai-baba554aa617>, <https://medium.com/artists-and-machine-intelligence/a-journey-through-multiple-dimensions-and-transformations-in-space-the-final-frontier-d8435d81ca51>, <https://jxmo.notion.site/The-Weird-and-Wonderful-World-of-AI-Art-b9615a2e7278435b98380ff81ae1cf09>, <https://ml.berkeley.edu/blog/posts/clip-art/>, <https://multimodal.art/apolinario-passos/>, <https://openai.com/research/dall-e>, <https://openai.com/research/clip>, <https://openai.com/dall-e-2>, <https://laion.ai/blog/laion-5b/>, <https://arxiv.org/abs/2110.01963>.

helpful. These are deep learning software generally trained on large collections of images scraped from the Internet, along with associated data (e.g., metadata).[335]

Once these models have collected this data, they are capable of generating new images based on user prompts, which are short textual phrases that the system interprets to produce an image.[336] The system breaks down the words and phrases of a prompt into smaller units called tokens, which are then matched with its training data and used to guide image generation.[337] The system then generates the image by leveraging the latent space of its mathematical models: through the exploration of thousands of potential combinations, it identifies patterns and metrics that enable the distribution of training data within this abstract, multidimensional space. As the models analyze the training data, their algorithms detect variables that enhance performance. In doing so, they construct a high-dimensional mathematical space – comprising hundreds of dimensions – within which clusters form, capturing the essential features of the data. Each point in this space can be seen as a kind of "recipe" for a possible image. The final phase of image creation involves a generative process known as diffusion. This begins with a state of so-called "noise", and, through a series of iterations, the model progressively denoises this representation within the latent space until, once decoded into pixels, it yields a composition that becomes intelligible to human viewers.

Due to the inherent degree of randomness typically in the process, the software will generally not produce exactly the same image twice in response to the same prompt, nor will it reliably recreate an image from a prompt – even when that prompt has been derived by the AI itself from the original image.[338] Similarly, submitting the same prompt to a different model – designed by other developers and trained on a distinct dataset – will yield a different result, as the image is generated within a different latent space.[339]

335 These are potentially hundreds of millions of images that constitute the so-called AI training data, often associated with an alternative text that website publishers normally upload at the same time as the images to allow accessibility via search engines.

336 <https://docs.midjourney.com/docs/prompts>.

337 A basic Midjourney prompt begins with the command/imagine prompt, followed by a more or less detailed textual description of the desired image.

338 <https://medium.com/@pramodima/why-cant-chatgpt-recreate-the-same-image-each-time-from-its-own-prompt-9e8534b37df6>. See also Brogden J and Erickson K, "On the Process of Image Creation with Artificial Intelligence: Rephotography Using Midjourney AI", forthcoming.

339 In short, deep learning can learn and imitate the style of an artist from training data, generating new works that resemble their aesthetic without directly copying any single existing image, just by referencing their name in a prompt, see *The text-to-image revo-*

A comparable operational logic underlies OpenAI's well-known ChatGPT, a neural network whose version 3.5 comprised what is often reported as around 175 billion parameters (the so-called "artificial synapses").[340] Unlike image generators, however, ChatGPT produces text rather than images. When a user inputs a text prompt into OpenAI's platform, the software selects the most contextually appropriate tokens (i.e. words or part of words) using complex statistical methods, drawing from massive datasets previously assembled or scraped from the web.[341]

Essentially, the system: (i) scans billions of pages of human-written text previously stored within it, (ii) generates a probability-based ranking of words that could logically follow the input text, and (iii) selects one of those words to continue the sentence. Every time the OpenAI system is asked to generate text, it attempts to produce a coherent continuation by asking itself, in essence: "Given the text written so far, what should the next word be"?[342] The level of detail, accuracy, and uniqueness in the images and texts generated by these tools generally depends on the quality and descriptive clarity of the input text. In this sense, the way a prompt is crafted plays a crucial role in determining the quality of the output produced by AI systems. The effectiveness of prompt engineering in generating high-quality results largely hinges on the user's ability to clearly articulate the desired image, text, or overall outcome.[343] Once again, the relationship between input and output is clear, and it is shaped by the triangulation with the prompt.

2.2 …The Dividing Line between "Ideas" and "Expression of Ideas"

Within the context of generative AI, the extraction, reproduction and elaboration of data from in-copyrighted works used to train an AI model and prompts

---

lution, explained, Vox. Available at: <https://www.youtube.com/watch?v=SVcsDDABEkM&t=297s>.

340 Laizure SC, "Caution: ChatGPT Doesn't Know What You Are Asking and Doesn't Know What It Is Saying" (2024) 29(5) Journal of Pediatric Pharmacology and Therapeutics 558 <https://doi.org/10.5863/1551-6776-29.5.558>.

341 <https://www.diariodiunlettoresquattrinato.com/post/chatgpt-e-produzione-narrativa-alcune-considerazioni?fbclid=IwAR1Vwk2rwSdMPh5aEVAgrn3PcEpy8KoyIctvROHErUjTBd4UOpLg-uGcvCk_aem_AdQ1B5AewviH5aWnr3SN5wswooWANAToYLWnPGGk37WYQmog5kb5E7pH2P3nkR74nQU>.

342 <https://www.diariodiunlettoresquattrinato.com/post/chatgpt-e-produzione-narrativa-alcune-considerazioni?fbclid=IwAR1Vwk2rwSdMPh5aEVAgrn3PcEpy8KoyIctvROHErUjTBd4UOpLg-uGcvCk_aem_AdQ1B5AewviH5aWnr3SN5wswooWANAToYLWnPGGk37WYQmog5kb5E7pH2P3nkR74nQU>.

343 Rossi A, "Opere in cerca d'autore: creatività, copyright e sistemi di Intelligenza Artificiale generativa di immagini" (2023) 4 Diritto di Internet.

entered in the system by the final user (input side), as well as the creation of an output that can possibly meet the requirements of an intellectual work both become integral part of an algorithmic process[344] – one with a purpose and structure fundamentally different from what is traditionally understood as a "creative process" under copyright law and the dialogical nature it is meant to embody according to certain legal traditions.[345]

First, contrarily to the human-led creative process, the AI-driven one appears to be largely detached from any intention to express meaning, let alone to convey informative content or a specific idea. Rather, it is primarily aimed at maximizing the probability of successfully achieving predefined objectives.[346] Recital 6a of the compromise text of the AI Act dated June 14, 2023,[347] was emblematic in this sense, stating that "machine learning refers to the computational process of *optimizing* the parameters of a model from data, which is a mathematical construct generating an output based on input data" (emphasis added).[348]

Second, what has long been regarded as the standard three-step sequence in the creation of a work – idea, expression of the idea, and fixation in a tangible medium[349] – is increasingly being questioned. This is part of a broader trend in the digital age, which has already challenged the third phase of the creative process: with the spread of the Internet, works that are never externalized in a tangible medium have proliferated.[350] Moreover, with the advent of AI, also the boundary between the idea (which is not protected) and the expression of the idea (which is protected)[351] is becoming increasingly blurred.

344 Drexl, Hilty et al (n 321).

345 Sganga C, Propertizing European Copyright (Edward Elgar Publishing 2018) <https://www.elgaronline.com/view/9781786430403.xml> accessed 9 August 2025, 17–49.

346 See Council of State, Section III, Judgment No. 7891, 25 November 2021.

347 It was then amended, and ultimately the relevant expressed reference was excluded from the AI Act final text.

348 See also Bensamoun and Farchy (n 4) (English version): "Flow Machines, an artificial intelligence project created in 2012 by a team led by François Pachet, then director of Sony Computer Science Laboratories Paris, is presented as a tool for optimizing musical composition".

349 Ubertazzi LC, Commentario breve alle leggi su proprietà intellettuale e concorrenza (6th edn, CEDAM 2016) 1464.

350 Romano R, L'opera e l'esemplare nel diritto della proprietà intellettuale (CEDAM 2001).

351 Giving "form" to ideas within the meaning of copyright law has hitherto meant expressing them "in the external world" in a structure "bearing the imprint of a personal elaboration" (cf. Mongillo R, Opere dell'ingegno, idee ispiratrici e diritto d'autore (Edizioni Scientifiche Italiane 2015) 30).

Traditionally, it has been the notion of originality – understood, in the EU[352], as the "author's own intellectual creation", that is, the author's free exercise of choice among multiple options and the expression of their personality[353] – that has served to distinguish these two stages, thereby justifying the activation of copyright protection.[354]

In the context of algorithmic "creative" processes, creativity is either absent at all,[355] either anticipated to an earlier stage (conception phase, including design and specifications given to the AI)[356] or deferred to a postproduction

352 Hartmann et al (n 228) 39.

353 As is well known, in the civil law tradition, particularly in French jurisprudence, originality is seen as the result of a conscious act of creation (*acte de création consciente*), forming the basis for protection under *droit d'auteur*. In contrast, the common law tradition defines it through the lens of the author's skill, labor, and judgment in producing a work. In civil law systems, originality reflects the author's freedom and independence in choosing how to express their ideas. It is understood as an expression of the author's personality – their unique "personal touch" – realized through an autonomous and original act of creation.

354 Greco P and Vercellone P, I diritti sulle opere dell'ingegno (Torino 1974) 37 ff.

355 It is often argued that freedom of choice – traditionally linked to creativity – cannot be ascribed to an algorithm. Some scholars contend that the natural person initiating an algorithmic creative process may lack the "minimal personal autonomy" (Ginsburg JC, "The Concept of Authorship in Comparative Copyright Law" [2003] SSRN Electronic Journal <http://www.ssrn.com/abstract=368481> accessed 9 August 2025) and the freedom of choice (Iaia V, "Le derive della creatività nel diritto d'autore. Originalità, interessi finanziari, concorrenza" (26 September 2022) <https://doi.org/10.13119/11385_222500>) – or, more precisely, the freedom of expressive choices – traditionally associated with creativity. The individual may not, in fact, have sufficient scope for the kind of expressive arbitrariness that is essential to manifest human intent, assuming such intent is indeed required under copyright law.

356 Hartmann et al (n 228). It should be noted that, in providing guidance to the 30 national committees in charge of drafting the Reports for the Study Question, AIPPI (See AIPPI, Study Question "Copyright in artificially generated works" (2019) www.aippi.org) had identified a creative moment relevant for the purposes of copyright protection in the phases preceding the processing of the work by the algorithm and, in particular, in the act of programming, training or managing the AI software and, on the basis of this, had come to postulate that the subject who put it in place could be attributed the status of author. As some authors have pointed out, even in art contexts in which the use of AI systems is not contemplated at all, there is a similar "tendency to shift creative activity from the final and concluded expression of an idea to an earlier stage" (translation by the author), see Rossi G, "L'intelligenza artificiale e la definizione di 'opera dell'ingegno'" (2019) AIDA XXVII, 275. Action painting is an illustrative example of such a shift, as wellntence. Every time the as Fontana's "concetto spaziale" or Marina Abramović's performance art. See also Sanseverino G, "Ex machina. La novità e l'originalità dell'invenzione 'prodotta' dall'AI" (2019) AIDA XXVII, 16).

one (redaction phase, including editing and finalization of the output).[357] However, the phase of the elaboration of an idea itself (the execution phase, including the production of draft versions of the output)[358] has become increasingly entangled with the mathematical mechanisms underpinning AI and the data it draws upon, including data selected by others or even automatedly by the system itself. In fact, especially in works fully generated by AI – if such a thing ever truly exists, as will be seen – the expression of ideas is a stage that pertains exclusively to the software and its functioning, not to the human being involved in the process. It is the (more or less "autonomous") functioning of the algorithm that, by executing inputs and prompts, processes (unprotectable) ideas and translates them into a form that is, at least theoretically, eligible for copyright protection.

Also, it has been pointed out that, when dealing with algorithmic processes – which may be fully automated[359] or even incorporate elements of randomness[360] – it remains far from clear whether the free and creative choices possibly expressed in the conception and redaction phase, depending on the specific circumstances, are genuinely expressed in the final AI-assisted

357 Hartmann et al (n 228). Human authors involved in algorithmic processes still play an essential role during the conception phase, and their contribution can also be significant in the redaction phase. In line with this idea, it has been argued that, according to the conception-and-execution theory of authorship, authorship is "based on two basic pillars: a mental step (the conception of a work) and a physical step (the execution of a work)" and "in many cases, either the upstream human being who programs and trains a machine to produce an output, or the downstream human being who requests the output, is sufficiently involved in the conception and execution of the resulting work to claim authorship. See Ginsburg JC and Budiardjo LA, "Authors and Machines" (2010) 34(2) Berkeley Technology Law Journal 343.

358 Hartmann et al (n 228).

359 It has been held, for example, that an artist instructing the algorithm with a command such as "Paint pictures of different types of children with big sad eyes, using dark backgrounds", would not be creating creative paintings "even if each painting were unique and technically perfect", precisely because the algorithm's process would not be sufficiently heuristic, see Amabile T, Creativity in Context (Westview Press 1996).

360 It has been held that a "work in the abstract protectable" could not be said to have come into existence when "due to the accentuated randomness of such a result" it is impossible to foresee the aesthetic result of the process in a sufficiently complete manner, see Fabbio P, "Opere protette e requisiti di tutela nel diritto d'autore UE" (2016) AIDA, 290. *Contra*, however, Ginsburg and Budiardjo (n 357) argue that "copyright theory tolerates some degree of randomness in a work's execution". However, even they question the limits of this tolerance, asking "is there a point at which the putative author has surrendered so much control over the execution that the independence of the work's embodiment calls into question whether her initial conception of the work was anything more than a general idea?"

output.[361] And that, ultimately, lies at the heart of ongoing scholarly debates, namely that the causal link between the human input and the (potentially original) final output has become progressively more tenuous.

In such a context, as also highlighted in the 2021 Policy Statement by the Max Planck Institute, it may in fact be impossible to pinpoint precisely where the dividing line lies between the input and output phases of the algorithmic "creative" process.[362] Moreover, in the case of artificial neural networks, the study suggests, the functions embedded within individual neurons may already possess independent informational value. Pushing the argument to its logical extreme, these internal functions could arguably be seen as autonomous "portions" of the final output – what might be described as "micro-outputs". If such micro-outputs were to be recognized as independently relevant from a copyright standpoint, they could effectively shift the point at which authorial protection is activated.

Identifying the precise caesura between the input and the output side of the algorithmic "creative" process is of critical importance, as it ideally determines both the moment of a work's legal coming into being and the threshold at which copyright protection is triggered.[363] But within the intricate web of mathematical "nodes" that make up a neural network, one question arises: where exactly could one locate the transition from mere ideas to their expressive form? In other words, at what point – whether in temporal terms, logical steps, or computational processes – does the moment of "expression of the idea" actually occur within the AI-driven creative process?

3 The Subjects

3.1 The Human Authorship as an Implicit Requirement of Protection

In the context of algorithmic "creative" processes, important questions arise concerning the definition of "author" and whether this category could, or should, be extended to nonhuman agents. In recent years, substantial debate has emerged on this issue, primarily focusing on whether such agents can indeed be regarded as creators of intellectual works eligible for copyright pro-

361 The IViR/JIIP also acknowledges this not-so-straightforward outcome, cautiously noting: "Assuming these choices are expressed in the final AI-assisted output", see Hartmann et al (n 228). This conditional phrasing underscores the core uncertainty: whether and to what extent the human's creative input is truly reflected in the resulting work.

362 Drexl, Hilty et al (n 228).

363 Drexl, Hilty et al (n 228).

tection.[364] This issue, however, is not entirely new, as the question of "what makes one an 'author' in copyright law" has long been recognized as a "perennial question".[365]

Nevertheless, to date, especially in international forums[366] and analyses,[367] there is broad support for the view that authorship must only be attributed to a natural person. According to this idea, the so-called "human authorship" is, in fact, an implicit requirement of copyright legislation.[368]

A clear position in this regard has been taken thus far by the ambitious proposal of the Wittem Project for the adoption of a European Copyright Code.[369] Article 2.1 of the proposed Code explicitly states that "the author of a work is the natural person or group of natural persons who created it". Fur-

---

364 Among the most emblematic positions in favor of the recognition of nonhuman authorship, see Abbott and Rothman (n 321).

365 Ginsburg and Budiardjo (n 357).

366 To get an idea of the approach to the topic taken by various national legal systems, see the reports drawn up by more than 30 countries worldwide on the AIPPI Study Question (n 356); as well as the reports drawn up on the occasion of the ALAI's annual international congress in Paris (22 and 23 June 2023) on the topic of "*Droit d'auteur, droits voisins et intelligence artificielle*".

367 By way of example only, Gervais D, "The Machine as Author" (2020) 105 Iowa Law Review, 2053; Ginsburg, "People Not Machines" (n 321) 131; Ginsburg and Budiardjo (n 357) 343; Guadamuz A, "Do Androids Dream of Electric Copyright? Comparative Analysis of Originality in Artificial Intelligence Generated Works" in Hilty RM, Lee JA and Liu KC (eds), Artificial Intelligence and Intellectual Property (Oxford University Press 2021) 147; Gervais D, "The Human Cause" in Abbott R (ed), Research Handbook of Artificial Intelligence and Intellectual Property (Edward Elgar 2022); Frosio G, "Four Theories in Search of an A(I)uthor" in Abbott R (ed), Research Handbook of Artificial Intelligence and Intellectual Property (Edward Elgar 2022). See also the US Copyright Office, Copyright and Artificial Intelligence: Part 2 – Copyrightability: A Report of the Register of Copyrights (January 2025) <https://www.copyright.gov/ai/Copyright-and-Artificial-Intelligence-Part-2-Copyrightability-Report.pdf>: in Section III, the USCO emphasizes that human authorship is widely recognized as a globally shared principle, even though the debate remains open in nearly all jurisdictions. This principle is acknowledged in several legal systems, including those of China and Japan.

368 As Ginsburg aptly observed in this regard: "much of Copyright Law in the US and abroad makes sense only if one recognizes the centrality of the author, the human creator of the work". See Ginsburg, "The Concept of Authorship in Comparative Copyright Law" (n 355).

369 In 2010, a group of academic experts in the field put forward the proposal for the adoption of a European Copyright Code, aimed at promoting greater harmonization and improving the functioning of the EU market for intellectual works (see Wittem Project, European Copyright Code (EPC), 2010, <https://www.ivir.nl/copyrightcode/>). In the introductory report to the Code, the authors specify that "The European Copyright Code is the result of the Wittem Project that was established in 2002 as a collaboration between copyright scholars across the European Union concerned with the future devel-

thermore, the accompanying commentary clarifies that the expression "in so far as"[370] in Article 1.1 – according to which a work qualifies as long as it constitutes "its author's own intellectual creation" – is not merely a condition for the existence of copyright but also serves to define its limits. This reconstruction is of great interest. However, the European Copyright Code remains a soft-law instrument with purely persuasive value. Despite having received support from the European Commission,[371] it has not been formally adopted and legal scholarship has noted that the prospect of the Code being enacted as binding law remains quite remote.[372]

Nonetheless, the requirement of human authorship can also be inferred from other legal sources, although only indirectly. For example, at the normative level, it can be derived from the Berne Convention, which appears to refer

opment of European copyright law. The project has its roots in an International Network Program run by three Dutch universities (Radboud University of Nijmegen, University of Amsterdam, and Leiden University) and sponsored by the government-funded Dutch ITeR Program. The aim of the Wittem Project and this Code is to promote transparency and consistency in European copyright law. The members of the Wittem Project share a concern that the process of copyright law-making at the European level lacks transparency and that the voice of academia all too often remains unheard. The Group believes that a European Copyright Code drafted by legal scholars might serve as a model or reference tool for future harmonization or unification of copyright at the European level. Nevertheless, the Group does not take a position on the desirability as such of introducing a unified European legal framework".

370 See Art. 1 of the European Copyright Code of the Wittem Project (n 369), "Copyright subsists in a work, that is to say, any expression within the field of literature, art or science in so far as it constitutes its author's own intellectual creation". Article 12 (Term of Protection) states, however, that "Whenever the term of protection of a work, other than a photographic work or a work of applied art, is calculated on a basis other than the life of a natural person, such term shall be no less than 50 years from the end of the calendar year of authorized publication, or, failing such authorized publication within 50 years from the making of the work, 50 years from the end of the calendar year of making", admitting that there may be cases where the term of protection of rights may in some cases be "calculated on a basis other than the life of a natural person".

371 Communication from the Commission to the European Parliament, the Council, the European Economic and Social Committee and the Committee of the Regions of 24 May 2011, A Single Market for Intellectual Property Rights. Boosting creativity and innovation to provide economic growth, jobs, and first-class products and services in Europe, COM(287)2011.

372 Bently L, Sherman B, Gangjee D and Johnson P, Intellectual Property Law (5th edn, Oxford University Press 2018) 56–57.

to a human author when using the terms "author" and "authorship",[373] according to a "humanistic principle".[374] As several scholars have observed, "it seems logical that when the Berne Convention speaks of 'author' or 'authorship', it refers to a human author".[375] This interpretation is supported, *inter alia*, by the wording of Article 7 of the Convention, which states: "the term of protection granted by this Convention shall be the life of the author and fifty years after his *death*" (emphasis added). The inclusion of moral rights under Article 6bis, which are explicitly granted to "authors", further suggests that the minimum standards of copyright protection are triggered only by human acts of creation. Finally, Article 3 refers to the nationality or residence of the author in determining the scope of application of the Convention. This strongly points to the idea that the term "author" is to be interpreted as referring to a human being.

A similar conclusion can be drawn with regard to the TRIPs Agreement and the World Intellectual Property Organization (WIPO) Copyright Treaty. While neither instrument provides an explicit definition of "author", both refer directly to the Berne Convention and rely on its principles for all matters not expressly regulated.[376] Moreover, the WIPO describes intellectual property as being rooted in creations of the mind – so, arguably, the human intellect.[377] Furthermore, this interpretation is reinforced by the recognition of intellectual property rights as fundamental rights. Human rights instruments

---

373 On this point, see Deltorn and Macrez (n 44) commenting on the Berne Convention for the Protection of Literary and Artistic Works (adopted 9 September 1886, last amended 28 September 1979).

374 ALAI, "Resolution Concerning the Impact of Artificial Intelligence on Copyright" <https://www.alai.org/en/resolutions-and-positions/> accessed 9 August 2025.

375 Deltorn and Macrez (n 44) 8, recalling Ricketson S, "People or Machines: The Berne Convention and the Changing Concept of Authorship" (1991) 16 Columbia-VLA Journal of Law & the Arts 1.

376 See Art. 1 of the WIPO Copyright Treaty (adopted 20 December 1996, entered into force 6 March 2002) 2186 UNTS 121: "(1) This Treaty is a special agreement within the meaning of Article 20 of the Berne Convention for the Protection of Literary and Artistic Works, as regards Contracting Parties that are countries of the Union established by that Convention. This Treaty shall not have any connection with treaties other than the Berne Convention, nor shall it prejudice any rights and obligations under any other treaties. (2) Nothing in this Treaty shall derogate from existing obligations that Contracting Parties have to each other under the Berne Convention for the Protection of Literary and Artistic Works (...)"; and Art. 9 of the TRIPs Agreement (n 83): "Members shall comply with Articles 1 through 21 of the Berne Convention (1971) and the Appendix thereto. However, Members shall not have rights or obligations under this Agreement in respect of the rights conferred under Article 6bis of that Convention or of the rights derived therefrom (...)".

377 WIPO, What is Intellectual Property? <https://www.wipo.int/publications/en/details.jsp?id=4528> accessed 9 August 2025.

support, indeed, the requirement of a human author. For example, the Universal Declaration of Human Rights and the International Covenant on Economic, Social, and Cultural Rights appear to presuppose the presence of a human author behind an intellectual creation.[378] Particularly, the Universal Declaration of Human Rights protects the moral and material interests of authors of scientific, literary, and artistic works.

Human authorship seems also implicit in the EU context, where, albeit only with reference to sectoral regulations, Directive 96/9/EC on the legal protection of databases provides that "The author of a database shall be the natural person or group of natural persons who created the base or, where the legislation of the Member States so permits" - hence, only by way of exception - "the legal person designated as the rightholder by that legislation" (art. 4). Similarly, Directive 2009/24/EC on the legal protection of computer programs adopts an analogous definition of authorship in Article 2.

Through interpretative analysis, the requirement that the author of an intellectual work must be a human being can also be inferred from various provisions of the InfoSoc Directive, which suggest that the concept refers specifically to a natural person.[379] For example, the Directive grants authors the right to authorize others to reproduce their works (Article 2(a)), communicate them to the public (Article 3(1)), and distribute them (Article 4(1)). It is debatable how nonhuman entities – such as animals or machines – could meaningfully exercise such rights. This issue becomes even more complex given that the Court of Justice of the European Union has interpreted the Directive as granting authors the exclusive initial entitlement to economic rights – something nonhuman entities cannot possess or exercise.

Human authorship would, however, be consistent with the inherently anthropocentric orientation of the EU copyright law system, which requires that the qualification of a subject matter as a protected work be grounded in human intellectual effort and authorship.[380] Moreover, the very structure of the entire regulatory framework – which protects not only the economic inter-

378 Geiger C, "Copyright as an Access Right: Securing Cultural Participation Through the Protection of Creators' Interests" in Giblin R and Weatherall K (eds), What If We Could Reimagine Copyright? (ANU Press 2017) 73, Max Planck Institute for Innovation & Competition Research Paper No 15-07 <https://ssrn.com/abstract=2643304> accessed 9 August 2025, 11.

379 Fritz J, "The notion of 'authorship' under EU law – who can be an author and what makes one an author? An analysis of the legislative framework and case law" (2024) 19(7) Journal of Intellectual Property Law & Practice 552 <https://doi.org/10.1093/jiplp/jpae022>.

380 Ibid.

ests of creative industry professionals but, above all, the moral interests of authors – further supports the view that the prerequisite for copyright protection is, and must be, the presence of a natural person at the origin of the creative process.

National laws within the EU also tend to follow the same principle. By way of example, in the Italian legal system, the requirement that the author must necessarily be a natural person can be inferred, at a systematic level, from several provisions of the Italian Copyright Act (*Legge Italiana sul Diritto d'Autore*).[381] One such provision is Article 25, which states – consistent with international and EU norms – that the duration of copyright is "the entire life of the author and until 70 years after the death of the author".[382] Additional support for this interpretation can be found in Article 2576 of the Italian Civil Code and Article 6 of the Copyright Act, both of which define the original basis for the acquisition of copyright as the creation of the work, conceived as a specific expression of intellectual labor – thus implying the need for a human intellect behind it.

Case law at the EU level appears to further support this interpretation. However, it does not address the issue of authorship directly; instead, it approaches it through the lens of the originality requirement, as traditionally understood, as well as through the expression "the author's own intellectual creation" which serves to define the concept of work. In this regard, the Italian national report submitted in the context of the AIPPI Study Question on Copyright and AI,[383] while recalling European case law, notes that "the Court of Justice of the European Union has stated on several occasions that copyright applies only to original works, and that originality must reflect the author's own intellectual creation" (see Case C-5/08, Infopaq International A/S v Danske Dagblades Forening). The report further specifies that "this is usually understood

381 See "*Legge 22 aprile 1941, n. 633 a protezione del diritto d'autore e di altri diritti connessi al suo esercizio*". It is worth specifying that Italian law does not provide an express definition of "author", providing only that the title of the acquisition of copyright is the creation of the work, as a particular expression of intellectual work (see Article 2576 of the Italian Civil Code and Article 6 of the Italian Copyright Law). However, the references made in the legal text have been generally held sufficient to sustain that, according to a literal interpretation, the notion of "author" – being linked to the expression of intellectual work and, therefore, creativity – implicitly presupposes the qualification of the same as a natural person. This interpretation has now been confirmed by Law no. 132 of 23 September 2025, whose Article 25 amended Article 1 of the Italian Copyright Act by adding the adjective "human" ("opere dell'ingegno umano"), while clarifying that works created with the assistance of AI tools remain protected provided they result from the author's own intellectual work.

382 Italian report on the AIPPI Study Question (n 356).

383 Ibid, 2.

as implying that a human author is required for a work to benefit from copyright protection". Similarly, in 2020, the European Parliament explicitly reaffirmed the principle that originality is necessarily linked to a human author[384] – thus underscoring the core of the debate: namely, that the primary criterion for copyright protection should be the capacity of a creative work to reflect the free and personal choices of its author.

The main criticism of the idea that human authorship requirement is an implicit feature of a number of legal orders is that, at the time when most relevant legislation across the world was adopted, it was even inconceivable that intellectual works could be created by entities other than human beings. As long as humans were the only entities capable of producing intellectual works, they were naturally regarded as the sole possible authors eligible for copyright protection. According to this view, the emergence of the new current technological contexts calls into question the validity of these foundational assumptions.

However, such objections are increasingly met with scepticism – both in legal scholarship[385] and case law.[386]

3.2 The Position of the US Copyright Office

Indeed, this very issue has recently been addressed by the United States Copyright Office (USCO), which has acknowledged the potentially disruptive role of AI in the creative process and has nonetheless taken a clear stance in affirming the fundamentally human nature of the concept of authorship. Its engagement with what has been termed the "difficult questions of authorship" dates back several decades. In fact, as early as its 1965 Annual Report, the Office recognized the impact of "developments in computer technology" and the

384 European Parliament, Report on Intellectual Property Rights for the Development of Artificial Intelligence Technologies, 20 October 2020, 2020/2015(INI): "works autonomously produced by artificial agents and robots might not be eligible for copyright protection, in order to observe the principle of originality, which is linked to a natural person, and since the concept of 'intellectual creation' addresses the author's personality".

385 As a matter of fact, the only element of copyright law that has remained consistent over time has been precisely the necessary existence of a natural person author to whom a creative act can be attributed. In a perspective of European Union analysis, see Kop M, "AI & Intellectual Property: Towards an Articulated Public Domain" (2020) 28(1) Texas Intellectual Property Law Journal 304; See also Bensamoun and Farchy (n 4) and art. 2.1 of the European Copyright Code of the Wittem Project (n 369).

386 See in Chapter 8.

complex questions they were beginning to raise regarding the authorship requirement for "works 'written' by computers".[387]

The position of the USCO is particularly significant in the current context, especially considering that the most prominent legal disputes – as will be discussed – are emerging primarily within the US technological landscape. In its Compendium of USCO Practices, the USCO stated that "to qualify as a work of 'authorship', a work must be created by a human being" and that it "will not register works produced by a machine or mere mechanical process that operates randomly or automatically without any creative input or intervention from a human author".[388]

Building on this principle, which establishes human authorship as a fundamental requirement for copyright protection, the USCO has consistently denied registration to works produced by a machine or as mere mechanical process that operates randomly or automatically without any creative input or intervention from a human author.[389]

To support this position, the USCO referred to a passage from the landmark *Bleistein v. Donaldson Lithographing Co.* judgment, according to which "a very modest grade of art has in it something irreducible, which is one man's alone. That something he may copyright".[390]

The underlying assumption of this approach has consistently been that "intellectual creation" must necessarily be a product of the human mind.[391] This interpretation was reaffirmed in a February 2022 decision, in which the USCO rejected the registration of an image generated by the AI system Creativity Machine. In that decision, the Office argued that copyright protection extends only to "the fruits of intellectual labor that are 'founded in the creative powers of the [human] mind'".[392]

---

387 US Copyright Office, Sixty-Eighth Annual Report of the Register of Copyrights for the Fiscal Year Ending June 30, 1965 (1966) 5 <https://www.copyright.gov/reports/annual/archive/ar-1965.pdf>.

388 US Copyright Office, Compendium of US Copyright Office Practices § 101 (3rd edn 2021) ("Compendium (Third)"), section 313.2 "Works that lack human authorship".

389 US Copyright Office, "Compendium (Third)" (n 388).

390 Bleistein v Donaldson Lithographing Co 188 US 250 (1903).

391 However, as pointed out by Rossi, "L'intelligenza artificiale e la definizione di 'opera dell'ingegno'" (n 356) 271, the expression "creative powers of the mind" was initially used by the US Copyright Office only to support its arguments as to what is meant by "originality", not to imply that a work must necessarily derive from an author (mind) in order to be considered protectable.

392 A Recent Entrance to Paradise (n 135).

More recently, in the context of a broader initiative undertaken since early 2023,[393] the USCO launched a series of activities on copyright and AI,[394] in which it acknowledged its approach to the nature of authorship.

In particular, as part of this initiative, the Office published a new Registration Guidance[395] (March 2023), in which it outlined the key aspects of its approach to the registration of works containing material generated by AI technology.

Among these, particular emphasis was placed on the central importance of the presence of a natural person "behind" a work for it to qualify as such. In particular, the Office reiterated the principle, grounded in settled case law, that "the term 'author', as used in both the Constitution and the Copyright Act, does not include nonhuman entities".[396] In the context of generative AI, the Guidance explains, this means that if a work's "traditional elements of authorship" are generated by an AI system, the work lacks the requisite human authorship and, therefore, cannot be registered.[397] The Guidance further clarifies that applicants seeking to register works containing AI-generated material must disclose this fact at the time of application. To determine whether a work is eligible for protection, the Office conducts a preliminary inquiry into whether it is "essentially one of human authorship" – that is, whether the computer (or other device) was merely used as a tool – or, conversely, whether the elements traditionally attributed to an author (such as literary, artistic, or musical expression, or choices in selection and arrangement) were actually conceived and executed by an AI system. In cases involving AI-generated content, this initial assessment is followed by an analysis of whether the AI's contributions amount to mere "mechanical reproduction" or reflect an "original mental conception" attributable to a human author. The Guidance concludes that such determinations must necessarily be made on a case-by-case basis, as the classification of the creative process – whether mechanical or authorial –

393 "In response to growing Congressional and public interest, the Office launched a comprehensive AI Initiative in early 2023. The Initiative identified a number of steps that the Office would take to further explore the copyright policy questions surrounding AI, including hosting public listening sessions and publishing a notice of inquiry", see Notice of Inquiry (NOI), <https://www.copyright.gov/ai/docs/Federal-Register-Document-Artificial-Intelligence-and-Copyright-NOI.pdf>.

394 Notice of Inquiry (NOI) (n 393).

395 <https://www.federalregister.gov/documents/2023/03/16/2023-05321/copyright-registration-guidance-works-containing-material-generated-by-artificial-intelligence>.

396 US Copyright Office, "Copyright Registration Guidance, Works Containing Materials Generated by Artificial Intelligence" 88 FR 16190 (16 March 2023) <https://copyright.gov/ai/ai_policy_guidance.pdf>, 2.

397 Ibid.

depends on the specific circumstances, including how the AI system operates and the manner in which it is used.

The report "Copyright and Artificial Intelligence. Part 2: Copyrightability", addressing the challenges posed by generative AI,[398] is also part of this initiative launched in 2023. According to the report, one of the central issues raised by these technologies concerns the nature and scope of the concepts of "author" and "authorship", examining the factors that should be considered when assessing whether AI-based outputs may qualify for copyright protection. On this point, in support of the idea that the notion of "author" must be understood as referring exclusively to a natural person, the report cites the 2023 decision of the US District Court for the District of Columbia, which, for the first time before a federal court, ruled on the copyrightability of an output generated by AI. In that case, the Court affirmed that "copyright law protects only works of human creation" and that "human authorship is a bedrock requirement of copyright".[399]

3.3 The Human Factor in the Algorithmic Creative Process

3.3.1 Authors of the Output?

Assuming that the presence of a human author is a prerequisite for considering a work as original, a number of questions arise, as to what human activity

398 US Copyright Office, Copyright and Artificial Intelligence: Part 2 (n 367). This publication is part of the results of the Notice of Inquiry (NOI) launched at the beginning of 2023 (n 393). At the core of this strategy – which also led, in March 2023, to the publication by the USCO of a policy statement regarding registration guidance for works incorporating AI-generated content – is the intent to offer, by virtue of its strategic role as the administrative authority responsible for assessing the requirements for copyright protection, a distinct perspective on the emerging issues raised by technological developments in the field of intellectual creation.

The document is divided into five sections: Section I, after identifying the main issues that the use of artificial intelligence may raise in relation to copyright, provides a historical overview of the evolution of this area of law in response to technological advancements and describes the Office's ongoing AI initiative; Section II offers a brief overview of the technologies involved and the existing legal framework, particularly with regard to questions concerning the requirement of human authorship, originality, and the idea/expression dichotomy; Section III outlines insights from the international landscape on the subject addressed by the Report; Section IV presents policy considerations on whether – or to what extent – copyright protection should be extended to AI-generated content; finally, Section V summarizes the conclusions reached, outlining the Office's positions and final recommendations.

399 Thaler v Perlmutter 687 F Supp 3d 140 (D.D.C. 2023).

is involved in the process by which works generated by AI come into existence, and, specifically, to what extent, and at what stages, human intervention is necessary for the purposes of authorial protection.

Indeed, numerous actors, both natural and legal persons, may participate in the algorithmic process, assuming specific roles and qualifications that differ appreciably from those of individuals normally engaging with a "traditional" creative process. Upstream – in the development and deployment of an AI system – the contributors are especially varied. Not only are software designers and programmers involved in implementing an AI model, but hardware developers also may have a crucial role. Furthermore, since AI systems typically undergo a training phase, those responsible for the training process must also be considered among the contributors to that process.

Further key figures in the creation and use chain of an AI system can be manufacturers, distributors, deployers and end users.

Interestingly, the EU AI Act groups a range of actors along the AI value chain under the collective label of "operators"[400] defining them as "provider, product manufacturer, deployer, authorized representative, importer, or distributor" and, in turn, (i) the provider as "natural or legal person, public authority, agency or other body that develops an AI system or a general-purpose AI model or that has an AI system or a general-purpose AI model developed and places it on the market or puts the AI system into service under its own name or trademark, whether for payment or free of charge"; (ii) the deployer as "a natural or legal person, public authority, agency or other body using an AI system under its authority except where the AI system is used in the course of a personal nonprofessional activity"; (iii) the authorized representative as "a natural or legal person located or established in the Union who has received and accepted a written mandate from a provider of an AI system or a general-purpose AI model to, respectively, perform and carry out on its behalf the obligations and procedures established by this Regulation"; (iv) the importer as "a natural or legal person located or established in the Union that places on the market an AI system that bears the name or trademark of a natural or legal person established in a third country"; and (v) the distributor as "a natural or legal person in the supply chain, other than the provider or the importer, that makes an AI system available on the Union market".

Even before that, however, the European Parliament resolution of October 20, 2020, containing recommendations to the Commission on a liability

400 See Art. 3(8) of the AI Act.

regime for AI,[401] had already addressed the definition of the concept of "operators". It merely distinguished, however, between: (i) a "frontend operator", i.e., "any natural or legal person who exercises a degree of control over a risk connected with the operation and functioning of the AI system and benefits from its operation"; and (ii) a "backend operator", i.e., "any natural or legal person who, on a continuous basis, defines the features of the technology and provides data and essential backend support services, thereby also exercising a degree of control over the risk connected with the operation and functioning of the AI system". Although these definitions are drawn from a proposal that has not been adopted, they remain useful from an interpretative standpoint.

It is clear that they will need to be coordinated with other roles relevant to the production processes of intellectual works. Among these, when AI systems are employed in the creative field, it is reasonable to identify, with some approximation, at least the following:[402] those who created the "original" works used to train AI systems; those who curate the selection of works for training datasets; those who, in the case of supervised learning, assign "labels" – keywords and metadata – to each selected item, enabling the model to be trained; those who choose a form of "signal representation", i.e., a format that transcribes information into a machine-readable form; those who decide on the type of AI model to be used (e.g., a neural network), its architecture, parameters, and the training methods (such as the cost function); those who, during training, observe, select, and use the generated outputs to adjust the model or characteristics of the supervised learning system; and finally, those who intervene in the "postproduction" phase to select and modify the outputs of the generative model or to reintroduce them into the training dataset.

Further parties potentially involved in various aspects of the creative process – each with distinct and legitimate interests – include investors, principals, users, licensees, and others.[403] The simultaneous presence of multiple actors raises several complex questions, chief among them whether any of these figures can be identified as the "author" within the meaning of relevant legislation.

Indeed, while it is true that the emancipation of creation from the human factor, even in the case of AI-generated works, is only partial,[404] and

401 See Article 3 of the European Parliament Resolution of 20 October 2020 with recommendations to the Commission on a liability regime for artificial intelligence (2020/2014 (INL)), "Artificial Intelligence Liability Regime", available at <https://www.europarl.europa.eu/doceo/document/TA-9-2020-0276_EN.html>.

402 Bensamoun and Farchy (n 4) 26.

403 Ibid, 27.

404 For instance, in the music realm, one commentator has noted: "as they stand, these models are black boxes containing an agent that uses probabilistic rules to arrange

that human involvement remains essential to the production of intellectual works, this observation alone does not justify the inference that such works can be attributed to an author in the traditional sense (even though according to some commentators, a human in this process can always be identified, however *éloigné*[405]).

The risk is that, on a "minimalistic" view of human contribution, the threshold for copyright protection may be deemed satisfied merely by the involvement of a natural person, regardless of whether their participation in the "creative" algorithmic process is substantial or merely marginal.[406]

Indeed, many of the individuals involved at various stages of the algorithmic creation chain – from the upstream phase of training dataset(s) selection to downstream tasks such as postproduction or curation, including intermediate steps such as the selection of the signal representation modality or the choice of the model[407] – may not contribute creatively at all, limiting their role to purely technical, or even mechanical, functions.[408]

It is, at the very least, debatable whether such human contributors – even in the event that the output is considered creative – can be meaningfully classified under the traditional notion of author, at least as conceived in *droit d'auteur* systems, and this circumstance calls for reflection on the possible disruption of the conventional syllogism: author = creativity = creative product.

3.3.2 Authors of the Intellectual Works Used to Train the AI

Machines are capable of emulating human creative output because they are trained on a vast amount of human works, from which they extract the patterns that underpin their generative capacities. At the core of the generative AI value chain lies the process of machine learning, which involves ingesting large volumes of data to identify patterns - patterns that the system then uses

---

tokens. Curation, composition, and performance are required to make the generated transcriptions become music", see Bob BL, Sturm J, and others, "Music Transcription Modeling and Composition Using Deep Learning" (2016) arXiv:1604.08723 <https://arxiv.org/abs/1604.08723> accessed 9 August 2025.

405 Bensamoun and Farchy (n 4).

406 Rossi, "L'intelligenza artificiale e la definizione di "opera dell'ingegno" (n 356) 275.

407 Bensamoun and Farchy (n 4) 26. See also Militsyna K, "Human Creative Contribution to AI-Based Output – One Just Can('t) Get Enough" (2023) XX GRUR International 1, according to whom in an algorithmic "creative" process, "the search for human-made decisions extends to the creation of a generative AI system. Thus, all human-made decisions in the creation process can be grouped into two categories: i) those that are taken to create a generative AI system; and ii) those that are made to generate output".

408 Deltorn and Macrez (n 44) 10.

to, generate new knowledge, and extract meaningful insights. The increasing technological capability of generative AI to replicate human creations is expected to significantly disrupt the market for human authorship, as these systems can produce content more rapidly and at a lower cost. Consequently, human creators are likely to face growing substitution, with potential income losses across fields such as journalism, literature, music, and visual arts.[409]

This potential disruption of creative markets has direct implications on the protection of authors' rights and interests. While the use of generative AI does not directly modify the legal definition of authorship in relation to the works used for training, it nonetheless substantially weakens the ability of original authors to effectively exercise their rights.

These concerns have been highlighted by several creative and cultural stakeholders in recent years. For example, the Authors Guild, the largest professional organization representing writers in the United States, has taken a firm stance in its defense.[410] In a 2023 statement accompanying an open letter addressed to major AI companies, including OpenAI, Alphabet, Meta, Stability AI, and IBM, the Guild argues that "the output of AI will always be derivative in nature. AI regurgitates what it takes in, which is the work of human writers. It's only fair that authors be compensated for having 'fed' AI and continuing to inform its evolution".[411]

In this letter, authors and creators collectively urged AI industry leaders to obtain permission for the use of copyrighted material, provide fair compensation for the past and ongoing use of their works, and ensure remuneration for the use of their works in AI-generated output, regardless of whether such outputs are deemed infringing under current legal standards.

Moreover, in October 2024, several organizations, including CEPI, ECSA, ENPA, and EVA, issued a joint letter, occasioned by the already-ongoing discussions on the implementation of the EU AI Act. According to the letter, practices such as unauthorized and large-scale appropriation of creative content for model training result in illegal commercial gains and confer unfair competitive advantages on AI companies, in direct violation of European

409 Senftleben, "Generative AI and Author Remuneration" (n 330).

410 Frosio G, "Should We Ban Generative AI, Incentivize it or Make it a Medium for Inclusive Creativity?" in Bonadio E and Sganga C (eds), A Research Agenda for EU Copyright Law (Edward Elgar) <https://ssrn.com/abstract=4527461> or <http://dx.doi.org/10.2139/ssrn.4527461>, 18.

411 Authors Guild, 2023: <https://actionnetwork.org/petitions/authors-guild-open-letter-to-generative-ai-leaders>.

copyright rules, and the AI Act could be a critical regulatory opportunity to impose accountability within the AI industry.[412]

The disruption of creative markets and its broader impact on individuals lies at the core of a wide-ranging debate that involves ethical, legal, sociological, economic, and political dimensions. A key aspect emerging from this discussion is the widely held belief that, notwithstanding the ongoing debates on whether the use of in-copyright materials falls in the scope of exception or limitation or not (see Chapter 7), it is only fair for human creators, whose works serve as the foundation for AI-generated content, to receive compensation when such content displaces the very demand for human creativity that made AI systems viable in the first place.

This is why, as it will seen, a growing body of legal scholarship supports the introduction of fair remuneration mechanisms for authors of the works used to train AI, such as levies or compulsory licensing schemes, as a way to counterbalance what these scholars describe as the parasitic appropriation of portions of the literary and artistic market by generative AI.

Yet, the problem persists for works that have already been incorporated into training datasets. In such cases, only *ex post* remedies may be considered, though their legal and technical feasibility remains highly uncertain.[413]

---

412 In this letter, they advocated for a sustainable and transparent licensing market that aligns with fair competition principles and secures remuneration for authors and rightsholders. The Act, they argued, should not only prevent unauthorized use of protected works, but also promote responsible innovation within a clearly defined legal framework. Also, the European Writers Council (EWC) added its voice to this chorus of concern, issuing a public statement on the adoption of the AI Act (n 5) in December 2024. While acknowledging that "if properly enforced, the AI Act will be a step in the right direction", the EWC emphasized that the regulation risks not going far enough to establish a meaningful and coherent strategy for the cultural and creative sectors. The EWC recognized the transformative potential of AI and its possible benefits across society, including in the realm of culture. However, it also highlighted the opaque and unregulated training practices of existing generative AI models, which have been developed through the massive, unauthorized scraping of copyright-protected content and personal data from the internet, without consent or remuneration for creators. The statement further warned of the risks posed by deepfakes and other forms of AI-manipulated content, which threaten democratic processes, authors' moral rights, and the public's trust in digital content.

Accordingly, the EWC called for all future initiatives on AI to be grounded in the principles of transparency, consent, and fair remuneration for authors and performers, urging policymakers to place ethical and human-centric AI governance at the heart of European innovation strategies.

413 A French legislative proposal to grant rights over AI-generated outputs to the authors of the training datasets also attempts to address this issue. However, such a solution must be regarded as fundamentally impracticable, given the sheer number of authors (potentially thousands or even millions) whose works are included in the vast datasets

Might it be said that, pending ongoing discussions over solutions applicable *ex tunc* or at least *ex nunc*, and assuming that the use of works for AI training cannot be justified under any exception or limitation, these individuals have effectively become authors… without an "author's right"?

4 The Subject-Matter

The use of generative AI to create text, video, images, and other similar content may call into question the very notion of "intellectual work", a notion that is not indeed without contradictions and whose necessarily flexible nature gives rise to tensions that affect at least two key aspects of the ongoing debate in this context.

Adopting once again the input/output dialectic, an important distinction emerges, as regards the subject-matter of copyright protection, between the two sides of the process. On the input side, the core issue is not whether the works used to train AI systems qualify as intellectual works – a point generally undisputed[414] – but rather their potential indirect exploitation through the extraction of data from them, often following unlawful access. This is confirmed by numerous examples, including the judicial cases that will be discussed in Chapter 7 – where many authors have voiced concerns about the use of their works without consent, claiming harm or infringement

By contrast, the contradictions surrounding the very concept of a work become particularly evident on the output side of the process. Determining whether, in a given case, an AI-based output qualifies as an intellectual work – or conversely, whether it should be regarded as belonging to an entirely different category of goods[415] – requires a concrete assessment of whether the conditions for copyright protection are met, and, more fundamentally, whether authorial protection can be conceived at all in such a context. As will be better

---

employed to train AI systems. If implemented, this approach could also lead to a decline in investment in the AI sector, thereby harming the competitiveness of any jurisdiction that adopts it, Geiger, "Elaborating a Human Rights Friendly Copyright Framework" (n 321) 8.

414 Nonetheless, there are important indirect implications on the input side for how we understand and apply the notion of intellectual work. If the reproduction or use of data extracted from such works were, in principle, deemed unlawful under copyright law, one might argue that copyright protection extends beyond the original works themselves to include – indirectly but effectively – the data and informational content derived from them.

415 This ambiguity is also reflected in scholarly discourse, where a growing part of the literature is opting for more neutral terms such as "outputs" or "products" to describe what generative AI produces.

pointed out in Chapter 8, a number of doctrinal reflections have already addressed this issue.

Nonetheless, due to the resemblance between the outputs of algorithmic decision-making processes and traditional creative works, a more abstract line of inquiry has emerged in the literature, particularly within French scholarship.[416] This inquiry seeks to explore the possibility of considering these outputs as at least "abstractly protectable", taking into account the characteristics of algorithmic outputs in abstract terms, while acknowledging that the evaluation of originality – which would determine whether they are actually protected in a specific instance – must ultimately be conducted on a case-by-case basis.

Notwithstanding its potential speculative character, such an abstract analysis can nonetheless prove useful in a systemic perspective, as it exposes the many contradictions arising from the potential conceptual overlap between AI-generated outputs and conventionally conceived intellectual works.

4.1 The "*Souplesse*" of the Concept of "Intellectual Work"

As is well-known, the element upon which, or in relation to which, the exclusive rights of the copyright holder are exercised is the intellectual work, as the object of copyright protection. Unlike other intangible goods, which are often defined in negative terms (as "things", "products", "objects" that are not material), an intellectual work can be defined positively, as the "product of the human mind" or the "result of a process of an intellectual nature".[417]

Such a definition of an intellectual work is, however, vague and "*souple*",[418] and, combined with the circular nature of copyright legislation, has given rise to long-standing debates. Indeed, as has been noted, the circularity of this legal framework makes the definition of its "subject matter of copyright (the

---

416 Benazeraf JA, La qualification d'œuvre de l'esprit à l'épreuve du procès: probatio diabolica? in Bensamoun A, Labarthe F and Tricoire A (eds), L'oeuvre de l'esprit en question(s). Un exercice de qualification (mare & martin 2015), 189; Benazeraf JA and Barthez V, Rapport de mission. La preuve de l'originalité (Conseil Supérieur de la propriété littéraire et artistique (CSPLA) 2020), footnote 89.

417 Spedicato (n 56) 32.

418 The term is used, with reference to originality, in Bensamoun and Farchy (n 4). This *souplesse* is largely due to the "inevitably elusive character" of this concept of copyright law, and especially to the difficulty of encapsulating in general and abstract terms the criteria used to define certain elements of the notion of "work". See also Fabbio (n 360) 286.

work), its protectability (originality), its subject (the author), and sometimes even its owner"[419] so intertwined that they may sometimes overlap.[420]

The *souplesse* of the discipline and the circularity of its core notions are, at once, among copyright law's greatest strengths – making it, for example, resilient against censorship pressures – and the source of long-standing uncertainties.

At least two sources of confusion stem from the elusive and at times tautological nature of key concepts in authorship legislation. The first concerns the often-nonlinear interaction between national, regional (e.g., EU), and international legal frameworks.[421]

Indeed, in an international context such as that in which intellectual works circulate – especially when they are digital or otherwise intended for online use – the differing perspectives adopted by case law, legislators, and legal scholarship at the national, regional, and international levels become particularly significant.

The transnational dimension of copyright law, when combined with the principle of copyright territoriality, which makes protection enforceable on a territory-by-territory basis, gives rise to an often-inconsistent overlap between judicial decisions, statutory provisions, and doctrinal interpretations: frequently, seemingly similar concepts reflect profoundly different legal cultures.[422] This can result in misunderstandings or, at the application stage, in evolutionary reinterpretations of traditional copyright categories, introducing

---

419 Bensamoun and Farchy (n 4) 25.

420 With regard to the originality requirement, see Iaia V, "To Be, or Not to Be…Original Under Copyright Law, That Is (One of) the Main Questions Concerning AI-Produ ced Works" (2022) 71(9) GRUR International 793 <https://ssrn.com/abstract=4528143>: "There is no common agreement on its meaning – and its subsequent applications – as the ethereal notion of originality has been interpreted several times by legislators, courts, and scholars, reaching manifold, and sometimes oppositional outcomes". See also Benazeraf and Barthez, Rapport de mission (n 416); Fishman LR, "Comparing concepts of originality in EU, Lithuanian and US law: photographs, new clips, databases, plot lines, TV formats, and other new uses of copyright works" in Mira T Sundara Rajan (ed), Cambridge Handbook of Intellectual Property in Central and Eastern Europe (CUP 2019) 80–109; Rosati E, "Why originality in copyright is not and should not be a meaningless requirement" (2018) 13 JIPLP 597–598.

421 Rotolo F, "Creatività vs. originalità: la qualificazione di "opera dell'ingegno" nell'era dell'intelligenza artificiale" (2022) 2 Rassegna di Diritto della Moda e delle Arti.

422 Ajani G, "*E Pluribus Unum* (?): Illusioni dell'armonizzazione e utilità dell'ontologia" (2007) 36 Rivista di estetica 13, 13–25, who pointed out that "There is in fact a difference between the contextual meaning of a term (or an expression) and the conceptual meaning of the same term: whereas the former meaning must be derived by observing contextual conditions, the latter concerns the type of information that can be received regardless of linguistic contexts".

elements that are foreign to the legal frameworks in which those categories originally developed.

An example of this is the apparent lack of full correspondence between the notion of "originality" – favored by the European Union (that has developed an autonomous concept of it[423]) and international law as the core requirement for the protection of intellectual works – and that of "creativity" underpinning an *acte de création consciente*, which appears to be more commonly used in certain national legislations (such as in Italian and French law) to refer to the "*quid proprium*" to an intellectual production.

The second source of uncertainty increasingly noted in legal scholarship lies in the growing perception that concepts such as creativity, originality – and, at times, even novelty – are being treated as inherent attributes of the work itself, as its constituent elements (requirements of the work), rather than as legal requirements for accessing authorship protection (requirement to access protection[424]). The distinction between the two ways of perceiving originality or creativity becomes evident when drawing a line between abstractly protectable works and actually protected works.[425]

4.2 The Impacts of AI on the Subject-Matter

The definition of abstractly protectable works is a classic topic in copyright law – one that may also be regarded as strategically significant from a systemic perspective. By establishing the balance point between the various interests involved *in abstracto* and *ex ante*,[426] the analysis of the notion of a "protect-

423 Among many authors, see in this regard Margoni T, "The Harmonization of EU Copyright Law: The Originality Standard" in Mark Perry (ed), *Global Governance of Intellectual Property in the 21st Century* (Springer International Publishing 2016) <http://link.springer.com/10.1007/978-3-319-31177-7_6> accessed 9 August 2025.

424 Riccio GM, "The Influence of the Court of Justice of the European Union on National Courts in Copyright Cases" in Pollicino O, Riccio GM and Bassini M (eds), Copyright and Fundamental Rights in the Digital Age. A Comparative Analysis in Search of a Common Constitutional Ground (Edward Elgar 2020) 174; Pardolesi R and Romano R, Attuazione e tutela dei diritti, I – La concorrenza e la tutela dell'innovazione (Giuffrè 2009) 117. Given that a necessary and sufficient element for the onset of authorial protection is the "expression" of an idea (see on this point Mongillo (n 351) 1 ff.) and that no prerequisites are required for intellectual works, creativity/originality and novelty could be understood at most as a filter for access to protection.

425 In this view, originality or creativity should be more appropriately understood as a criterion for identifying an actually protected work, rather than as part of the abstract definition of what constitutes a protectable work. However, the boundary between the two is difficult to trace, due to the circularity of copyright-related concepts.

426 Fabbio (n 360) 281.

able work" serves to delineate the "raw material" of copyright. Alongside rules on exceptions and limitations, term of protection, geographical limits, statutory and mandatory licenses, collective rights management, free uses (including fair use and fair dealing), and the idea/expression dichotomy, including the exhaustion principle,[427] it plays a key role in ensuring that all competing interests are appropriately safeguarded, especially in the current context of profound shifts in the balance of power among the different actors involved in the cultural production value chain.

The theoretical tool of the "protectable work" – by postulating an abstract notion of "intellectual work" that does not depend on its concrete original/creative character – allows for an initial distinction between what may be appropriated through exclusivity mechanisms and what must, in any case, remain part of the public domain.

Although primarily theoretical, this line of analysis has regained momentum in the context of generative AI, at least among a part of the EU copyright scholarship.

In this framework, the assessment in the abstract of what qualifies as an "intellectual work" must be regarded as a prerequisite (or, more precisely, a preliminary analytical step) with respect to the concrete assessment of this condition of access to protection[428].

Building on this premise, the question of whether AI-based outputs qualify as intellectual works eligible for copyright protection may be addressed through at least three analytical approaches.

The first of these has been advanced by IViR and JIIP in their 2020 report "Trends and Developments in Artificial Intelligence",[429] which identifies four key criteria for an AI-assisted output to qualify as a "work" under copyright law: (i) the production must fall within the literary, scientific, or artistic domain; (ii) it must involve human intellectual effort; (iii) it must exhibit

427 Mezei P, Copyright Exhaustion: Law and Policy in the United States and the European Union (Cambridge Intellectual Property and Information Law, CUP 2018) 6–23. According to Mezei, "Another doctrine that attempts to balance competing interests is exhaustion. It sets limitations for the author's exclusive right of distribution, along with the ownership interests of lawful acquirers of copies of protected subject matter. According to Friedrich-Karl Beier, "the principle of exhaustion is nothing more than a figurative expression for the simple legal idea that once genuine goods have been marketed, subsequent distribution should not be impeded by [IPR] actions".

428 Fabbio (n 360) 303.

429 Hartmann et al (n 228).

originality or creativity, typically through a creative choice;[430] and, finally, (iv) it must be expressed in an output[431]

According to this study, such an evaluation must take into account not only the extent of the human contribution to (and intervention in) the creative process, but also the degree to which each creative choice is expressed in the specific case. Within this framework, however, the distinction between "works protected in the abstract" and "concretely protectable works" is blurred, since the former requires an assessment in concrete of originality and creativity.[432] Notwithstanding the remarks that follow on the first point, it is worth noting that, as regards the second, the IViR/JIIP study emphasizes that, in order to meet the originality and creativity requirement, the creative act must be free from any constraints[433] – whether rule-based, technical, functional, or informational.

According to a similar, though slightly more comprehensive, perspective, the following areas of inquiry become particularly relevant:[434] (i) whether the subject matter under analysis qualifies as a "good" in legal terms; (ii) whether the legal goods fall in the domains of literature, art, and science and the categories exemplified in copyright law statutory provisions (e.g., musical, choreographic, sculptural, architectural works, etc.);[435] and (iii) the positive

430 In the continental European tradition, the notion of originality and creativity identifies the element that allows a work to be regarded as the result of the author's free and personal choices. In particular, the requirement for access to copyright protection is manifested in the author's "free and creative choices" and in the "discretionary choices" made when determining how to express an idea from among the many possible ways of doing so, thereby reflecting the author's personality – what is often referred to as their "personal touch" (See Case C-145/10 Eva-Maria Painer v Standard VerlagsGmbH and Others [2011] ECR I-12533, para 92).

431 Hartmann et al (n 228). See also Hugenholtz PB and Quintais JP, "Copyright and Artificial Creation: Does EU Copyright Law Protect AI-Assisted Output?" (2021) 52 IIC 1190, 1200–1207.

432 *Contra,* the concept of "work in the abstract" is not exhausted in the definition of its creative/original character, which, rather, should be understood as a requirement for access to protection and not as its constitutive element: "*l'originalité ne définit pas l'œuvre d'esprit*", but at most, "*elle conditionne sa protection*", see Benazeraf, "La qualification d'œuvre de l'esprit à l'épreuve du procès" (n 416) 189; see also Benazeraf and Barthez, Rapport de mission (n 416).

433 See also Iaia, "To Be, or Not to Be…Original Under Copyright Law" (n 420), recalling the Painer case: "Free from external constraints, so that the author would be able to express a sufficient level of arbitrariness" (Case C-145/10 Eva-Maria Painer v Standard VerlagsGmbH and Others [2011] ECR I-12533).

434 Fabbio (n 360) 303.

435 See paragraph 1 of Article 2 of the Berne Convention, which states that "the expression "literary and artistic works" shall include every production in the literary, scientific and

determination of what cannot be protected, even in the abstract, through the assessment of criteria such as human intellectual activity, manifestation of the idea, sufficient concreteness, and structural coherence. This also includes the examination of the fundamental dichotomy between expressive form and free ideas.[436]

With regard to the first profile, in order to qualify an AI output as a work abstractly protectable, at least two levels of evaluation are required. The first concerns whether the asset can be considered an "economic" good – that is, whether it possesses significant economic value and is capable of being traded. The second relates to a judgment on the meritoriousness of the interest to be protected.[437] Indeed, not all economically valuable goods are legally recognized as such: it is the perceived merit of the interests involved that determines the transition from the category of economic good to that of legal good. Within this framework, an intellectual work is not only an economic good, but also, in abstract terms, a good capable of satisfying a range of interests deemed worthy of protection – first and foremost, cultural and social interests. Whether the same can be said of AI-based outputs depends on several considerations, the first of which is that such outputs can clearly qualify as economic goods, though it remains uncertain whether they are

---

artistic domain, whatever may be the mode or form of its expression, such as books, pamphlets and other writings; lectures, addresses, sermons and other works of the same nature; dramatic or dramatico-musical works; choreographic works and entertainments in dumb show; musical compositions with or without words; cinematographic works to which are assimilated works expressed by a process analogous to cinematography; works of drawing, painting, architecture, sculpture, engraving and lithography; photographic works to which are assimilated works expressed by a process analogous to photography; works of applied art; illustrations, maps, plans, sketches and three-dimensional works relative to geography, topography, architecture or science". This definition applies to the EU, because even though it is not a signatory to the Berne Convention, it is bound to comply with it as a result of other international commitments, specifically those following from the Agreement on Trade-Related Aspects of Intellectual Property Rights (TRIPs Agreement (n 83)) and the WIPO Copyright Treaty (adopted 20 December 1996, entered into force 6 March 2002) 2186 UNTS 121. As a result, the EU must comply with Articles 1 to 21 and the Appendix of Berne, see Jongsma D, "The Nature and Content of the Three-Step Test in EU Copyright Law: A Reappraisal" in Rosati E (ed), Handbook of European Copyright Law (Routledge 2020) <https://ssrn.com/abstract=3665934> or <http://dx.doi.org/10.2139/ssrn.3665934>.

436 Fabbio (n 360) 282–283.

437 Pugliatti S, Gli istituti del diritto civile (Milan 1943) 299. The debate on the meritoriousness of interests has occupied generations of civil law scholars and cannot be revisited in detail here. However, insofar as it is relevant to the present analysis, the examination of the deservingness of interests in copyright law and the function attributed to intellectual property will be addressed more extensively in Chapter 9.

deserving of legal protection. Indeed, they often hold market value and are subject to commercial exchange.[438] A prominent example is the case of Edmond de Belamy, discussed in the Introduction to this manuscript, in which a work generated by the AI system of the Obvious collective was sold at auction for more than US$ 400,000.[439] Another case in point is that of the music tracks produced by AIVA Technologies, whose commercial potential – particularly for advertising, cinema, and gaming – was explicitly pursued from the outset.[440] It thus seems difficult to deny that AI content holds significant economic relevance and is fully integrated into existing market dynamics – whether within the art world or the broader creative industries. More complex, however, is the evaluation of whether these goods also satisfy interests that are not only economic. The answer to this question, as will be further explored in Chapter 9, depends on deeper normative and policy considerations underpinning the entire copyright system and cannot be separated from the broader analysis of the ultimate functions of this legal framework.

As for the second profile, – indeed one shared with the IViR/JIIP reconstruction – an AI-generated output can be considered abstractly protectable if it falls within the domains of literature, art, or science, and corresponds to categories of works such as musical, choreographic, sculptural, or architectural works, among others. The prevailing view today is that this statutory list of covered areas is merely illustrative[441] and that the assessment of whether a given asset falls within one of them should not be conducted in an overly restrictive manner. Consequently, the question of whether AI-based outputs belong to the domains traditionally covered by copyright law – or at least analogically comparable to them – is, for the most part, not particularly controversial. The examples discussed in Chapter 2 clearly illustrate that they do.

---

438 Gervais, "The Machine as Author" (n 367).

439 Bensamoun and Farchy (n 4) 24.

440 <https://www.digitaltrends.com/music/artificial-intelligence-taryn-southern-album-interview/>.

441 There is, indeed, a growing tendency to regard the lists of applicable domains and categories of works found in major Western legal systems as non-exhaustive. Some scholars argue that the technique of employing closed lists of abstractly protectable works should largely be seen as a legacy of the past, as it may at times deny protection to certain works "without objective functional justification, see Fabbio (n 360), 303; see also Rosati E, "Closed subject-matter systems are no longer compatible with EU copyright" (2014) <http://papers.ssrn.com/sol3/.papers.cfr?abstract_id=2468104>, Rosati E, "Originality in US and UK copyright experiences as a springboard for an EU-wide reform debate" (2010) 41(5) IIC 524, 542.

More problematic, however, is the analysis relating to the third and final logical step generally required for recognizing a work as abstractly protectable: i.e., the assessment of whether AI-based outputs can, in principle, transcend the realm of mere "free ideas". In an EU perspective, this step entails determining whether the output qualifies as an "author's own intellectual creation".[442]

As is well known, this formula – the AOIC standard – was originally found in Directive 96/9/EC (the so-called Database Directive) and Directive 2009/24/EC (the Software Directive),[443] and, with respect to photographic works, in Directive 93/98/EEC (the Term of Protection Directive).[444] It was subsequently elevated to a general standard for intellectual productions only following the landmark ruling in Infopaq International A/S v. Danske Dagblades Forening, where the Court stated that copyright applies to "an object that is original in the sense that it is the author's own intellectual creation".[445]

Clarifying the scope of the notion of the author's own intellectual creation has therefore been regarded as essential for fulfilling the third step in the assessment of a "work in the abstract" within this framework, both in legal scholarship and in case law. To summarize in a few words what has been the subject of extensive debate – at the risk of oversimplifying an issue that would warrant far more detailed treatment – it may be said that, according to the Court of Justice, the AOIC test is fulfilled when the following conditions are met.[446] First, the form of the elements for which protection is claimed must not be solely dictated by their technical function.[447] Second, there must be room for the author to exercise "creative freedom" – protection is excluded

442 Regarding the idea that the "Author's own intellectual creation" standard can be useful to define what is a "work" in the abstract, being "clearly an open standard, susceptible to further specification, in general and in relation to individual categories of works", see Fabbio (n 360) 293.

443 Article 3(1) of Directive 96/9/EC (the Database Directive); Article 1(3) of Directive 2009/24/EC (the Software Directive).

444 According to the Court, this expression was already implicitly derivable from the Berne Convention, see Case C-5/08 Infopaq International A/S v Danske Dagblades Forening [2009] ECR I-6569, par. 32 et seq. Notably, the same expression "author's own intellectual creation" was also used in 2010 in the European Copyright Code (ECC) of the Wittem Project (n 369).

445 Case C-5/08 Infopaq International A/S v Danske Dagblades Forening [2009] ECR I-6569, para. 37.

446 Fabbio (n 360) 290 ff.

447 Case C-393/09 Bezpečnostní softwarová asociace – Svaz softwarové ochrany v Ministerstvo kultury [2010] ECR I-13971 (BSA), paras. 49 et seq.

when no such freedom is possible.[448] Moreover, the author must have made free and creative choices in the development of the work.[449] The mere deployment of effort (labor) and possession of technical skill (know-how) are not sufficient unless they result in an original selection or arrangement of the various elements.[450] Finally, the author must be able to express their creative spirit in an original manner, particularly through the way in which they combine and organize elements that may not, in themselves, be eligible for protection.[451]

Such an assessment becomes particularly challenging in the context of AI-based creations, where it is often impossible to define, in the abstract, the degree and nature of human contribution in the generative process.

In any case, this latter profile of analysis once again lies at the intersection between the theoretical analysis of the notion of an "abstractly protectable work" and the practical assessment of the requirements for protection (originality/creativity). It illustrates how any attempt to delineate the operative scope of these concepts must inevitably contend with the inherent circularity of the underlying notions.

According to a third perspective, to assess whether AI-based outputs can be framed as "abstractly protectable works", an interpretation found in French legal scholarship may also be relevant. According to this view, the substance of the concept of the author's own intellectual creation depends on the presence of at least three elements: (i) the asset must constitute a creation of form; (ii) the creation must be, at least potentially, the result of a conscious process; and (iii) it must be attributable to a human creator, understood as the author.[452]

The third element of this assessment has already been addressed in detail in Paragraph 3 of this Chapter.

As for the first element necessary to qualify a creation as an "abstractly protectable work", the relevant notion of form should not be understood as material form, but rather as "expressive form", that is, the "expression" referred to in Article 2 of the WIPO Copyright Treaty.[453] This expression is understood

448 Joined Cases C-403/08 and C-429/08 Football Association Premier League Ltd and Others v QC Leisure and Others [2011] ECR I-9083 (FAPL), paras. 98 et seq.

449 Case C-145/10 Eva-Maria Painer v Standard VerlagsGmbH and Others [2011] ECR I-12533.

450 Case C-604/10 Football Dataco Ltd and Others v Yahoo! UK Ltd and Others EU:C:2012:115, para. 42.

451 Case C-406/10 SAS Institute Inc v World Programming Ltd EU:C:2012:259, para. 67.

452 Bensamoun A, "Intelligence artificielle et propriété intellectuelle" in Loiseau G and Bensamoun A (eds), Droit de l'intelligence artificielle (LGDJ 2022), 253 ff.

453 WIPO Copyright Treaty (adopted 20 December 1996, entered into force 6 March 2002) 2186 UNTS 121.

as the specific manner in which the author's thought is objectified (i.e., turned into an object or product) and made manifest (i.e., rendered perceptible or knowable).[454] According to this approach, it is precisely this criterion – the "*expression sensible d'une idée*"[455] – that renders a creation perceptible to the senses and thereby marks the boundary between the protected expression and the unprotected idea.

Finally, with regard to the second element, the requirement of consciousness – although not universally accepted[456] – implies un minimum de *maîtrise intellectuelle du processus créatif* [a minimum degree of intellectual mastery of the creative process].[457] This element not only excludes from protection, at least in principle, the creations of children[458] but also presupposes the third and final criterion: the presence of a human author.[459] From this perspective, the human being (third element) is the only subject capable of attributing intellectual meaning to the form produced and of manifesting a creative intention,[460] a general authorial intent,[461] that is, the intention to produce an original creation, whatever its nature. Such intention presupposes not really the capacity to act,[462] but at least a deeper "self-awareness, an idea, an inner

454 Spedicato (n 56) 43.

455 Bensamoun, "Intelligence artificielle et propriété intellectuelle" (n 452) 253 ff.

456 Vivant M and Bruguiere JM, Droit d'auteur et droits voisins (4th edn, Dalloz 2019), no. 119; Larrieu J, "Le robot et le droit d'auteur" in Mélanges A Lucas (LexisNexis 2014) 465 ff., spec. 467, Michaux B, "Singularité technologique, singularité humaine et droit d'auteur" in Mélanges Poullet, Droit, normes et libertés dans le cybermonde (Larcier 2018) 401 ff., spec. 410.

457 Lucas A, Lucas-Schloetter A and Bernault C, Traité de la propriété littéraire et artistique (5th edn, LexisNexis 2017), no. 57.

458 Binctin N, "L'influence de l'intelligence artificielle sur les mécanismes de la propriété intellectuelle" in Bruguiere JM and Geiger C (eds), Penser le droit de la pensée – Mélanges en l'honneur de Michel Vivant (1st edn, Dalloz 2020).

459 Bensamoun and Farchy (n 4) 33.

460 Binctin (n 458) 60.

461 See European Commission, Directorate-General for Communications Networks, Content and Technology, and others, <https://commission.europa.eu/about/departments-and-executive-agencies/communications-networks-content-and-technology_en>, 75, 82–83.

462 The prevailing doctrine recognizes the independence of artistic capacity from the capacity to act. As for the Italian System, see De Sanctis V, La protezione delle opere dell'ingegno. Le opere letterarie e scientifiche, le opere musicali e le opere informatiche, vol II (Giuffrè 2003) 70; Ascarelli T, Teoria della concorrenza e dei beni immateriali (3rd edn, Giuffrè 1960) 720; Greco and Vercellone (n 354), 213, who admit the protectability of works created under the influence of psychotropic substances or by persons in a state of mental illness.

archetype, a judgment, and a will to express".[463] However, the correlation between consciousness and the creation of intellectual works remains a matter of ongoing and intense debate[464] – and, in the context of AI-generated content, is closely tied to increasingly explored concepts such as randomness and control over the creative process.[465]

Indeed, randomness and control undeniably influence the extent to which, and whether, the intentions of the authors – whoever they may be – can be reflected in the final output, assuming such intentions are relevant to the act of creation and the creative process itself – a point that, as noted, should not be taken for granted.

In the context of generative AI, the intentions relevant to determining whether AI outputs can be regarded as "intellectual works" may be limited

463 "Creative activity is realized through a progressively free, personal (or multi-personal) process structured in a series of phases that make it possible to grasp the primary personal nature characterizing the original work, such as, in particular, self-awareness, the idea, the archetype, inner judgment, expression, the *medium* and concretization", see Iaia, "Le derive della creatività nel diritto d'autore" (n 355) 236.

464 The role of the author's intention in the critical interpretation of a work of art has long been debated, with positions ranging from Extreme Intentionalism to Anti-Intentionalism. On one side of the spectrum, lie intentionalism: "Intentionalism in aesthetics is, quite generally, the thesis that the artist's or artists' intentions have a decisive role in the creation of a work of art, and that knowledge of such intentions is a necessary component of at least some adequate interpretive and evaluative claims.1 In this paper, I develop and defend this thesis". See Livingston P, "Intentionalism in Aesthetics" (1998) 29(4) New Literary History 831 <https://www.jstor.org/stable/20057514>, who also claims that "intentionalist strictures make the focus of appreciation shift radically away from the text or structure and toward the life and mind of the artist". On the other side of the spectrum, lie Anti-intentionalism: "A premise of many anti-intentionalist arguments (...) is that if a work has determinate meanings and value, they must be immanent in the artistic text or structure. This sort of empiricism in aesthetics is vulnerable to some powerful criticisms. Not all of the artistically or aesthetically relevant features of a work of art are intrinsic properties of the text; some are relational and can only be known when the text or structure is cognized correctly in the context of its creation" (Ibid). However, More moderate perspectives have also emerged, such as those which conceptualize works as possessing relational properties that establish a dialogue between the "reader of a book" and its author. According to one of these moderate approaches, "the artist who, within "natural and logical limits", makes the work, and choos[es] and settl [es] on categories and meanings", remains a central figure in the creative process. As has been argued, "intentions are mental states having semantic contents, various psychological functions, and practical consequences but not always the targeted results" (Ibid).

465 According to a leading view, if "an author is a human being who exercises subjective judgment in composing the work and who controls its execution", then the absence of the latter – namely, of a certain degree of control – implies the presence of randomness in the creative process, which must be carefully taken into account. See Ginsburg, "The Concept of Authorship in Comparative Copyright Law" (n 355).

to the mere desire to express an idea (however obscure or inscrutable) that is nonetheless conveyed, in some form, through the AI's output.[466] This corresponds to what part of the legal scholarship has termed "categorial intentions", which govern not what a work is to mean but how it is to be fundamentally conceived or approached".[467] In this idea, the intention to create, for example, a sculpture and to have it understood as such constitutes a categorial intention, whereas the intention to express rage through the artwork is a semantic intention.[468] Within an algorithmic creative process, the only identifiable intention may thus be a categorial one – such as when a prompt directs the system to "create a painting" – regardless of the specific expressive content of the resulting output. Whether this limited form of intention suffices to classify the output as an intellectual work depends on the circumstances of the case... which inevitably brings us back to the initial observation regarding the inherent circularity of the notions at stake.

However, whatever assessment is adopted to determine the abstract protectability of AI outputs, it seems difficult to exclude *a priori* that such outputs could, at least in principle, satisfy all the criteria expressed above – subject, of course, to the inherent flexibility of such considerations and the blurred nature of the underlying boundaries. Whether this framework will ultimately suffice to ground actual copyright protection for AI-based outputs depends, once again, on a more concrete evaluation of the originality requirement and on the policy function that copyright protection is meant to serve, issues that will be addressed in Chapters 8, 9, and 10.

In any case, given the undeniable circumstance that AI outputs may plausibly fall within the statutory categories of literary, artistic, or scientific works, recognizing, *de facto* or *de jure*, the protectability of such outputs without first satisfying all the logical steps required to establish their abstract protectability may rise the risk of indirectly affecting the very notion of an intellectual work.

466 This approach relies on the distinction between semantic and categorial intentions, which is grounded primarily in the content of the intentions themselves and pertains more specifically to the particular aspects of the artwork the artist envisions. Livingston (n 464).

467 Ibid, 1188; see also Levinson J, "Extending Art Historically" in J Levinson, The Pleasures of Aesthetics (OUP).

468 Levinson (n 467), 150–71, spec. 158, no 8.

5 Some Conclusions

The advent of generative AI and its application in the cultural and (re)creative sectors risks triggering significant disruptions in the field of copyright law, whether *de facto* or *de jure*.

De facto, this may occur if the creation – through, for example, private autonomy – of exclusive rights over AI-generated outputs is accepted on the same terms as those granted under copyright law. *De jure*, this risk arises if current legislation is either reinterpreted- possibly for the flexibility and circularity of the concepts at stake without sufficient safeguards, or amended to extend copyright protection to works generated entirely by AI, without any human creative contribution.

With regard to the creative process, it has been observed that when the creation of a work results from an automated, algorithmic operation – where information processing may potentially be the exclusive or predominant domain of a machine – the boundary between free ideas and the protected expression of those ideas becomes increasingly blurred.

Ordinarily, the expression of an idea is the result of a free and conscious choice made by the author from among countless possible ways to give form to that idea; it marks the concrete moment in which the work comes into existence.

However, in a process where any creative judgment by a natural person is absent from the execution phase, when can it meaningfully be said that the transition from free ideas to expressed ideas has taken place? This question is all the more important because such a transition is not only a precondition for, but also the very foundation of, the application of copyright law. And how can one claim that the "creative judgment" is reflected in the output itself, in the way that the romantic notion of authorship[469] – as a personal "blueprint" of the author – would seem to require?

With regard to the subjects – both natural and legal persons – who may potentially be involved in the creation of an output using AI systems, the range of actors extends far beyond the end-users or professional deployers of such systems. Numerous other contributors play fundamental roles in the algorithmic creative process, including those responsible for the design, programming, implementation, and distribution of the system, each with their own distinct qualifications. These roles can only partially be assimilated to the traditional concept of "author", as their contribution, even when substantial, may remain purely technical. Compounding this, significant uncertainty

469 Ajani, "Contemporary Artificial Art and the Law" (n 321).

also surrounds the role, prerogatives, legitimate expectations, and even the very rights of the human creators of the thousands – if not millions – of works already incorporated into AI training datasets.

With regard to the subject matter, it has been observed that AI challenges the very definition of what constitutes an "intellectual work": from the input-side perspective, the potential protection of the works used to train generative AI could indirectly extend to their informational content, which, according to the classic idea/expression dichotomy, should remain outside the scope of copyright; from the output-side perspective, as well, uncritically recognizing AI-based outputs as intellectual works – without first assessing whether they meet all the steps to qualify as abstractly protectable – risks reinterpreting the very boundary between what is and is not eligible for copyright protection.

Taken together, these tensions – over the algorithmic "creative" process, the subjects, and the subject matter – are not merely technical issues internal to copyright doctrine. They are the point at which the broader pressures traced throughout this book come to bear on the foundations of the discipline: the redefinition of these classic categories is precisely where the privatisation of knowledge either advances or is held back. Whether their reinterpretation entrenches the propertarian drift or is steered toward copyright's social function is, ultimately, the question that the remainder of this study seeks to address.

SECTION 3

At the Core of the Input–Output Debates

CHAPTER 7

Legal Issues on the Input Side of the Creative Process

1 Preliminary Remarks

One of the most contentious aspects of the input phase of the algorithmic "creative" process concerns the use of data for training and testing AI systems. Most current AI tools rely on deep learning algorithms designed to generate content – such as images, text, video, dialogues, or code – based on user prompts. Generative AI, in particular, focuses on the creation of outputs across multiple media formats including text, images, video, and music. Prominent examples of such models include ChatGPT, Stable Diffusion, and DeepSeek.

As noted above, generative AI systems do not create *ex nihilo*. They rely on pre-existing data and works as training material. Machine learning algorithms are capable of recognizing patterns and stylistic features, through a deductive approach, by analyzing existing literary and artistic works. As Geiger has aptly noted, generative AI can mimic human creativity precisely because it has been exposed to human-created content during training.[470]

The higher the quality and comprehensiveness of the training data, the more sophisticated the output generated by AI systems tends to be.[471] For this reason, training such systems typically involves the use of vast amounts of data, often aggregated into large-scale datasets compiled through text and data mining (TDM) techniques or specifically curated for training purposes. These datasets may encompass a wide range of content types, frequently including personal data.[472] A prominent example of the diversity of data potentially included in AI training datasets is the use of text-image pairs

470 Geiger, 'Elaborating a Human Rights Friendly Copyright Framework' (n 321).

471 For an in-depth discussion of the technical foundations of machine learning from an IP perspective, Drexl, Hilty et al. (n 228). For a recent and insightful analysis of the legal implications of machine learning inputs and outputs, including issues of copyright liability and exceptions, see Guadamuz A, 'A Scanner Darkly: Copyright Liability and Exceptions in Artificial Intelligence Inputs and Outputs' (2024) 73(2) GRUR Int 111.

472 The circumstance that much of the data used to train generative AI systems also qualifies as personal data, thus triggering the application of data protection law, complicates the issue at stake. As noted by Pasa, the use of such data possibly creates an overlapping

employed to train so-called text-to-image models, such as Stable Diffusion or DALL·E. These data combine textual and visual elements to enable the models to associate visual structures, compositions, and perceptible features in images with corresponding textual descriptions.

The potentially vast diversity of datasets used to train generative AI has been made possible thus far because of the use of specific techniques to source enormous quantities of data from open-access online repositories, as well as content generated specifically for training purposes (synthetic data).[473] Synthetic data, which may include AI-generated visuals or other type of content that closely resemble real-world images in both appearance and statistical characteristics, are generally considered lower-quality substitutes for real data. As such, they are typically used only when access to real data is impractical, costly, or constrained by legal or regulatory restrictions.[474]

From a copyright perspective, neither public domain works nor synthetic data generally raise significant legal concerns, with the primary issues associated with these types of data being limited to the sheer scale of their use.[475] For example, one major concern with these data arises beyond copyright when it

---

regulatory space where copyright and data protection regimes intersect – both in terms of the types of content involved, the subjects whose rights are at stake, and the responsibilities imposed on data controllers and AI developers (Pasa B, 'Copyright and Data Protection' in Senigaglia R, Irti C and Bernes A (eds), Privacy and Data Protection in Software Services (Springer 2022), 111–123). The European General Data Protection Regulation (GDPR), for instance, imposes stringent obligations concerning the collection, use, and storage of personal data, including requirements of transparency, consent, and proportionality.

473 Rossi, 'Opere in cerca d'autore' (n 343).

474 Although the use of synthetic data in the training of generative AI models is not yet widespread, its transformative potential is increasingly acknowledged. According to a forecast by Gartner, by 2030 synthetic data is expected to surpass real data in prevalence for training AI models. See Goasduff L, 'Is Synthetic Data the Future of AI?' (Gartner, 22 June 2022) <https://www.gartner.com/en/newsroom/press-releases/2022-06-22-is-synthetic-data-the-future-of-ai>; Toews R, 'Synthetic Data Is About To Transform Artificial Intelligence' (Forbes, 12 June 2022) <https://www.forbes.com/sites/robtoews/2022/06/12/synthetic-data-is-about-to-transform-artificial-intelligence/>; Mischitelli M, 'I dati sintetici nuova frontiera dell'intelligenza artificiale: opportunità e limiti' (Agenda Digitale, 14 July 2021) <https://www.agendadigitale.eu/sicurezza/privacy/i-dati-sintetici-nuova-frontiera-dellintelligenza-artificiale-opportunita-e-limiti/>.

475 For instance, concerns related to the exploitation of public domain content have been highlighted by some reports, such as leaked internal documents from NVIDIA suggesting that the company was downloading the equivalent of 80 years' worth of video content per day from platforms like YouTube for scraping purposes. This has prompted fears of potential market disruption, even where the content is in the public domain. See <https://www.404media.co/nvidia-ai-scraping-foundational-model-cosmos-project/>.

is extracted or generated based on vast amounts of publicly available internet content, which may embed and amplify societal biases. The internet, being a massive repository of human-generated content, "inherently contains a myriad of biases and prejudices that exist within society". When such data are used without critical filtering or ethical consideration, synthetic datasets may inadvertently serve as a conduit for perpetuating and intensifying these biases.[476]

Aside from these cases, the primary legal and ethical concerns surrounding TDM activities for AI training emerge when the data used by AI systems include (parts of) copyrighted material. This may consist of excerpts from traditionally created artistic works or, when compiled into datasets, portions of copyright-protected databases. In a 2022 interview with *Forbes*, David Holz – founder of the AI image generation platform Midjourney – acknowledged that millions of images sourced from the web to train the AI model included content that are protected under copyright law.[477]

2 The Issue

Whenever the data used to train AI are in-copyright works, the core legal question is (i) whether such use qualifies as "text and data mining activities" and/or (ii) whether this use constitute a form of indirect exploitation of an intellectual work that should entitle rightsholders to exercise their exclusive rights, including the right to compensation?[478]

From a strictly legal standpoint, whether the training of generative AI models using copyrighted content constitutes copyright infringement is a complex and highly contested issue. The volume of ongoing litigation (see Paragraph 3 of this chapter) highlights the unresolved and contentious nature of this issue.

Before delving into how different jurisdictions, particularly the United States, have addressed this issue, a few preliminary considerations are in order. Arguably, the data used to train AI systems are not, in themselves, protected by copyright, as they often consist merely of portions of copyrighted works. More importantly, these data have often been deemed to serve an

476 Hao S, Han W, Jiang T, Li Y, Wu H, Zhong C, Zhou Z and Tang H, 'Synthetic Data in AI: Challenges, Applications, and Ethical Implications' (arXiv preprint, 3 January 2024) arXiv:2401.01629v1 [cs.LG].

477 "David Holz's responses regarding the data used for training are not specific either. They range from 'a big scrape of the Internet', 'the open data sets'136 and the data based on the users' preferences regarding the use of Midjourney to '12 training datasets'"; see Militsyna, 'Human Creative Contribution to AI-Based Output' (n 407), 946.

478 Rossi, 'Opere in cerca d'autore' (n 343).

informational purpose that remains within the limits of the idea/expression dichotomy.[479] As such, the use of such data should not, in principle, require prior authorization under copyright law.

In fact, it is generally accepted that mere facts or data "as such" – for example, raw weather data or simple factual occurrences – do not fall within the scope of copyright protection. This exclusion rests on a conceptual foundation that regards facts as the basic building blocks of human knowledge.[480] As has been observed, affording copyright protection to factual data would be equivalent to granting exclusive rights over the letters of the alphabet, thereby hindering the ability to generate new knowledge or expression.[481]

In line with the notion that facts and data as such do not fall within the scope of copyright protection, certain jurisdictions have adopted particularly permissive approaches to the use of data in the context of AI training. Notably, Japan has emerged as a frontrunner in embracing a liberal stance. In June 2023, the Japanese government issued an AI-guideline proposal on the training of generative AI,[482] reinforcing its earlier legislative move from 2018 that allowed the use of copyrighted works for machine learning purposes, provided the use was not "for enjoying or causing another person to enjoy the ideas or emotions expressed in such work".[483] The new 2023 guidelines go even further: they clarify that machine learning engineers are permitted to use any data they can access "regardless of whether it is for non-profit or commercial purposes, whether it is an act other than reproduction, or whether it is content obtained from illegal sites or otherwise".[484]

This approach echoes the position of several scholars who emphasize the importance of not demonizing TDM activities per se. In its opinion on the EU Copyright Directive,[485] indeed, the European Copyright Society (ECS) argued that TDM should be permitted for at least two reasons. First, under the idea/expression dichotomy, TDM does not engage with protected expression but rather with patterns and correlations that are not themselves subject to copy-

479 As noted in Chapter 6, the dichotomy "free idea/expression of idea" is the tool used by copyright to maintain a careful balance between the interests at stake: while it protects original expressions – defined in EU law as the "author's own intellectual creation" manifested through free and creative choices – it expressly excludes from protection basic, unoriginal elements necessary for the advancement of knowledge and culture.

480 Margoni T, 'TDM Opt-Outs: Legal and Technical Considerations' in R Dreyfuss and others (eds), The Regulation of AI through IP (2025) 7.

481 Ibid.

482 Geiger, 'Elaborating a Human Rights Friendly Copyright Framework' (n 321).

483 Article 30-4 of the Japanese copyright act.

484 Geiger, 'Elaborating a Human Rights Friendly Copyright Framework' (n 321).

485 CDSM Directive (n 116).

right. Second, TDM does not interfere with the normal exploitation of a work, nor does it constitute a market substitute (i.e., infringing works that undermine markets for the author's works). According to the ECS, the process does not generate any of the economic incentive effects that copyright law is intended to support, nor does it involve using a work as a work.

Moreover, according to this view, TDM can be considered a (fair) activity that underpins the development of generative AI, potentially fostering innovation, expanding access to knowledge, and promoting scientific and artistic progress.

This consideration becomes even more compelling when AI training is conducted for research purposes, directly implicating the fundamental right to scientific inquiry and the public interest in the free circulation of knowledge.[486] In the context of scientific research – which is, as known, strongly driven by input-output mechanisms – all scientific outputs are potentially also "input information" for new productive processes. Therefore, any disruption in this input-output dynamic may significantly hinder the advancement of research and knowledge. From this perspective, it has been even argued that TDM can be grounded in human rights, such as the right to science and culture and the freedom of artistic expression enshrined in key international instruments, including Articles 19 and 27(1) of the Universal Declaration of Human Rights (UDHR), Articles 15(1)(a) and (b) of the International Covenant on Economic, Social and Cultural Rights (ICESCR), and Articles 11 and 13 of the EU Charter of Fundamental Rights (EUCFR).

Why, then, do TDM activities remain so contested? The answer lies in two considerations.

First, as has been argued, "the creation of a training corpus through web scraping or database extraction often entails the prior reproduction and storage of protected works".[487]

Second, even where no storage of protected works occurs, the mere unauthorized access to such works may itself constitute an infringement, unless

486 It must not be forgotten that Generative AI technologies also have substantial potential in scientific contexts. As highlighted by Scientific American, a differentiated regulatory approach may be warranted depending on the purpose for which machine learning is deployed. In this regard, Text and Data Mining (TDM) emerges as a critical tool for research across numerous domains. According to some, differentiated approaches with regard to the purpose of the ML should be adopted in order to allow at least some kind of models to take advantage of TDM activities; see <https://www.scientificamerican.com/article/we-need-smart-intellectual-property-laws-for-artificial-intelligence/>.

487 Lucchi N and Hunter S, 'Generative AI and Copyright – Training, Creation, Regulation' (2025) <https://www.europarl.europa.eu/RegData/etudes/STUD/2025/774095/IUST_STU(2025)774095_EN.pdf> accessed 9 August 2025, 30.

covered by a statutory exception. Indeed, according to a prevailing formalistic interpretation of the reproduction right – both in jurisdictions such as the United States, where the first decisions on the merits have begun to emerge, with diverging outcomes, and in EU law, which does not exempt TDM from the requirement of "lawful access" to works- [488] in order to extract and mine data, it is first necessary to have or obtain lawful access to the original protected content, either because the use qualifies as a form of free use, or because authorization has been granted by the rightsholders.

A growing body of legal scholarship is engaging with these issues, attempting to resolve the question raised at the beginning of this paragraph. However, the matter remains far from settled and is addressed differently across jurisdictions. In the United States, for example, the debate centers on the uncertain applicability of the fair use doctrine to TDM activities and the broader training of generative AI systems. Similarly, under the EU legal framework, significant ambiguity persists as to whether the processes involved in machine learning fall within the scope of the TDM exceptions provided by Articles 3 and 4 of the Directive on Copyright in the Digital Single Market.

3 The US Experience

A significant portion of the current debate over the use of copyrighted works to train generative AI systems hinges on whether the ingestion of in-copyright works for the purposes of machine learning and text and data mining qualifies as fair use.

Major AI developers argue that their training activities involving protected content should fall within the scope of this doctrine. This position is reflected in the nearly 10,000 responses submitted by leading companies in the generative AI sector to the US Copyright Office's Notice of Inquiry (NOI), issued on August 30, 2023, as part of its initiative on Copyright Law and AI.[489]

---

488 On critical reflections on the formalistic interpretation of the concept of "reproduction right", see Orlando S, 'Il diritto di Text and Data Mining (TDM) non esiste' (2023) 1 Rivista italiana di informatica e diritto. As for the concept of "lawful access" the EU legal framework, including the Copyright in the CDSM Directive (n 116), offers little clarity on when content is "lawfully available" for such purposes. A purpose-driven interpretation has been advanced by some scholars (Margoni, 'TDM Opt-Outs' (n 480)) suggesting that the requirement of lawful access should be interpreted as relating to the behavior of the user, rather than the legal status of the source. See more on this point in Chapter 10.

489 Notice of Inquiry (NOI) (n 393).

A substantial portion of the legal scholarship also supports this view.[490] This strand of scholarship relies on the key judicial precedents of Authors Guild v. Google and Authors Guild v. HathiTrust, arguing that these cases – both addressing large-scale digitization and computational analysis of copyrighted works for non-expressive, transformative purposes – demonstrate how the fair use doctrine provides strong legal support for the permissibility of TDM activities. In particular, in Authors Guild v. HathiTrust, the digitization and full-text indexing of copyrighted books by a university library was deemed a legitimate fair use.[491] In particular, the US court held that scanning and storing full copies of in-copyright books, as well as enabling the data mining of their content, qualified as "transformative use" because these activities neither reproduced expressive content for public dissemination nor substituted for the original works. The purpose, enabling data mining and improving accessibility for visually impaired readers, was indeed to extract factual information, not to expose the copyrighted expression. Similarly, in Authors Guild v. Google,[492] which centered on claims that Google's book-scanning project constituted infringement, the court ruled that displaying limited text snippets and using complete works for non-expressive search functionality did not harm the market for the original books. Consequently, the court rejected the infringement claims and held that the project qualified as fair use.[493]

Although these precedents have become foundational to arguments supporting the application of the fair use doctrine, it is important to recognize that these rulings predate the rise of modern generative AI systems and the unprecedented scale at which they now operate. Consequently, the question of fair use remains far from resolved.[494]

Generally speaking, the US doctrine of fair use permits the use of protected works without the prior authorization of the rightsholders, for example for

490 Rossi, 'Opere in cerca d'autore' (n 343).

491 Authors Guild v HathiTrust 755 F3d 87 (2d Cir 2014).

492 Authors Guild v Google 804 F3d 202 (2d Cir 2015).

493 This way, the court dismissed all three arguments advanced by the plaintiffs: that users' ability to read parts of the books amounted to a market substitute; that Google had infringed their derivative rights by providing search functionalities that could have been licensed; and that the storage of digital copies posed a security risk that could lead to widespread unauthorized distribution, thereby devaluing their copyrights.

494 However, some guidance can be found in the most recent report by the US Copyright Office, Copyright and Artificial Intelligence: Part 3 (n 198) – which, at the time of writing, is still in its pre-print form.

purposes of research and teaching.[495] Where fair use is found to apply, the copying of protected content, otherwise unlawful, becomes fully lawful, with no obligation to pay compensation to the copyright holder.[496]

Fair use has long served as a key instrument for balancing competing interests within copyright law framework. As emphasized by the US Supreme Court in Stewart v. Abend, 495 US 207 (1990), it should be understood to function as a flexible exception, designed to prevent a rigid application of copyright rules in circumstances where such rigidity would stifle the very creativity that copyright law aims to encourage.[497] First, it enables the peaceful coexistence of private rights in authored works with public rights of access and expression – allowing limited, unlicensed use of copyrighted material when such use serves a socially beneficial function. Moreover, fair use functions as an exception that actively supports and encourages new forms of creativity.[498] Finally, over time, it has helped to temper claims of infringement in ways that promote technological innovation.[499]

The doctrine has been developed by American courts since the mid-nineteenth century. The decision generally regarded as the doctrinal origin of US fair use is Folsom v. Marsh, 9 F. Cas. 342, 348 (C.C.D. Mass. 1841) (No. 4,901). However, earlier antecedents can be traced to the English common law tradition, particularly the late eighteenth-century "fair abridgement" cases.[500] The doctrine was later codified in Section 107 of the Copyright Act of 1976.

The fair use framework is "broad, supple, indeed manipulable" – an openness that has enabled the doctrine to remain responsive to novel forms of communication and cultural production.[501] Rather than setting out a closed set of acceptable uses, in fact, the US law sets out a general framework. Indeed,

495 Belisario E and Riccio GM, 'L'IA distruggerà la creatività?' (*Legge Zero* newsletter #32, 7 July 2024) <https://leggezero.substack.com/p/lia-distruggera-la-creativita-legge>.

496 Ginsburg JC, 'Fair Use for Free, or Permitted-but-Paid?' (2014) 29 Berkeley Tech LJ 1383 <https://scholarship.law.columbia.edu/faculty_scholarship/692>, 1385.

497 Rossi, 'Opere in cerca d'autore' (n 343).

498 The doctrinal roots of fair use in support of new creativity are traceable to 1841 Supreme Court opinion in Folsom v. Marsh, 9 F. Cas. 342 (C.C.D. Mass. 1841) (No. 4901). Notable examples of modern creative fair use include Campbell v. Acuff-Rose Music, Inc., 510 U.S. 569 (1994) (a commercial parody by 2 Live Crew); Cariou v. Prince, 714 F.3d 694 (2d Cir. 2013) and Blanch v. Koons, 467 F.3d 244 (2d Cir. 2006) (both involving appropriation art); and Bill Graham Archives v. Dorling Kindersley Ltd., 448 F.3d 605 (2d Cir. 2006), which upheld the use of reduced reproductions of concert posters in a biography (see Ginsburg, 'Permitted-but-Paid' (n 496) 1389).

499 Ginsburg JC, 'Fair Use in the United States: Transformed, Deformed, Reformed?' (2020) 2020 Sing JLS 265 https://scholarship.law.columbia.edu/faculty_scholarship/2676 2.

500 Ginsburg, 'Fair Use for Free, or Permitted-but-Paid?' (n 496), 1389.

501 Ginsburg, 'Fair Use in the United States' (n 499) 5.

the list of permissible uses provided in Section 107, such as criticism, comment, news reporting, teaching, scholarship, and research, is merely illustrative. Consequently, the inclusion of a use in the list does not guarantee that it qualifies as fair, and the absence of a use from the list does not preclude it. However, most of the listed examples involve contexts in which the copied material is re-used within a newly created work by the person who carried out the copying, reflecting the doctrine's underlying emphasis on transformation and public benefit.[502]

The statute outlines four factors that courts must consider in order to assess the applicability of this doctrine: (i) the purpose and character of the use, including whether such use is commercial or for nonprofit educational purposes; (ii) the nature of the copyrighted work, particularly distinguishing between works that are more "creative and expressive" and those that are more "factual and functional"; (iii) the amount and substantiality of the portion used in relation to the work as a whole; (iv) the effect of the use upon the potential market for, or value of, the copyrighted work.

These are flexible and interdependent factors, whose application has been the subject of numerous judicial decisions over the years.

Their flexibility has long been regarded as one of its principal virtues, since these broad, adaptable, and at times deliberately open-ended criteria have allowed courts to accommodate evolving modes of creativity, expression, and technological mediation.

However, this very adaptability risks also introducing a significant degree of unpredictability in the US legal framework. Scholars have argued that the indeterminacy in how the fair use factors may be applied in any given case generates legal uncertainty for creators, users, and innovators alike – especially in the context under consideration[503] – and that the openness of this doctrine may raise systemic equity concerns and expose underlying asymmetries in the distribution of legal risk and reward. Moreover, over time, this flexibility has even been observed to risk a collapse of the traditional four-factor framework

502 Ginsburg, 'Fair Use in the United States' (n 499) 4.

503 In particular, the absence of clear boundaries in fair use jurisprudence may tend to disproportionately affect new entrants and independent creators, who often lack the legal and financial resources to navigate an ambiguous legal landscape. As a result, they may be more likely to self-censor or refrain from engaging in innovative activities, in contrast to larger, well-resourced entities. As a corollary, this legal uncertainty facilitates the consolidation of power, with dominant players in the tech sector leveraging fair use in strategic litigation, both defensively and offensively to entrench their control over emerging technologies. See Frosio, 'Should We Ban Generative AI, Incentivise it or Make it a Medium for Inclusive Creativity?' (n 410) 5.

into a predominantly single-factor inquiry, rendering the judicial analysis highly discretionary. Yet, in the realm of AI, the debate appears to have revived the need for more rigorous and genuinely multi-faceted assessments.

Given the ideological weight of the doctrine and its central role in balancing public and private interests, answering the question of its applicability in this domain also means, indirectly, confronting critical questions about whose interests fair use is ultimately understood to serve. More specifically, commentators have asked whether recognizing fair use for AI training will primarily benefit large technology companies, which rely on the mass ingestion of data for model development; whether it can meaningfully safeguard freedom of expression and creative reuse for human authors and independent users; or, alternatively, whether it will instead serve the long-term vitality of cultural industries by fostering innovation, diversity, and access.

In May 2025, the Part 3 of the Copyright and Artificial Intelligence report (hereinafter, the "Report") by the USCO was released in a "pre-publication version" seeking to provide a primer on these questions by framing, from the Office's perspective, the issue of whether AI training activities fall within the scope of the fair use doctrine.[504]

The USCO clarified that the use of copyrighted works for training artificial intelligence systems is generally to be considered transformative and, as such, in principle capable of satisfying the first factor of the fair use doctrine (the purpose and character of the use) – by far the most complex to assess, together with the fourth factor (the effect of the use upon the potential market for, or value of, the copyrighted work). Training, in the Office's view, entails the transformation of "a massive collection of 'training examples' into a statistical model capable of generating a wide range of outputs across a variety of new and different situations".[505]

Nevertheless, whether such use ultimately qualifies as fair use in any specific case still depends on further assessments, including the concrete analysis of the other factors. In what follows, the focus will be placed primarily on the

---

504 The "pre-publication version" was issued by the Office just a few days before Librarian of Congress Carla Hayden's departure and the removal of Shira Perlmutter from her position as Register of Copyrights and Director of the USCO. These events, which have stirred the waters within the US Copyright Office, have made it difficult to predict the direction the USCO will take on this matter – and even to speculate on when, or if, the Report will ever be published in its final version.

505 US Copyright Office, Copyright and Artificial Intelligence: Part 3 (n 198).

first and fourth ones, as they are widely regarded as the most controversial in the context of generative AI training.[506]

Briefly speaking, among the four statutory factors of fair use, the first has received a broad attention in both legal and scholarly analysis especially following the US Supreme Court's landmark decision in Campbell v. Acuff-Rose (1994).[507] This decision introduced the notion of "transformative use", namely a use that "adds something new, with a further purpose or different character, altering the first with new expression, meaning, or message" – in short, a use that brings "new expression, meaning, or message" to the original material.[508] Many observers credit (or, in some cases, blame) the doctrinal recognition of transformative use for the recent expansion of fair use, which has "come to favour increasingly parasitic derivative works and business models that rely heavily on copyrighted content".[509]

Interestingly, apart from the transformative nature of the use, part of the evaluation under the first factor also concerns its commercial character, as will be examined shortly. Particularly, courts have held that a commercial purpose may weigh against fair use; however, this consideration typically carries less weight when the secondary use is highly transformative.

The interdependence between transformativeness and commerciality creates an indirect correlation between the first and fourth factors – namely, the effect of the use upon the potential market for, or value of, the copyrighted work – which has become increasingly relevant in light of technological developments. The more transformative a use is, the less significance courts tend to assign to its commercial character, and the less likely the use is to be regarded

---

506 "The second factor, the nature of the copyrighted work, 'calls for recognition that some works are closer to the core of intended copyright protection than others.' The use of more creative or expressive works (such as novels, movies, art, or music) is less likely to be fair use than use of factual or functional works (such as computer code). The unpublished nature of a work can also weigh against a fair use determination. Those commenters who discussed the second factor asserted that it will often weigh against fair use because training datasets usually include expressive works, even if they contain less creative or unprotectable material as well (...) On the third factor, the question is whether 'the amount and substantiality of the portion used in relation to the copyrighted work as a whole, ... are reasonable in relation to the purpose of the copying'. This factor 'harken[s] back to the first [factor]' because '[t]he extent of permissible copying varies with the purpose and character of the use.' It also bears on the fourth factor insofar as more extensive copying can increase the risk that the use will serve as a market substitute for the original'" (US Copyright Office, Copyright and Artificial Intelligence: Part 3 (n 198), 53 ff.).

507 *Campbell v. Acuff-Rose*, 510 U.S. 579 (1994).

508 Ginsburg, 'Fair Use in the United States' (n 499) 2.

509 Ibid, 2.

as a market substitute for the original work.[510] This doctrinal evolution is most clearly reflected in Authors Guild v. Google (the Google Books case), where the court afforded little weight to the commercial nature of Google's activities.[511]

Yet in the context of generative AI, the analysis of the purpose of the use becomes particularly complex. Because the creation and training of AI systems often involve distinct acts and multiple actors, identifying the relevant use with sufficient particularity is critical for assessing the first and fourth factors.

3.1 Fair Use's First and Fourth Factors in the Era of AI

The first fair use factor "focuses on whether an allegedly infringing use has a further purpose or different character, which is a matter of degree, and the degree of difference must be weighed against other considerations". As noted, courts typically emphasize two elements within this factor: transformativeness and commerciality.[512]

The notion of transformative use was introduced in the mid-Nineties and has since become the doctrinal anchor for a broader reading of the first factor, particularly in cases involving technological uses of copyrighted works,[513] linking the idea of "transformativeness" to Campbell's reference to "something new, with a further purpose".[514] More recently, in *Andy Warhol Foundation*

510 Ginsburg, 'Fair Use in the United States' (n 499), 6.

511 Ginsburg, 'Fair Use in the United States' (n 499) 16.

512 However, some courts have also evaluated whether the defendant had lawful access to the work. See, e.g., Copyright Alliance Initial Comments at 52–53; The Authors Guild Reply Comments at 6 (Dec. 6, 2023) ("[T]he knowing use of pirated copies in the service of a commercial enterprise should weigh against fair use"). In this regard, in the USCO's view, the knowing use of a dataset that consists of pirated or illegally accessed works should weigh against fair use without being determinative.

513 Ginsburg, 'Fair Use in the United States' (n 499) 2. This development marked a shift from transformative work to transformative purpose, thereby allowing courts to excuse even the full-scale reproduction of copyrighted works in digital form. This evolution paved the way for a range of technological fair uses – uses that did not necessarily involve commentary, criticism, or creative engagement, but instead enabled new forms of access, searchability, or utility. Since fair use is defined as a non-infringing use, even these commercially driven uses could lawfully appropriate entire works without compensation to the original rightsholders.

514 Campbell's reference to "something new, with a further purpose" came to be interpreted as encompassing uses that repurpose existing works to serve a new function – even without adding new expression – so long as the use was functionally distinct and served a broader public interest.

v. Goldsmith, the US Supreme Court clarified that adding new expression, while relevant, does not automatically render a use transformative. Rather, a use is justified only when it has a purpose that also furthers the goal of copyright, promoting the progress of science and the arts, without unduly diminishing the incentive to create.

The US Copyright Office, in the already mentioned Part 3 of the Report on generative AI and Copyright, has observed that generative AI models may simultaneously serve transformative and non-transformative purposes. Indeed, many AI models are designed to perform multiple functions, some of which may be distinct from the purposes of the copyrighted works used for training, thus becoming transformative. The nature of the purpose in the specific case, however, depends on the use that is made of the model. Indeed, in USCO's view, AI training should not be understood as inherently transformative, not even if considered as human learning (as some have argued thus far), as fair use does not excuse all human acts done for the purpose of learning either.[515]

Another aspect of the first fair use factor is, as said, commerciality. This inquiry concerns the potential unfairness of exploiting copyrighted works for financial gain without payment. Notably, in the context of generative AI, several commenters have warned against classifying dataset curation or model training as genuinely non-commercial. Indeed, such practices may initially occur for non-commercial or research purposes, yet the resulting datasets or models may later be adapted for commercial applications.

However, as the USCO notes, "the crux of the profit/nonprofit distinction is not whether the sole motive of the use is monetary gain but whether the user stands to profit from exploitation of the copyrighted material without paying the customary price"[516] – a principle particularly relevant because even paradigmatic fair uses, such as news reporting or criticism, are often carried out for profit.

Nonetheless, the complexity of AI development, often involving distinct acts and multiple actors, makes it critical to identify the specific use with sufficient particularity, i.e. on a case-by-case basis.

As for the fourth factor – "the effect of the use upon the potential market for, or value of, the copyrighted work" – in Part 3 of the Report, the USCO considers its evaluation to be among the most critical in the context of generative AI. There are growing concerns that AI training and outputs can affect the market for or the value of the underlying works, whether through lost sales, market dilution, or lost licensing opportunities.

---

515 US Copyright Office, Copyright and Artificial Intelligence: Part 3 (n 198).

516 Ibid, spec 48.

According to the USCO Report, "when a model is capable of generating substantially similar outputs that directly substitute for works contained in the training data, this may result in lost sales". Furthermore, "even when a model's outputs are not similar to any specific copyrighted work, they may still negatively impact the market for the works used in training". Finally, the Report emphasizes that lost revenue in actual or potential licensing markets can also constitute market harm, because copyright owners could in principle receive compensation for any use of their works. The relevant markets are those that are "traditional, reasonable, or likely to be developed".[517]

Importantly, when addressing this factor in the generative AI domain, scholars have started to move beyond the traditional focus on direct market substitution and lost sales. They have started to acknowledge, instead, the necessity to account for broader and more complex forms of market harm.

Accordingly, it has been argued that, given their nature and the markets they operate in, AI-generated outputs can compete both directly and indirectly with human-created works, potentially producing chilling effects on artistic creativity and undermining the economic incentives that copyright law is designed to protect.[518] This includes not only potential loss of revenue but also the erosion of professional opportunities and the displacement of original creators in creative industries.

Hence, a more nuanced interpretation of the fourth factor has been proposed, arguing that such an interpretation would align with the statutory language of Section 107, which refers not only to the "effect of the use upon the potential market for" a work (direct impact) but also to its "value" (indirect market impact) – two concepts that are not necessarily interchangeable. As has been observed, the "linguistic disjunction" between market and value within the fourth factor suggests that "value" should be interpreted more broadly than mere direct commercial exploitation, potentially encompassing a wider range of authorial and creative interests.[519]

In this view, a work can generate economic and cultural value not only directly, but also indirectly, for example by serving as a reputational asset or as a "draw" that supports related works and ancillary commercial opportunities (enhancing the visibility of an artist's portfolio, boosting demand for live performances, merchandise, or commissioned projects, etc.). Uses of generative AI that erode this broader ecosystem of value – such as by diminishing the

517 US Copyright Office, Copyright and Artificial Intelligence: Part 3 (n 198) 62 and ff.

518 Geiger, 'Elaborating a Human Rights Friendly Copyright Framework' (n 321).

519 Ginsburg, 'Fair Use in the United States' (n 499) 35.

uniqueness or recognizability of an author's creative voice – may therefore inflict harm even in the absence of direct market substitution.[520]

Yet, to date, very little case law or secondary literature has engaged directly with the proposition that "value" encompasses more than traditional market or licensing potential.[521]

Whether this interpretation will emerge as a decisive issue in one of the pending US court cases on generative AI remains to be seen. Nonetheless, whatever stance the courts ultimately take on this subject-matter, these decisions are poised to grapple with all these questions and could either reshape or reinforce the boundaries of the fair use doctrine in the age of artificial intelligence.

3.2 The Cases

As artificial intelligence continues to advance across creative sectors, several high-profile lawsuits have emerged in the US against major AI developers such as OpenAI, Meta, Anthropic and Stability AI.[522] By early spring 2025, the number of active copyright lawsuits against AI companies in the United States alone had reached forty, illustrating the scale and intensity of these legal battles.[523] Globally, similar actions have been initiated across several jurisdictions,[524] yet the majority have been filed in the US, which is unsurprising

520 These concerns become particularly acute in cases where an author's public and professional identity is built less on the commercial performance of individual works and more on the consistent cultivation of a distinctive artistic reputation. In such cases, unattributed or derivative uses – even from freely accessible material – can cause disproportionate harm to the overall value of the author's creative output. Where, depending on the artistic or economic strategy of the author, the "currency" of authorship is not only monetary but reputational, misappropriation can severely impact the author's standing in the public eye and the integrity of their oeuvre; see Ginsburg, 'Fair Use in the United States' (n 499) 37.

521 Ginsburg, 'Fair Use in the United States' (n 499) 35.

522 Frosio G, 'Generative AI in Court' in N Koutras and N Selvadurai (eds), Recreating Creativity, Reinventing Inventiveness – International Perspectives on AI and IP Governance (Routledge 2024) <https://doi.org/10.4324/9781003260127-2>.

523 As of March 2025, there are 40 copyright lawsuits pending in the US against companies developing AI; see <https://chatgptiseatingtheworld.com/2025/03/24/latest-map-of-all-40-copyright-suits-v-ai-in-u-s/>.

524 This includes cases in United Kingdom (Getty Images (US) v. Stability AI Ltd.; in France (*Syndicat national de l'édition* - National Publishing Union v. Meta- at the Tribunal Judiciaire de Paris), in Germany (GEMA v. OpenAI and GEMA v. Suno at the Munich Regional Court, and Kneschke v. LAION at the Hamburg Regional Court (n 564); in the Netherlands (DPG Media et al. v. HowardsHome (n 564)); in China (Shanghai Character License Administrative Co. v. TAB, before the Guangzhou Internet Court); in India (Asian News International v. OpenAI, heard in the New Delhi Court) and in Canada

given that the country hosts the headquarters of nearly all major generative AI companies.

The outcomes of these US cases will inevitably carry global ramifications and influence regulatory and judicial developments well beyond national borders.[525] Indeed, as commentators have noted, these decisions will not only determine liability and potential damages for possible copyright infringements, but could also reshape the development, deployment, and accessibility of generative AI technologies worldwide, including the European Union.[526] Notwithstanding that, the significant differences between US and EU copyright regimes, as will be noted, may lead courts to reach divergent conclusions, creating coordination challenges across jurisdictions.

The list of the litigations worldwide continues to grow, yet some preliminary considerations can be drawn through the recurring legal arguments emerging from this growing body of generative AI copyright cases.

One of the central contentions raised by plaintiffs across jurisdictions is that the outputs of AI systems are heavily reliant on copyrighted source materials, and that these technologies would not be able to function without ingesting and replicating expressive elements of protected works. Particularly, plaintiffs have consistently alleged that training data have been often acquired through unauthorized web scraping, bypassing both contractual restrictions and legal safeguards protecting intellectual property. In certain cases, the situation is further aggravated by the alleged use of illegally sourced content, such as torrent files from shadow libraries like Library Genesis.[527]

(CanLII v. Caseway AI at the Supreme Court of British Columbia, and Toronto Star News v. OpenAI at the Ontario Superior Court of Justice).

525 Belisario E, 'New York Times e OpenAI troveranno un accordo?' (Leggezero newsletter#6, 7 January 2024) <https://leggezero.substack.com/p/new-york-times-e-openai-troveranno>.

526 Belisario (n 525). Even in scenarios where monetary compensation is awarded to plaintiffs, the broader impact would stem from a judicial determination that training models on copyrighted data without authorization is unlawful. Should courts uphold this position, the legal usability of models already trained through such methods would be severely compromised. Moreover, the entire model development process would become more burdensome, requiring negotiated licensing agreements with each rights holder – a process that would likely be prohibitively expensive and logistically impractical for all but the most capitalized actors. As a result, the cost of developing AI systems would increase dramatically, with clear knock-on effects for reliability, market accessibility, and pricing for end users.

527 It is the same concern raised at the EU level; see the reflections around the concept of "lawful sources", "lawful access", and lawful use" in Chapter 10.

In response, defendants have typically adopted a twofold defense strategy. First, they have frequently moved for early dismissal of the claims, arguing for example that the plaintiffs have failed to identify any specific copyrighted works that were unlawfully reproduced or directly incorporated into AI-generated outputs. A number of courts have, in some instances, agreed with this line of reasoning.[528]

Second, defendants have invoked the fair use doctrine as the principal legal justification for the use of copyrighted content in model training. Particularly, companies such as OpenAI, Google, Meta, and Anthropic have consistently argued that the ingestion of copyrighted materials for training purposes constitutes a transformative use, aimed at enabling new forms of expression rather than replacing the original works.

Interestingly, in some of the emerging lawsuits in the music sector – such as those brought against Udio and Suno[529] – defendants contend that training AI

528 Some courts have pronounced the insufficient evidence of harm or irreparable damage in some cases under discussion. For instance, in Raw Story Media, Inc. and AlterNet Media, Inc. v. OpenAI (SDNY, Case 1:24-cv-01514), the case was dismissed in November 2024 not on the merits of the copyright claim but for lack of Article III standing (https://admin.bakerlaw.com/wp-content/uploads/2025/01/ECF-117-Raw-Story.pdf). Several cases have followed a similar pattern. In Andersen et al. v. Stability AI, Midjourney, and DeviantArt (Case 3:23-cv-00201.), a federal judge in September 2023 dismissed most claims but allowed the core copyright infringement claim to proceed (Geiger, 'Elaborating a Human Rights Friendly Copyright Framework' (n 321)). Also, in a 2024 action against Anthropic, major record labels – including Universal – sought a preliminary injunction, which the District Court of California denied (Case 5:24-cv-03811-EKL, https://storage.courtlistener.com/recap/gov.uscourts.cand.431519/gov.uscourts.cand.431519.321.0.pdf). The court found no demonstrable user misconduct or knowledge of infringement by Anthropic, leading to the case's dismissal; see Belisario E, La Ghiblificazione delle immagini IA (e i suoi effetti sul copyright) (Leggezero newsletter#67, 30 March 2025) <https://leggezero.substack.com/p/la-ghiblificazione-delle-immagini>.

529 In June 2024, the Recording Industry Association of America (RIAA) – representing major record labels such as Universal Music Group (UMG), Sony Music Entertainment, and Warner Records – filed two separate lawsuits against Suno Inc. and Uncharted Labs Inc., the respective creators of the music-generating platforms Suno and Udio AI. The actions were filed in the District Court of Massachusetts and the Southern District of New York, respectively (Belisario and Riccio, 'L'IA distruggerà la creatività?' (n 495)). The central allegation in both cases is that the defendants engaged in the "unlicensed copying of sound recordings on a massive scale" for the purposes of training their AI models. According to the RIAA, thousands of copyrighted musical works were reproduced without authorization or compensation, in clear violation of copyright law. The plaintiffs are seeking statutory damages of up to $150,000 per infringed work. Both Suno and Udio have admitted, in their respective legal filings, to using copyrighted audio recordings during the model training process, but they argue that such use is lawful under the US fair use doctrine. They defend their technologies as tools that empower users to generate

to recognize and generate musical patterns qualifies as "quintessential fair use", likening the process to that of a student learning a musical genre through attentive listening rather than rote reproduction. In particular, Suno publicly stated that "learning is not infringing", and emphasized that its training practices mirror those of major technology firms – including OpenAI, Google, and Apple – which also reportedly use publicly available internet content to develop their models.[530] The USCO, as noted above, does not embrace these positions, reasoning that even human learning is not automatically entitled to fair use protection merely by virtue of being a human act.

To date, only a handful of judicial rulings have addressed whether training AI systems on copyrighted materials qualifies as fair use, while most cases remain pending. However, further rulings are expected as more reach the summary-judgment stage. Among the many cases currently attracting attention,[531] two warrant closer examination for the significant developments they have seen.[532]

---

original musical compositions based on textual prompts. According to the RIAA, however, outputs from these platforms often include vocals or musical sequences that closely resemble those of globally recognized artists such as Bruce Springsteen, Michael Jackson, and ABBA. These cases bring to mind similar cases that are now being discussedin Europe, where the German performance rights organization GEMA filed a separate lawsuit on January 21, 2025, against Suno Inc. before the Munich Regional Court. GEMA accuses Suno of unauthorized processing of works from its extensive repertoire, including iconic songs such as Forever Young (Alphaville), Mambo No. 5 (Lou Bega), Daddy Cool (Frank Farian), Cheri Cheri Lady (Modern Talking), and Atemlos (Kristina Bach). According to GEMA, these tracks were used without license to train the AI model, resulting in AI-generated outputs that are "confusingly similar" to the originals in terms of melody, harmony, and rhythm (https://www.gema.de/en/w/press-release-lawsuit-against-suno). The lawsuit underscores a demand for fair remuneration: while Suno profits from subscription fees paid by users of its premium tool, it allegedly provides no compensation to the rights holders of the musical works it has systematically ingested into its training corpus. Notably, this is not GEMA's first action in the AI space. In November 2024, the organization also filed a suit against OpenAI, both in its US-based parent company and its European subsidiary, OpenAI Ireland Ltd. That case centers on the chatbot's unauthorized reproduction of copyrighted song lyrics, which the system reportedly generates upon user prompts (https://www.gema.de/en/news/ai-and-music/ai-lawsuit).

530 <https://www.theverge.com/2024/8/2/24211842/ai-music-riaa-copyright-lawsuit-suno-udio-fair-use>.

531 Among the ongoing cases, one of the most emblematic worth recalling is the lawsuit filed by The New York Times Company on December 27, 2023, against Microsoft and OpenAI in the Southern District of New York (Case No. 1:23-cv-11195). This litigation is one of the first that has come to symbolize the broader conflict surrounding unauthorized data scraping in the context of generative AI. The case has at its core the *New York Times*' allegation that the defendants unlawfully used the *Times*' copyrighted content –

The first is Bartz v. Anthropic, in which the court's order of June 23, 2025 represents the first substantive ruling on how fair use applies to generative models. However, the case was settled before the scheduled trial on damages for the pirated copies.[533] The second is Kadrey v. Meta, decided on June 25, 2025.[534]

In both cases – whose allegations largely mirror those raised in many other pending lawsuits[535] – the courts were called upon to assess the application of

---

such as news articles, investigative reports, editorials, reviews, and instructional materials – to train their large language models (LLMs), specifically ChatGPT and Bing Copilot, without authorization or compensation. Particularly compelling are the side-by-side comparisons provided in support of this allegation by *The Times*' legal team, which showcase ChatGPT-generated outputs that closely mirror original Times articles, presented as clear indicators of substantial copying. According to the complaint, the unauthorized use of its content by OpenAI and Microsoft undermines the economic viability of investigative journalism, while simultaneously contributing to a surge in the market valuations of the defendants (over $1 trillion for Microsoft and approximately $90 billion for OpenAI) (see Lavagnini S, 'New York Times contro ChatGpt: ecco tutti i diritti in gioco' (Agenda Digitale, 29 December 2023) <http://agendadigitale.eu/mercati-digitali/new-york-times-contro-chatgpt-ecco-tutti-i-diritti-in-gioco/>). The position of OpenAI in response to these allegations has mainly centered on the argument that the use of copyrighted material for training generative AI constitutes fair use. It claims that such use is transformative, as it contributes to the development of useful systems rather than expressive works, and that the material is not reproduced publicly but is used solely for training purposes. In April 2025, the federal judge presiding over the case denied OpenAI's and Microsoft's motion to dismiss the core copyright infringement claims, allowing the lawsuit to proceed.

532 For a first comprehensive analysis on the two decisions, see Samuelson P, 'Does Using In-Copyright Works as Training Data Infringe?' (Copyright Blog, 18 July 2025) <https://legalblogs.wolterskluwer.com/copyright-blog/does-using-in-copyright-works-as-training-data-infringe/>.

533 Case 3:24-cv-05417-WHA (Bartz v. Anthropic). In September 2025, "the parties filed a proposed settlement agreement. Anthropic agreed to pay $1.5 billion to settle claims that it downloaded pirated books to train its AI systems – the largest US copyright settlement in history. This sum would amount to an estimated gross recovery of $3,000 per infringed work. Anthropic agreed to also destroy the LibGen and PiLiMi datasets after the expiration of any litigation preservation or other court orders". On September 25, 2025, the court granted preliminary approval to the class settlement. See <https://www.bakerlaw.com/bartz-v-anthropic/>.

534 Case 3:23-cv-03417 (Kadrey v. Meta).

535 In Kadrey v. Meta (n 534), filed in the United States District Court for the Northern District of California (San Francisco Division) on July 7, 2023, the plaintiffs alleged Me ta's unauthorized use of their copyrighted works to train its AI systems, including those sourced from illegal online archives such as Library Genesis (LibGen) (https://www.wired.com/story/new-documents-unredacted-meta-copyright-ai-lawsuit/). First, they cl aim direct copyright infringement under 17 U.S.C.par. 106, arguing that they never authorized Meta to make copies of their works and derivative works, publicly display copies

the four statutory fair use factors. Ultimately, both judges concluded that the AI training purposes at issue were highly transformative, albeit arriving at that conclusion through different reasoning.

In Bartz v. Anthropic, Judge Alsup partially granted summary judgment in favor of Anthropic, holding that two of its uses of Bartz's books qualified as fair use – specifically, (i) training the Claude model and (ii) digitizing print books that Anthropic had lawfully purchased. However, the court denied summary judgment on the plaintiffs' piracy claim, finding that Anthropic's acquisition of "pirated" copies of books to populate its "central library" could not be justified as reasonably necessary for training LLMs.[536] The court emphasized that "[p]iracy of otherwise available copies is inherently, irredeemably infringing even if the pirated copies are immediately used for the transformative use [of training models] and immediately discarded".[537] Damages for the infringing copies will be determined at trial.

(or derivative works), or distribute copies (or derivative works) during the training process of the LLaMA language models. Second, the complaints allege vicarious copyright infringement, based on the premise that every output generated by the LLaMA models constitutes an infringing derivative work. Third, the lawsuit invokes the Digital Millennium Copyright Act (DMCA), asserting that Meta violated 17 U.S.C. § 1202(b) by removing copyright management information (CMI) embedded in the plaintiffs' works. In Bartz v. Anthropic (n 533), "author plaintiffs filed a class action complaint against Anthropic alleging Anthropic infringed their copyrights by using their copyrighted books to train its Claude LLMs for use with its AI services capable of generating writings that mimic the writing style of humans. (…) Anthropic sourced content for its library in various ways. It downloaded for free millions of pirated copies of books in digital form. In addition, it purchased millions of copyrighted books (some overlapping with those acquired from pirate sites), removed the bindings, scanned and stored the works in a digitized searchable format, and then discarded the paper originals. (…) However, according to the facts in the record, the training copies were not disseminated to the outside world. Rather, when each LLM was put into a public-facing version of Claude, it was combined with other software that filtered user inputs to the LLM and filtered outputs from the LLM back to the user. Ultimately, the plaintiffs did not allege any infringing copy of their works was or would ever be provided to users by the Claude service. The plaintiffs did, however, claim Anthropic infringed their copyrights by (1) pirating copies of their works for Anthropic's library and (2) reproducing their works to train Anthropic's LLMs". Moreover, "in support of their copyright infringement claims, the plaintiffs alleged, among other arguments, that use of their books to train Anthropic's LLMs could result in the production of works that compete and displace demand for their books. In addition, the plaintiffs alleged Anthropic's unauthorized use has the potential to displace an emerging market for licensing the plaintiffs' works for the purpose of training LLMs"; see <https://www.afslaw.com/perspectives/alerts/landmark-ruling-ai-copyright-fair-use-vs-infringement-bartz-v-anthropic>.

536 <https://www.bakerlaw.com/bartz-v-anthropic/>.

537 Samuelson, 'Does Using In-Copyright Works as Training Data Infringe?' (n 532).

By contrast, in Kadrey v. Meta, Judge Chhabria considered factor one an “easy win” for Meta, observing that “[t]here is no serious question that Meta’s use of the plaintiffs’ books had a ‘further purpose’ and ‘different character’ – that it was highly transformative.” He noted that plaintiffs did not meaningfully dispute Llama’s training purpose. Regarding the use of pirated books as training data, however, the court took a different approach than Judge Alsup’s: Judge Chhabria held that bad faith or good faith is largely irrelevant under the first factor, stating that what ultimately matters is whether the use is objectively fair, not the subjective conduct of the user.[538]

However, despite their different reasoning, both judges cautioned that a finding of high transformativeness under factor one does not automatically settle the fair use question, as the other three statutory factors must still be considered in full.

As for the second factor, which concerns the nature of the copyrighted work, both judges found that it weighed against a fair use finding. This is because Anthropic and Meta had deliberately used the plaintiffs’ expressive literary works, rather than factual or functional content, to train their models. Their creative nature heightened the degree of protection under copyright law. Regarding the third factor, which evaluates the amount and substantiality of the portion used, both courts concluded that Anthropic and Meta acted reasonably in copying the entirety of the plaintiffs’ works for training purposes. The judges recognized that training large language models (LLMs) generally requires complete copies of source material to function effectively, and therefore the wholesale reproduction was not inherently fatal under this factor.

More complex is the evaluation of the fourth factor.

Under this umbrella, as noted, fall several considerations, including the loss of licensing opportunities, the risk of lost sales, and the broader market effects in terms of potential market dilution.

On licensing opportunities, both judges concluded that the use of books as training data involves a market that authors are not entitled to control. They recalled established case law recognizing that copyright owners cannot monopolize certain markets for transformative uses.[539] Judge Chhabria, in particular, emphasized that (1) Meta’s model “is not capable of generating enough text from the plaintiffs’ books to matter”, and (2) “the plaintiffs are not entitled to the market for licensing their works as AI training data”.

538 Ibid.
539 Ibid.

With respect to lost sales, the courts similarly found no actual market substitution. In Kadrey v. Meta, Judge Chhabria accepted Meta's argument that its output filters prevent the model from reproducing more than small fragments of the plaintiffs' books. Likewise, in Bartz v. Anthropic, Judge Alsup observed that the plaintiffs had conceded that Anthropic's training copies did not reduce demand for their books. However, he reached a different conclusion regarding Anthropic's use of pirated copies: the company should have lawfully purchased the books to build its "central library", and for this specific use he found against Anthropic on fair use.

By contrast, the two decisions diverge when it comes to the issue of market dilution, which addresses the broader and more indirect ways in which generative AI may erode the value and ecosystem of creative works, even absent direct substitution.

This market dilution theory is both novel and unprecedented in copyright law.

During oral argument in Bartz v. Anthropic, Judge Alsup dismissed the theory as "science fiction",[540] thereby signaling a greater willingness to recognize fair use by rejecting the notion that indirect market dilution should factor into the analysis.

Judge Chhabria, in Kadrey v. Meta, took a more nuanced approach. While he agreed that no existing copyright precedent supports the market dilution theory, he also observed that this is likely because courts have never before confronted a phenomenon like generative AI, which can rapidly flood copyright markets with vast numbers of works.

He noted, however, that Kadrey's lawyers had advanced the wrong market-effects argument. Traditionally, copyright cases focus on direct market substitution, whereas generative AI raises concerns of indirect market substitution, a factor he believed should be given due weight. Judge Chhabria explained that the plaintiffs' theory – that Meta copied their works to create a product likely to flood the market with similar outputs, thereby causing market dilution – could have been a "potentially winning argument" if supported by evidence showing how current or anticipated outputs from Meta's models would dilute the market for their works. He especially remarked that plaintiffs in other generative AI cases would likely "decisively win the fourth factor" if, unlike Kadrey, they presented credible evidence of it.

However, based on the evidence presented in this particular case, he declined to support the market-dilution theory – while clarifying that his decision does not set a blanket precedent for all similar disputes.[541] In doing so,

540 Ibid.

541 <https://www.bakerlaw.com/kadrey-v-meta/>.

Judge Chhabria appeared slightly less inclined toward a broad fair use than Judge Alsup.

His concerns, centered on "the rapid generation of countless works that compete with the originals, even if those works aren't themselves infringing", are particularly significant. Indeed, they touch on the most delicate policy dimension of the fair use analysis, and they highlight once again the tension between this doctrine and the broader issue of the ultimate scope of copyright protection.

4 The EU Approach: The TDM Exceptions

4.1 The Three-Step Test for EU Limitations and Exceptions

Legal and regulatory scrutiny of generative AI is by no means confined to the United States: case law is beginning to develop across the EU too. Notable examples include National Publishing Union v. Meta in France; GEMA v. OpenAI and GEMA v. Suno before the Munich Regional Court; Kneschke v. LAION at the Hamburg Regional Court in Germany; and DPG Media et al. v. HowardsHome in the Netherlands.

Interestingly, public debate in the EU surrounding data scraping and unauthorized use of online content has increasingly focused on concerns that extend beyond copyright to encompass issues of privacy and competition law.[542]

---

542 A particularly strong stance has emerged, for example, from the Dutch Data Protection Authority, which has openly stated that web scraping – especially when involving personal data – is "almost always illegal" under European data protection law. Belisario E, AI Index 2024: lo stato dell'arte dell'IA (e delle sue regole) (Leggezero newsletter#23, 5 May 2024), <https://leggezero.substack.com/p/ai-index-2024-lo-stato-dellarte-dellia>. Furthermore, the French Competition Authority imposed a €250 million fine on Google (Alphabet) in May 2024. The fine was issued for training its generative AI system – Gemini – on content from French press outlets without prior authorization. The ruling also found that Google had penalized those media publishers who explicitly opted out of data use for AI training by removing or downranking their content across its services, thereby engaging in anti-competitive conduct (see https://www.autoritedelaconcurrence.fr/fr/article/droits-voisins-lautorite-prononce-une-sanction-de-250-millions-deuros-lencontre-de-google and Belisario E, La guerra dello scraping (Leggezero newsletter#24, 12 May 2024) https://leggezero.substack.com/p/la-guerra-dello-scraping-legge-zero). This case is interesting because it represents one of the first instances in Europe where a competition authority, rather than a copyright or data regulator, has taken enforcement action in response to AI training practices – highlighting the multi-dimensional legal risks faced by generative AI providers.

However, from a copyright perspective, the European legal framework diverges notably from that of the United States, primarily because the fair use doctrine has no equivalent in EU law.

Unlike the flexible US doctrine illustrated in the paragraphs above, European copyright legislation adopts a closed-list approach to exceptions and limitations, as set forth in Article 5 of the InfoSoc Directive (2001/29/EC), as well as in other provisions scattered across additional directives – including Articles 3 and 4 of the CDSM Directive, as will be discussed.

Among these exceptions, only narrowly defined activities (such as, in the case of Article 5, quotation, criticism, review, parody, or use for teaching purposes) are permitted. Even then, such uses must be proportionate and must neither interfere with the normal exploitation of the work nor unreasonably prejudice the legitimate interests of the rights holder.

Indeed, in the European Union, the application of exceptions and limitations to copyright is governed by the so-called three-step test, a doctrinal framework with international origins that continues to shape the permissible boundaries of copyright use.

The three-step test was first codified in Article 9(2) of the 1967 Berne Convention for the Protection of Literary and Artistic Works,[543] with specific reference to the exclusive right of reproduction. Article 9(1) grants authors the exclusive right to authorize the reproduction of their works "in any manner or form". However, paragraph 2 tempers this exclusivity by allowing national legislatures to introduce exceptions to reproduction rights in "certain special cases", provided that such exceptions do not conflict with the normal exploitation of the work or unreasonably prejudice the author's legitimate interests. Importantly, the Berne Convention applies this test only to the right of reproduction. However, the scope of the three-step test has been extended by Article 13 of the TRIPs Agreement to all exclusive rights enjoyed by copyright holders and not just the reproduction right.[544]

More specifically, and in brief, (i) the requirement that exceptions be confined to "certain special cases" means that they must be exceptional in nature and not overly broad in scope. This step requires that any exception or limitation apply only to clearly defined and specific cases. The term "certain" implies that such exceptions must be narrowly and precisely formulated within national legislation. However, it is not necessary to explicitly enumerate every possible situation to which the exception might apply, provided that its scope is

543 Berne Convention for the Protection of Literary and Artistic Works (adopted 9 September 1886, last amended 28 September 1979).

544 See also Article 10(1) and (2) of the WIPO Copyright Treaty (adopted 20 December 1996, entered into force 6 March 2002) 2186 UNTS 121.

known and sufficiently particularized;[545] (ii) the requirement that exceptions must not conflict with the normal exploitation of the work refers to what right holders may reasonably expect from potential or future markets. It encompasses "all forms of exploiting a work, which have, or are likely to acquire, considerable economic or practical importance".[546] The term should be understood as referring to uses for which rightsholders would ordinarily expect to receive remuneration – that is, uses that are regular, typical, or commercially standard;[547] (iii) finally, the requirement that exceptions must not prejudice the legitimate interests of the author (as set out in the Berne Convention) or of the rightsholder (under the TRIPs Agreement) implies that such exceptions must not cause disproportionate harm to the interests of owners of the rights. Notably, as has been observed, this latter requirement allows for the consideration of fundamental rights and freedoms – such as the right to privacy or freedom of expression – within the framework of the three-step test.[548]

The European Union has explicitly incorporated this international test into its legal order. Article 5(5) of the 2001 Information Society Directive (InfoSoc Directive) formalizes the test within EU copyright law, making it a mandatory standard for evaluating the legality of any exceptions or limitations set out in national legislation.

This approach was further reinforced with the adoption of the 2019 Directive on CDSM Directive, which introduced four new mandatory exceptions and limitations to copyright, including an exception for TDM for scientific research (Article 3) and the broader TDM exception for general purposes (Article 4), which are those potentially concerned by the algorithmic "creative" process.[549] Crucially, Article 7(2) of the CDSM Directive affirms that the three-

545 Wymeersch P, 'EU Copyright Exceptions and Limitations and the Three-Step Test: One Step Forward, Two Steps Back' (2023) 72(7) GRUR International 631 <https://doi.org/10.1093/grurint/ikad019>.

546 Senftleben M, Copyright, Limitations and the Three-Step Test (Kluwer Law International 2004) 177, 198–201.

547 The interpretation of "normal" is nuanced and has been the subject of extensive legal commentary. If "normal exploitation" were interpreted as including the full extent of all exclusive rights, the three-step test would risk being deprived of any meaningful limiting function; see Wymeersch (n 545).

548 Hugenholtz PB and Okediji R, 'Conceiving an International Instrument on Limitations and Exceptions to Copyright' (Amsterdam Law School Research Paper No 2012-43, Institute for Information Law Research Paper No 2012-37, 7 March 2012) <https://ssrn.com/abstract=2017629> or <http://dx.doi.org/10.2139/ssrn.2017629>.

549 The list of mandatory exceptions and limitations in the CDSM Directive (n 116) also includes: an exception to enable digital and cross-border uses for illustration in teaching (Article 5), and an exception for preservation activities by cultural heritage institutions (Article 6).

step test articulated in the InfoSoc Directive applies equally to all the new mandatory exceptions.

Indeed, the three-step test acquires particular significance when assessing whether copyright exceptions can apply to generative AI activities, especially training ones.

If the test were to be deemed applicable to TDM activities – a question on which scholarly opinions are still divided[550] – it remains uncertain whether TDM would ultimately meet the test's requirements.

Regarding the first step, the answer is far from straightforward. It depends on how one conceptualizes "certain special cases", for which there is little interpretative guidance in the EU,[551] and on how "training" is characterized, including whether this activity meaningfully differs, if at all, from text and data mining. According to some scholars, the sheer scale at which training takes place weighs against classifying it as a "special case".[552] Others, however, argue that as long as a copyright exception has sufficiently clear conceptual contours, it can withstand scrutiny under the "certain special case" requirement. This, they claim, was already recognized for uses of a private nature or for the creation of temporary copies, and would likewise apply to TDM activities carried out for AI training.[553] Policy considerations would also support

550 According to Senftleben, the scrutiny of TDM provision should only be relevant to "national and regional systems that bring TDM copies within the scope of the reproduction right and declare (parts of) the test applicable": "From the perspective of international copyright law, however, it is an open question whether the three-step test must be taken into account at all. There are good reasons to assume that copies made in the context of TDM form a special category of reproduction that falls outside the scope of the right of reproduction in Article 9(1) BC.16 The provision sets forth a broad exclusive right of reproduction covering reproduction "in any manner or form."17 Nonetheless, the deliberations at the 1996 WIPO Diplomatic Conference – leading to the adoption of the WCT and WPPT – show that the international copyright community has reserved for itself the freedom of taking individual decisions on each new category of reproduction that has not been considered previously. Arguably, TDM copies are such a new, formerly unknown reproduction category. It has been underlined around the globe that TDM does not concern reproduction in the traditional sense of making copies for the purpose of consulting and enjoying a work. In the TDM process, literary and artistic works are not used as works but as data input for a computational analysis"; see Senftleben M, 'TDM, GenAI and the Copyright Three-Step Test' (24 July 2025) <https://ssrn.com/abstract=5373903> 3.

551 Ibid.

552 Lucchi and Hunter (n 487) 42, 51.

553 Indeed, the use of protected material on a large scale – a broad spectrum of works, a large volume of copies – is already "a feature of several use privileges" that have been deemed "compatible with the three-step test at the international and national level", such as the private copying exception. See Senftleben, 'TDM, GenAI and the Copyright Three-Step Test' (n 550) 3.

this, grounded in the idea that the "three-step test is the primary tool in international copyright law for reconciling copyright protection with other societal objectives and values" and therefore "should be understood as an open, elastic framework that allows national policymakers to strike a proper balance".[554]

The other two steps, however, present even greater challenges. The second requires that the use "does not conflict with the normal exploitation of the work", and the third that it "does not unreasonably prejudice the legitimate interests of the author". Interestingly, as some scholars have noted, these criteria largely mirror the evaluations that US courts are called upon to make – namely, those reflected in the fourth fair use factor, which concerns "the effect of the use upon the potential market for or value of the copyrighted work".[555]

As highlighted in the US cases discussed above, and acknowledged by EU scholarship,[556] generative AI outputs can potentially compete with human-created works. This is less evident at the level of the individual work: no conflict with normal exploitation is likely to arise because TDM for AI training does not constitute a traditional, well-established mode of exploitation, and any potential impact would in any event be mitigated in the EU framework, which allows rightsholders to opt out.[557]

Nevertheless, even on this reading, the broader concern lies in the indirect, market-wide effects.

In the EU context too, as in the US, it has been observed that the ability of generative models to replicate the style, structure, or substance of protected works can indirectly undermine normal exploitation channels, including licensing and derivative markets.[558] Indeed, TDM for AI training can thus be regarded as the starting point of a broader, potentially parasitic appropriation of the market for human literary and artistic creations.

Moreover, this large-scale, uncompensated use – often occurring without transparency or consent – is likely to unreasonably prejudice authors' legiti-

554 Ibid, 4.

555 This convergence is not accidental: as a party to the Berne Convention and the TRIPs Agreement, the United States is itself bound by the three-step test, and the fourth fair use factor is one of the principal points at which the open-ended U.S. doctrine meets the test's requirement that a use not conflict with the normal exploitation of the work. As noted, "The individual fair use factors can forge a link with the criteria of the three-step test. The fourth factor in the U.S. fair use analysis, for instance, requires an assessment of 'the effect of the use upon the potential market for or value of the copyrighted work'. A line between this fair use factor and the prohibition of 'conflict with a normal exploitation of the work' can easily be drawn". See Senftleben, 'TDM, GenAI and the Copyright Three-Step Test' (n 550) 2.

556 Senftleben, 'Generative AI and Author Remuneration' (n 330).

557 Senftleben, 'TDM, GenAI and the Copyright Three-Step Test' (n 550) 15.

558 Lucchi and Hunter (n 487), 43.

mate interests, thereby implicating the third requirement of the three-step test.[559] If this is the case, both the second and third steps of the test may prove particularly difficult to satisfy.

Given these divided opinions, it remains debated whether generative AI activities can, in practice, comply with the current three-step test. Should a rigid interpretation of the test prevail – and in the absence of a balancing mechanism comparable to US fair use – many commentators predict that it will become considerably more challenging for AI developers to justify their practices under EU copyright law. Whether such rigidity can withstand the evolving demands of AI innovation remains uncertain, but it is clear that this tension warrants close attention.

4.2 The TDM Exceptions in the CDSM Directive

The 2019 Directive on Copyright in the CDSM Directive defines TDM as "any automated analytical technique aimed at analysing text and data in digital form in order to generate information which includes but is not limited to patterns, trends and correlations". The Directive introduces two key copyright exceptions for TDM: one limited to scientific research purposes (Article 3), and another – sometimes referred to as the "commercial" TDM exception – covering broader uses, including by private entities such as AI companies (Article 4).

Much has been written about the limited ambition of the provisions on text and data mining, and a detailed discussion of the matter lies beyond the scope of this section.[560]

What is crucial to emphasize, however, is that although the EU's closed-list approach to copyright exceptions – including those codified in Articles 3 and 4 of the CDSM Directive – offers limited flexibility in accommodating AI and other data-driven technologies,[561] these two provisions have nevertheless emerged as the most relevant legal basis, within academic discourse, for assessing the permissibility of AI training under EU copyright law.[562]

559 Ibid.

560 For a critical evaluation on the Directive, see Geiger C, Frosio G and Bulayenko O, 'Text and Data Mining in the Proposed Copyright Reform: Making the EU Ready for an Age of Big Data?' (2018) 49 IIC 814 https://doi.org/10.1007/s40319-018-0722-2; Geiger C, Frosio G and Bulayenko O, 'The Exception for Text and Data Mining (TDM) in the Proposed Directive on Copyright in the Digital Single Market – Legal Aspects' (Centre for International Intellectual Property Studies (CEIPI) Research Paper No 2018-02, 2 March 2018) <https://ssrn.com/abstract=3160586> or <http://dx.doi.org/10.2139/ssrn.3160586>.

561 Drexl, Hilty et al (n 571).

562 Geiger, 'Elaborating a Human Rights Friendly Copyright Framework' (n 321).

Article 3 establishes a narrowly tailored exception for TDM that is restricted to non-commercial scientific research and limited to use by recognized institutions, such as research organizations and cultural heritage institutions. Interestingly, while this exception facilitates academic and public-interest research, it excludes other important actors – such as journalists, educators, and others – thereby constraining innovation across these sectors.[563]

By contrast, Article 4 introduces a more expansive TDM exception that is not limited to specific institutions, thereby rendering it more relevant to commercial AI development. According to Article 4(1), Member States are required to provide for an exception allowing "reproductions and extractions of lawfully accessible works and other subject matter" for the purposes of text and data mining. Furthermore, Article 4(2) permits the retention of such reproductions and extractions for as long as is necessary to complete the TDM process – potentially addressing the existing concerns related to the storage and temporary reproduction of copyrighted materials during AI training.

However, the operability of this exception is limited by Article 4(3), which introduces a so-called "opt-out" mechanism. Under this provision, rightsholders may exclude their works from being used for TDM purposes by expressly reserving their rights.

Recent national case law among the EU Member States, such as Kneschke v. LAION and DPG Media v. HowardsHome, has started to interpret these provisions, but many doctrinal and technical questions remain unresolved,[564] as will be explained shortly.

Further clarity on the implications of this framework may emerge from this ongoing litigation. For now, however, the case law remains in flux, as courts have

563 European Copyright Society, 'General Opinion on the EU Copyright Reform Package' (2017) <https://europeancopyrightsociety.org/wp-content/uploads/2015/12/ecs-opinion-on-eu-copyright-reform-def.pdf>.

564 Hamburg District Court, 310 O.22723, LAION v Robert Kneschke [27 September 2024]; Amsterdam District Court, DPG Media BV and others v HowardsHome BV, C/13/737170 / HA ZA 23-690 [30 October 2024]; Goldstein P, Stuetzle C and Bischoff S, 'Kneschke vs LAION – Landmark Ruling on TDM Exceptions for AI Training Data – Part 1' (Copyright Blog, 13 November 2024) <https://legalblogs.wolterskluwer.com/copyright-blog/kneschke-vs-laion-landmark-ruling-on-tdm-exceptions-for-ai-training-data-part-1/>; Goldste in P, Stuetzle C and Bischoff S, 'Kneschke vs LAION – Landmark Ruling on TDM Exceptions for AI Training Data – Part 2' (Copyright Blog, 14 November 2024) <https://legalblogs.wolterskluwer.com/copyright-blog/kneschke-vs-laion-landmark-ruling-on-tdm-exceptions-for-ai-training-data-part-2/?output=pdf>; Valk E and Toepoel I, 'DPG Media et al vs HowardsHome – A National Ruling on DSM's Press Publishers' Rights and TDM Exceptions' (Copyright Blog, 16 January 2025) <https://legalblogs.wolterskluwer.com/copyright-blog/dpg-media-et-al-vs-howardshome-a-national-ruling-on-dsms-press-publishers-rights-and-tdm-exceptions/>.

only recently begun to engage with the practical application of the exceptions set out in the CDSM Directive in the context of AI development and training.

A key question therefore arises: do the EU's text and data mining exceptions extend to generative AI?

Yet the very prominence of Articles 3 and 4 is double-edged. Many scholars argue that the dual regime they establish is misaligned with generative AI and ill-suited to large-scale AI training.[565]

The reasons are several. First, while traditional TDM systems focus on analytical pattern recognition, aiming to extract factual or semantic insights from data, generative AI models, especially those based on transformer or diffusion architectures, are trained to synthesize new outputs by encoding and internalizing expressive features of the input content.[566] Hence, unlike standard TDM, generative training inherently involves expressive reproduction. In some scholars' view, this only means that TDM "is neither synonymous with AI training nor is it all that AI training entails".[567] However, for some other scholars this is a qualitative difference that places generative AI's training outside the intended scope of the current TDM exceptions.[568]

Moreover, the TDM exceptions were not arguably designed to accommodate machine-based activities at this scale, nor to facilitate commercial uses detached from scientific inquiry.[569] Article 4, for example, was primarily intended to remove contractual barriers to large-scale data analysis, not to authorize commercial ingestion of expressive works for synthetic generation purposes.[570]

Despite these concerns-generally rooted in the fact that the TDM regime predates today's generative AI capabilities,[571] - it is precisely this framework

565 Lucchi and Hunter (n 487), 29.

566 "During training, these models build multi-dimensional parameter spaces that allow them to reproduce style, structure, and composition, enabling outputs that closely resemble original creative works. This shift from extraction to expressive recombination marks a significant departure from the analytical logic that underpins the TDM exceptions". See Lucchi and Hunter (n 487) 30.

567 Rosati E, 'Copyright Exceptions and Fair Use Defences for AI Training Done for "Research" and "Learning," or the Inescapable Licensing Horizon' [2025] European Journal of Risk Regulation 1, 4.

568 Lucchi and Hunter (n 487), 29, who also argues that emerging scholarly consensus holds that training generative models constitutes reproduction, not mining, making Article 4 an inadequate legal basis for such activities.

569 Lucchi and Hunter (n 487), 30.

570 Ibid, 43.

571 "The TDM exceptions were not designed to cover machine learning by generative AI systems, meaning AI systems that can produce new works based on the learning from other existing works. This emerges very clearly from the preparatory works of the Direc-

that the EU legislature has chosen as its anchor: Article 4 of the CDSM Directive has been expressly referenced in the EU AI Act in art. 53, emphasizing that providers of general-purpose AI models must implement "a policy to comply with Union law on copyright and related rights, and in particular to identify and comply with, including through state-of-the-art technologies, a reservation of rights expressed pursuant to Article 4(3) of Directive (EU) 2019/790".

5 Generative AI Training and the AI Act

By expressly recalling in the AI Act the CDSM Directive's "copyright exceptions and limitations" (Recital 105), the EU has established a significant intersection between copyright law and the emerging regulatory framework for artificial intelligence.[572]

According to Recital 105, when a developer conducts text and data mining on protected content for the purpose of training a general-purpose AI model (GPAI), such activity constitutes a reproduction under copyright law. Consequently, it must either be authorized by the rightsholder or fall within one of the limitations and exceptions provided by law. Although it would be "myopic" to restrict the reference to this statutory exception,[573] Article 4 is certainly one of them, arguably together with Article 3 (TDM for scientific research).

To give effect to these principles, Article 53(1)(c) of the AI Act imposes a primary obligation according to which providers of general-purpose AI models must implement a copyright compliance policy. This policy must specifi-

---

tive, where the issue of generative AI and TDM exceptions is absent and has obviously been overlooked"; see Geiger, 'Elaborating a Human Rights Friendly Copyright Framework' (n 321). However, according to the European Parliament the TDM exceptions – including the opt-out mechanism – "provide balance between the protection of rightholders including artists and the facilitation of TDM, including by AI developers"; see <https://www.europarl.europa.eu/doceo/document/E-9-2023-000479-ASW_EN.html>.

572 Geiger, 'Elaborating a Human Rights Friendly Copyright Framework' (n 321).

573 Notably, as Rosati ('Copyright Exceptions and Fair Use Defences' (n 567) 4) notes, the analysis over the intersection between TDM activities and the AI training shouldn't even only focus on art. 4 CDSM Directive (n 116): "from a European (thus including both the EU and the UK) perspective, focusing on Article 4 DSMD alone to treat unlicensed TDM and AI training is myopic. As the recent decision of the District Court of Hamburg in LAION demonstrates, Article 3 DSMD has also the potential to be largely – and inappropriately – relied upon in the context of unlicensed TDM and subsequent AI training practices. That is so for two key reasons: the possibility – expressly allowed by the DSMD itself – for the beneficiaries of the exception to collaborate with third parties, including commercial AI developers; and the potentially (over)broad construction of key notions like 'research organization' and 'scientific research'".

cally identify and respect copyright reservations made under Article 4(3) of the CDSM Directive, using "state-of-the-art technologies" to detect and comply with rightsholders' opt-outs.

A second obligation, set out in Article 53(1)(d), requires developers to prepare and publish a sufficiently detailed summary of the content used to train their AI models. This summary must adhere to a template to be established by the newly formed AI Office, with the aim of ensuring greater transparency and accountability regarding the source materials used in model development.

Since transparency is a prerequisite for the exercise of rights and for the potential emergence of a functioning market for data licensing in the context of AI, these two obligations are inherently interconnected. In particular, the publication of a detailed training data summary (Article 53(1)(d)) is intended to enable rightsholders to give meaningful effect to the reservation of rights they may have expressed under Article 4(3) of the CDSM Directive. Without such disclosure, content creators would be unable to detect the unauthorized use of their works and would face significant obstacles in proposing licensing arrangements. The idea behind these conjunct provisions was that, by ensuring transparency regarding the training datasets of their models, AI companies would also fulfil their obligation under Article 53(1)(c).[574]

Both provisions are, in principle, intended to safeguard authors' legitimate interests and rightsholders' rights. Yet, given the challenges of implementation and enforcement, which will be discussed shortly, these measures risk remaining formalistic.[575] They outline a framework that, in theory, grants rightsholders greater control over the use of their works; in practice, however, such control may prove elusive. And even where effective, it is likely to benefit large intermediaries rather than individual creators – at least where the latter are not represented by a collective management organization (CMO).

Nevertheless, the AI Act's requirement to "put in place a policy to comply with Union law on copyright and related rights" remains significant, above all because it brings copyright – as a comprehensive framework – back to the center of the AI governance debate, and confirms that the legal and policy conversation is far from settled. The real challenge now lies in coordinating these emerging AI obligations with the complex architecture of EU copyright law, especially given that

574 Quintais, Generative AI (n 310).

575 "Even supposing that the transparency obligations introduced by the EU Artificial Intelligence Act could contribute to greater oversight of training practices, such obligations remain limited in scope. Indeed, the AI Act mandates only the disclosure of summary information – not specific datasets – and does not provide mechanisms for opt-out enforcement, real-time monitoring, or model-specific auditability"; see Lucchi and Hunter (n 487) 52.

the two regimes, as noted in Chapter 5, pursue different functions, are built on distinct principles, and operate under divergent territorial scopes.

5.1 Article 53(1)(C): Copyright Policies and the Opt-Out Mechanism

The obligation set out in Article 53(1)(c) of the AI Act is to "put in place a policy to comply with Union law on copyright and related rights, and in particular to identify and comply with, including through state-of-the-art technologies, a reservation of rights expressed pursuant to Article 4(3) of Directive (EU) 2019/790."

The expression "to comply with Union law on copyright and related rights" – which must be interpreted in light of Recital 106 of the AI Act – is notably ambiguous and open to interpretation. Some commentators have, for example, pointed out that it remains unclear how rigorously this compliance obligation will be enforced, and whether it requires proactive due diligence, reactive compliance mechanisms, or merely technical neutrality on the part of AI developers.[576]

However, the critical component of this obligation lies in the requirement to identify and comply with reservations of rights made under Article 4(3) of the CDSM Directive, raising questions about how they should operate in practice – under what conditions, through which technical means, and according to which legal standards.

First, it is unclear, whether, under Article 53(1)(c) of the AI Act, the opt-out mechanism can have retroactive effect and, specifically, whether a reservation made after the scraping of works can preclude the use of data already ingested.

Furthermore, Recital 106, intended to clarify the provision, is itself ambiguous, particularly in requiring GPAI providers to respect copyright obligations "regardless of the jurisdiction in which the copyright-relevant acts underpinning the training of those general-purpose AI models take place". While this language clearly seeks to prevent regulatory arbitrage, its practical implications remain uncertain for models trained outside the EU but deployed within it, which remain subject to the EU's transparency and compliance obligations.[577]

Moreover, scholars have also noted that coordination with Article 53(1)(d) of the AI Act may prove challenging. Although this provision introduces an obligation to disclose the composition of training datasets, it remains unclear how detailed such disclosure must be in order to comply with the AI Act. This is

576 Stieper M and Denga M, The International Reach of EU Copyright Through the AI Act (Institut für Wirtschaftsrecht, 2024).

577 On both these aspects, see Margoni, 'TDM Opt-Outs' (n 480).

particularly relevant when discussing the reservation of rights under Article 4(3) of the CDSM Directive. In the absence of a comprehensive reporting obligation requiring AI developers to specifically identify which copyrighted works have been mined or extracted for machine learning purposes, it becomes nearly impossible for rightsholders to detect whether their works have been used. This would be realistically possible only in clear-cut cases, such as when a generated output closely resembles the original work, or when recognizable markers, such as a watermark resembling that of Getty Images,[578] appear in an AI-generated image, indicating potential infringement.[579]

However, the most widely shared criticism of Article 53(1)(c) concerns the absence of effective enforcement mechanisms, as the AI Act provides no clear procedural standards for rightsholders to exercise their opt-out in practice. Indeed, one of the core challenges associated with the opt-out mechanism lies in the absence of standardized methods for its implementation. As recent policy analysis has shown, there is currently no generally accepted technical protocol for expressing rights reservations in an "appropriate" manner and in a "machine-readable format".[580]

Publisher-developed tools, artist-led platforms, proprietary systems introduced by AI companies, and other instruments are emerging to address this issue. Yet, it remains uncertain which of these will ultimately be adopted or supported by major AI developers.[581]

In light of these concerns, recent national case law in several EU Member States has begun to shed light on the practical interpretation of Article 4(3), even though most of these decisions do not directly involve generative AI.

---

578 <https://www.bakerlaw.com/getty-images-v-stability-ai/>.

579 Geiger C, 'Remuneration, Transparency and Copyright in the AI Act: A European Perspective' (International Association of Artificial Intelligence and Law (IAAIL), 2024).

580 <https://openfuture.eu/publication/defining-best-practices-for-opting-out-of-ml-training/>.

581 Some of them – including OpenAI, Microsoft, Google, and Stability AI – have acknowledged the relevance of opt-out mechanisms and have introduced voluntary compliance protocols. These include extensions to the robots.txt protocol that allow web publishers to signal their refusal to be included in training datasets. OpenAI, for example, maintains a dedicated form through which creators can request the exclusion of visual content from its DALL·E training corpus. Notably, among these companies, as of late 2023, only Google had explicitly framed its protocol as an implementation of Article 4(3) of the CDSM Directive (n 116), highlighting its alignment with EU copyright requirements. See Keller P, 'Generative AI and Copyright: The Convergence of Opt-Outs' (Kluwer Copyright Blog, 23 November 2023) <https://copyrightblog.kluweriplaw.com/2023/11/23/generative-ai-and-copyright-convergence-of-opt-outs/>.

In DPG Media et al. v. HowardsHome,[582] the Amsterdam District Court examined whether the plaintiffs, the Belgian media companies DPG Media, Mediahuis Netherlands and Mediahuis NRC (all active in the Dutch online commercial news sector), had appropriately reserved their TDM rights on their websites. The defendant was accused of unlawfully aggregating, through automated bots, news items from the publishers' websites in order to provide its alert service "HowardsHome Nieuws" (HowardsHome) to public institutions and private companies.

Regarding whether the defendant had lawful access to the works under Article 4(1) and Recital 14 of the CDSM Directive, the Dutch court found that the publishers had not sufficiently demonstrated that HowardsHome's alerts included or provided access to content behind their paywalls. Consequently, the court assumed that HowardsHome relied solely on publicly available information and therefore – at least in principle – had lawful access.

As to whether the DPG Media and Mediahuis had expressly reserved their rights in an appropriate manner, such as through machine-readable means, the judgment indicates that publishers had primarily targeted large AI bots (such as ChatGPT-User, CCBOT, and anthropic-ai, among others), but not specifically those used by HowardsHome. It is unclear from the ruling which bots were involved; however, the court ultimately held that the publishers' rights-reservation measures did not validly deny TDM permission to the bots used by HowardsHome.

This is because, as the court appears to imply, for an opt-out under the TDM exception to be effective, the parties it targets must be explicitly identified. It is possible that the Publishers' reservation, expressly directed at specific TDM actors, was also intended as an implicit reservation against all other TDM actors. However, the reasoning underlying the court's judgment appears to be that implicit reservations are insufficient, given the requirement for an expressly made reservation.

Interestingly, before reaching this conclusion, it first had to determine whether the statutory copyright limitation at issue complied with the Berne three-step test under the 2001 InfoSoc Directive, which the court found it did. Regarding the first step, the court held that the Dutch implementing law's specified exceptions are sufficiently well-defined to constitute a "certain special case". As to the second step, since it was not evident how signaling the Publishers' paywalled content would harm their business operations, the court found no conflict with the normal exploitation of the works. Finally, under the third step, the court determined that HowardsHome operates

582 Valk and Toepoel (n 564).

within the boundaries of the Dutch Copyright Act, and therefore the Publishers' legitimate interests were not unreasonably prejudiced.

That said, this judgment is interesting because it arguably implies that for the opt-out to be effective, generalized or implied reservations are insufficient.[583]

Another case in Germany, Kneschke v. LAION, has provided further insight into the interpretation of art. 4(3) of the CDSM Directive and, particularly, the "machine-readable" requirement. The plaintiff in this case was the author of the photograph at issue, which is protected as a photographic work under the German Copyright Act. The image had been lawfully made available to the public through the website of a stock-photo provider holding non-exclusive exploitation rights. The defendant downloaded the photograph from this website for AI training purposes, despite a usage restriction – prohibiting web scraping of published content – being declared in natural language on a subpage of the site.

The Hamburg Regional Court, when called to rule on the matter, suggested, albeit in *obiter dictum*, that natural-language declarations may qualify as machine-readable, thus aligning with the wording of Article 4(3) of the CDSM Directive and Section 44b(3) of the German Copyright Act. The court, though, did not definitively rule on whether the specific declaration in question satisfied all formal requirements.

Although these cases have begun to provide some, national-level, answers to the questions surrounding the interpretability of Article 4(3) of the CDSM Directive, many issues remain unresolved.[584]

The absence of standardized mechanisms for exercising opt-out rights currently appears to be the most pressing one at the moment, with significant implications for authors, rightsholders, and AI developers alike.

On the one hand, the opt-out mechanism poses a significant challenge for AI developers. Given that generative AI systems rely on the ingestion of vast datasets, the obligation to obtain individual authorizations for each work, where an opt-out has been exercised, would probably risk becoming unmanageable. This scenario will inevitably benefit large tech corporations, who pos-

583 Goldstein (n 564).

584 Pukas J and Nordemann JB, 'German Regional Court (Landgericht) of Hamburg paves the way to treat the reproduction of works as AI training data under the EU text and data mining exceptions' (Kluwer Copyright Blog, 25 October 2024) <https://legalblogs.wolterskluwer.com/copyright-blog/german-regional-court-landgericht-of-hamburg-paves-the-way-to-treat-the-reproduction-of-works-as-ai-training-data-under-the-eu-text-and-data-mining-exceptions/>.

sess the financial and legal capacity to manage such licensing regimes, while leaving start-ups and independent developers unable to compete.[585]

On the other hand, for individual authors and bigger rightsholders, the absence of harmonized and scalable procedures imposes a significant burden, as they must proactively issue opt-outs that are both legally and technically valid in order to protect their copyrights.

Indeed, this requirement can prove prohibitively demanding for many creators, either because they lack the technical literacy, financial means, or institutional support to navigate the opt-out process effectively, or because they are required to submit separate declarations to each entity training AI models. Moreover, the fulfilling of this requirement is complicated by the fact that the same work may appear on different platforms or under varying legal conditions due to multiple uploads by the same or different rightsholders, or the existence of infringing copies. As a consequence, contradictory opt-out declarations may arise,[586] and the transaction costs associated with managing multiple and potentially conflicting declarations increase significantly – an impact that proves especially disproportionate for individual and small-scale creators. The practical burden of exercising the reservation of rights, indeed, weighs more heavily on individual authors than on structured rightsholders such as intermediaries or industry players.[587] It is, therefore, likely that the governance of rights reservations – for example offering differentiated licensing terms for different use cases – will become more and more centralized or at least devolved to collective management organizations (CMOs) capable of reducing the difficulties of implementing and verifying the effectiveness of the opt-outs.[588]

Yet, what is more concerning in this regard is that, even when the opt-out is properly exercised, there is no guarantee that the benefits of subsequent licensing – needed to authorize AI training – will reach individual authors. In many cases, again, rights will be exercised by large rightsholders, leaving individual authors to renegotiate remuneration terms by themselves with publishers or producers.

585 Geiger, 'Elaborating a Human Rights Friendly Copyright Framework' (n 321).

586 Margoni, 'TDM Opt-Outs' (n 480).

587 Keller (n 581).

588 Collective management organizations have already begun to operationalize the opt-out at scale. On 12 October 2023, the French collecting society SACEM announced that it would opt out of AI model training on behalf of its repertoire. Relying on Article L122-5-3 of the French Intellectual Property Code, which implements Article 4(3) of the CDSM Directive (n 116), SACEM stated its intention to establish an exclusive licensing right over TDM uses, thereby requiring AI developers to negotiate permissions. See SACEM Press Release, 12 October 2023, <https://societe.sacem.fr/en/news/our-society/sacem-favour-virtuous-transparent-and-fair-ai-exercises-its-right-opt-out>.

5.2 Article 53(1)(D): The Obligation to Provide a Sufficiently Detailed Summary of Training Datasets

Article 53(1)(d) of the AI Act requires GPAI providers to draw up and publish a summary of the content used for training, that enables interested parties, particularly copyright and related rights holders, to exercise and enforce their rights. The objective is to provide meaningful and comprehensive information allowing parties with legitimate interests to understand whether and how their rights may have been affected. While the introduction of such an obligation is a welcome step, it presents a number of substantial implementation challenges.

On the one hand, these models are often trained on vast and heterogeneous datasets drawn from a multitude of sources – many of which are only partially documented or entirely opaque.[589] As a result, it may be difficult, if not technically unfeasible,[590] for AI developers to accurately reconstruct which specific works were processed or to retrospectively verify whether they were subject to an opt-out declaration. This uncertainty, compounded by the fact that the scope of the obligation must take "due account of the need to protect trade secrets and confidential business information" (Recital 107), contributes to the ambiguity surrounding the scope and level of detail of this disclosure obligation.

On the other hand, according to the regulation, the summary should be "generally comprehensive in its scope instead of technically detailed" and broad enough to allow rightsholders to determine whether their works have been used. According to this formulation, explicit reference could also be limited to major datasets used for training (e.g., Common Crawl, Re-LAION-5B), while only a narrative description could be required for any additional data sources consulted.[591]

Moreover, several structural and legal challenges further undermine the effectiveness of this transparency requirement, particularly when considered in relation to copyright compliance. These include:[592] (i) the low and inconsistent thresholds of originality across jurisdictions, which complicate the identification of what constitutes in-copyright content that may be used for

589 Geiger C and Iaia V, 'Towards an Independent EU Regulator for Copyright Issues of Generative AI: What Role for the AI Office (But More Importantly: What's Next)?' (2024) II Auteurs & Media 185 <https://ssrn.com/abstract=4914938> or <http://dx.doi.org/10.2139/ssrn.4914938>.

590 Geiger and Iaia, 'The Forgotten Creator (n 306).

591 Recital 107 of the AI act (n 5).

592 Quintais, Generative AI (n 310).

training purposes; (ii) the fragmentation of copyright ownership, often involving multiple rightsholders for a single work; (iii) the absence of a mandatory copyright registration requirement in most legal systems; and (iv) the general lack or poor quality of metadata linking digital content to its rightful owners.

For these reasons, while this AI Act's transparency obligation represent a significant policy effort to align AI development with copyright protection, its effective implementation will require further clarification, standardization, and possibly the development of new technological solutions to ensure meaningful compliance.

To address the need to operationalize the transparency and copyright obligations enshrined in the AI Act, according to art. 53(1)(d) and following Recital 107, the AI Office has developed a template that general-purpose AI model providers are required to use in order to publish such a "sufficiently detailed summary" of the training data employed during model development.[593]

The AI Office initiated this process through a multi-stakeholder consultation, which gathered over 430 contributions from a wide range of actors, including industry representatives, civil society organizations, academic institutions, and individual experts.[594]

Notably, from stakeholder feedback a substantial divergence between rightsholder representatives, NGOs and industry actors emerged, reflecting differing policy perspectives on this issue.[595] Rightsholders and NGOs argued for granular, work-by-work disclosure, arguing that information essential for the exercise of copyright and related rights must not be shielded under the guise of trade secrecy. By contrast, industry participants expressed concern that overly detailed disclosure requirements could jeopardize the security of AI systems or undermine commercial competitiveness. They therefore advocated for a broad interpretation of trade secrets and confidential business information to limit the scope of the summary obligation.[596]

593 <https://digital-strategy.ec.europa.eu/en/library/explanatory-notice-and-template-public-summary-training-content-general-purpose-ai-models>.

594 The development of the Code of Practice for general-purpose AI models proceeded in parallel with the implementation of the Template. Given the close interlinkage between these two initiatives, participants in the Code of Practice process – over 1,000 stakeholders – were invited to review and comment on the preliminary structure of the template, with feedback collected until 31 January 2025. (https://digital-strategy.ec.europa.eu/en/policies/ai-code-practice).

595 <https://ec.europa.eu/newsroom/dae/redirection/document/111909>.

596 This fundamental tension is acknowledged in Recital 107 of the AI Act (n 5), which seeks to strike a delicate balance. It states that the training data summary must be "comprehensive in scope" rather than technically detailed, and that it should be designed to

Content-wise, the Template is divided into three main sections. The first concerns the collection of general information, enabling the identification of both the provider and the model, as well as the general characteristics of the training data. The second focuses on the list of data sources, requiring the disclosure of the primary datasets used to train the model, such as large private or public databases. Notably, this section also calls for a comprehensive narrative description of the data scraped online by or on behalf of the provider – including a summary of the most relevant domain names – as well as a description of any other data sources employed (e.g., user-generated or synthetic data), in order to ensure a complete overview of the content used for training. The third section addresses the relevant data-processing aspects, particularly those affecting the exercise of copyright and related rights by parties with legitimate interests under EU law.

6 *Ad Interim* Considerations and Future Perspectives

At the heart of the current legal debate surrounding the input phase of the "creative" process lies the question of whether text and data mining activities for the purpose of AI training and testing are legally incompatible with the existing copyright framework governing the intellectual works from which such data are extracted. The answer to this question is likely to be shaped by ongoing copyright litigation concerning generative AI.

The growing body of case law currently unfolding before US courts on fair use – together with the first emerging cases and ongoing debate surrounding TDM exceptions in the EU – may serve as a flashpoint in the broader "negotiation" over the boundaries of intellectual property in the digital age. These developments invite a deeper examination of copyright law as a normative framework for addressing and guiding technological change, and, in light of such change, of what must ultimately be regarded as legally appropriable and what falls outside that scope.

The current wave of litigation echoes earlier chapters in the complex relationship between copyright and technological disruption, recalling previous legal battles over piano rolls, radio broadcasting, VHS recorders, cable television, peer-to-peer software, MP3 players, digital image thumbnails, and, more recently, services such as MP3Tunes, ReDigi, and Tom Kabinet – platforms that

---

facilitate enforcement by parties with legitimate interests, including rightsholders, while safeguarding the trade secrets of AI developers".

attempted to establish secondary markets for digital goods.[597] It also brings to mind the early days of Web 2.0, when platforms like YouTube and social media networks triggered a period of unprecedented content circulation. During that time, cultural industries responded with significant investments in anti-piracy enforcement, while comparatively neglecting digital innovation and support for creators.[598]

Indeed, these legal battles have frequently served as business strategies aimed less at fostering innovation and more at asserting control through copyright enforcement[599] and the current debate on generative AI is only the latest chapter of this "historical dance" between copyright and technological evolution.

The outcomes of the pending AI-related cases will shape not only the commercial viability of specific platforms, but also the broader trajectory of human and machine creativity in the twenty-first century.[600]

However, many fundamental questions are likely to remain unresolved even after the resolution of these cases as they may not be directly addressed in court proceedings.

For instance, systematic risks deriving from a large-scale exercise of the opt-out right under Article 4(3) of the CDSM Directive are unlikely to be dealt with through litigation. These include the potential impact on the quality and diversity of training datasets, and the consequent increased risk of reproducing biases. The existing literature has documented a number of examples illustrating the connection between flawed inputs and flawed outputs.[601]

As previously noted, TDM activities can play a valuable role in supporting the fair and inclusive development of AI. Yet if opt-outs are exercised at scale, they may lead to training datasets that are incomplete or skewed, ultimately compromising the performance and accuracy of AI models.

Moreover, if the EU's TDM exception mechanism proves less adaptable to the training of generative AI than the exceptions available in other jurisdictions, such as US fair use, the widespread exclusion of European content from training datasets could lead to the underrepresentation of European languages, cultures, and creative sectors – particularly if developers increasingly rely on data from jurisdictions with more permissive copyright frameworks.

597 Frosio, 'Should We Ban Generative AI, Incentivise it or Make it a Medium for Inclusive Creativity?' (n 410) 5.
598 Belisario and Riccio, 'L'IA distruggerà la creatività?' (n 495).
599 Frosio, 'Should We Ban Generative AI, Incentivise it or Make it a Medium for Inclusive Creativity?' (n 410) 7.
600 Ibid.
601 Geiger and Iaia, 'The Forgotten Creator (n 306).

More fundamentally, if read in light of the broader question of what we consider "appropriable" in the digital environment, the opt-out mechanism under Article 4(3), as recalled by art. 53(1)(c) of the AI Act, arguably shifts the balance back toward proprietary interests (albeit in a formal manner, disconnected from any concrete guarantee of remuneration for creators) at the expense of access and the circulation of informational content - thus raising pressing policy concerns.

Another key question is whether the EU approach, which places the burden on authors to actively protect their intellectual property via opt-out mechanisms, is truly preferable to a system in which generative AI providers would be obliged by default to verify that their use of a work does not infringe existing copyright. As several scholars have noted, this issue goes beyond the questions before the courts and would require a broader policy and regulatory assessment.[602]

Likewise, the lack of standardization in the opt-out mechanism is not an issue that can be resolved through court rulings alone. It raises significant policy concerns and calls for coordinated regulatory intervention. This process should be pursued through inclusive, multi-stakeholder dialogue, ideally initiated or supported by the European Commission.[603]

In the end, future solutions will require a combination of enforceable technical protocols and binding legal standards, potentially even prohibiting the use of AI systems that do not allow or respect legitimate opt-outs.

Moreover, there remains the unresolved issue of how to deal with past violations: whether and how redress mechanisms can be established to counterbalance the disproportionate power currently held by major AI providers.

The European Union, with its proactive regulatory approach and emphasis on fundamental rights, may well serve as a model in shaping these future challenges. However, implementing such solutions at an EU level raises complex questions of governance and enforcement that would go beyond European Union borders.

Against this backdrop, the EU could take the lead in proposing model solutions to counterbalance the risks raised by the uncompensated, large-scale exploitation of in-copyright works used to train generative AI. One of them could be a shared framework for a remuneration right and statutory licenses applicable to the use of copyrighted works in AI training. The functioning of statutory licensing schemes offers a promising pathway in this regard: unlike the opt-out, which forces authors to choose between excluding their works

602 Rossi, 'Opere in cerca d'autore' (n 343).

603 Keller (n 581).

from training (thereby impoverishing the datasets) and tolerating their uncompensated use, a statutory licence reconciles the two, allowing the volume of copyrighted content available for machine learning to be maximised while safeguarding the legitimate interest of authors in being remunerated for the commercial use of their intellectual labor.

What remains is to determine how these objectives can be effectively implemented and how they interact with copyright law when considered as a complex and comprehensive legal framework.

CHAPTER 8

Legal Issues on the Output Side of the Creative Process

1 Preliminary Remarks

The issue of whether outputs created by (or with the assistance of) generative AI models can be protected under copyright law has been the subject of extensive debate in recent years, particularly since such technologies began to attract widespread media attention.[604] This debate has intensified with the recent increasing number of legal disputes arising in many jurisdictions. However, as is well known, the roots of this discussion can be traced back much further, at least from the 1960s, particularly in the United States[605] – well before the phenomenon now commonly referred to as "generative AI" entered the public discourse.[606]

604 Inter alia, see Militsyna, 'Human Creative Contribution to AI-Based Output' (n 407); Iaia, 'To Be, or Not to Be...Original Under Copyright Law' (n 420); Hugenholtz and Quintais, 'Copyright and Artificial Creation' (n 438) 1190 ff.; Hartmann et al (n 228), 67–96; Gervais, 'The Machine as Author' (n 367); Kop (n 385); Deltorn and Macrez (n 44); Guizzardi S (n 189); Guadamuz, 'Do androids dream of electric copyright?' (n 367) 169–186; Bulayenko O, Quintais JP, Gervais D and Poort J, 'AI Music Outputs: Challenges to the Copyright Legal Framework' reCreating Europe Report (2022); Mezei P, 'From Leonardo to the Next Rembrandt: The Need for AI-Pessimism in the Age of Algorithms' (2020) 2 Institute of Comparative Law and Legal Theory 390–429; Bonadio E, 'Artificial Intelligence as Producer and Consumer of Copyright Works: Evaluating the Consequences of Algorithmic Creativity' (2020) 2 IPQ 112–137; Ramalho A, 'Originality Redux: An Analysis of the Originality Requirement in AI-Generated Works' [2019] AIDA 2–18; Spedicato G, 'Creatività Artificiale, Mercato e Proprietà Intellettuale' (2019) 4 Rivista di diritto industriale 253; Spina Alì G, 'The Times They Are AI-Changin': Copyright and Computer Generated Works' [2019] AIDA 367–399; Degli Esposti M, Lagioia F and Sartor G, 'The Use of Copyrighted Works by AI Systems: Art Works in the Data Mill' (2018) 11 European Journal of Risk Management 51–69.

605 US Copyright Office, Copyright and Artificial Intelligence: Part 2 (n 367) 2.

606 Notably, in the Treccani online encyclopedia, the expression "generative artificial intelligence" has been included among the neologisms of 2023; see <https://www.treccani.it/vocabolario/neo-intelligenza-artificiale-generativa_%28Neologismi%29/>. Current debates, in fact, frequently draw on theoretical frameworks developed by legal scholars over the past two decades regarding the so-called "computer-generated works". See Ginsburg and Budiardjo (n 357); Ginsburg, 'People Not Machines' (n 321); Goold PR, 'The Curious Case of Computer-Generated Works under the Copyright, Designs and Patents Act 1988'

Indeed, as early as 1965, the first "difficult questions of authorship" began to arise, prompted by attempts to register before the USCO a "musical composition created by a computer", as well as "an abstract drawing, and (…) compilations of various kinds, which were at least partly the 'work' of computers".[607] At the time, it was observed that "both the number of works proximately produced or 'written' by computers and the problems of the Copyright Office in this area will increase" and that in this framework "the crucial question appears to be whether the 'work' is basically one of human authorship, with the computer merely being an assisting instrument, or whether the traditional elements of authorship in the work (literary, artistic, or musical expression or elements of selection, arrangement, etc.) were actually conceived and executed not by man but by a machine".[608]

Since then, "computer-generated" works have continued to grow in both number and sophistication.[609] Today, the most significant challenges arise from machine learning (ML) models[610] – and, in particular, from the more "complex and dynamic" systems that are composed of layers of interconnected artificial neurons.[611] Since machine learning is currently the most widely adopted subfield of AI in the cultural and recreational sector, the following paragraphs will primarily focus on it, unless otherwise specified.

Despite the early emergence of the "questions of authorship", no legal system has yet introduced comprehensive and systematic legislative provisions to address whether intellectual works created or generated by AI software or hardware are eligible for protection under copyright law or other dedicated legal frameworks.[612]

[2021] 2 IPQ 120–129 https://ssrn.com/abstract=4072004; Ercolani S, 'Computer Generated Works' (1998) Il Diritto di Autore 605; Miller AR, 'Copyright Protection for Computer Programs, Databases, and Computer-Generated Works: Is Anything New Since CONTU?' (1993) 106 Harv L Rev 977, 1060–65; Samuelson P, 'Allocating Ownership Rights in Computer-Generated Works' (1985) 47 U Pitt L Rev 1185, 1186–87.

607 US Copyright Office, Sixty-Eighth Annual Report of the Register of Copyrights for the Fiscal Year Ending June 30, 1965 (1966) <https://www.copyright.gov/reports/annual/archive/ar-1965.pdf>, 5.

608 Ibid.

609 Notably, the variables that influence whether an AI-based output can be qualified as copyrightable include both the design of the AI system (i.e., its methods and models) and the manner in which it is trained (i.e., the data, processes, and techniques used). The overall performance of a given AI system depends on the combination of these factors; see Militsyna, 'Human Creative Contribution to AI-Based Output' (n 407), 942.

610 Drexl, Hilty et al (n 228) 2.

611 Ibid.

612 See, for example, the results of the AIPPI Study Question (n 356); see also Guizzardi S (n 189) 45.

At the EU level, it is worth noting that the AI Act does not address this issue directly. In fact, with regard to AI-generated content, the only relevant provision in the Act pertains to the risk of falsely attributing AI outputs to human authors. In this context, Article 50 of the AI Act introduces transparency obligations for both providers and deployers of AI systems, requiring them to ensure that users are informed when they are interacting with content that has been generated or manipulated by artificial intelligence.[613]

However, the regulation remains silent on the core question of whether AI-based outputs are eligible for protection.

In any event, although, as noted, no systematic solution has been adopted worldwide, various regulators have made efforts to address this issue thus far. One of the earliest attempts within the EU dates back to 2016, when the European Parliament, in its Draft Report 2015/2103(INL) of 31 May 2016 (No. 10), urged the European Commission to "elaborate criteria for an 'own intellectual creation' for copyrightable works produced by computers or robots".[614] However, this recommendation was dropped from the final Resolution (P8_TA (2017)0051) of 16 February 2017, leaving the debate unresolved.

Since then, other regulators have continued exploring potential legislative responses to this issue.

One of the first formally adopted approaches came from Ukraine, which, in its Copyright Law enacted on 1 December 2022, introduced explicit provisions regarding algorithmic outputs that do not qualify for copyright protection, but are subject to a distinct legal status. Specifically, Article 33 of the Ukrainian law establishes a *sui generis* right for non-original objects generated by a computer program, provided that they: (i) are distinct from existing works, (ii) are created without direct human involvement, and (iii) respect third-party rights throughout the production process.[615]

In most other jurisdictions, however, legislative initiatives remain at the draft stage.

Within the European Union, tentative efforts have been made, for instance, in France – where, as noted in Chapter 4, Bill No. 1630 (*Proposition de loi visant à encadrer l'intelligence artificielle par le droit d'auteur*) was submitted to the

613 In particular, AI-generated outputs must be clearly labeled in a machine-readable format, making them detectable as artificially produced or modified. This measure aims to foster user awareness about the nature and origin of algorithmic content; see Iaia V, Klein A and De Gaspari A, 'Stretching Copyright to AI-Generated Outputs: Case Law and Upcoming Regulations' (2025) ECTA Articles.

614 Draft Report 2015/2103 (INL) of 31 May 2016, No. 10 with recommendations to the Commission on Civil Law Rules on Robotics (2015/2103(INL)).

615 Iaia, Klein and De Gaspari (n 613).

National Assembly in September 2023 (prior to the adoption of the AI Act), with the aim to regulate artificial intelligence through the framework of copyright law.[616] Notably, Article 2 of the proposal stipulates that when a work is created by artificial intelligence without direct human intervention, the only rightsholders are the authors or rightholders of the pre-existing works that enabled the generation of the AI-produced content.

Italy has also taken steps toward regulating this matter. The already mentioned Law no. 132 of 23 September 2025, which outlines a national legal framework for artificial intelligence, includes specific provisions on the copyright protection of AI-based works.[617] In particular, Article 25, in addition to clarifying the scope of lawful reproduction and data extraction by AI systems (on the input side of the creative process), reaffirms the requirement of human intellectual contribution as a prerequisite for copyright protection. At the same time, it acknowledges the protectability of works created with the assistance of artificial intelligence tools, provided that such works result from the author's own intellectual effort.

However, as noted, these initiatives remain fragmented and tend to focus on notions such as "non-direct human involvement" (as seen in the Ukrainian law and the French bill) or works created "with the assistance of artificial intelligence", which are difficult to define concretely in practice. They also lack a systematic approach, especially with regard to the increasingly common cases of "hybrid works" resulting from the iterative process between a human and a machine.

Nevertheless, these approaches reflect the prevailing tone of most legal and academic discussions on the subject to date, which often remain exploratory in the absence of comprehensive legislative solutions.

Indeed, the dominant view regarding the protectability of outputs generated through algorithmic processes has long held that, in order to determine whether copyright protection may apply, a distinction must be drawn between

---

616 Notably, the proposal also assigns a central role to collective management organizations (CMOs), empowering them to manage the rights associated with such AI-generated outputs. In particular, CMOs are tasked with representing the relevant rightsholders, facilitating rights enforcement, and ensuring fair remuneration. At the time of writing, the bill remains under examination by the French *Assemblée Nationale*. It is interesting to note that, much like the AI Act, a second French proposal – Bill No. 675, Proposition de loi visant à identifier les images générées par intelligence artificielle publiées sur les réseaux sociaux, introduced on 3 December 2024 – imposes mandatory labeling requirements for AI-generated images published on social media platforms. As of the time of writing, this bill too remains under examination by the French *Assemblée Nationale*.

617 Law 132/2025 (n 234).

two types of content:[618] (i) outputs 'assisted' by a (non-autonomous) AI system, in which the AI functions merely as a tool within a creative process that remains under the control of, or at least supervised by, a human author; and (ii) outputs 'generated' by (autonomous) AI systems, produced with minimal or no human input – where the AI system itself is regarded as the originator.

This distinction – reflected, whether explicitly or implicitly, in the three proposals discussed above, as well as acknowledged by the European Parliament[619] – is typically grounded in the degree of autonomy exercised by the AI system during the creative process and/or the extent of human intervention involved.

Against this backdrop, AI-assisted outputs are generally considered eligible for copyright protection.[620] Within the EU legal framework, for example, it is generally assumed that "the current EU IP framework (…) [appears] broadly suitable to address the challenges raised by AI-assisted (…) creations"[621] and that it applies to this kind of works. This is due to the "human pre-eminence" in such works, which doesn't affect the classical legal qualifications of copyright.[622] Indeed, these outputs are still the result of human intellectual effort, with AI serving merely as a tool to support, enhance, or streamline the creative process. In such cases, the human input in the creative process plays a decisive role, enabling the expression of individual creativity – whether in the pre-production, execution, or post-production phase.[623] In these instances, AI is often compared to traditional creative tools such as brushes, typewriters, or cameras, as frequently noted in academic literature.[624]

---

618 Iaia, 'To Be, or Not to Be…Original Under Copyright Law' (n 420), and the bibliography cited therein.

619 See European Parliament resolution of 20 October 2020 on intellectual property rights for the development of artificial intelligence technologies, 2020/2015(INI), 2021 O.J. (C 404) 129, at § 14.

620 Among many, see Drexl, Hilty et al (n 228) 5.

621 European Commission, 'Communication to the European Parliament, the Council, the European Economic and Social Committee and the Committee of the Regions on "Unlocking the EU's Innovative Potential – An Action Plan on Intellectual Property to Support EU Recovery and Resilience"' (25 November 2020) COM(2020) 760 final, 7.

622 « *Les qualifications juridiques ne sont donc pas appelées à être modifiées* (…)»; see Bensamoun and Farchy (n 4) 25.

623 Iaia, 'To Be, or Not to Be…Original Under Copyright Law' (n 420).

624 In this view, whether a creator uses a paintbrush, a chisel, a camera, or a high-tech instrument, the underlying reasoning remains the same: once a human being creatively intervenes in the process, the instrument used becomes secondary. See Bensamoun and Farchy (n 4) 26.

By contrast, the legal status of AI-generated outputs – or more descriptively, "fully machine-generated" content[625] – remains uncertain. However, in the binary framework often adopted by commentators, such outputs are typically viewed as falling outside the scope of copyright protection and thus in the public domain. This is because AI-generated content is presumed to be created with no (or only minimal) human involvement.[626] This latter, even if present, is considered to be eclipsed by the "algorithmic contribution".[627]

However, the distinction between AI-assisted and AI-generated outputs is neither clear-cut nor entirely accurate, for several reasons (see Paragraph 1.1). Furthermore, it does not appear to have been particularly useful in resolving the first cases brought before national authorities and courts thus far (see Paragraph 1.2).

1.1 The Problematic Distinction between AI-Assisted and AI-Generated Outputs

As argued by Gervais, "the binary paradigm according to which machines are either mere tools in the hands of human users or generators of either random output (therefore, non-original, as it does not result from creative choices) or entirely pre-programmed (as in the videogame audiovisual output example) is obsolete".[628]

First, as noted above, this distinction has often relied, in the relevant literature, on an *a priori* categorization of AI systems as either autonomous or non-autonomous. However, the very notion of fully autonomous AI systems is arguably misleading.

In the fields of bioethics and philosophy, "autonomy" denotes respectively a "guiding principle of moral action, which includes different meanings: self-determination, self-decision, the right to freedom and privacy", as well as "the expression of the freedom of the will, both in its negative aspect of exclu-

---

625 Lucchi and Hunter (n 487), 9.

626 "To be more accurate, there is a human intervention, but it is limited to the pre-production (or programming) stage which encompasses the following activities: (i) the writing of the source code; (ii) the 'feeding' of the algorithm; (iii) and the selection of the objective(s) that AI should reach throughout the production process. Thus, there could be some – also new – entry points for human intervention to produce a work"; see Iaia, 'To Be, or Not to Be…Original Under Copyright Law' (n 420).

627 Iaia, Klein and De Gaspari (n 613). In these cases, as has been argued, excessive constraints on the ability to make free and creative choices at any stage of the process may prevent the output from meeting the requirement of originality. In this regard, see Hugenholtz and Quintais, 'Copyright and Artificial Creation' (n 438) 19.

628 Gervais, 'The Machine as Author' (n 367).

sion of any norm that does not derive from its own nature, and in its positive aspect of affirmation of the power of the spirit to give itself its own norm".[629]

Considering autonomy in these terms, it is difficult to claim that AI possesses a will or freedom of its own, distinct from that of the individuals who design, program, train, or operate it – unless one wishes to engage, from a primarily philosophical perspective, with the very meaning of human "freedom" and "will". However, this inquiry lies beyond the scope of this work. As Vivant aptly put it: *"Le robot pensant, si tant est qu'un robot puisse penser, fait beaucoup fantasmer… et penser peut-être".*[630]

Claims that AI "autonomously" generates outputs – where humans merely define the end goal without providing instructions on how to reach it – have already provoked significant controversy in the past[631] and are not supported by the current state of technological development:[632] "even if the connection between the human intervention and the AI-assisted output is increasingly remote, at this point in time it is hard to conceive of content that is generated through AI that involves no human agency whatsoever".[633] This was also acknowledged in the 2020 IVIR-JIIP report which states: "While AI systems have become – and will become – increasingly sophisticated and autonomous, this Report nonetheless assumes that fully autonomous creation or invention by AI does not exist and will not exist for the foreseeable future".[634]

In the current state of technological development, indeed, software and AI systems designed to address new problems through inductive reasoning and probabilistic analysis always operate on the basis of human contribution and remain, at least minimally, under human control. Even the most sophisticated systems, which learn and evolve by processing increasing volumes of external data, continue to depend on human-provided input and guidance – whether at the stage of the development of the AI software, the selection and curation of training data, the drafting of functional specifications, the supervision of the process of generation of an output, or the editing, post-production, etc.

However, relying primarily on a binary classification between autonomous and non-autonomous systems, the distinction between AI-assisted and AI-generated creations risks overlooking what should be considered the crux of the matter, i.e. the fact that what truly matters in the creation of a work, is not the mere presence or absence of human intervention – or its quantity – but

629 See Treccani Online Encyclopaedia, headword "autonomia", <https://www.treccani.it/enciclopedia/autonomia/> (translation by the author).

630 Vivant M, 'Intelligence artificielle et propriété intellectuelle' (n 188) 1.

631 Drexl, Hilty et al (n 228).

632 Ibid.

633 Hugenholtz and Quintais, 'Copyright and Artificial Creation' (n 438).

634 Hartmann et al (n 228); see also Sanseverino (n 356) 6, 19.

rather the quality of that contribution, which may or may not amount to a creative act.

The fact that an AI-based "creative" process involves some form of human intervention does not necessarily imply that the resulting activity meets the criteria for copyright protection.

It is not necessarily the case that a work created with the assistance of a non-autonomous AI system is more creative than a work generated by "autonomous" intelligent systems, and this is because human intervention, in the former as in the latter case, although perhaps present on a massive scale,[635] can be reduced to an activity of a merely technical nature.

Instead, for the purposes of copyright protection, the human contribution to the creative process should be assessed not merely in quantitative terms – i.e., the amount of human involvement – but in terms of the degree to which that input involves free and creative choices that meaningfully shape the final output.

This, in turn, depends not on the autonomy of the AI system but on the degree of automation within the algorithmic "creative" process.[636] This principle is also affirmed by the USCO in Part 2 of its Report on Artificial Intelligence and Copyright, which states that the distinction between copyrightable and non-copyrightable AI-based outputs "depends on how the system is being used, not on its inherent characteristics".[637]

Therefore, the focus of the analysis should not be on an abstract assessment of the AI's autonomy. Rather, it should shift to how the creative process unfolds in a specific case, requiring an examination of the "causation of originality"[638] in each instance. In particular, emphasis should be placed on the human-driven choices that imbue a given output with originality,[639] more

---

635 This is what it seems it happened in the "Théâtre D'opéra Spatial" case before the US Copyright Office, where a work generated with the aid of Midjourney, was deemed non-original even though the applicant claimed to have submitted over 624 prompts. See US Copyright Office Review Board, Decision of 5 September 2023 on, SR No 1-11743923581 (Théâtre D'opéra Spatial) <https://www.copyright.gov/rulings-filings/review-board/docs/Theatre-Dopera-Spatial.pdf>.

636 In other words, the key issue when assessing works produced by AI systems does not lie in the AI's capacity to be autonomous – that is, to think, to create, or to possess consciousness – but rather in how the creative process manifests in a specific instance.

637 US Copyright Office, Copyright and Artificial Intelligence: Part 2 (n 367) 12. To be more precise, the automation of a process can also be sometimes related to the architecture or model of the artificial intelligence system adopted, but it does not depend solely on the AI itself, rather on how it is used in a specific case.

638 Gervais, 'The Machine as Author' (n 367) 2099.

639 Gervais ('The Machine as Author' (n 367) 2105) defines an author as one who exercises "decision-making authority over what changes are made and what is included in a work".

than on a generalized evaluation of the AI system's capacity to autonomously generate outputs that resemble intellectual works.

Therefore, it is in relation to the degree of automation of the process (rather than the autonomy of the AI)[640] that the role of the human agent should be assessed – particularly the extent to which they exercise creative choices, whether freely or within constraints, and how those choices are reflected in the output and influence the outcome of the process in a discernible way.[641] It is the (potentially) automated nature of the process (if any) that may weaken the causal link between the human and the resulting work[642] – regardless of the quantity of user input – and may render the human creative control over the resulting output insufficient under copyright law,[643] particularly in terms of the "detailed conception" and "controlled execution" of the work, as theorized by some scholars as integral components of authorship.[644]

The considerations that follow will build on these premises to advance the idea that AI-generated content refers to outputs produced through an automated process which, although requiring some level of human involvement, may – by definition – entail no (qualitatively) creative input from any human being.

---

640 This notion has been recently defined by the Italian Council of State, as the "provision of action and control systems capable of reducing, to varying degrees, the extent and frequency of human intervention in the performance of a given activity" (see Italian Council of State, Section III, Judgment No 7891 of 25 November 2021). More generally, automation entails "the use of complex and sophisticated machines and procedures capable of regulating their own functioning and of controlling, through sensitive mechanisms, the quality of the output produced – particularly in relation to production cycles governed by process computers" (see Treccani Online Vocabulary, headword "automation", https://www.treccani.it/vocabolario/automazione/).

641 At the risk of oversimplifying a much more complex concept, an algorithmic process may be considered automated when its outcome is not – even indirectly – the result of discretionary choices made by the human agent involved. These are processes in which multiple layers of mediation separate the final output from the human inputs initially provided. In the context of AI-based processes, this may occur, for example, when: (i) the neural network architecture and the volume of mathematical operations underlying the AI's functioning are so extensive and complex that it becomes difficult to trace any meaningful correlation between the input data and/or prompt, the algorithm, the training dataset, and the resulting output; (ii) as a consequence, it is impossible to predict the nature or extent of the results produced by the process; (iii) human intervention is limited to purely technical or mathematical operations, such that no identifiable creative contribution or original intent to "create" a work can be discerned in the final output; and so on.

642 Iaia, 'To Be, or Not to Be…Original Under Copyright Law' (n 420).

643 Zarya of the Dawn (n 136).

644 Ginsburg and Budiardjo (n 357).

1.2 First Decisions from the US Copyright Office and Other National Authorities

The distinction between AI-assisted and AI-generated outputs has not featured prominently in the resolution of concrete cases brought before national authorities. Indeed, in the early proceedings that are emerging, administrative and judicial bodies – although acknowledging the need to take into account any use of the AI system as an assistive tool – tend to base their evaluation of copyright eligibility for AI-based outputs on concrete, fact-specific considerations that often bypass the need to formally classify the work as either "AI-assisted" or "AI-generated".

Instead, the focus is typically placed on assessing the nature and quality of the human contribution to the creative process. One of the first institutional bodies to develop a line of decisions in this area has been the US Copyright Office. Its position has been articulated through a series of key determinations on the copyrightability of works created with the assistance of AI, including cases involving the digital image "A Recent Entrance to Paradise" in February 2021;[645] the graphic novel "Zarya of the Dawn" in February 2023;[646] the digital art piece "Théâtre D'opéra Spatial" in September 2023;[647] and the two-dimensional graphic work titled "Suryast", in December of the same year.[648] These cases remain among the most prominent to date, and the list continues to grow as new applications for the registration of AI-based works are submitted and reviewed at an accelerating pace. As the first occasions globally in which a public authority has taken a stance on these issues, these cases warrant a brief discussion before delving into a more systematic doctrinal analysis of the protection of AI-based outputs.

In particular, the "A Recent Entrance to Paradise" case – which involved the so-called "Creativity Machine" developed by engineer Stephen Thaler[649] – deserves special attention, as it marked the US Copyright Office's first formal decision on an AI-based work.

The case originated in 2018, when Thaler submitted an application to register the image with the USCO, designating the Creativity Machine as the author

645 A Recent Entrance to Paradise (n 135).

646 Zarya of the Dawn (n 136).

647 Théâtre D'opéra Spatial (n 635).

648 US Copyright Office Review Board, letter of 11 December 2023, no 1-5PR2XKJ (Suryast) <https://www.copyright.gov/rulings-filings/review-board/docs/SURYAST.pdf>.

649 Stephen Thaler is also known for the DABUS system, through which he has challenged multiple jurisdictions to recognize AI-generated outputs under various intellectual property regimes, including patents and copyright. See www.artificialinventor.com.

and himself as the claimant, by virtue of his ownership of the AI model. The image – described by Thaler as a depiction of the afterlife, generated through the simulation of a near-death experience – was rejected on the grounds that it lacked human creative contribution, and thus could not qualify for copyright protection under US law.[650]

Following the initial refusal, Thaler appealed to the USCO Review Board, advancing two arguments: first, that US law does not explicitly exclude works created by AI from copyright protection; and second, that even non-human legal entities, such as corporations, are normally allowed to hold copyrights, and thus AI-based outputs should be afforded similar recognition. The Review Board upheld the USCO's initial decision, affirming that copyright protection requires a contribution from a natural person and that a link between human intellect and creative expression is always indispensable. Addressing Thaler's first argument, the Board reiterated that under the US Copyright Act, protection is limited to "original works of authorship". As for the second claim, the Board dismissed the analogy between AI systems and corporate entities, noting that unlike AI, corporations can enter into legal agreements and assume responsibilities under contract law. The matter eventually reached the US federal courts, first the District Court of Columbia[651] and then the Court of Appeals for the District of Columbia Circuit[652] which – respectively in August 2023 and March 18, 2025 – confirmed the position previously taken by the US Copyright Office and upheld the denial of Stephen Thaler's application to register the work, reaffirming that, under the Copyright Act of 1976, copyright protection is reserved for works originally created by a human being.[653]

This case is interesting because it reflects the effort by the US authorities (USCO and judicial courts) to maintain the integrity and coherence of copyright law in an era increasingly influenced by post-human creative processes.

---

650 A Recent Entrance to Paradise (n 135).

651 <https://www.wipo.int/wipolex/en/judgments/details/1840>; see also US District Court for The District of Columbia, Thaler v. Perlmutter, et. al., no. 22-1564 (BAH). For further discussion, see Campus G, 'Artificial Intelligence, Machine Learning and Creativity in Visual Art: What Are the Protectability Requirements? Part 1: The Italian Supreme Court's "Floral Fractal" Case' (5 September 2023) Kluwer Copyright Blog <https://copyrightblog.kluweriplaw.com/2023/09/05/artificial-intelligence-machine-learning-and-creativity-in-visual-art-what-are-the-protectability-requirements-part-1-the-italian-supreme-courts-floral-fractal-case/> accessed 9 August 2025.

652 <https://media.cadc.uscourts.gov/opinions/docs/2025/03/23-5233.pdf>.

653 In this occasion, the Court expressly affirmed that "copyright law protects only works of human creation", and that "human authorship is a bedrock requirement of copyright" (Thaler v. Perlmutter, 687 F. Supp. 3d 140, 142 (D.D.C. 2023).

For this reason, it has been regarded as significant primarily in terms of legal principle.[654] Nonetheless, according to some commentators, the practical implications of this human authorship requirement, as affirmed in the case, are relatively limited. As Judge Millett noted, the decision does not prevent the protection of works created with the assistance of artificial intelligence: it just moves the reflections on identifying the human individual who designed, operated, or employed the AI system[655]— thus bringing the analysis back to the starting point of our analysis.

Another noteworthy case is that of the graphic novel "Zarya of the Dawn", for which the USCO decided to partially revoke the initially granted copyright registration after learning, via social media, that the images had been generated using an AI system. The Office limited protection to the literary elements of the work and their composition with the visual components, treating the "selection and arrangement of the images and text in the Work" as a compilation. In contrast, it denied protection for the Midjourney-generated images, on the grounds that they lacked sufficient human modification to meet the minimum threshold of creativity.

The USCO maintained this same restrictive approach in the "Théâtre D'opéra Spatial" case, refusing registration for the image – also generated via Midjourney – even though the applicant claimed to have submitted 624 prompts and further edited the output using Photoshop and Gigapixel AI. The primary reasons given were the applicant's failure to disclose the algorithmic origin of the image and the resulting impossibility of clearly distinguishing the human contribution from that of the AI.

This case illustrates that, for the USCO, the (high) number of human interventions – a quantitative criterion – in the creative process (624 prompts, along with further edits) is not sufficient to consider the output copyrightable and, rather, a qualitative assessment of the human input is necessary. In this specific case, it was found that "the steps in that process were ultimately dependent on how the Midjourney system processed Mr. Allen's prompts".[656]

Another case placed specific emphasis, similarly to this one, on the exploration of the iterative process between the human being and the machine. It was decided in December 2023 and concerned the registration of a two-dimensional graphic work titled "Suryast". The work was the result of an AI-

---

654 Blaszczyk M, 'Thaler v Perlmutter: Human Authors at the Center of Copyright?' (Legal Blogs, 8 April 2025) <https://legalblogs.wolterskluwer.com/copyright-blog/thaler-v-perlmutter-human-authors-at-the-center-of-copyright/#:~:text=On%20March%2018%2C%202025%2C%20the,be%20authored%20in%20the%20first>.

655 Blaszczyk (n 654).

656 Théâtre D'opéra Spatial (n 635), 6.

based process in which an AI system named "RAGHAV" was used to merge Vincent van Gogh's famous painting "The Starry Night" with an original photograph by Ankit Sahni – the applicant – depicting a sunset. The only additional input provided by Sahni was a numerical value indicating the degree of stylistic influence Van Gogh's painting should exert on the final image.

Although Mr. Sahni acknowledged the AI system as a co-author, both the US Copyright Office and its Review Board denied the application for registration, determining that the human input did not meet the minimum level of creativity required for copyright protection. According to their assessment, the algorithm – rather than the human – was chiefly responsible for the final outcome. Because US copyright law currently excludes non-human authorship, the work was considered to be in the public domain.

All these decisions reflect a growing tendency within the USCO to adopt a proceduralized approach to creativity, almost placing an obligation on authors to document the iterative stages of their creative process to obtain copyright protection.

This trend can be explained by the requirement to "identify the nature and origin of the creative choices, if any", in order to determine "the subsistence of copyright during an infringement case".[657] From this perspective, such proceduralization may be the only workable approach to ensure a minimum level of legal certainty, especially given the complex and multifaceted nature of copyrightability when it comes to AI-generated outputs. However, as some commentators have noted, this approach could conflict with the principle that "authors" should not be obliged to "disclose or document their creative process to be granted copyright protection", since the creation of the work alone – at least when done through traditional means[658] – should suffice.

That said, similar decisions on the matter have taken a different direction in other jurisdictions. In contrast to the generally restrictive stance of the USCO, the Beijing Internet Court has adopted a more receptive approach to AI-based processes in 2023, recognizing copyright protection for an image generated using Stable Diffusion.[659]

The case concerned an image that the defendant had published on his blog after removing the watermark and without the author's consent. The plaintiff

---

657 Bulayenko, Quintais, Gervais and Poort (n 604) 75.

658 Ibid.

659 For a commentary on this, see Wang Y and Zhang J, 'Beijing Internet Court Grants Copyright to AI-Generated Image for the First Time' (Legal Blogs, 2 February 2024) <https://legalblogs.wolterskluwer.com/copyright-blog/beijing-internet-court-grants-copyright-to-ai-generated-image-for-the-first-time/>. See also Iaia, Klein and De Gaspari (n 613).

successfully brought an infringement claim, arguing that the image was entitled to copyright protection in his favor, and the court awarded damages in the amount of 500 CNY.

The court applied a four-element test to determine whether the disputed image constitutes a work under Chinese Copyright Law: (i) belonging to the fields of literature, art, or science; (ii) possessing originality; (iii) having a form of expression; and (iv) being a result of "intellectual achievement". By focusing on the "intellectual achievement" and "originality" elements, the court considered that the plaintiff's intellectual effort resided in the selection of the initial prompts, the adjustment of parameters to tailor the output to the desired result, and the choice of the final image – a discretionary and creative decision that marked the end of the production process. In support of his claim, the plaintiff submitted the original prompt along with 120 additional prompts used in post-production.

The court emphasized that machines remain instruments of human creativity, and that the decisive factor is the presence of sufficient human intervention in the creative process. This decision aligns with an earlier ruling from 2019, in which the Nanshan District People's Court recognized copyright protection for an article generated by Dreamwriter, an AI system designed to produce literary content. In that case, the court found that the article was the product of a form of creative collaboration involving the programmers and data curators ("feeders") who had developed and operated Dreamwriter. Emphasizing the central role of human involvement in the generation of the text, the court held that Article 11 of the Chinese Copyright Law was applicable. This provision attributes authorship to the individual(s) under whose intention, direction, and responsibility the intellectual work is created.[660]

In EU, too, the debate surrounding the copyrightability of AI-generated outputs is beginning to gain traction in case law – and the emerging position appears cautious, yet nonetheless somehow aligned with the abstract possibility to grant copyright protection to creative AI-based outputs. A notable example is an Italian Court of Cassation's judgment that had the opportunity to address for the first time in Italy the recognition of a digital work created with the aid of a software as an intellectual work. In Order No. 1107 of 16 January 2023,[661] the Italian Supreme Court was called upon to decide whether an

660 Iaia, Klein and De Gaspari (n 613).

661 C. Cass., 16 January 2023, no. 1107. On this point, see Campus, 'Artificial Intelligence, Machine Learning and Creativity in Visual Art' (n 651; see also Traina Chiarini R, 'Può essere protetta l'opera creata da A.I.? La questione arriva in Cassazione' (1 March 2023) Quotidiano Più <www.altalex.com> accessed 9 August 2025: "With Order No. 1107 of 16 January 2023 the Court of Cassation confirmed the rulings of the judges on the merits,

output created with the aid of a graphic software could be attributed the character of creativity. The Court described creativity as the "personal and individual expression of an objectivity belonging to the categories listed, by way of example, in Article 1 of the Italian Copyright Act". The case involved RAI, the Italian national broadcaster, which had been accused of unlawfully reproducing a visual artwork depicting a flower – created by the claimant using the said software – during the broadcast of the 2016 Sanremo Music Festival. Both the Court of Genoa and the Court of Appeal had found the reproduction to be unlawful, and the Cassation Court confirmed these findings. Arguing that "the image was not a mere reproduction of a flower, but involved a genuine reworking of it", the Italian Court of Cassation held that the lower courts had provided sufficient justification for its finding of creativity in this image. However, some of the factors cited in support of that finding raise questions as to their actual relevance to the concept of creativity. These included the circumstance that users had responded positively to the image; that the image had gained online visibility, evidenced by a high number of views, likes, and comments; and that RAI itself had implicitly acknowledged its symbolic value by highlighting it as a representation of the event. Whether such elements are genuinely indicative of creative authorship is, at the very least, debatable.

However, although the Court ruled on the matter only incidentally,[662] it made an important statement regarding the use of software in the creative process: the use of such tools is "certainly not sufficient" to disqualify a work as lacking creativity. Rather, the Court suggested that it simply requires a "more rigorous scrutiny of the degree of creativity" in order to assess whether, and to what extent, the use of the tool has supplanted or absorbed the human author's own creative elaboration. Accordingly, the Court concluded that, insofar as the human contribution can be shown to prevail over the role of

---

the Court of First Instance and the Court of Appeal of Genoa, and rejected the appeal of RAI Radiotelevisione Italiana S.p.A, considering the work 'The Scent of the Night', created by a young Genoese architect and used by RAI as the set design of the Sanremo Festival in 2016, as an original work deserving of copyright protection whose reproduction without authorisation constituted an infringement of the author's rights. In fact, the Supreme Court recognised that the work in question, consisting of a digital image with a 'fractal' floral subject matter, i.e. 'characterised by self-similarity, i.e. by the repetition of its forms on different scales of size', was sufficiently creative and original, in that it was capable of 'reflecting the personality of its author, manifesting his free and creative choices', and that the set design of the festival took up this work, thereby commercially exploiting it".

662 RAI's grievance on the erroneous classification of the image in question as an intellectual work for its being generated by a software was raised for the first time before the court of Cassation and therefore deemed inadmissible from a procedural point of view.

the software, there is no reason to deny copyright protection to the individual who made use of such a tool in the creation of the work.

2 Is It Possible to Protect AI-Generated Outputs under Copyright Law?

To draw a line through the discussion above, the distinction between AI-assisted and AI-generated outputs is central to most theoretical analyses and has played a key role in shaping initial regulatory responses to the phenomenon. However, framing this distinction solely in terms of the AI system's autonomy tends to place excessive emphasis on the quantity of human contribution, rather than on the more relevant question of the evaluation of its quality – namely, whether the input is creative or non-creative within the specific process. This approach also overlooks the fact that certain "original" outputs – despite involving a quantitatively significant human contribution – may not be deemed creative, and vice versa.[663]

So far, judicial authorities have preferred to adopt a case-by-case approach to this subject-matter, which has at times been more permissive, and at other times more restrictive. Nevertheless, a more systematic reflection on the copyright status of AI-based outputs is needed. Such a reflection would help guide legal responses not only in clear-cut cases where AI is used purely as an assistive tool, but also in more ambiguous scenarios: i.e. those in which AI-based outputs fall into the grey area between AI-assisted and AI-generated works - and ultimately occupy a space between what can be considered "creative expressions of ideas" and "free ideas". Indeed, many AI-created works exist along a spectrum, resulting from the iterative human use of AI tools, and do not fit neatly into this binary classification.[664] The US Copyright Office itself acknowledges this complexity in Part 2 of its Report on Artificial Intelligence and Copyright, where it emphasizes that between the two poles (AI as a tool supporting human creativity and AI as a substitute for it) lies a broad spectrum of intermediate cases. Each, it stresses, requires a careful, context-specific assessment based on the particular facts of the case.[665]

663 To agree with such a statement, it suffices to consider that the condition of originality has been recognized by the CJEU even in products of very low creative value, "as long as there is creative human intervention in the final result"; see Geiger, 'Elaborating a Human Rights Friendly Copyright Framework' (n 321) 14.

664 Lucchi and Hunter (n 487).

665 US Copyright Office, Copyright and Artificial Intelligence: Part 2 (n 367) 12.

The following reflections examine the terms of the ongoing debate within legal scholarship concerning "fully generated" and "hybrid" outputs – both of which will be collectively referred to as "AI-generated works" unless otherwise specified – since, as seen, the "clear-cut cases" of AI-assisted outputs generally do not raise significant legal challenges in the context of copyright protection. For the purposes of this analysis, AI-generated outputs will include not only those created through fully automated processes involving no human intervention (to the extent such full autonomy is even possible), but also those in which human involvement is present but questionably creative/original in comparison to the threshold required under existing copyright standards (the paradigmatic example being the human limited to "pushing the button"). Accordingly, the category of AI-generated content, as used here, also encompasses those cases in which the human contribution is neither clearly identifiable nor entirely absent, due to a dominant role played by the software.[666]

This broad definition will be adopted to underscore the fact that, from a copyright law perspective, systematic considerations should take into account not only works "entirely" - if they ever exist - generated by AI, but also hybrid outputs that fall along the spectrum of human–AI collaboration (which could be seemingly "original" but not in the meaning understood in continental authors' right traditions).

2.1 Public Domain, Copyright Law, and Other Nuances

According to a first perspective, aligned with an approach that emphasizes the centrality of the human person, AI-generated creations cannot and should not be granted copyright protection.

Specifically, in light of the personalistic principle,[667] it would be undesirable to adopt interpretations of copyright law that disregard, on the one hand, the necessary presence of a human author in relation to creative works, and on the other, the traditional meaning attributed to the concept of originality and creativity.

---

666 It is what some scholars have termed AI-genassisted works, which, for the purposes of this analysis, fall within the notion of AI-generated content: AI-genassisted works "stand in the middle among AI-assisted and AI-generated works (...). They are in the blurred territory between, respectively, clear human intervention and its absence due to the predominant role played by the software. This is the case, for instance, with works created using AIVA, an AI-based software that generates music". See Iaia, 'To Be, or Not to Be...Original Under Copyright Law' (n 420).

667 As well as the "principle of human primacy"; see Bensamoun and Farchy (n 4) 26.

Indeed, at a European Union level, among the objectives of the EU agenda in this area is not only the aim of ensuring a "high level of protection" for intellectual property rights in order to promote culture, but also the goal of preserving an anthropocentric approach to AI, ensuring that it complies with ethical principles and human rights, and that it "remains an instrument at the service of people and the common good".[668]

As early as 2015, Stefano Rodotà warned against "inadequately channelled innovation",[669] emphasizing that, when it comes to transformations driven by profit or interests concerning individuals, the response cannot be entrusted to artificial intelligence, but must come from collective intelligence, hence from politics and the decisions it is called upon to make.

Within this framework, according to which granting protection to AI-generated outputs would not be desirable, some scholars argue that such works should, in any case, be considered part of the public domain[670] and, where necessary, they suggest that legal instruments outside the scope of intellectual property law should be employed instead.

Treating AI-generated outputs as belonging to the public domain in all cases is a solution that certainly has the merit of preserving the integrity of traditional copyright categories – such as "work", "creativity/originality", "author", and "creative process" – by preventing their instrumentalization. It also takes a principled stance against an uncritical expansion of intellectual property rights.

---

668 European Parliament, 'Report on Intellectual Property Rights for the Development of Artificial Intelligence Technologies' (Committee on Legal Affairs, 2 October 2020) <https://www.europarl.europa.eu/doceo/document/A-9-2020-0176_EN.html> 5.

669 As pointed out by Grieco M (https://www.linkiesta.it/2021/02/etica-intelligenza-artificiale-diritto-tecnologia), "Rodotà warned against inadequately channelled innovation. For him, the only solution to a drift that, in the name of progress, de-responsibilises man, is law. Europe has long been moving in this direction. Unlike in the United States or Asia, the European Parliament has, over the years, embarked on a regulatory path to regulate the use of AI and analyse its economic impact. In addition to ensuring development in line with the rest of the world – in Europe, an investment in AI is estimated at between EUR 2.4 and 3.2 billion – the EU is including in the debate issues related to ethics, responsibility and rights, such as property rights: in this way, not only is awareness of the tool created, but trust is instilled in citizens and an awareness that takes personal freedoms into account".

670 For a defense of the public domain solution, see, *inter alia*, Kop (n 385); Stokes S, 'Art and Copyright: Some Current Issues' (2006) 1(4) Journal of Intellectual Property Law & Practice, 277; De Cock Buning M, 'Artificial Intelligence and the Creative Industry: New Challenges for the EU Paradigm for Art and Technology by Autonomous Creation' in Barfield W and Pagallo U (eds), Research Handbook on the Law of Artificial Intelligence (Edward Elgar 2018) 529 ff. *Amplius*, Boyle J, 'The Second Enclosure Movement and the Construction of the Public Domain' (2003) 66 Law and Contemporary Problems 33.

Moreover, this represents the most "guarantor" option for protecting the current legal framework, particularly within legal traditions that adhere to a personalistic – even romantic[671] – conception of copyright, such as authors' rights systems.[672]

Furthermore, some argue that placing AI-generated outputs in the public domain would help counterbalance the risks associated with an overly broad protection, namely, the risks that, with copyright umbrella protection to such productions, entire sectors of the creative industry could be displaced and become the exclusive domain of AI systems.[673]

Given AI's vast productive capacity, which can generate huge quantities of content at high speed and low cost, this could, in this view, result in a saturated copyright landscape, leaving limited creative space for human authors. Such a development could have a chilling effect on human creativity – by undermining authors' ability to earn from their creative work, for instance – and undermine long-term cultural production.[674]

To cite the USCO, in Part 2 of the Report on Artificial Intelligence and Copyright, "there are already indications that AI-generated content has impacted some creators' ability to be compensated for their work. Musicians and songwriters, for instance, have been impacted by the proliferation of AI-generated content on streaming services. UMG reported that 'content over-supply', produced by an estimated 170 million AI-generated music tracks, currently threatens to dilute human creators' royalties. AI-generated works have also threatened to reduce the pool of royalties available to human creators through the Mechanical Licensing Collective".[675]

That said, according to a certain perspective, the scope of the public domain – the "mirror image" of copyright – should be defined in the negative; that is, by identifying what is not eligible for copyright protection.[676]

---

671 Ajani, 'Contemporary Artificial Art and the Law' (n 321).

672 Hartmann et al (n 228) 69.

673 With reference to music, see Bensamoun and Farchy (n 4) 25.

674 Geiger, 'Elaborating a Human Rights Friendly Copyright Framework' (n 321) 17.

675 US Copyright Office, Copyright and Artificial Intelligence: Part 2 (n 367) 37.

676 Ciani Sciolla J, Il pubblico dominio nella società della conoscenza. L'interesse generale al libero utilizzo del capitale intellettuale comune (Giappichelli 2021). Notably, however, « *Valérie-Laure Benabou écrit notamment que " Les exceptions apparaissent en effet, et de plus en plus, non comme un simple 'négatif' des droits conférés au plan individuel au titulaire, mais en tant que véritable système d'organisation alternatif au droit exclusif et collectiviste* », in Rochfeld J, Martin GJ and Cornu M, L'échelle de communalité. Proposition de réformes pour intégrer les biens communs en droit, Rapport finale della «Mission de Recherche. Droit & Justice» (2021) 57.

This includes works or sets of information that are freely accessible to anyone with an interest in them, "either because they do not meet the requirement of originality (ontological public domain) or because the term of protection has expired (temporal public domain)".[677] This therefore would include not only the cases envisaged by the legislator in which the exceptions and limitations of copyright apply (functional public domain), but also those that originate from private autonomy as a result of the owner's adherence to free exploitation regimes of the work characterized by different levels of openness (e.g. *copyleft* licenses – the so-called voluntary public domain).[678]

Thus conceived, the public domain could be regarded as the default option for AI-generated works – for sure the preferable one for all the outputs that are the result of a generative AI fully automated process:[679] a work created "solely"[680] by an AI should certainly be excluded from copyright protection.

However, this is not true for "hybrid" works, which could well fall within the scope of copyright instead, depending on where the threshold for the "sufficient human involvement" is set, "provided, of course, that the criteria of originality and existence of the creative choices are met".[681]

It is precisely in that "provided that" where the most critical tension lies. Advocating an automatic placement of all AI-generated outputs into the public domain leaves, in fact, several key questions unresolved: Which ones? What does "solely created" mean? What about outputs in the grey area? When can AI be considered a mere tool?

Again, the problematic point here is not so much whether the AI has "solely" created the work (in which case, notwithstanding some opposing views, it is normally accepted that copyright would not apply[682]), but rather how to determine – even in principle, if that is ever possible, and not merely

677 Iaia, 'Le derive della creatività nel diritto d'autore' (n 355); see also Dusollier S, 'Scoping Study on Copyright and Related Rights and the Public Domain' (WIPO 2010) CDIP/4/3/REV./STUDY/INF/1, 6, according to whom "The public domain is generally defined as encompassing intellectual elements that are not protected by copyright or whose protection has lapsed, due to the expiration of the duration for protection".

678 Lombardi EM, 'Innovazione digitale e incidenza sul paradigma proprietario: notazioni sul fenomeno "copyleft"' in Diritto privato. Nuovi orizzonti (Edizioni Scientifiche Italiane 2020).

679 Geiger, 'Elaborating a Human Rights Friendly Copyright Framework' (n 321) 12 ff.

680 Interestingly enough, the term used by Geiger ('Elaborating a Human Rights Friendly Copyright Framework' (n 321) 12 ff.) is reminiscent, and not surprisingly, of the term used in Article 22 of Regulation (EU) No. 2016/679.

681 "If a work solely created by an AI cannot be protected by copyright, works for which the creators use the AI as a tool in the production process can be, provided of course that the conditions of originality and the existence of creative choices are met"; see Geiger, 'Elaborating a Human Rights Friendly Copyright Framework' (n 321) 12 ff.

682 *Inter alia*, see ultimately Lucchi and Hunter (n 487).

on a case-by-case basis – when AI functions as a tool and when it effectively replaces human creative activity.

In short, the option that denies *tout court* copyright protection to AI-based outputs carries the drawback of leaving these fundamental questions unanswered, at least with regard to works in the grey zone. This perspective defers the resolution of these issues either to a later moment (increasingly imminent), or relies on a highly granular, case-by-case assessment, thereby postponing the necessary development of a more comprehensive and principled legal response.

In any case, even setting aside the considerations discussed above, this solution presents two additional, indirect, drawbacks related to the blanket non-recognition of AI-generated outputs as creative or original under copyright law. First, it risks incentivizing the creation of exclusivity over such outputs through mechanisms of private autonomy, such as contractual agreements or technological restrictions.[683] Second, given the increasing difficulty of distinguishing between traditional (human-created) works and AI-generated outputs, creators who make use of generative AI tools might be disincentivized from disclosing their use of these technologies, particularly in the absence of any legal protection. Even if a transparency obligation were imposed *ex lege* (as envisioned, for instance, by the AI Act), ensuring effective enforcement would be highly challenging in practice.

For these and other reasons, those who oppose the public domain perspective argue that a total denial of protection for AI-generated works is not a realistic option.[684]

First and foremost, denying protection to AI-based content has been deemed implausible given that (i) works created by artificial intelligence are, at present, clearly economic goods; and (ii) the interests surrounding such works could arguably merit protection – in the EU context, for example, in light of the objectives set out in both the European Intellectual Property Agenda and broader AI policy.

Furthermore, arguments in favor of granting protection to AI-generated outputs highlight that the use of AI in the cultural sector does not necessarily hinder creativity and, in fact, it may enhance it.[685] For example, in the music

683 In that case, remedies of a contractual nature could apply; see Ricolfi M, 'Il diritto della proprietà intellettuale nella società algoritmica: fra metamorfosi e continuità' (2022) AIDA.

684 Ramalho A, 'Ex Machina, Ex Auctore? Machines That Create and How EU Copyright Law Views Them' (2018) <http://copyrightblog.kluweriplaw.com/2018/11/12/ex-machina-ex-auctore-machines-that-create-and-how-eu-copyright-law-views-them/> accessed 9 August 2025.

685 Bensamoun and Farchy (n 4) 25.

industry, it has been suggested that AI systems could serve as "untapped sources of inspiration", encourage unprecedented forms of "dialogue between the musician and the machine",[686] and expand access to creative tools.

It has also been argued that "undoubtedly, these new techniques open the way to uncharted territories in terms of creative explorations, not only to the experienced composer but, also, to the untrained amateur".[687] Even those with minimal musical training may be able to produce enjoyable compositions – so much so that AI music composers may inspire millions of music consumers to start creating their own songs.[688]

Based on these premises, among those who advocate for the protection of AI-generated outputs, some propose complementary reforms (*de iure condendo*), while others support the application of existing legal frameworks (*de iure condito*). Within the latter perspective, two main options are worth highlighting and will be further developed in the following paragraphs: (i) the application of copyright law (quasi) in its existing form, though with a modified function; and (ii) the possibility of relying on existing related rights legislation;[689] while, those who argue for *de iure condendo* solutions primarily advance the idea of introducing a *sui generis* right for AI-generated outputs.

Before delving into these positions in greater detail, it must be acknowledged, however, that more moderate positions exist between those advocating these solutions and those supporting the inclusion of AI-generated content in the public domain. These intermediate views favor alternative forms of protection.[690]

On the side of those opposing protection for AI-generated outputs, for example, some argue for applying to the phenomenon the paradigm of competition law[691] or the protections offered against unfair competition,[692] including for slavish imitation and parasitic conduct. Proponents of this

---

686 Deltorn and Macrez (n 44) 6.

687 Ibid.

688 Ibid.

689 Ramalho, 'Ex Machina, Ex Auctore?' (n 684); as well as Hartmann et al (n 228).

690 Ajani, 'Contemporary Artificial Art and the Law' (n 321).

691 Colangelo G, 'A Competition Policy Analysis of Copyright Protection in Generative AI' (Singapore Journal of Legal Studies, 2 April 2025) <https://ssrn.com/abstract=5201510> or <http://dx.doi.org/10.2139/ssrn.5201510>. Notably, however, in Andersen v. Stability AI Ltd., Judge William H. Orrick III dismissed the plaintiffs' unfair competition claims, noting that they were preempted by the Copyright Act and that the plaintiffs had failed to allege plausible facts in support of their theory that users of a text-to-image model could be deceived. See No. 23-CV-00201, 2023 WL 7132064, at *14 (N.D. Cal. Oct. 30, 2023).

692 Foong C, 'GenAI Models and Copyright Infringement: Doctrinal Challenges and Regulatory Gap-Filling Using Unfair Competition Principles' (2025) 48(4) University of New

approach contend that competition rules can serve as an effective governance tool to prevent free riding by third parties. Nevertheless, reliance on competition law or on unfair-competition remedies, even where these can operate alongside other legal frameworks does not resolve the normative question of whether specific protection for AI-generated creations is desirable or necessary (also) from a copyright perspective.

On the side of those who argue for some form of legal protection, although outside the framework of copyright and related rights, an alternative position worth noting is the suggestion that trade secret law could be applied to AI-generated content. However, this approach appears unconvincing in the context under consideration. AI-generated outputs, especially in the context in which they are often produced (e.g., user-generated content platforms), are generally intended for widespread dissemination. Their economic value lies precisely in their potential for broad circulation. By contrast, trade secret protection requires that the protected information: (i) is secret – that is, not generally known or readily accessible to experts in the field; (ii) is subject to reasonable measures taken by those in lawful control of the information to maintain its secrecy; and (iii) derives economic value specifically from its secrecy.[693]

2.2 The *De Lege Lata* Solutions

2.2.1 An (Almost) Classic Copyright

2.2.1.1 The Abstract Viability of the Copyright Solution

A part of the legal scholarship argues that AI-generated outputs should be granted copyright protection either in their own right or, alternatively, as an "extension" of the generative software that produced them.[694] If protected as

South Wales Law Journal (forthcoming) <https://ssrn.com/abstract=5327096> or <http://dx.doi.org/10.2139/ssrn.5327096>.

693 Art. 2(1) of Directive (EU) 2016/942. More generally; see Iaia, 'Le derive della creatività nel diritto d'autore' (n 355).

694 Hristov K, 'Artificial Intelligence and the Copyright Dilemma' (2017) 57(3) IDEA: The IP Law Review 453. However, the protection of the outputs as part of the AI software is difficult to endorse. While some scholars argue that such a solution could encourage investment in the "creative" capacities of artificial intelligence, it is essential to recall that the object of copyright protection is fundamentally different: in the case of software, protection applies to the source code itself, not to its generative potential. The latter must be regarded as a mere idea – something that, by its nature, is not subject to copyright protection unless it is concretely expressed in a perceivable form.

such, a further strengthening of the legal framework would, in this view, not only be possible, but also desirable.

Granting full copyright protection to AI outputs as such, they contend, should be done – if for no other reason – on the basis of the principle of technological neutrality and, more broadly, the principle of non-discrimination between intellectual works.[695]

According to these principles, works of a creative nature should be protected under copyright law "regardless of the mode or form of expression". Indeed, as previously noted, from an "objective" standpoint, AI-generated products are often indistinguishable from "traditional" creative works. As stated in the January 2020 report by the French *Conseil supérieur de la propriété littéraire et artistique* (CSPLA) on artificial intelligence and culture, the output of an AI system constitutes *"une réalisation culturelle qui ressemble à une œuvre"*. The principle of non-discrimination between different kinds of intellectual works is enshrined in the positive law of several legal systems. For instance, Article 1(1) of the Italian Copyright Law, as amended by Law No. 132/2025, provides that "works of the human mind of a creative nature belonging to literature, music, the visual arts, architecture, theatre, and cinematography, whatever the mode or form of expression even where created with the aid of artificial-intelligence tools are protected under this law". Similarly, in the French system, Article L112-1 of the Intellectual Property Code states: "The provisions of this Code protect authors' rights over all works of the mind, regardless of their genre, form of expression, merit, or purpose".[696] This principle excludes the possibility of differentiating the level of protection afforded to works based on their genre, mode of expression, merit, or intended use. This same logic finds further support in current case law concerning works created using more traditional tools, where courts have increasingly ruled against infringers even in cases involving works of trivial or low-level originality.[697] Indeed, the threshold of originality has been so diluted – with AI-based creativity arguably exceeding the average human standard found in the trivial works that have received copyright protection thus far – that, on this reasoning, protection could in principle extend even to the results of automated processes.

However, the application of (quasi) unchanged copyright to works of AI has also been considered a viable path for other reasons. First, it would align with the EU's objective of ensuring strong (and extended) protection of intellectual prop-

695 Bensamoun and Farchy (n 4) 26 and 31.

696 Article L112-1: *"Les dispositions du présent code protègent les droits des auteurs sur toutes les œuvres de l'esprit, quels qu'en soient le genre, la forme d'expression, le mérite ou la destination"*.

697 Iaia, 'To Be, or Not to Be…Original Under Copyright Law' (n 420).

erty, and because, as some argue, the original rationale behind the introduction of copyright law was more concerned with the monopoly over the distribution of intellectual works than with the protection of authors themselves.[698]

Indeed, as a significant part of legal scholarship has pointed out, copyright did not historically emerge as a right aimed at protecting personalistic interests – even though its object has traditionally been "pure works of art"[699] that arguably bear a connection to their human creator: at its early-modern origins, in the age of printing privileges, copyright was not concerned with fostering intellectual creativity or originality of expression. Rather, it was shaped more by the logic of "publication" than by that of "authorship".[700] The first forms of protection for authors' intellectual creativity began to emerge only after the liberal revolutions that prompted the reform of absolutist states between the eighteenth and nineteenth centuries. This period witnessed, among other developments, the rise of natural law claims asserting that individuals should have a right to the products of their creative work. At the same time, the idea took hold that the "cultural progress of the governed" in the newly emerging states should be actively promoted.[701] It was only with the Industrial Revolution of the nineteenth century, that growing attention was devoted, even within copyright law, to the development of theories centered on the flourishing of human personality rights.[702]

Second, the application of copyright to AI-generated outputs is considered possible in light of the paradigmatic precedent set by the recognition of photographic works as copyright-protected subject matter. Although legal scholarship initially expressed skepticism about whether photographic works truly involved creative input or could meaningfully enrich the cultural heritage,[703] it was ultimately accepted that such works do contribute to it and that the use of a camera cannot be viewed as a disruptive element in the creative process.

That said, determining whether the "classic" rules of copyright law can be applied to AI-based outputs requires a case-by-case analysis – an approach that, as the case law above illustrates, seems unavoidable, although some higher-level principles would be desirable from a systemic perspective. Cer-

698 Ardizzone et al. (n 183).

699 Di Cataldo, 1991, 21, cited in De Sanctis (n 462) 571–572.

700 Clerico G and Rizzello S (eds), Diritto ed economia della proprietà intellettuale (CEDAM 1998) 70 ff.; Bertani M, Diritto d'autore europeo (Giappichelli 2011).

701 Bertani M, Diritto d'autore europeo (Giappichelli 2011) 10.

702 In particular, this period witnessed the emergence of political and cultural movements which, while advocating for more efficient forms of appropriation consistent with the capitalist market economy, also called for increasingly robust protection of authors' personal interests; see Bertani, Diritto d'autore europeo (n 701) 27–28.

703 De Sanctis (n 462) 58.

tainly, protection must be excluded whenever the work is the result of merely technical human intervention. However, in cases involving highly automated creative processes, drawing a clear line between technical and creative human input remains complex. For example, a relatively trivial yet "original" work may emerge from a sophisticated prompt, even though its creation may ultimately be the outcome of a largely random operation performed by the AI.

It could be debated (and indeed it has been) whether randomness should be seen as a disruptive element in the assessment of originality. However, many scholars, aligning with the idea that originality requires a certain degree of control over the creative process,[704] argue that randomness can stand in the way of recognizing the free and creative choices necessary for a work to qualify as original.

2.2.1.2 The Originality Requirement for Copyright Protection

If an almost classical form of copyright were to be recognized for AI-generated outputs, some brief considerations should be made regarding the requirement that such outputs must satisfy in order to qualify for protection.

In most legal systems worldwide, the protection of an intellectual work is not subject to any constitutive formalities. A partial exception, as is well known, is the United States, where, for US intellectual works, registration with the Copyright Office is a prerequisite for initiating infringment proceedings.

In other legal systems, including that of the European Union, the mere creation of the work constitutes both a necessary and – unlike other exclusive rights in the field of intellectual property – a sufficient condition for copyright to arise.

As discussed in Chapter 6, creation has traditionally been understood to unfold through three phases of the creative process: the idea (conception), the expression of the idea (execution), and its externalization on a tangible medium (fixation).[705]

As for the externalization on a material support, as noted, the advent of the Internet has significantly challenged this third phase, giving rise to a new category of works that circulate without ever being fixed on any physical medium.[706]

Regarding instead the distinction between the first two phases of the process – which marks the dividing line between protectable expressions and

704 US Copyright Office, Copyright and Artificial Intelligence: Part 2 (n 367).
705 Ubertazzi (n 349) 1464.
706 Romano (n 350).

unprotectable ideas – this demarcation hinges on the fulfilment of the requirements for protection: the common feature of all copyright-protected creations is that they are, first and foremost, "works of the mind" endowed with originality or creativity.

Given the absence of constitutive formalities for the protection of intellectual works, the assessment of whether a given work meets the threshold of originality or creativity remains particularly relevant in operational terms.

In the continental European tradition, the requirement for access to copyright protection is manifested in the author's "free and creative choices", which function as non-dictated elements of the work.[707]

This notion goes beyond the mere effort or expertise (skill and labor) invested in the creation of a work, unless such factors are reflected – at the level of expressive form – in choices that manifest the author's personality (their "personal touch").[708] What is required is the presence of genuine creative freedom.[709]

It is worth noting that, in a seminal work from the 1990s, entitled Creativity in Context,[710] Amabile argued that for a work to be considered "creative", the process by which it is produced must itself be characterized by creativity. In her view, among the other conditions identified, the process must be heuristic, meaning that "the path to the outcome" must not be "clear and straightforward".[711] Accordingly, intellectual creations originate from a process that is at once technical – entailing the selection of ideas and materials – and idealistic, embodying the so-called creative spirit.

This element reflects the author's personal choices and is what makes an original work ontologically distinct from other legally regulated goods, even when the result stems from a mechanical or automated "creative" process. According to this perspective, it is "the very process of creating the work, of which the result is only the end point, the expression"[712] – rather than its specific characteristics – that determines whether the work can be considered creative.[713]

---

707 Fabbio (n 360) 290.

708 Case C-145/10 Eva-Maria Painer v Standard VerlagsGmbH and Others [2011] ECR I-12533, para 92.

709 Joined Cases C-403/08 and C-429/08 Football Association Premier League Ltd and Others v QC Leisure and Others [2011] ECR I-9083 (FAPL), paras. 98 et seq.

710 Amabile (n 359), building on her earlier "The Social Psychology of Creativity" (1983).

711 Ramalho, 'Ex Machina, Ex Auctore?' (n 684).

712 Rossi, 'L'intelligenza artificiale e la definizione di "opera dell'ingegno"' (n 356) 275.

713 In this vein, the creativity of the artefact resides and must be assessed in the dimension of the process: it is, in fact, the latter upstream – which may be, depending on the case,

In light of the above, the question of whether AI-generated outputs can be protected under copyright law does not have a straightforward answer and requires an evaluation of whether the creative process is "heuristic enough", i.e. it is not subject to external constraints (rule-based, technical, functional, or informational),[714] nor entirely automated, and the human contribution is more than merely technical.

Moreover, the AI-based outputs should align with the existing case law on creativity. By way of example, it has been recognized that literary works may reflect creativity in the author's choice, arrangement, and combination of words;[715] photographic works may demonstrate it through specific compositional decisions, the use of lighting, or the characterization of the subject (such as pose or clothing);[716] databases, through the selection and organization of materials and the criteria used to structure the data;[717] and musical works, through the shaping of a melodic line, or the choice of a specific genre or rhythm.[718] Conversely, works in which the selection of elements is dictated exclusively by technical or functional constraints, leaving no room for creative freedom, are not considered creative (it is the so-called technical exclusion principle).[719] This includes, for example, creations whose form is entirely determined by utilitarian functions[720] or which follow standardized formats.[721]

This is by no means an easy assessment and will inevitably have to be conducted on a case-by-case basis, despite the need of legal certainty and of systematization of the entire framework.[722]

However, if copyright protection were ultimately to be recognized for such AI-generated works, certain systematic considerations would become neces-

---

creative or merely technical-mathematical – that defines, downstream, whether the work can be considered creative or not.

714 Hartmann et al (n 228) 69.

715 Case C-5/08 Infopaq International A/S v Danske Dagblades Forening [2009] ECR I-6569, para. 45: in the present case, the question was whether an extract of a press article amounting to only 11 consecutive words was a "partial reproduction" within the meaning of Article 2 of Directive No. 2001/29.

716 Opinion of the Court in Burrow-Giles Lithographic Co. v. Sarony, 111, U.S. 53.

717 Ubertazzi (n 349) 1690.

718 C App Milan, IP Section, 30 August 2010, *Universal Music Italia srl v Première Music sarl, Cywie, Rivière, Abramo Allione, Edizioni Musicali srl, Montagné and Barbelivien* in *AIDA* 2011, Repertory I.2.4.

719 Trib Milan, 4 June 2013, in www.iusexplorer.it.

720 Ubertazzi (n 349) 1468.

721 Trib Rome, 5 June 2008, in AIDA 10, 1330; Trib Milan, 26 February 1998, in AIDA 98, 884.

722 See Chapter 9.

sary. There is, in fact, a risk that the threshold for originality may come to be understood as progressively lower, or that its very nature may change, leading to a transformation of the concept in objective terms. This could be an indirect consequence of the emergence of AI systems that merely simulate creativity – traditionally conceived as the outward expression of the author's personality – yet are capable of producing outputs which, from an ostensibly objective perspective, are virtually indistinguishable from human-made works and may even appear original.[723] For the purposes of this analysis, as noted above, AI-generated works are the result of human input and labor, but do not necessarily serve as a blueprint of the author's personality. Consequently, classifying such work as original despite its being the outcome of an automated process could ultimately mark a rupture with the traditional conception of originality, rooted in the author's personal touch, and shift towards a more objective understanding that of a *"nouveauté dans l'univers des formes"*-[724] in which originality is treated as an intrinsic quality of the work rather than the subjective expression of the author's personality.

That would not be entirely novel, however. Indeed, even within the strongly personalistic French system,[725] the concept of originality has apparently already undergone a similar transformation – from a subjective to a purely objective meaning – in which it is increasingly regarded as inherent to the intrinsic characteristics of works rather than to the link between them and their author. In particular, in addition to being inappropriate, the subjective approach has over time been characterized as "anachronistic" and "unrealistic":[726] anachronistic, because it ignores the scholarship that, since the end of the nineteenth century, "refuses to see in the work anything other than the work itself";[727] unrealistic, because the subjective definition of originality as "the imprint of the author's personality" fails to give a true account of what is

723 According to the January 2020 report of the *Conseil supérieur de la propriété littéraire et artistique* (CSPLA) on artificial intelligence and culture, the AI exactly « comme la personne humaine » is capable of producing « *effectivement une forme qui peut être objectivement appréhendée comme une œuvre* ». The report further characterizes the output of a "creative" AI as « *une réalisation culturelle qui ressemble à une œuvre* »; see Bensamoun and Farchy (n 4).

724 As for French law, see Vivant and Bruguiere, 'Droit d'auteur et droits voisins' (n 456), no 271; Gautier PY, Propriété littéraire et artistique (11th edn, PUF 2019).

725 Notably, the reference to the notion of *empreinte de la personnalité de l'auteur,* with regard to *oeuvres d'esprit,* adopted in later years by the jurisprudence of the Court of Justice of the European Union, first appeared in a ruling of the Paris Court of Appeal in 1862, Paris Court of Appeal, 10 April 1862, D. 1863, 1, 53.

726 Bensamoun and Farchy (n 4) 41.

727 Ibid, 40.

provided for in positive law.[728] Ultimately, this notion is said to have been inherited from a romantic vision of creation that mythologized the poet or the artist, often shifting attention away from the work itself to the torments of its creator,[729] and which no longer corresponds to factual reality.

2.2.1.3 Authors of AI-Generated Outputs

If copyright protection were to be granted to AI-generated outputs, another question arises as to who would be attributed authorship over such content.[730]

A number of doctrinal approaches have been proposed thus far, including the idea that AI could be regarded as a co-author alongside the human contributors involved in the algorithmic creative process.[731] According to a leading scholarly view, however, "asking whether a computer can be an author", or a co-author "is the 'wrong' question". In fact, "even the most technologically advanced machines of our era are little more than faithful agents of the humans who design or use them".[732] Instead, "the 'right' question addresses how to evaluate the authorial claims of the humans involved in either preparing or using the machines that 'create'".[733]

---

728 Lucas, Lucas-Schloetter and Bernault (n 457) no 119, no 125, 145.

729 Délégué Y, 'Mallarmé, le sujet de la poésie' (2001) 101(5) Revue d'histoire littéraire de la France, 1426, according to whom « *On pointe ainsi le caractère anachronique d'une notion héritée d'une vision romantique de la création qui 'avait mythifié le poète, 'l'artiste', en déplaçant souvent sur les tourments de sa personne l'intérêt qu'on devait porter à l'œuvre seule'* ».

730 One peculiar approach was outlined for example by a French legislative proposal dated 12 September 2023. The proposal suggested placing the machine learning process under the exclusive control of the rightsholders whose works are used during training. It further recommended that authorship of the AI-generated output be attributed to all authors whose works were included in the training dataset. Additionally, it required that any such output be clearly labeled as an "AI-generated work" and accompanied by a list of all the authors whose works had been used in the training process. However, such a solution must be regarded as fundamentally impracticable, given the sheer number of authors (potentially thousands or even millions) whose works are included in the vast datasets employed to train AI systems. This approach could also lead to a decline in investment in the AI sector – in particular, among start-ups, which are typically unable to clear rights for all the works used during training – thereby harming the competitiveness of any jurisdiction that adopts it. See the French National Assembly, Bill of 12 September 2023, No. 1630, available at <https://www.assemblee-nationale.fr/dyn/16/textes/l16b1630_proposition-loi.pdf>. For a critical analysis, see Geiger and Iaia, 'The Forgotten Creator (n 306), Geiger, 'Elaborating a Human Rights Friendly Copyright Framework' (n 321) 8.

731 Bao A and Zeng Y, 'Allowing AI Co–Authors Is a Disregard for Humanization' (2024) Accountability in Research 1 <https://doi.org/10.1080/08989621.2024.2420812>.

732 Ginsburg and Budiardjo (n 357).

733 Ibid.

A particularly emblematic position in line with these questions has been taken by the French scholarship, according to which the author of an AI-generated output could, in theory, be identified either as the "designer" of the AI system or its "deployer".[734]

With regard to the first hypothesis, the designer may be considered the "indirect" author of the work, insofar as they are capable of exerting significant influence over the creative process by designing the inference model within which the output is generated.[735] This approach has the advantage of attributing authorship to an identifiable entity, arguably closely connected to the AI's functioning – a figure that, in the French tradition, may well be a legal person.[736] However, it does not resolve the practical issue of determining who, among the various individuals involved, can in fact be considered the designer of the system: the algorithm's programmer? The developer? The person responsible for the training phase? The one selecting the data? The copyright holder of the AI software? Or perhaps the project coordinator? Moreover, the definition of "system developers" itself remains subject to interpretative uncertainty. As noted by Miller, this category "includes a wide range of roles and professions, such as designers, technicians, finance providers, instructors, and operators" and these concerns "become even more salient when AI systems are developed in projects, which are temporary organizations whose team members may not be available once the project terminates".[737]

A similar approach was adopted by the Italian expert group responsible for drafting the national report for the 2019 AIPPI Study Question, "*Copyright in artificially generated works*", according to which authorship could be attributed to the individual who defines the specific goal or objective to be achieved by the AI system. More specifically, it has been argued that when a human sets the particular aim to be pursued by an AI entity, they may be considered the author of the resulting work – provided that the instructions reflect a degree of creativity and have had a tangible impact on the final output.

This hypothesis finds a degree of parallelism with the well-known Section 9 of the UK Copyright, Designs and Patents Act (CDPA) of 1988, which, in the case of

---

734 Bensamoun and Farchy (n 4) 35.

735 Bensamoun and Farchy (n 4) 37.

736 The designer defines the field of possibilities in which the AI will then evolve. In this case, the AI ultimately only executes the creative framework established by the designer. This assumption has the advantage of identifying a human person who will have maintained very close links with the machine; see Ibid, 35.

737 Miller GJ, 'Stakeholder Roles in Artificial Intelligence Projects' (2022) 3 Project Leadership and Society.

"computer-generated" literary, dramatic, musical or artistic works,[738] designates as the author "the person by whom the arrangements necessary for the creation of the work are undertaken".[739] The CDPA allows for the protection of "computer-generated works", defined in Section 178 as works "generated by a computer in circumstances such that there is no human author of the work". Pursuant to Section 9(3), authorship is attributed to the individual who undertakes the necessary arrangements for the creation of the work. However, these provisions have been regarded by some scholars as conflicting with Section 1 of the same Act, which establishes that copyright protection applies only to works that are original.[740] According to this idea, the very notion of "authorless works" constitutes a conceptual paradox – even within the framework of this act.[741]

Moreover, in 2021, the United Kingdom Intellectual Property Office (UKIPO) launched a public consultation on whether the current legal framework should be revised in light of advancements in generative AI. Noting the absence of case law applying the relevant provision to AI-generated works, the UKIPO acknowledged that "[i]t is unclear whether removing [protection for computer-generated works] would either promote or discourage innovation and the use of AI for the public good". Consequently, in its June 2022 response, it decided to maintain the existing legislation, while leaving the door open to potential future reforms.[742] This uncertainty would likely extend to any other regulatory framework that chooses to adopt a similar approach.

---

738 *Section 178(b)* of the *UK Copyright, Designs and Patents.*

739 Deltorn and Macrez (n 44) 12. The same is provided for by Section 21(f) of Ireland's Copyright and Related Rights Act 2000. In both UK and Irish legal systems, a computer-generated work is essentially defined as a work lacking human authorship. Exclusive economic rights over such works are conferred upon a human subject by virtue of a *fictio juris*, whereas moral rights are excluded.

740 The UK copyright law, in fact, on the one hand "provides for protection of authorless works, ascribing authorship to the person making the necessary compositional arrangements", yet, on the other hand, considers a work without "authorial originality" as unprotectable (cf. Section 1 of the law): "[it] provides for protection of authorless works, ascribing authorship to the person making the necessary arrangements, but according to Section 1, without authorial originality, no works are protectable"; see Blaszczyk M, 'Contradictions of Computer-Generated Works' Protection' (Kluwer Copyright Blog, 6 November 2023) <https://copyrightblog.kluweriplaw.com/2023/11/06/contradictions-of-computer-generated-works-protection>.

741 See also in this sense Blaszczyk M, 'Impossibility of Emergent Works' Protection in US and EU Copyright Law' (2023) 25(1) North Carolina Journal of Law & Technology.

742 The question, however, has since been reopened: in a fresh consultation launched in December 2024 (closed on 25 February 2025), the UKIPO has put the future of the "computer-generated works" provision back on the table. However, at the time of writing, the outcome of that consultation is still awaited.

As for the option of considering the deployer of the AI system as the author, it certainly has the advantage of simplicity and technical feasibility, as it identifies as the author the one who has the actual availability of the artificial intelligence and uses it under their authority. Such a solution circumvents the problematic need to distinguish between AI-assisted and fully AI-generated creation and, according to Samuelson, may also appear reasonable insofar as the individual or entity who has, arguably, acquired a license to use the system would then benefit from protection.[743]

However, identifying the individuals or entities deploying the AI systems remains challenging[744] – for example, in the case of digital platforms hosting such systems (e.g. Midjourney, to name but one), where, according to this idea, the (professional) deployers could possibly be considered as the "author" of potentially massive quantities of outputs.

In its report Copyright and Artificial Intelligence, Part 2 "Copyrightability", the USCO appears to acknowledge that the author of an AI-generated output – if one exists – should be identified as the user of the AI system. However, to determine authorship, if any, in AI-generated outputs, the USCO states that it is first necessary to analyze the categories of human contribution to generative AI outputs. In particular, such contributions may occur through (i) crafting prompts that provide specific instructions to the system; (ii) incorporating pre-existing intellectual works or other expressive inputs, including via prompts, that may influence the output; and (iii) modifying and reworking AI-generated outputs.

Regarding the third category of human intervention, the report affirms that copyright protection may be granted for the creative selection, coordination, or arrangement of AI-based material, as well as for its modification, adaptation, refinement, or enhancement, provided that these interventions amount to an original contribution. To this end, the USCO draws an analogy with derivative works, defined under 17 U.S.C. § 101 as "a work based upon one or more preexisting works", thereby implicitly recognizing that the resulting content may, at the very least, build upon pre-existing material processed by the AI. By contrast, with regard to the first two types of human contribution, the Report clarifies that if a human-created work is used as an expressive input and is incorporated – even partially and in a perceptible manner – into the final output, the corresponding portion of that input may qualify for copyright protection. It remains unclear, however, whether authorship (if any) on the remaining portions of the work should be attributed to other actors along the

743 Samuelson, 'Allocating Ownership Rights in Computer-Generated Works' (n 606) 1185.
744 Miller, 'Stakeholder Roles in Artificial Intelligence Projects' (n 737).

AI value chain, or whether the works in question would simply fall into the public domain. Instead, USCO argues that simple prompts are insufficient to establish authorship over the resulting output for the natural person providing them, as such instructions do not reflect sufficient human control over the generative process.[745]

2.2.1.4 Multi-authorial Works?

Under another perspective, an interesting alternative solution to solve the "questions of authorship" of AI-generated outputs, could be to consider such outputs – not merely as the authorship, if any, of the AI designer, programmer, or user individually taken – but rather as works with a "complex structure", that is, works that are "simple in an objective sense" but "composed or complex in a subjective sense".[746] Given their multi-authored nature, if copyright protection were to be considered applicable to such works, and in the absence of specific *ex contractu* agreements among the parties involved in the creative process, reference could alternatively be made to the legal regimes governing collective works or works of joint authorship.

These collaborative forms of creation are not uniformly conceptualized across legal systems, especially when it comes to statutory definitions. In the UK, for instance, works of joint authorship are considered a subset of collective works. Section 178 of the Copyright, Designs and Patents Act 1988 (CDPA) defines a collective work broadly as either: "(a) a work of joint authorship, or (b) a work in which there are distinct contributions by different authors, or in which works or parts of works of different authors are incorporated".[747] The position differs in other jurisdictions.

Within the EU, in the absence of a harmonized definition of either joint authorship or collective work, it is left to the discretion of national laws and courts to determine whether a collaborative creation should be classified as a joint work, a collective work, or simply as two or more distinct works by different authors.[748] This results in a lack of legal certainty, particularly regarding

---

745 Prompts indeed are to be understood as mere ideas or suggestions, which – by their nature – are not eligible for copyright protection, unless they are themselves expressed in a creative form. Even in such cases, however, authorship does not extend to the output generated by the AI system as a result of those prompts. See US Copyright Office, Copyright and Artificial Intelligence: Part 2 (n 367).

746 De Sanctis (n 462) 38.

747 Angelopoulos C, 'The Myth of European Term Harmonisation: 27 Public Domains for the 27 Member States' (2012) 43(5) IIC 567, Amsterdam Law School Research Paper No 2012-82, Institute for Information Law Research Paper No 2012-48 <https://ssrn.com/abstract=2145862> or <http://dx.doi.org/10.2139/ssrn.2145862>, 7 ff.

748 Ibid, 4.

key questions such as: how should the collaborative effort be qualified in order for the resulting work to be recognized as a joint or collective work? Does it reflect a common intellectual endeavor – i.e., shared authorship in the conception of the work? Or is the collaboration primarily economic or organizational in nature? Or, again, is it merely a factual circumstance? Each of these perspectives may lead to a different legal classification with significant practical implications as well – for instance, in the application of rules governing the duration of copyright protection.[749]

That said, an analysis of the suitability of the legal framework governing collective works for AI-generated outputs would offer valuable insights. Bearing in mind that, due to the fragmented legal landscape, its concrete applicability would necessarily require a jurisdiction-by-jurisdiction analysis – which is beyond the scope of this analysis – it is nonetheless worth recalling that, although with slight variations,[750] collective works are commonly understood

749 In this regard, although the Directive 2006/116/EC of the European Parliament and of the Council of 12 December 2006 on the term of protection of copyright and certain related rights (codified version) [2006] OJ L372/12 explicitly refers to both categories of multi-authored works, it fails to provide a consistent definitional framework to distinguish between them. Art. 1(4) of the Term Directive: "Where a Member State provides for particular provisions on copyright in respect of collective works or for a legal person to be designated as the rightholder, the term of protection shall be calculated according to the provisions of paragraph 3 ["70 years after the work is lawfully made available to the public"], except if the natural persons who have created the work are identified as such in the versions of the work which are made available to the public"; Art. 1(2) of the Term Directive: "In the case of a work of joint authorship, the term referred to in paragraph 1 shall be calculated from the death of the last surviving author".

750 For instance, in the United States, section 101 of the Copyright Act of 1976 defines a collective work as "a work, such as a periodical issue, anthology, or encyclopedia, in which a number of contributions, constituting separate and independent works in themselves, are assembled into a collective whole". In the European context (see Angelopoulos (n 747) 7 ff.), Article 2(5) of the Berne Convention (Paris text 1971) provides that: "Collections of literary or artistic works such as encyclopaedias and anthologies which, by reason of the selection and arrangement of their contents, constitute intellectual creations shall be protected as such, without prejudice to the copyright in each of the works forming part of such collection". In countries such as France, Italy, Spain, the Czech Republic, and the Netherlands, national laws provide relatively similar definitions of collective works. In France, Article L113-2 of the *Code de la propriété intellectuelle* defines an *œuvre collective* as "a work created at the initiative of a natural or legal person who edits it, publishes it and discloses it under his direction and name and in which the personal contributions of the various authors who participated in its production are merged in the overall work for which they were conceived, without it being possible to attribute to each author a separate right in the work as created". In Spain, Article 8 of the *Ley de Propiedad Intelectual* defines a collective work as a work created on the initiative and under the direction of a natural or legal person, who edits and publishes

as works that consist of contributions from several authors, assembled and published under the direction of a natural or legal person who holds the copyright in the work as a whole. The ownership of the "work as a whole" is typically distinct from the ownership of the individual contributions, which means that the contributing authors may retain the right to publish their work elsewhere. Such works are thus normally the result of multiple creative (and economic!) contributions by two or more individual authors.[751]

In collective works, as in the case of AI-generated creations, at least two distinct activities of a potentially creative nature can be identified: on the one hand, the contributions of the individual authors; on the other, the activity of selecting, arranging, and coordinating these works into a single, coherent whole.[752]

Just as the act of coordinating and organizing individual works has been recognized as creative in some jurisdictions (e.g. the Italian one) – and, notably, as pre-eminent over the contributions of the individual authors, who are not considered co-authors of the unified work[753] – so too could the activity of using (i.e., coordinating the functioning of) AI systems be regarded as a form of creative activity.

However, a problematic aspect of applying the legal framework of collective works to AI-generated outputs lies in the nature of their creation. These outputs often result from multiple human interventions that are not easily distinguishable – for example, those of the AI system designer, the program-

---

it under his or her name, and which consists of the combination of contributions by various authors so integrated into a single, autonomous creation that it is not possible to assign to any of them a separate right in the entire work (Angelopoulos (n 747) 7 ff.). In the Czech Republic, a collective work is defined as a work created with the participation of more than one author, at the initiative and under the management of a natural or legal person, and made available to the public under that person's or entity's name, where the individual contributions are not capable of independent use. In the Netherlands, Article 5 of the Copyright Act provides that "if a literary, scientific or artistic work consists of separate works by two or more persons, the person under whose guidance and supervision the work as a whole has been made or, if there is no such person, the compiler of the various works, shall be deemed the author of the whole work, without prejudice to the copyright in each of the works separately". In Italy, collective works are described as works "constituted by the bringing together of works or parts of works, which have the character of an autonomous creation, as the result of selection and coordination for a specific literary, scientific, didactic, religious, political or artistic purpose, such as encyclopaedias, dictionaries, anthologies, magazines and newspapers". Such works are "protected as original works" under Article 3 of the Legge sul diritto d'autore.

751 Chimienti L, Diritto di Autore 4.0. L'intelligenza artificiale crea? (Pacini 2020) 28.

752 As for the Italian case law, see Court of Milan, Judgment 26/10/2017.

753 Piola Caselli E, *Codice di diritto d'autore* (UTET 1943).

mer, the data curator, the trainer, the deployer, or the end user. By contrast, the components of a collective work must generally be distinguishable and autonomous, insofar as they are independently creative, in order to qualify as parts of a collective work.

Unlike collective works, the works of joint authorship do not imply the distinguishability of individual human contributions.[754] Rather, the qualification of a work as jointly authored is generally linked to some variation[755] of the basic formula: collaboration between two or more individuals, plus inseparability of their contributions.

The point of divergence among legal systems lies in the interpretation of this second element – whether inseparability should be understood in factual, economic, or intellectual terms.[756]

---

754 Ibid.

755 For instance, in the United States, a joint work is defined in Section 101 of the US Copyright Act as "a work prepared by two or more authors with the intention that their contributions be merged into inseparable or interdependent parts of a unitary whole". According to Section 201(a), the authors of a joint work are granted co-ownership in the resulting copyrighted work. In the European Union, the notion of joint authorship is indirectly referenced in Article 1(2) of the Term Directive, which provides that in the case of a work of joint authorship, the term of protection is 70 years after the death of the last surviving joint author. However, the directive does not offer a definition of the concept itself. In France, Article L113-2 of the French *Code de la propriété intellectuelle* defines an *œuvre de collaboration* broadly as "a work in the creation of which more than one natural person has participated". The emphasis here lies on concerted creative effort, a "community of inspiration" and mutual control (Angelopoulos (n 747) ff.). Furthermore, Article L113-3 allows joint authors – unless otherwise agreed – to exploit their respective contributions independently, provided that this does not prejudice the exploitation of the overall work. In Italy, pursuant to Article 10 of the Italian Copyright Law, a work qualifies as one of joint authorship if and insofar as it is created "with the indistinguishable and inseparable contribution of several persons". The law further provides that, in such cases, copyright shall belong to all the joint authors in common. Similar definitions are found in other European jurisdictions. Article 7 of the Spanish Intellectual Property Act and Article 10 of the UK's Copyright, Designs and Patents Act (CDPA) follow comparable approaches, focusing on the inseparability of contributions and the joint nature of the creative effort. (Angelopoulos (n 747) 7 ff.). In the Netherlands, although the Dutch Copyright Act does not provide an explicit definition of joint authorship, case law from the *Hoge Raad* (Dutch Supreme Court) has taken a similar position. Under this approach, a work is considered jointly authored when no single contributor can identify a substantial and independent part of the work as solely their own, without the involvement of the other contributors. Conversely, in the Czech Republic, Article 10(2) of the Czech Copyright Act defines a work of joint authorship as a work created up to the point of completion through the joint creative activity of two or more authors, where the individual contributions, regardless of whether they can be distinguished, are not capable of being used independently. In this case, economic rather than factual indivisibility appears to be the decisive criterion.

756 Angelopoulos (n 747) 5 ff.

However, the application of the joint authorship regime to AI-generated outputs raises other concerns. Firstly, as some legal scholars within the Italian system have argued, for the joint authorship framework to be applicable, the individuals involved must contribute more than merely technical or logistical support.[757] In practice, though, the human involvement in the "creative" algorithmic process often consists of purely technical and/or mathematical activities – for example, arguably, those carried out by programmers, data curators, or the developers responsible for training the model: even where such tasks involve discretion, they may fall short of the threshold of creativity required for authorship under copyright law.

Moreover, if one were to recognize the applicability of such a legal framework to AI-generated creations, it would also likely follow that the rules governing the civil law institution of co-ownership should apply. This is the case in Italy, for instance, where co-owned works are subject to the regime set out in Articles 1100 et seq. of the Italian Civil Code. Under these provisions, the consent of all co-authors is required for certain acts concerning the work (such as its publication, if unpublished, modification, or exploitation in a form different from the original publication). In the event of an unjustified refusal by one or more co-authors, judicial authorization would be necessary to proceed.[758]

It is, however, difficult to imagine the practical applicability of such rules in a sector where the individuals involved in the creative process operate with profoundly different purposes (e.g., entertainment vs. economic investment), roles (e.g., technical support vs. artistic contribution), legal status (e.g., natural vs. legal persons), and qualifications (e.g., users, investors, researchers, market operators). These actors may never have come into direct contact, may operate under different jurisdictions, and may be physically located in entirely different parts of the world. However, collective bargaining mechanisms and standard licensing terms of AI systems – in other words, contractual remedies – could offer a useful means of addressing such complexity.

2.2.1.5 Critical Considerations

In the light of the above, opting for the application of copyright protection to AI-generated outputs, from a *de lege lata* perspective, is certainly an option that has been explored and supported in many theoretical reflections.

Nonetheless, this approach must be carefully assessed. First, although there is an underlying (albeit debatable) hope that granting copyright to

757 Ubertazzi (n 349) 1505.

758 See Article 10(3) of the Italian Copyright Law.

the results of automated AI processes might stimulate creativity[759] by recognizing broader control over AI-based outputs and ensuring economic returns for those involved in their creation, there is currently a lack of empirical evidence to support such a claim. Nor is there any concrete indication that this form of protection would foster investment in the sector.[760] On the contrary, a 2022 study by the European Commission has highlighted potential negative consequences of extending exclusive rights to AI-generated outputs. As the report notes, "the feedback received seems to indicate that an additional right in favour of machine-generated outputs might have negative impacts on the traditional creative sectors".[761]

Moreover, applying copyright to generative AI would *de facto* require an evolutionary reinterpretation of the originality requirement, effectively entailing a major paradigm shift in copyright law, at least as developed in the EU legal framework. Such a shift risks transforming originality into a disguised "novelty requirement" and copyright into a purely market-based right, rather than preserving its function as both an economic incentive and a means of protecting moral interests, as well as a guarantor of the free circulation of information and ideas.

In this vein, a strand of legal scholarship – adopting an approach more closely aligned with common law traditions – has argued that the "convergence of copyright and market requirements is not surprising because, although authors' rights may include the concept of moral protection of the author, copyright is essentially a market right".[762] It has also been described as a *de facto* tool that fosters investment and capital accumulation by large corporations,[763] ultimately becoming increasingly confined to the mainstream culture, and the authorized culture.[764]

Clearly, if this view is adopted, the consequences on the ultimate function and legal nature of copyright as a legal institution should be carefully assessed.

---

759 US Copyright Office, Copyright and Artificial Intelligence: Part 2 (n 367).

760 Geiger, 'Elaborating a Human Rights Friendly Copyright Framework' (n 321) 17.

761 European Commission: Directorate-General for Communications Networks, Content and Technology, Crowell & Moring, IMC University of Applied Sciences Krems, Philippe Rixhon Associates, Technopolis Group and UCLouvain, 'Study on Copyright and New Technologies – Copyright Data Management and Artificial Intelligence' (Publications Office of the European Union 2022) <https://data.europa.eu/doi/10.2759/570559>, 21.

762 "La convergenza tra i requisiti del copyright e i requisiti del mercato non è una sorpresa perché, anche se il diritto d'autore può comprendere il concetto della protezione morale dell'autore, il copyright è essenzialmente un diritto del mercato"; see Macmillan F, 'Il diritto d'autore nell'era digitale: verso il declino dell'originalità dell'opera?' in Resta G (ed), L'Armonia del Diritto: Contributi ad una riflessione su diritto e musica (Roma TreEpress 2020) 109, 113.

It would have to be acknowledged, for instance, that the protection of the author's personality would, if at all, be delegated to institutions which would remain external to the core framework of copyright law – which is at odds with statutory provisions of authors' right legal traditions.

Moreover, the protection of the author's moral interests, as well as broader societal interests in the promotion of culture and free access to creative works, would increasingly fall within the discretionary power of the judiciary in individual cases. Judges would be called upon to consider copyright as potentially antagonistic to these values and, in the absence of an internal balancing mechanism within copyright law – unless the regime of exceptions and limitations is interpreted more flexibly – would be forced to rely on the external balancing of fundamental rights. Indeed, the possible choice to extend copyright protection to AI-generated works could mark the definitive breakdown of the traditional interdependence between the moral and economic prerogatives normally granted to the author solely by virtue of the creation of the work.

In defining the appropriate form of protection for AI-generated outputs, careful consideration must therefore be given to these concerns, in order to avoid an excessive curtailment of the general interest in access to creative works and the promotion of cultural development in society, in favor of the particular (and private) economic interests of the AI end users or industries that produce or deploy artificial intelligence in the creative and cultural sectors.

2.2.2 The Application of the Related Rights Discipline

The application of related (or neighboring) rights could, in theory, circumvent the challenges posed by a forced reinterpretation of the originality requirement, as well as those concerning authorship and the creative process. This is because these alternative forms of protection are generally aimed at safeguarding economic interests[765] and do not, at least in some instances, require the presence of a natural person as author.

Within the EU framework, reference is typically made to the related rights granted to performers (e.g., singers, actors), producers of phonograms (e.g.,

763 Copyright has arguably become a "strumento per favorire l'investimento e l'accumulazione di capitale da parte delle grandi imprese"; see Macmillan, 'Il diritto d'autore nell'era digitale' (n 762), 118.

764 Macmillan, 'Il diritto d'autore nell'era digitale' (n 762), 116.

765 Sganga C, 'The Many Metamorphoses of Related Rights in EU Copyright Law: Unintended Consequences or Inevitable Developments?' (21 April 2021) (Forthcoming) GRUR Int 10/2021 <https://ssrn.com/abstract=3831543>.

record labels) and to videograms (e.g., film producers), and broadcasting organizations (e.g., television and radio operators).

It has been argued that "in light of the general absence in related rights law of a requirement of human authorship or originality, and its rationale of rewarding economic or entrepreneurial activity, related rights will accommodate AI-assisted output in cases of insufficient human creative input".[766]

As noted in a seminal Position Statement by the Max Planck Institute, protection under the current related rights regime is primarily based on the logic of investment protection,[767] which supports the view that such rights may apply even in the absence of a high level of originality as in the case of AI-generated works. Unlike copyright, these rights do not arise from an act of intellectual creation but rather from an act of industrial activity (e.g., phonogram production) or professional performance (e.g., performing arts), which is protected as such, and in parallel with the author's right.

Recognizing AI-generated outputs solely under the framework of related rights would have the merit of preserving the internal coherence of copyright law and its anthropocentric foundation, without forcing an interpretive stretch of its legal categories.[768]

The most critical limitation of this solution lies in the fact that related rights are narrowly defined and apply only to specific categories expressly established by law. Whether these rights can be extended to AI-generated outputs ultimately depends on whether such outputs fall within those legally predetermined categories. Accordingly, an analysis of the legal basis of each relevant related right would not be avoided in order to determine whether the corresponding framework is, in fact, applicable to the AI-generated outputs in each given case. Even if the answer were affirmative in certain cases, a broad range of AI-generated works would nonetheless fall outside the scope of protection, simply because they do not meet the express legal definitions.

Moreover, it must be acknowledged that the absence of originality as a requirement across all related rights is a matter of debate: not all related rights are entirely exempt from the originality or human authorship thresholds.[769] Conversely, it could also be questioned whether a related right can exist in the absence of the foundational conditions for copyright protection – namely, the existence of a work that is at least abstractly eligible for such protection. In this regard, the observations of certain strands of French legal scholarship are

766 Hartmann et al (n 228).

767 Drexl, Hilty et al (n 228).

768 Bonadio E and Lucchi N, 'How Far Can Copyright Be Stretched? Framing the Debate on Whether New and Different Forms of Creativity Can Be Protected' (2019) Intellectual Property Quarterly 115.

769 Bensamoun and Farchy (n 4).

noteworthy, particularly those challenging the recognition of related rights over productions that, due to the absence of human input and/or creative character, may not qualify as "intellectual works" at all.[770]

2.3 The *De Lege Ferenda* Solution

According to a strand of legal scholarship, the foreseeable further evolution of AI technologies and the emerging uses of those already in the market may soon render the current regulatory framework obsolete and legislative intervention is both necessary and appropriate. The proposed solution would be to introduce a new *sui generis* right for AI-generated creations within the existing legal system, akin to the protection currently granted to database makers.[771]

Indeed, this is the path already taken by Ukraine. As noted in Chapter 8, Art. 33 of the Ukrainian Copyright Law now establishes a *sui generis* right for non-original "objects" generated by software, distinguishing them from works created by humans using software, which are explicitly excluded from this

---

770 With reference to the right of performers, « the protection offered by the neighboring rights regime implies, for these persons, the existence of a copyright on the work performed » (« la protection que confère le régime des droits voisins implique, pour ces acteurs, l'existence d'un droit d'auteur sur l'œuvre interprétée »); see Bensamoun and Farchy (n 4) 30. A similar wording is also present in the Italian Copyright Law (i) with reference to the related right of phonogram producers, at Art. 72, according to which the person who takes the initiative and the responsibility for the first fixation of the sounds resulting from an interpretation or performance or of other sounds or representations of sounds has certain specific (related) rights as "producer of phonograms", "without prejudice to the rights due to the author under Title I"; (ii) at Art. 79, with reference to "those engaged in the activity of radio or television broadcasting"; (iii) in Arts. 85-ter and 85-quater, respectively for "whoever, after the expiry of the terms of protection of copyright, lawfully publishes or communicates to the public for the first time a work not previously published" and "whoever publishes, in any manner or by any means, critical and scientific editions of works in the public domain" (Sections 85-ter and 85-quater of the Copyright Act specify, in fact, that the respective provisions apply 'without prejudice to the moral rights of the author") and (iv) in Art. 88 for the photographer "with respect to photographs reproducing works of figurative art".

771 Ciani Sciolla (n 676) 286; Dias Pereira AL, 'A Copyright Human-Centred Approach to AI?' (2021) 70(4) GRUR International 323; Scalzini S, 'Fattispecie costitutiva del diritto d'autore' in Genovese A and Olivieri G (eds), Proprietà intellettuale. Segni distintivi, brevetti, diritto d'autore (Wolters Kluwer 2021) 976; Lauber-Rönsberg A and Hetmank S, 'The Concept of Authorship and Inventorship Under Pressure: Does Artificial Intelligence Shift Paradigms?' (2019) 14(7) Journal of Intellectual Property Law & Practice 576; Papadopoulou A, 'Creativity in Crisis: Are the Creations of Artificial Intelligence Worth Protecting?' (2021) 3 Journal of Intellectual Property, Information Technology and E-Commerce Law 408.

protection. This distinction between "objects" and "works" aims to prevent overlap between the *sui generis* right and copyright.

The Ukrainian precedent, however, also illustrates the limits of a purely national response: since the debate on the subject essentially unfolds transnationally, isolated national solutions may prove insufficient. Ideally, the regulatory intervention should be at least European in scope – if not even at a global level. More specifically, the intervention of the EU legislator could consist in the development of shared criteria and tests at the European level, aimed at overcoming "the conceptual and substantive constraints of the respective national traditions", and could thus "create the prerequisites for a harmonisation or, as the case may be, a broader and deeper standardisation than has been achieved so far" – something that would not be possible merely through legal interpretation: "there are regulatory aspects that (…) only the legislator can effectively harmonise".[772]

In this light, introducing a *sui generis* right to protect AI-generated outputs (thereby "circumventing" the issue of the absence of the originality requirement) is not only theoretically possible but arguably desirable.

A similar approach has already been adopted in the past with regard to the makers of databases, that have the right to "prevent extraction and/or re-utilization of the whole or of a substantial part, evaluated qualitatively and/or quantitatively, of the contents of that database".[773] Indeed, the *sui generis* right in question grants the party who has assumed the entrepreneurial risk of creating the database the right to prohibit the extraction or re-utilization of the whole or a substantial part of the database – without prejudice, of course, to any existing rights in the content of the collection or its individual parts.[774] The protection in question is conditional upon the maker of the database – whether a natural or legal person – having made an investment,[775] whether financial, material, or human, in the "obtaining, verification, or presentation" of the database's content.[776]

Adapted to the specificities of the AI sector, such a *sui generis* right – by possibly preventing unauthorized economic exploitation[777] – would allow

772 Fabbio (n 360) 301.

773 Art. 7 Directive 96/9/EC of the European Parliament and of the Council of 11 March 1996 on the legal protection of databases.

774 cf. Art. 102-bis (3) of the Act.

775 Interesting in this regard is the wording in Article L341-1 French Code de la proptiété intellectuelle, according to which the maker of a database, "producteur", is "la personne qui prend l'initiative et le risque des investissements correspondants".

776 Bensamoun and Farchy (n 4) 44.

777 Ibid, 45.

those who undertake the risk of investing in this field (whether a deployer or an end user) to obtain a return on their investment.

A regulatory framework similar to that envisaged for makers of database could, in fact, align coherently with the declared objective of supporting and protecting investments in the field of AI and the creative industries that rely on it.[778]

However, opting for the introduction of a *sui generis* right would necessitate a number of considerations concerning its practical implementation.

First and foremost, the new regulatory provision should be coordinated with what is envisaged by the AI Act, especially regarding general purpose AI models.

Moreover, it would be essential to provide a clear and precise definition of the right,[779] including its exact scope.

For example, the right to reproduction and communication to the public over the output could be limited, recognizing it only in cases of commercial use, in order to allow free use for non-commercial purposes, so as to reduce the scope of exclusivity to purely parasitic behavior.[780] This new form of protection could coexist with any other existing rights in the work and could also apply to outputs that are co-creations between a human being and an AI system, combining human creativity and artificial intelligence.[781] However, it would still be necessary to determine who, in the absence of a specific agreement, should be considered *ex lege* the holder of such a right, and whether this "owner" should also be recognized as the "author" of the work. Drawing on the wording already adopted in UK law, the owner could be identified as "the person by whom the arrangements necessary for the creation of the work are undertaken".[782]

---

778 Bensamoun and Farchy (n 4) 45.

779 In this regard, criticism has already been raised, for example, in relation to the new Ukrainian legislation. The law's vague criteria for distinguishing between non-original objects and human-created works – particularly with respect to the threshold of human involvement – raise concerns about legal certainty. Moreover, the law fails to clarify to whom the sui generis right should be attributed (e.g., the software developer or the end user), thereby creating additional uncertainty; see Iaia, Klein and De Gaspari (n 613) 45.

780 Bensamoun and Farchy (n 4) 45.

781 <https://www.gov.uk/government/consultations/artificial-intelligence-and-ip-copyright-and-patents/artificial-intelligence-and-intellectual-property-copyright-and-patents#:~:text=Works%20generated%20by%20a%20computer,be%20protected%2C%20as%20described%20above>.

782 See Section 9(3) of the UK CDPA. Other regulatory options that could be considered include recognizing ownership of the right in the hands of the AI designer or user – albeit with all the complexities such solutions inevitably entail. For instance, it would be

As for the duration of protection, it should be chosen to reflect the effort or investment made in the creation of the works. According to the UKIPO's 2022 response to consultation, too long a duration could discourage the production of AI-based outputs and investment in AI technology.[783] Opting for a shorter duration, instead, would reflect the speed with which an AI is capable of creating works, even with minimal human effort or contribution, and would, at the same time, incentivize the dissemination of creations, which would fall into the public domain after a considerable amount of time.

In this regard, some argue that it should last five years,[784] while others favor the idea of setting the temporal extension of protection at 25 years, starting from the date of publication of the work, inspired by Art. 4 of Directive 2006/116/EC.[785] Indeed, this has been the approach adopted by the Ukrainian legislator. However, the 25-year duration of the right has been criticized as excessive.[786]

Finally, concerning the protection requirements necessary to make such a right operational, the French CSPLA study suggested the possibility of introducing an investment-based criterion – similar to that used for databases. This investment would need to be significant, both quantitatively and qualitatively, and could be complemented by an additional requirement, such as the novelty of the creation.[787]

Another possible approach would be to introduce an additional condition reflecting a form of "artistic value", as already envisaged in other areas of intellectual property law.

---

necessary to assess the feasibility of such an approach in relation to creative content generated within the framework of UGC platforms such as MidJourney, DALL·E, and ChatGPT, particularly given that OpenAI's Terms and Conditions appear to recognize individual users as the authors of their respective creations.

783 <https://www.gov.uk/government/consultations/artificial-intelligence-and-ip-copyright-and-patents/artificial-intelligence-and-intellectual-property-copyright-and-patents#:~:text=Works%20generated%20by%20a%20computer,be%20protected%2C%20as%20described%20above>.

784 <https://www.gov.uk/government/consultations/artificial-intelligence-and-ip-copyright-and-patents/artificial-intelligence-and-intellectual-property-copyright-and-patents#:~:text=Works%20generated%20by%20a%20computer,be%20protected%2C%20as%20described%20above>.

785 Directive 2006/116/EC of the European Parliament and of the Council of 12 December 2006 on the term of protection of copyright and certain related rights.

786 Iaia, Klein and De Gaspari (n 613) 45.

787 « *Il serait aussi possible, si la volonté politique était en ce sens, d'ajouter à ce cadre une condition d'implication ou d'investissement* (*matériel, humain ou financier*) »; see Bensamoun and Farchy (n 4) 43.

As with design works – whose protection applies to "those industrial sectors and creations where the greatest economic interests are at stake, and where interference with the functioning of the internal market is therefore most intense"[788] – AI-generated works are often mass-produced and may have industrial applications. To prevent distortions of competition, the requirement of artistic value could serve to raise the threshold of protection for such automatically generated works. The desirability of the introduction of such requirements, however, would have to be carefully considered and supported by clear and transparent policy objectives.

In any case, much like the extension of existing legal frameworks (such as copyright or related rights) to AI-generated creations, the proposal to introduce *ad hoc* protection is not without its critics.

First and foremost is the concern that, according to some,[789] introducing a new right for AI-generated content would increase the risk of misattribution of such creations, given the far less advantageous regime they would enjoy over human creations. In fact, the same critical issues arise here as in the hypothesis that all AI-assisted outputs automatically fall into the public domain. Indeed, in some cases, someone might falsely claim authorship over a work that was actually generated by AI for the sole purpose of benefiting from longer copyright protection. In particular, some have argued that, due to the clear resemblance between traditional creative works and those generated by AI, challenging the authenticity of authorship claims may prove difficult (if not altogether unfeasible) especially in corporate environments where industrial secrecy is paramount.[790]

From this perspective, any transparency obligations provided for in the T&Cs of the service (e.g., the platforms hosting the generative AI)[791] or those set out in the AI act would also risk being ineffective, as it would be difficult in such a context to ensure their enforcement.

Even if one wishes to overcome these critical issues, however, such a solution risks proving unsatisfactory from a systematic standpoint.[792] As has been

788 Fabbio (n 360) 298.

789 See German Report of the AIPPI Study Question (n 356).

790 Bensamoun and Farchy (n 4) 45.

791 E.g. OpenAI' T&Cs, where it is specified that in the case of sharing content created with its own applications "the role of AI in formulating the content' must be 'clearly disclosed in a way that no reader could possibly miss, and that a typical reader would find sufficiently easy to understand"; see https://openai.com/policies/sharing-publication-policy (last accessed November 2023).

792 For example, specific reflections should be made with respect to the rights of performers in the works of AI, since normally their right is based on the performance of a classical intellectual works; see Bensamoun and Farchy (n 4) 45.

correctly argued, whenever a new area of exclusive rights is to be introduced, it is necessary to adopt a cautious approach: before contemplating the introduction of a new right in these terms, it is essential to provide a demonstration that it is indispensable for developing innovation in a given sector.[793]

In fact, the implementation of a specific *ex novo* framework can only be considered acceptable if the associated social costs are lower than the associated net benefits.[794]

Moreover, this solution could potentially be reduced to yet another "exception to the rule" of copyright, in a way that is alien to the objectives of promoting the advancement of culture and artistic productions. Finally, it potentially underestimates the scale of generative AI and its broader implications within the context of knowledge capitalism.

To counter the overwhelming power of the big players – potentially represented here in three main roles[795] by intermediaries in the creative industry, providers of artificial intelligence, and gatekeepers of online platforms[796] – it may be necessary to move beyond the mere addition of another derogation from the traditional copyright regime, and instead engage in a broader, more structural reflection.

3 Is It Desirable to Protect AI-Generated Outputs under Copyright Law?

The conventional distinction that scholars and policy institutions tend to draw between AI-assisted and AI-generated outputs, when addressing the issue of protection for AI-based creations, is essentially an overly dichotomous representation of the two ends of the spectrum in which the "creative" process may unfold when generative AI is used to produce intellectual works. This distinction reflects the varying degrees of human involvement and algorithmic contribution in different creative processes: in a highly automated process, human input is minimal – both quantitatively and, possibly, qualitatively non-creative – while the algorithmic contribution is dominant; in a less automated process, the opposite is true: the human input is potentially creative

793 Geiger C, 'The Construction of Intellectual Property in the European Union: Searching for Coherence' in Geiger C (ed), Constructing European Intellectual Property: Achievements and New Perspectives, EIPIN Series Vol 1 (Edward Elgar 2013) 21.

794 Ginsburg and Budiardjo (n 357) 455–456.

795 Macmillan, 'Il diritto d'autore nell'era digitale' (n 762).

796 See Art. 2 in conjunction with Art. 3 of the EU DMA (n 284).

and sufficient to exert control over the process such that authorship can be attributed to the resulting output and copyright applied.

Such a distinction is certainly valid from a theoretical standpoint, provided it is based not on the autonomy of AI systems but rather on the degree of automation (not of the AI itself, but of the creative process). However, it often struggles to maintain logical coherence when applied to concrete cases. Nonetheless, this distinction reflects what has been described as the "resistance" of the personalistic theory of copyright,[797] which, in judicial and doctrinal assessments regarding the protection of AI-based outputs, still gives pre-eminence to the human being – that is, to the evaluation of whether a human made free and creative choices.

Although it remains necessary to determine how the "principle of human primacy"[798] will and should be applied in specific cases, the primacy of the human designer is, in general, a widely shared principle at the international level, as discussed in Chapter 6.

On the basis of these premises – and bearing in mind the limitations inherent in the classification of AI-based content in "generated" and "assisted" ones – from the analysis above it is clear that different solutions can be proposed for the legal treatment of such AI creations. These range from the opposing approaches of the application of copyright protection, and placement in the public domain, to more intermediate solutions, such as the application of regulatory frameworks external to copyright law (e.g., antitrust regulation), protection through related rights, or the *de lege ferenda* introduction of a *sui generis* right, etc. All of these options have been examined thus far and are respectively supported by different strands of legal scholarship.

Answering the question of whether AI-generated works are eligible for protection is, in theory, possible from each of these perspectives – each offering its own advantages and drawbacks, as shown above. Yet, while these theoretical approaches are all viable, (i) their practical applicability remains limited: the assessment of the protectability of AI-generated outputs continues to be, and perhaps will always remain, a case-by-case matter. Moreover, (ii) favoring one solution over another depends on broader considerations and should arise from a more systematic reflection – one that places at its core the aim of contributing, through this very question as well, to the broader governance of the phenomenon of generative AI in cultural and (re)creative domains.

As to the first point (i), the still pending decisions in the United States' cases will likely shed more light on how US courts and the Copyright Office interpret

797 Iaia, Klein and De Gaspari (n 613).

798 Bensamoun and Farchy (n 4) 26.

and assess the interplay between human and algorithmic contributions in the creative process. In EU, the Court of Justice of the European Union – together with national courts – will continue to play a crucial role in establishing standards and guiding principles in the absence of a harmonized statutory framework.

While responses may need to remain case-specific, however, the imperative of legal certainty requires nonetheless that they be anchored in widely shared principles – ideally at the international level, given the inherently transnational nature of the phenomenon at stake – bringing the analysis to the second point (ii).

Infact, when placed within the broader matter at hand, that is the governance of a phenomenon deeply embedded in a specific socio-economic context (knowledge capitalism) and situated within a distinct historical moment of intellectual property law, the central question surrounding the protectability of AI-generated works needs to shift from "Is it possible to protect them?" to "Is it desirable to do so?"

Answering this question requires, first and foremost, a conscious acknowledgment (and possibly a clear stance) on not only the functions copyright is believed to fulfil at present, but also those it ought to serve in the future.

SECTION 4

Closing the Circle

CHAPTER 9

The Way of the Social Function of Copyright Law

1 Connecting the Dots

As two facets of the same broader concern, the analysis of issues relating to the input and output phases of the algorithmic creative process has been central to the overarching goal of this manuscript, which is to explore how the use of generative AI in the creative sector can be regulated more effectively, and more appropriately, while also reflecting on the role that law (particularly copyright law) has played, currently plays, and could play in the future in governing this phenomenon.

As discussed in the previous chapters, the debate surrounding generative AI is highly fragmented, with numerous voices often in tension with one another. In this proliferation of perspectives, the role of law is frequently overshadowed – sometimes by the momentum of technological innovation, and sometimes by the pressures of economic interests.

Even the most cautious commentators – those who resist both uncritical technological enthusiasm and the market-driven logic that increasingly shapes today's landscape – tend to focus their interventions primarily on ethics. Ethical considerations are often invoked by these observers as a means to counterbalance the potential negative consequences of the phenomenon. However, while undoubtedly essential, such reflections frequently have the unintended effect – at least in public discourse – of obscuring the role that law itself can play, including through the legal instruments already available within its own tradition.

As a result, the role of law in relation to this phenomenon remains far from clear, both for (industry) operators and lawyers and for the broader public.

Reactions to these technologies tend to swing between two extremes: dismissiveness on the one hand, and sensationalism on the other.

The aim of this work is not to demonize these tools, nor to downplay the relevance of technology-driven or market-oriented considerations. On the contrary, the manuscript fully acknowledges the immense value that these technologies can bring – whether in research, in creative endeavors, in automating repetitive tasks, in detecting illnesses, in analyzing data, or in advancing knowledge and innovation. At the same time, however, it recognizes the risks they entail, beginning from the premise that one of the core functions of law is precisely to distribute resources and to allocate risks.

 HTTPS://DOI.ORG/10.1163/9789004730731-011

From a descriptive standpoint, adopting an input–output dialectic is necessary because, as the analysis so far has shown, the two sides of the process raise distinct technical and operational issues, engage different legal provisions, and rest on different underlying premises.

Yet this dialectic alone is insufficient, as the inherently iterative nature of the creative process makes clear. This holds for several reasons: yesterday's datasets and prompts determine today's outputs, and today's outputs, in turn, may become the inputs of tomorrow's creative processes. Moreover, the apparent distinction between what constitutes the input of an algorithmic process and its resulting output tends to dissolve when viewed through the lens of a broader phenomenon: that of datafication. Ultimately, in the era of datafication, both input and output are nothing but data – extracted, collected, combined, processed, recombined.

Copyright law, while traditionally responsive to technological developments, does not always interact clearly or consistently with the transformations brought about by datafication. As it is generally designed to protect original expressions of ideas rather than mere ideas, data, or information, its precise role in this context remains uncertain.

Tracing back the solutions proposed so far by scholars and courts reveals a fragmented regulatory framework, marked by unclear objectives and frequent instrumentalization.

This is hardly encouraging, especially if one considers datafication as part of today's socio-economic landscape of knowledge capitalism. As previously noted, this context is shaped by well-defined power dynamics, driven by at least two,[799] if not three, major actors: on one side, the giants of the AI industry; and on the other, the traditional intermediaries of the creative industries, alongside – arguably – the suppliers and gatekeepers of online platforms that frequently host generative AI systems.[800]

These actors pursue objectives that extend well beyond the mere provision, through generative AI, of creative services across the cultural domains – be it in music, literature, or other forms of art – and are driven by interests that often guide the direction of the current debate and shape the range of the solutions advanced by the legal scholarship.

On the input side, for instance, the discussion unfolds on two interconnected levels, both shaped by differing views on how broadly the needs of these actors should be accommodated within the copyright framework. At a first level, it concerns whether copyright exceptions and limitations should be interpreted restric-

799 Macmillan, 'Il diritto d'autore nell'era digitale' (n 762).

800 Art. 2 and Art. 3 of the DMA (n 284).

tively or expansively, and whether the international three-step test ought to function as a rigid or rather a flexible tool. At a second level, it addresses the scope and permissibility of TDM activities, both under the doctrine of fair use in the United States and under Articles 3 and 4 of the CDSM Directive in the European Union. In the EU context, for example, the discussion involves: (i) whether training activities should be regarded as acts of TDM or not – specifically, whether to attribute value to the expressive re-elaboration of data during training or treat the process as purely analytical; (ii) whether, consequently, training amounts to an act of reproduction under copyright law; (iii) if so, whether rightsholders should be allowed to rely on an opt-out mechanism; and (iv) the degree of rigidity that should be accorded to the requirement of "lawful access".

Each of these stances, reflected in scholarly opinions, court decisions, and policy documents, reveals different conceptions of copyright and its relationship to technology and power structures. They also mirror differing understandings of how knowledge, embedded in the data ingested by algorithms and capable of generating further knowledge, may or may not be appropriated through exclusive rights.

On the output side, similar concerns emerge, as the questions raised and the solutions advanced are closely tied to the extent to which the current regulatory framework is seen as accommodating or not the interests of these three dominant actors. As noted, the debate on whether AI-generated outputs should be regarded as protectable under copyright, whether their protection should instead be entrusted to other legal instruments – either internal or external to the copyright framework broadly understood (including related and *sui generis* rights) – or whether they should ultimately be treated as part of the public domain. Answering these questions inevitably requires addressing how originality is to be understood: whether in objective or subjective terms, whether the threshold for originality should be raised or lowered, and whether originality can or must reflect the author's personality.

Once again, the positions adopted by scholars, courts, and policymakers reveal not only their perception of copyright law but also their underlying view of the broad framework itself, including its surrounding architecture: as an individualistic rather than a collective construct, and as a body of law serving purely private interests or also pursuing broader public goals.

As a result, the positions taken by operators, commentators, and policymakers on the algorithmic creative process as a whole – from the distinction line between "idea" and "expression", to the nature and quality of human intervention in algorithmic creation, to the status of the "data" ingested by AI and the "data" it produces – become a litmus test of how these actors perceive and conceptualize copyright law, also in the face of possible *de facto* and *de jure* shifts in its classical categories.

The fact that these issues are situated within the broader framework of the ongoing "technological paradigm shift" is neither accidental nor is it trivial to consider in the analysis of the matters at stake. Bringing this dimension to light is useful because it allows the different positions taken in the debate to be recomposed into a coherent picture: many of them, once situated within this paradigm shift, reveal themselves as essentially market-driven. This is evident, for example, in the stances of those who (i) favor a restrictive interpretation of exceptions and limitations and of the three-step test, (ii) adopt a rigid reading of the notions of "reproduction" and "lawful access", or (iii) advocate for a lower threshold of originality as a requirement for copyright protection.

Taken together, in fact, these positions can be seen as manifestations of what has been described in the literature as (a non-technical) copyright propertization.[801]

First, they reflect a broader trend toward the privatization of knowledge, which, as noted in Chapter 1, implies the progressive application of proprietary logics to what until recently belonged to the common heritage of knowledge, such as mere ideas and non-creative expressions of those ideas. This privatization has often been conceptually justified by invoking the tragedy of the commons,[802] but in practice it has served to legitimize the gradual erosion of the public domain in the name of strong IP protection, presented as a tool to avoid market failures associated with commons regimes.

Moreover, these positions may be read in the light of the extractive and accumulative model of knowledge capitalism, which allows the market logics of AI industries and large cultural intermediaries to prevail over the protection of authors' interests, particularly those of individual creators.

These positions, indeed, often reflect an uncritical acceptance of prevailing market logics, which are the responsible for the growing tension between the traditional copyright framework and the role it is increasingly expected to play in contemporary society. In doing so, they leave unaddressed some of the most

801 Sganga, 'Propertizing European Copyright' (n. 345).

802 Hardin G has argued that, absent appropriate incentives supported by a network of guarantees to sustain the work leading to invention, the production of such goods would be insufficient. This view, set out in 'The Tragedy of the Commons' (1968) 162 Science 1243, rests on a twofold theoretical foundation: first, the postulates of the economic analysis of information; and second, following the motto "private property saves lives", the Hayekian theses on the superiority of private property regimes over forms of public regulation. In this regard, see Resta, 'La privatizzazione della conoscenza e la promessa dei beni comuni' (n 59), 286.

pressing risks posed by the AI disruption – such as, to name a few, the concentration of power in the hands of a few major players, labor market displacement, market dilution, the lack of remuneration for creators, and the homogenization of cultural outputs (as described in greater detail in Chapter 2). All these phenomena should be regarded as integral considerations within a healthy regulatory framework, as their neglect ultimately heightens barriers to accessing cultural expressions and – at a higher level of abstraction – to culture and knowledge themselves.

This is precisely why, in order to regulate the use of generative AI in the creative sector through the lens of copyright law not only more effectively but also more desirably – that is, mitigating the risks arising from an uncritical acceptance of the ongoing privatization of knowledge within the emerging paradigm of knowledge capitalism – the response must be sought not solely in technical tools and operational solutions, but in a principled assessment of the function we wish to attribute to copyright law.

Indeed, outlining a better governance framework for this phenomenon on the copyright side requires a holistic view of the problem,[803] one that fully considers the role of copyright in relation to innovation. As has been observed, "a more holistic view that accounts for the role of IP law across the AI innovation cycle would be beneficial".[804]

Outlining such a governance model through copyright law is no easy task. The very expression "copyright wars"[805] used to describe these debates, along with the evident fragmentation of the current normative framework – despite its resilience, exemplified by the principle of human pre-eminence reaffirmed even in the age of AI – demonstrates how copyright law has long been pulled in different directions by competing interests.

The regulatory environment, in fact, already appears to be significantly deformed by the pursuit of objectives that bear little relation to the original purposes of copyright law, and it risks being strained even further in the AI era, as suggested by the *de facto* and *de jure* transformations that AI technologies may imply.

The challenge is further compounded by the transnational dimension of the phenomenon, which demands a delicate coordination among the (at least) three

803 Drexl, Hilty et al (n 228).

804 Ibid.

805 See, e.g., Baldwin P, The Copyright Wars: Three Centuries of Transatlantic Battle (Princeton University Press 2014); Johns A, Piracy: The Intellectual Property Wars from Gutenberg to Gates (University of Chicago Press 2010); Decherney P, Hollywood's Copyright Wars: From Edison to the Internet (Columbia University Press 2012); Macmillan F, '"Speaking Truth to Power": Copyright and the Control of Speech' in Pollicino O, Riccio GM and Bassini M (eds), Copyright and Fundamental Rights in the Digital Age. A Comparative Analysis in Search of a Common Constitutional Ground (Edward Elgar 2020), 20.

major geopolitical blocs and the complex balancing of the diverse forces at play. The EU's own difficult, non-linear experience with the adoption of the AI Act – and the equally intricate process of its implementation through templates and codes of practice – offers a telling example. Globalization, moreover, complicates the formation of a public opinion capable of underpinning collective decision-making, tending to deprive societies of the conditions for democratic political deliberation and leaving economic logics as the dominant force.[806]

Above all, the task is challenging because AI technology, the governance of knowledge, and IP regulation are not neutral instruments and are, moreover, deeply interdependent. Because of this interdependency, any attempt to regulate AI and copyright with the aim of identifying the most desirable governance model inevitably affects knowledge and its accessibility.[807] Since knowledge is cumulative by nature, building upon pre-existing layers, any attempt to enclose it reveals its full disruptive potential.

Hence, striving for a more socially desirable governance of this phenomenon is no easy task, yet it is all the more important. It requires acknowledging that the proprietary, exclusivist approach – pervasive as it may be – is neither inevitable nor necessarily the best, or only, option to regulate the balance of freedom, access, and control over knowledge.

This becomes evident when one adopts a functionalist perspective of the analysis, which evaluates the interests involved as a basis for meaningful reflection and, ultimately, workable solutions. In this context, the relevant interests are both private and collective, and the relationship between them is becoming increasingly uncertain. The demands for individualization and personalization – hallmarks of the so-called "second" and "third modernity", already embedded two decades ago in the business models of Apple and Google and reflective of one of the private interests at stake – interact ambiguously with the general interest, including that in preserving culture and a pluralistic cultural environment.

In copyright law too, the supposedly symmetric forces of individual and collective interests upon which this framework is founded shape its very essence and underpin its constitutional status across many legal traditions, from the US to the EU.[808] Yet, the answers given to questions such as what

806 Barcellona M, 'La metafora dei beni comuni: l'Impero, lo Stato e la democrazia nel tempo del capitale cognitivo' (2016) 3 Democrazia e Diritto.

807 Even when formally granted, access to it does not necessarily translate into effective usability, thereby exposing it to problematic trajectories where it risks becoming increasingly enclosed in the hands of few actors; see Barcellona (n 806).

808 On one hand are the private interests of authors, involving control over their work, its uses, and corresponding remuneration, consistent with a humanist approach to copyright; on the other hand, are collective interests, centered on the promotion of culture

qualifies as a protected work, where to draw the line between idea and expression, how to define the creative process, and whether and how inputs or outputs are protectable under copyright, will directly affect the – already unstable – equilibrium of these interests.

Nonetheless, the ambition to protect both sets of interests often remains a matter of principle, one that increasingly struggles to align with reality. As will be further illustrated soon, the "corporate copyright" trope highlights how copyright law may increasingly struggle to pursue public interests, while its growing fragmentation renders it highly susceptible to instrumentalization.

What is needed, therefore, is a more sustainable reconsideration of copyright law, one that involves a re-systematization of the discipline at (at least) the EU level – passing through a reassessment of the constitutional significance of copyright and a renewed focus on its social function – ultimately enabling its reconstruction as a pluralistic framework.

Such a process is only prompted by the emergence of generative AI, which has amplified the need for a comprehensive reconsideration of this legal framework, but the disruption brought by generative AI is merely the epiphenomenon of broader tensions that have long surrounded copyright law.

2 Re-systematization of Copyright Law

2.1 The "Copyright Corporate Trope" and the Need for a Re-systematization of the Discipline

The debate on generative AI unfolds against the backdrop of at least two ongoing intellectual property crises, which, over the past two decades, have provided fertile ground for European and international policymakers to pursue a steady strengthening of IP rights: a crisis of public legitimacy[809] as well as a crisis in the effectiveness of the very mechanisms of "appropriation" on which it rests.

At the heart of these crises lies a deep tension between the ongoing transformation of copyright and the traditional justifications advanced by both

---

and aligned with the constitutional or broader public interest dimension of intellectual property.

809 Geiger, 'The Social Function of Intellectual Property Rights' (n 87); Ginsburg, 'How Copyright Got a Bad Name for Itself' (n 186); Dusollier, 'Open Source and Copyleft: Authorship Reconsidered?' (n 186).

scholars and legislators for granting exclusive rights over the intangible assets that constitute creative works.

Under strong pressures (including the challenge of approximating the profoundly different traditions of common law and civil law[810]) and lobbying influences,[811] copyright law has increasingly been reshaped as a regime primarily serving the economic prerogatives of authors and, especially, of the creative industry's intermediaries. This evolution has often occurred to the detriment of both the moral rights central to civil law traditions, with their strong personalist imprint, and of a more collective, societal conception of copyright. In practice, copyright has gradually shifted from a legal technique designed to protect interests often antagonistic to those of industry into a mechanism primarily serving industrial and commercial interests.[812] Indeed, originally intended to protect authors and provide them with incentives to create, it has come to be widely perceived as a system that primarily benefits "large, impersonal, and unlovable corporations".[813] This dynamic is captured by what the literature has termed the "corporate copyright" trope:[814] the recognition that the bulk of copyright's modern expansion has disproportionately enriched intermediaries – publishers, studios, record labels, and digital platforms – rather than individual creators or the public. Most authors and creative professionals, in fact, derive only limited benefits from copyright compared to the far greater advantages accruing to the firms that mediate between creators and audiences.[815]

---

810 Scarciglia R, Metodi e comparazione giuridica (3rd edn, Wolters Kluwer 2021).

811 Spina Alì G, 'Why Intellectual Property Does Not Belong in the Constitution(s): Four Considerations' (2020) 42(8) European Intellectual Property Review, 464, Geiger C, 'Implementing Intellectual Property Provisions in Human Rights Instruments: Towards a New Social Contract for the Protection of Intangibles' in Geiger C (ed), Research Handbook on Human Rights and Intellectual Property (Edward Elgar 2015) 662–664.

812 Spada P, 'Banche di dati e diritto d'autore (Il "genere" del diritto d'autore sulle banche di dati)' (1997) AIDA, 17 ff.; see also Geiger, 'Copyright as an Access Right' (n 378) 3: "Copyright, originally conceived as a tool to protect the author and to provide incentives for him to create for the benefit of society, is nowadays more and more perceived as a mechanism to the advantage of "large, impersonal and unlovable corporations"; see *contra* Chimienti (n 571) 26, footnote 2.

813 Geiger, 'Copyright as an Access Right' (n 378) 3.

814 Hughes J and Merges RP, 'Copyright and Distributive Justice' (2017) 92 Notre Dame L Rev 513.

815 This imbalance reflects the dual-incentive structure of copyright, which is meant to reward both authors and the industries investing in their work. In practice, however, the latter are far more powerful, better organized, and better positioned to shape copyright's evolution through lobbying and policy influence. The result is a system in which

Moreover, this shift, paired with the pervasive datafication of all human interactions, has pushed for the expansion of IP protection even to many of the "new economic goods".[816]

Together, these dynamics are producing a progressive and extensive "restyling" of intellectual property law, whose theoretical framework appears now increasingly fragile.[817]

Such restyling has frequently been justified by the utilitarian rationale of copyright, which has historically relied on the "tragedy of the commons" argument theorized by Hardin: the idea that free access to information leads to inefficiency,[818] and that granting exclusive rights is therefore necessary to foster creativity and innovation.

However, a growing body of critical scholarship has highlighted a widening gap between the doctrinal narrative of such utilitarian justification (law in the books) and its real-world functioning (law in action).[819]

In particular, within the knowledge capitalism framework,[820] copyright is becoming no longer "an engine for the creation of ideas, nor a tool for enhancing cultural development" (incentivizing creativity and innovation), but rather a limitation on the circulation of ideas and on their re-use or re-elaboration.[821]

In line with this restyling of copyright law, what was once framed as a balanced system serving both private and public interests now arguably appears instrumentalized to pursue functions that are skewed toward the private side and often alien to its original purpose. Even its core concepts (authorship, creativity, originality, the very notion of "intellectual work")[822] risk being increasingly reframed, to the point that recent scholarship has begun to highlight this evolution, de-romanticizing the often misleading narrative that has traditionally surrounded the legislation.[823]

This dynamic becomes even more pronounced in the context of generative AI. As illustrated in Chapter 6, the growing use of generative AI in artistic and (re)creative domains amplifies the risk of a market-driven reinterpretation of

---

industry gains are prioritized, while creators and the public interest are increasingly marginalized; see Macmillan, 'Speaking Truth to Power' (n 805).

816 Clerico and Rizzello (n 700), 175; Resta G (ed), 'Diritti esclusivi e nuovi beni immateriali' (Utet Giuridica 2010).

817 Ibid.

818 Resta, 'La privatizzazione della conoscenza e la promessa dei beni comuni' (n 59) 185.

819 Macmillan, 'Speaking Truth to Power' (n 805) 20.

820 Ibid, 21.

821 Ibid.

822 Ibid.

823 Ibid.

foundational copyright categories, further destabilizing the fragile equilibrium between private and public interests.

This is why a change in perspective is needed.

To counterbalance the drifts of the corporate copyright trope, indeed, a comprehensive reassessment and systematization of copyright law may become indispensable. The advent of generative AI – while raising issues that are not new in nature but certainly different in scale – offers a unique opportunity to reappraise this framework. More specifically, it underscores the urgency of a coherent systematization that revolves around two fundamental principles: on the one hand, the centrality of human authorship; on the other, the preservation of free and shared knowledge.

In line with the ambitious proposals advanced by part of the doctrine, it may be necessary to "eradicate the economic-centric grafts" that have progressively distorted copyright, and to recover the constitutional dimension of this institution within the value framework of the right to science and culture, or even freedom of expression.[824]

2.1.1 A Manifesto for a Sustainable Intellectual Property

Contrary to the claims of some scholars who regard intellectual property as one of the "black beasts" of knowledge capitalism, the matter is not settled by the nature of IP itself: it depends largely on the general theories of justification adopted, which ultimately reflect specific legal policy choices. The motivations that prompt the legislature to artificially create exclusive spaces attributable to IP rights may, in fact, also be grounded in values other than those primarily defended by industry.

Yet, it is undeniable that "restyled" intellectual property – tellingly renamed pseudo-IP[825] – is now often shaped by a few influential economic actors, who can increasingly assert themselves on a global scale as the "winners" of today's capitalist system.

Against this backdrop, which inverts the means-to-end relationship between IP protection on the one hand, and the protection of authors and the promotion of culture on the other, a revisitation of this framework in a sustainable key of the system becomes essential.

---

824 Iaia, 'Le derive della creatività nel diritto d'autore' (n 355) 237.

825 Caso R, 'Michelangelo's David and Cultural Heritage Images: The Italian Pseudo -Intellectual Property and the End of Public Domain' (Kluwer Copyright Blog, 2023) <https://legalblogs.wolterskluwer.com/copyright-blog/michelangelos-david-and-cultural-heritage-images-the-italian-pseudo-intellectual-property-and-the-end-of-public-domain/> accessed 9 August 2025.

Sustainable intellectual property is intellectual property not in opposition to, but in support of other fundamental rights and, especially, the right to freedom of expression and information.

It is an intellectual property that benefits the community and integrates with the prerogatives of the law protecting free competition, especially in a context where the established and lasting concentration of power of such market players is extremely strong, as in the digital context.[826]

A sustainable intellectual property is a more transparent intellectual property, which, guided by the principle that economic freedom and the exercise of property cannot conflict with social utility, also pursues general and collective interests, including the protection of future generations.

It is a pluralist and inclusive intellectual property, grounded in the principle of solidarity[827] and the protection of human dignity – whose inviolable character and binding force, requiring respect and protection (Art. 1, EU Charter of Fundamental Rights), give it the potential to act as a genuine principle of market regulation.[828]

It is an intellectual property system in which the utilitarian argument for incentivizing research and promoting culture is not abandoned, but instead shifts from being the insurmountable premise and ultimate goal of public action to becoming its guiding constraint.[829]

Sustainable intellectual property is, therefore, intellectual property that certainly takes into account the technological, social, economic, and cultural changes taking place, but without yielding to the temptation — often driven by sectoral interests — to unreasonably compress the interests of the society in favor of the interests of the industry.

The sustainable reinterpretation of intellectual property, far from denying the nature of intellectual property as a law protecting relations between private individuals and its fundamental role in regulating the market, nevertheless presupposes that it can also pursue the general interest, giving concrete effect to the objectives long enshrined in European and international charters, which otherwise risk being reduced to mere rhetorical declarations.

---

826 Camardi C, 'Contratti digitali e mercati delle piattaforme. Un promemoria per il civilista' (2021) 4 Jus Civile.

827 Balduzzi R, 'La "liberalizzazione" dei diritti di proprietà intellettuale sui vaccini. Profili costituzionali e internazionali' (2022) 2 Quaderni costituzionali – Rivista italiana di diritto costituzionale 261.

828 Senigaglia R, 'La dimensione patrimoniale del diritto alla protezione dei dati personali' (2020) 2 Contratto e Impresa, 760–783.

829 Balduzzi (n 827) 265.

2.1.2 The Pillars of an EU Re-systematization

The method of systematization offers a means to restore coherence to a given normative framework by reconnecting it with the common "principles, concepts, and dogmas"[830] elaborated by legal tradition over time.

In this context, such a method is essential to address the growing fragmentation of the system, a problem particularly acute in the EU, where the absence of harmonization has produced what some have described as a "systematic chaos generated by the incompatibility of EU and national copyright models".[831]

This re-systematization should be built upon a set of interrelated pillars.

Given the inherently transnational nature of the phenomenon, such a re-systematization should, at the very least, be pursued at the EU level.

Moreover, copyright has to be understood as a property right, one that has constitutional rank, as expressly recognized in the EU by Article 17(2) of the Charter of Fundamental Rights of the European Union (the "Nice Charter"). As a property right with constitutional value, copyright must conform to the constitutional construction of property that both the EU and its Member States have developed over time.[832]

A constitutional reading of property rights brings to light their internal limitations: according to such view property is not conceived as an absolute and purely exclusivist entitlement, but as a right that is internally limited by the need to pursue a social function. In this sense, copyright should no longer be regarded as a monolithic right of exclusion but as a plural normative framework encompassing diverse operational regimes.

These regimes may be conceived as lying along a spectrum, a graduated scale, where some are closer to the exclusivity pole, while others are oriented toward inclusivity. This approach resonates with the Italian theory of *beni comuni*[833] and the French doctrine of the *échelle de communal-*

830 Sganga, 'Propertizing European Copyright' (n. 345).

831 Sganga C, 'EU Copyright Law Between Property and Fundamental Rights: A Proposal to Connect the Dots' in Roberto Caso and Federica Giovanella (eds), Balancing Copyright Law in the Digital Age (Springer Berlin Heidelberg 2015) <http://link.springer.com/10.1007/978-3-662-44648-5_1> accessed 9 August 2025.

832 Sganga, 'Propertizing European Copyright' (n. 345).

833 Rodotà S, Il terribile diritto. Studi sulla proprietà privata e i beni comuni (3rd edn, il Mulino 2013); Marella MR (ed), Oltre il pubblico e il privato. Per un diritto dei beni comuni (Ombre corte 2012); Mattei U, Beni comuni. Un manifesto (Laterza 2011); Angiolini C, 'La reconnaissance de l'intérêt commun en rapport avec les droits fondamentaux au sein des beni comuni en Italie' in J Rochfeld, GJ Martin and M Cornu (eds), L'échelle de communalité. Proposition de réformes pour intégrer les biens communs en droit (2021); Barcellona (n 806).

ité.[834] This latter, in particular, conceptualizes property as a flexible institution capable of serving private and collective interests in a scalable way, providing tailored arrangements of prerogatives according to the extent and relevance of the community's specific interest in each case.

Thus reshaped, copyright can be understood as an "inclusive" property right,[835] able to embrace societal values that safeguard constitutionally significant interests extending beyond the immediate concerns of the industry, functioning as a vehicle for ensuring public access to cultural artifacts[836] other than protection to intellectual works and their authors. Within this spectrum, the balance between public and private prerogatives will vary depending on the type of work involved and the nature of its use.

The landing point of this re-systematization could take two complementary directions.

On the one hand, this approach could pave the way for legislative intervention, operating *ex ante* and offering the dual advantages of greater legal certainty and the preservation of a more holistic vision of copyright. Yet pursuing this path is particularly challenging, as it remains far from a political priority within the EU. The AI Act itself, for instance, does not engage with such systematic considerations; it merely calls for the implementation of copyright policies to demonstrate compliance with Article 53(1)(c), without addressing the substance of the issue.

On the other hand, re-systematization could, from an *ex post* perspective, help establish clearer and more transparent criteria to guide fair-balance assessments and other judicial tests.

2.2 The Constitutional Foundation(s) of Copyright

In recent decades, alongside the rise of pseudo-IP and the corporate copyright trope, a parallel trend has emerged: initial critical reflections and isolated acts of dissent against this IP restyling have evolved into organized movements, increasingly advocating for the reorganization of innovation-stimulating regimes in line with socially beneficial objectives.[837]

---

834 Rochfeld, Martin and Cornu (n 676).

835 Dusollier S, 'The Commons as a Reverse Intellectual Property – from Exclusivity to Inclusivity' in Helena Howe and Jonathan Griffiths (eds), Concepts of Property in Intellectual Property Law (1st edn, Cambridge University Press 2013) <https://www.cambridge.org/core/product/identifier/9781107300880%23c04182-11-1/type/book_part> accessed 9 August 2025; Dusollier S, 'Propriétés Inclusives' (2024) 29 Lex Electronica 81.

836 Geiger, 'Copyright as an Access Right' (n 378).

837 Resta, 'La privatizzazione della conoscenza e la promessa dei beni comuni' (n 59) 291.

This trend is also evident in legal scholarship, where the resistance to pseudo-IP is increasingly coalescing around a new narrative that highlights the ongoing constitutionalization of intellectual property in the EU[838] – a process driven first by legislation and subsequently reinforced through case law – which increasingly relies on fundamental rights in shaping and applying IP norms,[839] also horizontally.[840]

In this context, fundamental rights perform a twofold function in the field of intellectual property: they provide the basis for external limitations to IP law,[841] and they also shape its scope through internal limitations, reinforcing its status as a constitutionally relevant right.

Depending on the philosophical perspective and the relevant theory of justification, the constitutional foundation of IP has been identified, at a minimum,[842] as: (i) a fundamental property right; (ii) a fundamental personality right; (iii) a right ensuring both freedom of (artistic) expression and individual access to culture and science; or (iv) a right instrumental to the fundamental right to culture, fostering innovation and the dissemination of knowledge.

In this first sense, copyright is conceived as a fundamental right insofar as it constitutes a property right. In this regard, John Locke's theory has been deemed particularly influential, often complemented - albeit inaccurately - by a Kantian interpretation that frames copyright as a natural right.[843]

838 Geiger C, "Constitutionalizing" Intellectual Property Law? The Influence of Fundamental Rights on Intellectual Property in Europe' (2006) 37(4) IIC 371; Geiger and Izyumenko (n 12). Interestingly, the constitutionalization of intellectual property is not, as is well known, an isolated phenomenon and, indeed, is part of the broader strand of the constitutionalization of civil law as a whole. On this point, see Camardi C, 'Brevi riflessioni sull'argomentazione per principi nel diritto privato' (2017) 5 Rivista di Diritto Civile, 1130.

839 Geiger and Izyumenko (n 12).

840 Sganga, 'Propertizing European Copyright' (n. 345).

841 With regard to the first aspect, the extensive case law of the Court of Justice of the European Union and the European Court of Human Rights is emblematic. By way of example, the CJEU decisions in *Funke Medien, Pelham,* and *Spiegel Online* (Funke Medien NRW GmbH v Bundesrepublik Deutschland EU:C:2019:623, Case C-476/17, Pelham GmbH and Others v Ralf Hütter and Florian Schneider-Esleben EU:C:2019:624 and Case C-516/17 Spiegel Online GmbH v Volker Beck EU:C:2019:625) have addressed the proper balance between intellectual property and other fundamental rights, such as the rights to privacy and freedom of expression, at times limiting the former in light of the latter, conceived as its outer boundaries.

842 See also the taxonomy outlined by Macmillan: "firstly, copyright as a fundamental property right; secondly, copyright as a fundamental personal and/or cultural right; thirdly, copyright as a means to encourage cultural innovation and diffusion of that innovation"; see Macmillan, 'Speaking Truth to Power' (n 805).

843 Macmillan, 'Speaking Truth to Power' (n 805) 22.

In short, under this approach, property is protected to safeguard individual freedom; the person is therefore indirectly protected through the protection of the property they create.[844] The author, as a "creator of property", gains personal protection through the direct protection of the work they have brought into being.[845]

At the international level, the reconstruction of copyright as a fundamental property right has often been linked to Article 15(1)(c) of the UN International Covenant on Economic, Social and Cultural Rights (ICESCR). Yet some scholars argue that this interpretation is unfounded: the provision recognizes the right of authors to have their "moral and material interests" protected, but it does not mandate the granting of property rights as the means to achieve this protection.[846]

At the level of national law, the French tradition offers an emblematic example, historically affirming that "The most sacred, the most legitimate, the most unassailable, and, if I may say so, the most personal of all properties, is the work, the fruit of the mind of a writer".[847] However, the French Constitution, like most other national constitutions, do not contain expressly any reference to intellectual property, nor does it define it as "property" right.[848]

At the European Union level, instead, a positive foundation of the recognition of IP rights as property rights is found in Article 17(2) of the Charter of Fundamental Rights of the European Union (Nice Charter). This provision has been interpreted as not only affirming the nature of intellectual property as a property right within the EU, but also as elevating it to the status of a fundamental right.[849]

---

844 Rahmatian A, 'Originality in UK Copyright Law: The Old "Skill and Labour" Doctrine Under Pressure' (2013) 44 IIC – International Review of Intellectual Property and Competition Law 4, 13.

845 Ibid.

846 "The baselessness of The argument that the grant of private property rights over intellectual output is mandated by Article 15(1)(c) of the International Covenant on Economic, Social and Cultural Rights is fairly evident from its text, which recognises the rights of authors to have their 'moral and material interests' protected, but says nothing about the grant of private property rights in order to achieve this end"; see Macmillan, 'Speaking Truth to Power' (n 805).

847 On this oft-quoted phrase from Le Chapelier, the reporter for the French decree on copyright in 1791, see the analysis of Bently L and Kretschmer M (eds), 'Le Chapelier's report (1791), Primary Sources on Copyright (1450–1900)' <http://www.copyrighthistory.org> accessed 9 August 2025.

848 Sganga, 'Propertizing European Copyright' (n. 345) 112. Countries having IP in their constitutions are, inter alia, Portugal (Art. 42(2)), Sweden (ch. 2 sect. 19); Slovakia (Art. 43(1)), Slovenia (Art. 60), Czech Republic (Art. 34), Russia (Art. 44(1)).

849 Sganga, 'Propertizing European Copyright' (n. 345) 4.

However, neither the consecration of intellectual property as a "fundamental right as a property right" based on art. 17(2) of the Nice Charter has been free from controversy. Criticism has focused on several points: the laconic wording of the provision in the Nice Charter, which appears inconsistent with its stated objective to "put a stronger emphasis on the growing importance of IP for the EU, particularly in light of the large number of legislative acts enacted in the field",[850] leaving its interpretation uncertain; the fact that the recognition of IP as a fundamental right has often served as a legal basis for policies expanding its exclusive scope;[851] and, finally, the failure to account for the composite nature of intellectual property or for the philosophical justifications that typically underlie fundamental rights.[852] In particular, the inclusion of IP in Article 17(2) of the Charter of Fundamental Rights of the European Union, if interpreted merely as a consecration of the economic weight of this area of law,[853] risks portraying intellectual property as an end in itself, rather than as a means for the pursuit of broader societal interests[854] – contrary to the usual reading of fundamental rights.

According to a second conception, copyright is protected first and foremost as the author's personality right: as a human being, everything the author creates and which bears the features of the author's personality also obtains protection.[855]

850 Sganga, 'Propertizing European Copyright' (n. 345) 112. See the explanatory note of the Praesidium (Praesidium, Explanations relating to the Charter of Fundamental Rights [2007] OJ C-303/17, 23) and by the comment redacted by the Commission's Network of Independent Experts on Fundamental Rights (EU Network of Independent Experts on Fundamental Rights, Commentary of the Charter of Fundamental Rights of the European Union, http://ec.europa.eu/justice/fundamental-rights/files/networkcommentaryfinal_en.pdf, June 2006), 165 ff.

851 Geiger C, 'Intellectual Property Shall Be Protected? – Article 17(2) of the Charter of Fundamental Rights of the European Union: A Mysterious Provision with an Unclear Scope' (2009) European Intellectual Property Review 113 ff.; Sganga, 'Propertizing European Copyright' (n. 345).

852 Shestak JJ, 'The Philosophical Foundations of Human Rights' in Symonides J (ed), Human Rights: Concepts and Standards (UNESCO/Ashgate Publishing 2002) 31.

853 The inclusion of intellectual property in Article 17(2) of the European Charter of Fundamental Rights could be understood as an expression of a mere "'activism of the Community legislator' and the 'economic weight' of this area of law. And indeed, in the way it is formulated, the statutory provision in question would seem to presuppose the predominant role of the investor"; see Geiger, 'Intellectual Property Shall Be Protected?' (n 851) 113 ff.

854 Ibid.

855 Rahmatian (n 844) 15.

This view, more than in copyright systems, is supported in *droit d'auteur* jurisdictions, where the author's work is protected through the protection of the author's person.[856] This approach, like the view that conceives copyright as a fundamental property right, often finds its justification in Kant's philosophy of natural rights.[857] Unlike the former, however, it does not take into account the Lockean theory of property rights[858] and postulates, instead, a copyright that is primarily intended to protect the author's interest in "the collective appreciation of their work" and, more generally, "in the recognition of the authorship of their actions".[859]

Within this conception of copyright, the "development of the person"[860] and the author's freedom of thought are regarded as prevailing over purely economic considerations.[861]

Adjacent to this conception is the third approach, that regards copyright as a fundamental right insofar as it also guarantees: (i) the freedom of (artistic) expression of the creator, and (ii) the right of access to information, culture, and science – the so-called rights to culture and to science.[862]

This is what part of the literature refers to as the "expressive foundation of IP",[863] according to which copyright is an integral component of the broader right to freedom of opinion and expression. This includes not only the right to express one's thoughts, but also the right "to seek, receive, and disseminate information and ideas by any means and regardless of frontiers"[864] (the right to express oneself, impart and receive information).[865]

Such an understanding reflects a dialogic conception of copyright, viewing it as a tool to foster dialogue between an author and their audience,[866] and it has the merit of emphasizing the close link between copyright and information governance.

---

856 Rahmatian (n 844) 15.

857 Macmillan, 'Speaking Truth to Power' (n 805) 23.

858 Ibid, 23.

859 Ubertazzi (n 349) 1456.

860 Italian Constitutional Court, no. 88/361, in Ubertazzi (n 349) 1456.

861 De Sanctis (n 462) 81.

862 Geiger, 'Copyright as an Access Right' (n 378) 9.

863 Geiger, 'Copyright as an Access Right' (n 378) 9.

864 See Art. 19 Universal Declaration of Human Rights, as well as Art. 10 ECHR, para. 1 and Art. 11(1) of the Nice Charter.

865 Geiger, 'Copyright as an Access Right' (n 378) 9.

866 Such an approach is in line with the view of Kant, who believed that the *opus mysticum* represents the dialogue between author and audience, in respect of which the publisher acts as a mediator. See Limonata, The Copyright Debate, History of European Civilisation edited by Umberto Eco (2014), in www.treccani.it.

The foundations of this conception of copyright can be found in several constitutional charters, at the national, regional, and international levels.

At the national level, the 1978 Spanish Constitution provides an emblematic example:[867] it protects the rights to "literary, artistic, scientific, and technical production and creation" as part of the broader right to freedom of expression and information.[868] As one commentary on Article 20 of the Spanish Constitution aptly notes, freedom of expression is integral to intellectual property, since its absence stifles artistic creativity, scientific research, and the philosophical search for truth: "intellectual property is the riverbed or the iter where freedom of expression passes by".[869]

At the regional level, the instrumental role of copyright in expanding or restricting freedom of expression and access to information is clear from Article 11(2) of the Charter of Fundamental Rights of the European Union (Nice Charter), which specifies that the rights to freedom of opinion and information require respect for the freedom and pluralism of the media – and arguably, by extension, of the creative and original content they convey.

At the international level, this view aligns with both Article 15(1) of the International Covenant on Economic, Social and Cultural Rights (ICESCR) and Article 27(2) of the Universal Declaration of Human Rights (UDHR), which affirms that "everyone has the right freely to participate in the cultural life of the community, to enjoy the arts, and to share in scientific progress and its benefits".

On this normative and, above all, ideological basis,[870] this position has been regarded by part of the literature as far more acceptable than the view that

867 Indeed, it can be inferred from Article 20 of the Spanish Constitution that the purpose of intellectual property is, at least in part, to guarantee freedom of expression and the public's right to information – a logic that could be further traced in Article 15(e) of the 1984 Liberian Constitution, when it refers to the "commercial aspect of expression in […] copyright infringement", and in Article 13 of the Central African Constitution of 2004, which incorporates the protection of "freedom of intellectual, artistic and cultural creation" within the broader right to freedom of expression and information; see Geiger, 'Copyright as an Access Right' (n 378) 13.

868 Otero C, 'La protección constitucional del derecho de autor: Análisis del artículo 20.1 b/ de la Constitución española de 1978' (1986) 2 La Ley 370, 1986.

869 See analyses by Izyumenko E, 'Freedom of Expression as a Rationale for IP Protection' (2023) 72(9) GRUR International 840–852 <https://doi.org/10.1093/grurint/ikad071>.

870 Macmillan, 'Speaking Truth to Power' (n 805) 23–24: "The claim, which covers a broad range of sub-positions, that copyright is a fundamental personal, cultural and/or political right, is generally based on the Kantian concept of natural rights. Prised apart from the Lockean property rights discourse, this position has much more going for it in a normative sense. At its most general, it also seems coherent with Article 15(1)(c) of the UN

grounds the fundamental-rights nature of copyright in property rights.[871] However, it remains contested whether this approach accurately reflects the actual role of copyright in today's legal and economic environment: "the arguments underpinning this second justificatory discourse have considerable appeal, although the claim that they reflect the reality of copyright law is open to debate".[872]

The fourth conception of copyright as a fundamental right views it as a functional instrument for the promotion of culture. Under this approach, the justification for granting exclusive rights over intellectual creations lies "in the interest of (...) promoting cultural progress (...) or to ensure, in competition, the triumph of those works that the public deems most worthy".[873]

This view, arguably consistent with the very objectives enshrined in the Statute of Anne (not by chance formally titled "An Act for the Encouragement of Learning"[874]), finds support in several international instruments. As early as the 1990s, the WIPO Copyright Treaty explicitly emphasized in its preamble "the paramount importance of copyright protection as an incentive for artistic and literary creation".[875] This principle was subsequently reaffirmed in the Directive 2001/29/EC, which noted that the protection of copyright and related rights contributes to the preservation and development of creativity in the interest not only of authors, performers, producers, and consumers, but also of "culture, industry and the public in general" (Recital 9)[876]. A similar approach was later adopted by Directive 2004/48/EC, whose Recital 1 states that "the protection of intellectual property (...) is important not only for the promotion of innovation and creative activity, but also for the development of employment and increased competitiveness" (Recital 1).[877]

International Covenant on Economic, Social and Cultural Rights and with Article 27(2) of the Universal Declaration on Human Rights, on which the former provision is based. The idea that a person is entitled to the 'moral and material' benefits of their intellectual creation is intuitively pleasing and, assuming that the moral interest includes the right to control the use of one's work, it also chimes nicely with empirical research demonstrating that it is this aspect of copyright that is particularly important to authors even in the absence of material benefits".

871 Macmillan, 'Speaking Truth to Power' (n 805) 23.

872 Macmillan, 'Speaking Truth to Power' (n 805) 24.

873 Ascarelli (n 462) 84.

874 Macmillan, 'Speaking Truth to Power' (n 805) 25.

875 WIPO Copyright Treaty (adopted 20 December 1996, entered into force 6 March 2002) 2186 UNTS 121.

876 See also Recital 22 of Directive 2001/29/EC.

877 Directive 2004/48/EC.

In this conception of copyright law, the promotion of culture serves both as the justification for the protection designed by this legal framework and as the criterion for defining its scope – an idea often referred to as the "Progress Clause" borrowing the expression from US constitutional law. Under this principle, copyright's exclusive rights are conferred only insofar as they facilitate the progress of the community,[878] operating through a "social contract" between the author and society.[879]

By virtue of this contract, this framework serves a dual function. On the one hand, it incentivizes the creation of intellectual works – pursuing cultural, economic, and technological progress – by granting the author a reward in the form of a private right that ensures exclusive control over the work. On the other hand, the author, in return, enriches the community by guaranteeing access to the works produced.

From this perspective, the cultural-progress conception of copyright shares certain affinities with the incentive theory. This vision often emphasizes the close interrelation between the author's primary role[880] and the broader public interest, conceived as a means-to-end relationship. Its key distinction, however, lies in its foundation: rather than relying on purely economic arguments, it is grounded in values enshrined in fundamental rights.

This approach also shares affinities with the conception of copyright as a right aimed at fostering the personal development of authors and freedom of expression – an affinity that, as some scholars note, can lead to overlaps among all the categories of constitutional foundations for copyright law.[881]

Although the arguments advanced by the positions[882] of those viewing copyright as "fundamental to" cultural production and those treating it as

---

878 Geiger, 'Copyright as an Access Right' (n 378) 11.

879 Geiger C, Droit d'auteur et droit du public à l'information (Litec 2004) 27 ff.

880 « *L'intérêt privatif des auteurs et des inventeurs150 à l'octroi d'un contrôle exclusif de l'exploitation de leurs œuvres et inventions, porteur d'un éventuel retour économique, est bien entendu central dans les régimes de propriété intellectuelle. Mais ce droit individuel et exclusif est aussi compris comme le moyen de la diffusion dans la société des contenus culturels et des innovations essentiels à son progrès* »; see Rochfeld, Martin and Cornu (n 676) 53. See also Geiger, 'Copyright as an Access Right' (n 378) 11.

881 "This is strange because theoretically the arguments are quite different. However, in an intellectual environment that has not always been notable for the quality of its theoretical engagement, there has been a tendency to roll these two cautiously pro-copyright positions together. As Waldron notes, this is a consequence of a type of inductive reasoning that 'moves from encouragement to incentive to benefit to reward to desert, so that something which starts off as a matter of desirable social policy ends up entrenched in an image of moral entitlement'"; see Macmillan, 'Speaking Truth to Power' (n 805).

882 Macmillan, 'Speaking Truth to Power' (n 805) 25.

"instrumental to" it differ from a theoretical perspective, they arguably share a common normative foundation,[883] as both rest on the assumption that cultural production and circulation of artifacts are essential goods of society.[884]

There is, in fact, a certain complementarity between the two conceptions. One protects an individual, constitutionally relevant interest, resulting in a question of "moral entitlement".[885] The other protects a more general interest, responding instead to a form of "desirable social policy".[886]

This complementarity reflects the enduring tension between individual and collective prerogatives that underlies the very foundation of copyright. Its balance – although, as has been noted, "constantly pursued without distinction of time and place" – has taken many different normative forms over the centuries, depending on the weight accorded, at any given historical moment, to either "the individual interests of authors or cultural intermediaries [or] the interests of the community to have more or less access to protected works".[887]

2.3 The Social Function of Copyright Law

2.3.1 Copyright's Social Function as the Result of the Integration of Its Constitutional Foundations

Among the fixed points emerging from the discussion so far is that (i) copyright is, at least in part, a property right – but, as has been observed by Sganga, this aspect alone is ultimately insufficient to justify the absolute and inviolable conception typical of eighteenth-century Western legal traditions;[888] (ii) at the same time, copyright serves an expressive function and plays a central role in promoting culture, operating at the intersection of private and public interests.

Discarding any of the mentioned constitutional foundations for copyright would be neither wise nor necessary. Indeed, they all can serve as a starting point for broader reflections on the very function of copyright law: in fact, taken together, these three constitutional conceptions of copyright – as a proprietary right, a personality and freedom of expression right, and a functional

883 In this sense, the conception of copyright as instrumental to the advancement of culture can also be found in Article 27(1) of the Universal Declaration of Human Rights and Article 15 of the International Covenant on Economic, Social and Cultural Rights.

884 Macmillan, 'Speaking Truth to Power' (n 805) 25.

885 Ibid.

886 Ibid.

887 Bertani, Diritto d'autore europeo (n 701) 69.

888 Sganga, 'Propertizing European Copyright' (n. 345).

right for the protection of culture – embody the very essence of copyright's social function.

When reinterpreted through the prism of sustainable intellectual property and within the framework of fundamental rights, the social function it pursues can be comprehensively understood as the "stimulus to, and protection of, cultural production and its diffusion".[889]

The conceptions of copyright as a right of personality and freedom of expression, and as functional to the protection of culture are more intuitively framed as pursuing this social function. By contrast, reconstructing the foundation of this copyright's function within the framework of its qualification as a property right is a more indirect task and, at the EU level, it involves recalling their constitutional understanding as developed in many Member States.

2.3.2 Social Function as Internal Limit of Property and Intellectual Property

The idea of a property right as able to pursue a social function was first confined to the context of private law[890] and only later, during the Enlightenment, extended to the field of intellectual property and copyright.[891]

In the general discipline of private law, the notion of property constrained by social-utility requirements appears, more or less explicitly, across several legal systems.

In Germany, the theory of the social function of private law (*Sozialbindung des Privatrechts*) was decisive in this respect. It maintains that all individual rights are inherently limited by the interests of the community as a whole. Emerging at the end of the nineteenth century, it later became a cornerstone of German private law. Under this approach, the entire legal system is imbued with a social dimension, seeking an ideal compromise between the interests of the individual and those of society. As an illustration of this approach, its proponents often referred to the *Treu und Glauben* clause in § 242 BGB, which imposes a general duty of good faith in contractual relationships. Transposed to the field of property, this principle implies the exclusion of any exer-

889 Macmillan, 'Speaking Truth to Power' (n 805) 25.

890 As early as the thirteenth century, the theologian and philosopher Thomas Aquinas expressed the view that positive law could only be considered just and legitimate to the extent that it aimed at the common welfare. This idea was later reiterated by many philosophers of law; see Geiger, 'The Social Function of Intellectual Property Rights' (n 87) 153.

891 Geiger, 'Copyright as an Access Right' (n 378) 6.

cise of ownership that would unreasonably, and therefore abusively, prejudice others.[892]

In France, the notion of limited private property in the name of its social function is not expressly codified, but it has been reconstructed from the writings of jurist Josserand, who rejected the supposed unlimited nature of ownership and observed that it contains "a multitude of obstacles, barriers, borders that restrain its movement and oppose its expansion".[893]

Within the Italian system, the pioneering reflections of Rodotà (1981), Rescigno (1972), Sacco (1968), and Salvi (1986) laid the foundations for rethinking the concept of private property as capable of serving a social function. This vision is explicitly reflected in Article 42(2) of the Italian Constitution, which limits property in accordance with the requirements of "social utility". The article states that "private property is recognised and guaranteed by law, which determines the ways in which it may be acquired, enjoyed, and its limits in order to ensure its social function and to make it accessible to all". This has been interpreted to mean that, in light of the social utility it must serve, the limits of property are not exceptional derogations, but rather structural and inherent elements of its very *modus essendi*.[894] When understood as such, they serve as a directive for legislators, functioning as a common denominator to systematize the diverse sector-specific regimes in which property is operationalized and to regulate the use and distribution of resources ("*utilizzazione e distribuzione delle risorse*").[895] As such, property rights are grounded in broader considerations of public welfare and accessibility.[896]

---

892 Sganga, 'Propertizing European Copyright' (n. 345) 222.

893 Josserand L, De l'esprit des droits et de leur relativité (2nd edn, Dalloz 1939, reissued 2006) 16.

894 Angiolini (n 833) 505; Macario F, 'Commento all'art 42 della Costituzione Italiana' in R Bifulco, A Celotto and M Olivetti (eds), Costituzione commentata (UTET giuridica, Torino 2006); Macario F and Miletti MN, La funzione sociale nel diritto privato tra XX e XXI secolo. Atti dell'incontro di studio, Roma 9 ottobre 2015 (RomaTre Press 2017).

895 Rodotà 1960, 1272; revised in Rodotà 1981, 324, cited in Macario (n 894).

896 According to prominent Italian scholars, the principle of social function has played a dual role. On the one hand, it has served as the normative core around which diverse forms and legal regimes of private property have been structured. On the other, it has helped to erode, or even neutralize, the traditional barrier created by the supposed exceptional nature of limitations on private property. This barrier had long prevented the integration of the numerous special legal regimes governing property into a coherent general theory. Doctrinal approaches were slow to reflect this evolving reality, constrained by interpretive traditions that regarded such limitations as exceptional and therefore peripheral within the broader system of legal reasoning. As Gambaro (Gambaro A, Il diritto di proprietà, in Tratt Cicu-Messineo (Milano, 1995) 47) noted, the growing influence of these special laws and the constitutional principle of social func-

Property is likewise conceived as naturally limited by the pursuit of social utility under Article 17(1) of the Charter of Fundamental Rights of the European Union, which expressly recalls the possibility for legislation to impose constraints on the indiscriminate use of property in the general interest, and under Article 1 of Protocol No. 1 to the ECHR, which similarly enshrines the possibility of imposing restrictions in the name of the public interest.[897]

Accordingly, at both the European Union and international levels, individual property rights are not conceived as absolute, but as inherently limited by the interests of the broader community.[898]

That said, extending the principle of the limited nature of property to intellectual property has been less immediate and far more controversial. A telling example in the EU is the literal wording of Article 17(2) of the Nice Charter, which makes no reference to public-interest limitations and thus seems to place intellectual property legislation beyond the reach of the social-function theory.[899]

Despite the reference in the first paragraph to property's subjection to social-utility limits, the silence of the second paragraph has been interpreted by this strand of scholarship as reflecting a conception of copyright as an "absolute" property right.

However, at the EU level, the social-function paradigm can be extensively applied to intellectual property rights in light of at least two considerations.

First, intellectual property is a specific manifestation of the right to property: hence, the two paragraphs of Article 17 must be read as intrinsically connected, and it is precisely this constitutional dimension of copyright that provides the foundation for such an interpretation. Also, as Geiger has observed,

---

tion demand a reconceptualization of property not as a monolithic and absolute right, but as a flexible institution shaped by multiple legislative and constitutional layers. As early as 1954, Pugliatti authoritatively argued that the Constitution requires full normative effect to be given to Article 42(2), which serves as a unifying and systematic principle. In his words, it is "the cement, the unifying idea, the systematic organizing principle which, as such, transcends the specific legal episode, breaks through the exceptional character of the provision, establishes connections between particular norms, and fills in gaps – wherever one can recognize a concrete and specific implementation of social needs through the institution of property" (Pugliatti S, La proprietà nel nuovo diritto (Giuffrè, Milano 1954) 278; see also Pugliatti S, La proprietà e le proprietà con riguardo particolare alla proprietà terriera (Giuffrè 1954); Macario (n 894)).

897 "This limited nature of the right to property was clearly envisaged by the drafters of both the Charter and the ECHR. As the *travaux préparatoires* of the First Protocol to the ECHR demonstrate, a newly introduced property paradigm was viewed as being of a "relative" nature as opposed to the absolute right to own property in a sense it was understood by Roman law"; see Geiger, 'Copyright as an Access Right' (n 378) 16.

898 Geiger, 'Copyright as an Access Right' (n 378) 7.

899 Sganga, 'Propertizing European Copyright' (n. 345) 113.

it is precisely the inclusion of intellectual property within the constitutional protection of property that "has extended the social function of property to intellectual property".[900] This constitutional recognition requires taking into consideration the constitutional frameworks of the EU Member States when interpreting IP rights. Accordingly, "the joint reading of Article 17 CFREU and the Member States' common constitutional traditions proposes a framework where the propertization of copyright opens a plethora of new interpretative opportunities and, to some extent, a partial paradigm shift":[901] among these opportunities is that to conceive property, and intellectual property as well, as a right internally limited by its social-function objective.

Second, as has been aptly observed, "perhaps more than classical individual private property", intellectual property "is not conceived solely for the selfish interest of the owner in their thing; it also inherently encompasses society, the public, and the users of the intangible creations it protects. It thus carries a strong communal dimension, in which the notion of commonality naturally unfolds".[902]

3 A "Pluralistic" Framework for (Intellectual) Property Law

3.1 From Exclusive to Inclusive Property

As a "concept steeped in history and ideology, as well as in rhetorical suggestions",[903] the use of the term "property" with reference to intellectual property has often been the cause of long-standing misunderstandings. Even in the context of reflections on generative AI, the crux of many debated issues lies in the problematic relationship that intellectual property maintains with property law.[904]

The greatest source of misunderstanding undoubtedly concerns the very nature and scope attributed to this institution, which has been termed, not by chance, as "terrible right", recalling the words of Stefano Rodotà.[905]

Rooted in the absolutist conception of ownership that emerged during the codification era, and closely tied to industrialization, the Western legal tradi-

900 Geiger, 'Copyright as an Access Right' (n 378) 15.
901 Sganga, 'Propertizing European Copyright' (n. 345) 224.
902 Rochfeld, Martin and Cornu (n 676) 53.
903 Iannarelli A, '"Proprietà", "immateriali", "atipicità": i nuovi scenari di tutela' in Resta G (ed), Diritti esclusivi e nuovi beni immateriali (Utet Giuridica 2010) 74.
904 Ibid, 83.
905 Rodotà (n 833).

tion model for property has earned the epithet "terrible right" for being characterized by the near-unlimited power it granted to private actors over economic goods,[906] and for having historically legitimized the overexploitation and misuse of natural resources, while failing to provide adequate protection for unowned or collectively held lands and environmental assets.

In light of the historical significance attributed, during this era, to property – conceived as deeply intertwined with, if not the very counterpart to, individual freedom, and able to define the "horizon of meaning" of the new bourgeoisie, in stark contrast to the preceding feudal system[907] – it is easy to understand the central role (private) property assumed in the codification movements of the 1800s and the symbolic weight attached to the notion of property as "full and exclusive".

Based on differing perceptions of the prerogative to "exclude" third parties from the use, enjoyment, and disposal of an asset, two main conceptions of property have emerged, reflecting the respective approaches characteristic of the civil law and common law traditions. Firstly, the civil law tradition has depicted it as a tree with the trunk representing the core element of exclusivity and the branches symbolizing the various prerogatives and powers of owners, which can be adjusted or combined depending on the legal and factual characteristics of the asset. In this view, property is primarily understood as the relationship between an individual and a material object.[908] By contrast, in the common law tradition, property is conceptualized as a set of relationships between individuals, all interacting with one another through a defined structure of rights, powers, privileges, and immunities, alongside their corresponding duties and liabilities. These entitlements over an object are often described as a "bundle of sticks", with the right to exclude representing only one of them, the absence of which – unlike in the civil law tradition – does not automatically disqualify a legal interest from being considered "property".[909]

---

906 Salvi C, L'invenzione della proprietà. La destinazione universale dei beni e i suoi nemici (Marsilio Editori 2021) 11.

907 Barcellona (n 806).

908 See more extensively Mattei U, Quarta A, Valguarnera F and Fisher RJ, Property Meeting the Challenge of the Commons (Springer 2023).

909 Mattei (n 908). Interestingly, the concept of "bundle of rights" was primarily "proposed by a critical legal scholar, Hohfeld (1913), who argued that private ownership is not an absolute right but what remains from the rights governed by state laws, local ordinances, private nuisance regulations, and institutions, and has intrinsic constraints. An owner has a set of rights to use, manage, and transfer within these limits, and can assign certain rights to other people"; see Takamura G, Nishide T, Kanazawa Y and Hayashi M, 'Bundle of Rights Reversed: Anticommons in a Japanese Common Property Forest Due to Legalization' (2021) 15(1) International Journal of the Commons 259 https://doi.org/10.5334/ijc.

In recent years, as in other areas of law, a convergence between civil law and common law traditions has been underway.[910] With respect to property, however, this convergence has been far from linear. On the one hand, as a byproduct of broader phenomena such as digitalization and globalization – which have reinforced the dominance of economic structures in the governance of global challenges – an expansion of the "exclusivity-driven" model of property, as already noted, has gained increasing traction.[911] On the other hand, diverse political and theoretical reflections have emphasized a weakening of the exclusivity "trunk", accompanied by a growing recognition of new configurations of power in the circulation of assets, particularly intangible ones.[912]

Building on this evolution, and indeed moving beyond it, an increasing number of scholars have begun to rethink this institution – either by analyzing the scope and the implications of commons regimes[913] or by directly questioning the very paradigm of property itself.[914]

These debates, grounded in the very idea that property possesses an "internal" capacity to serve general interests objectives, are revealing a gradual shift from property as a monolithic right to a plural institution. According to this renewed conception of property – or rather, of "properties"[915] – there is no

---

1080 262. Schlager and Ostrom (1992) use this concept to show that the property rights to common property resources are not exclusive to a community with homogeneous members but correspond to the coexistence of different rights holders of various positions (Ibid, 262).

910 Marini (n 152).

911 This trend reflects a broader shift toward what Piketty has termed proprietarianism and is closely linked to the emergence of "Knowledge capitalism". The evolution of this new form of capitalism underpins the processes of commodification and the expansion of exclusive rights over resources that previously belonged to the public domain. It offers a compelling explanation for the accelerating privatization of intangible assets. In this regard; see Boyle (n 670).

912 An illustration of this is the proliferation of streaming services that allow people to "enjoy" a song, a movie, etc., without granting them full property to it.

913 Ostrom E, The Governing of Commons: The Evolution of Institutions for Collective Action (Cambridge University Press 1990); Dusollier, 'Propriétées Inclusives' (n 835); Dusollier, 'The Commons as a Reverse Intellectual Property' (n 835).

914 See, *inter alia*, Boyle (n 670); Rochfeld, Martin and Cornu (n 676); Rodotà (n 833); Pugliatti S, Gli istituti del diritto civile (Milan 1943); Salvi (n 906); Pugliatti, 'La proprietà nel nuovo diritto' (n 896); Pugliatti, 'La proprietà e le proprietà' (n 896); Quarta (n 33); Resta, 'Diritti esclusivi e nuovi beni immateriali' (n 816); Cascione C, Il diritto privato dei beni pubblici. Modelli di appartenenza e circolazione (Cacucci 2013); DeLong JV, Epstein RA, Lepage H and Palmer T, La proprietà (intellettuale) è un furto? (Rubbettino Editore 2006).

915 Pugliatti, 'La proprietà e le proprietà' (n 896).

longer a single paradigm of ownership, but rather as many forms of property as there are distinct configurations of interests in relation to the specific asset at issue.

As a consequence, even legal systems in which the absolutist conception of property had thus far remained unchallenged have begun to signal the desirability of a shift toward the theorization of a more "inclusive" property regime(s), seeking to preserve the core of exclusive ownership while simultaneously acknowledging third-party entitlements to access and benefit from (natural) resources, and promoting active community involvement in their governance.

Inclusive property regimes are plural and should not be viewed as opposed to the exclusive paradigm, because the property framework is not a binary model but rather a spectrum: a continuum of operational regimes whose axes are the degree of inclusivity versus exclusivity and the degree of individuality versus communality.[916]

In this conception, the theorization of inclusiveness could be seen as closely tied to that of the social-function paradigm of property, serving as a dynamic illustration of the different forms that the exercise of ownership can take in pursuing general interests' objectives.

Movable boundaries already exist between public and private property, between tangible and intangible assets, and even within "the sphere of the inappropriable, present both outside and inside" the domain of ownership. What is needed is merely their re-systematization.

An attempt in this direction is offered by the French doctrine of the *échelle de communalité* that reinterprets the right to property as a legal institution that can, and indeed should, be reorganized along a scale of protections.[917] According to this theory, the regime governing certain types of goods is structured along a spectrum of appropriability, which varies with the degree and extent of the relevant general interest attached to those goods. As the doctrine explains, "*les biens reconnus porteurs d'un intérêt commun seraient appropriables selon certaines gradations*":[918] at one extreme, goods for which no general-interest component exists would be subject to the highest degree of exclusivity; at the other, goods in which the general interest is paramount would demand the maximum degree of inclusiveness.

916 Dusollier, 'The Commons as a Reverse Intellectual Property' (n 835) 84.
917 Rochfeld, Martin and Cornu (n 676).
918 Ibid, 34.

3.2 Copyright Law as a Pluralistic Property Right

In line with the evolution of the "terrible right" toward a pluralistic and inclusive framework, copyright law too – although traditionally "presented as a universality, a unitary whole"[919] – is, or at least should be, understood as a legal system capable of encompassing a broad spectrum of operational solutions, applied modularly depending on the interests at stake in each concrete case.

It is indeed a system able of protecting both individual and collective interests in a scalable manner,[920] through mechanisms such as the delimitation of its object (original works), its content (specific moral and economic rights), and its duration, as well as through the regime of exceptions and limitations.

The aptitude of copyright to embody a scalable property paradigm[921] lies in the very nature of the goods it protects, which – being immaterial, non-excludable, and non-rivalrous – are inherently destined for collective use. The exclusivity surrounding copyright-protected creations is, in fact, the result of a legal construct that restricts their use by the general public by virtue of the social contract between the author and the society, and the cultural, scientific, technical, or informational value embodied by intellectual works.[922]

Their legal regime, more than addressing the "selfish" relationship between an owner and their "thing" – the so-called dominium in classic Anglo-Saxon doctrine – concerns the organization of the circulation and exploitation of the intangible good, reconciling the interests of the creator, the right holder, the intermediaries of the creative industry, and ultimately society as a whole, the final beneficiary of creation and innovation.

Until now, copyright has predominantly been conceived as a unitary framework, with its classical categories stretched to fit justifications that ultimately have undermined their own purpose. This approach, which treats an ever-growing number of practical situations as mere derogations, has weakened the overall system and exposed the discrepancy between the statements of principle found in both domestic and European Union law and the operational reality shaped by market forces.

---

919 Bensamoun A, 'Libre propos sur l'existence d'un droit de l'oeuvre applicable aux créations issues de l'intelligence artificielle' in Bruguiere JM and Geiger C (eds), Penser le droit de la pensée – Mélanges en l'honneur de Michel Vivant (1st edn, Dalloz 2020) 18.

920 Iannarelli (n 903) 75, footnote 2.

921 See R Rochfeld J, 'Penser autrement la propriété: la propriété s'oppose-t-elle aux "communs" ?' (2014) 3(XXVIII) Revue internationale de droit économique 351.

922 Geiger, 'Copyright as an Access Right' (n 378) 4.

In reality, however, copyright is inherently inclusive, as many intermediate situations exist between strict exclusivity and open access.[923] It is therefore more accurate to understand copyright as having a composite nature: a right that operates along a spectrum. On one end lies protection, understood as ensuring that authors fairly share in the fruits of the commercial exploitation of their works; on the other lies access, meaning the protection and organization of access to intellectual works and participation in cultural life.[924]

A vision of copyright as a plural framework, capable of internally accommodating such diverse regimes, nonetheless requires more systematic operationalization and interpretation. One way to achieve this is by translating the *échelle de communalité* into copyright law. Applied to this field, the theory reveals how copyright could serve as a paradigmatic example of a ladder-structured property framework, naturally tempered by limits and exceptions that operate differently depending on the specific interest at stake.

Under this conception, the configuration of rights that make up copyright integrates from the outset not only the interests of authors and rightsholders, but also those of users – whether market operators, creators who access and transform the work to generate new intangible goods, or end-users who simply enjoy the work.

923 Dusollier, 'The Commons as a Reverse Intellectual Property' (n 835).

924 Geiger, 'Copyright as an Access Right' (n 378).

CHAPTER 10

Operationalizing the Social Function of Copyright Law

1 An Inclusive Copyright Law in the Age of AI

Conceiving copyright as an inclusive right means acknowledging it as a form of property, which – insofar as it is framed within a constitutional framework – is aimed at fulfilling the social function of promoting culture, fostering a pluralistic cultural environment, safeguarding artistic freedom of expression, and ensuring access to information.

Inclusive copyright does not deny that a property right lies at its core; rather, it rejects a strictly exclusive conception of it. It recognizes spaces of flexibility within its framework, grounded in the understanding that "exclusivity" does not necessarily entail "exclusion", and that the modern vision of property as "jealous, solitary, and absolute" is merely a "historical accident".[925] In this pluralistic perspective, property can accommodate different operational regimes, depending on the specific work involved, the nature of its use, or the context in which it is exploited.

This approach already reflects what is, at least in part, the reality of copyright – which has, in principle, always pursued both public and private interests, even if this dual perspective has at times been obscured in practice. Re-examining copyright through a systematic lens along these lines can enhance the coherence of the entire framework and foster the emergence of a new narrative.[926]

Such a narrative would operate on multiple levels, including at least the reassessment of: (i) the delimitation of the concept of "intellectual work" and its relationship to the public domain; (ii) the scope of exceptions and limitations; (iii) the operation of the three-step test.

In the age of AI, this shift is not merely descriptive but also normative, carrying significant implications for the future evolution of copyright law and its capacity to address contemporary challenges.

While the reading proposed hereinafter is not the only one compatible with copyright's constitutional foundations — other configurations of the balance

925 Dusollier, 'Propriétées Inclusives' (n 835), citing Paolo Grossi.
926 Dusollier, 'Propriétées Inclusives' (n 835).

 | HTTPS://DOI.ORG/10.1163/9789004730731-012

between exclusivity and access could, in the abstract, be derived from the same premises — what is argued is that an inclusive, pluralistic reading is the only one capable of responding adequately to the conditions of the present moment. In the age of knowledge capitalism — where information has become the primary means of production and its extractive, accumulative logics tend to concentrate control over knowledge in the hands of a few dominant actors — a strictly exclusivist reading would not merely be one option among others: it would actively amplify the systemic risks identified in Chapter 2, from the erosion of cultural pluralism and the homogenization of creative outputs to the displacement of individual creators and the enclosure of the public domain. It is precisely as a counterweight to these concentration effects, and as a means of preserving the dialectic between the individual and collective dimensions of the discipline, that the inclusive reading recommends itself not only as legitimate, but as the most, if not the only, defensible one in the current context. The choice, in other words, is not deduced from the premises as a matter of logical necessity, but justified by the function copyright is called upon to serve in this precise historical and economic conjuncture.

1.1 The Input Side

"Intellectual works", "exceptions and limitations" and "three-step test" are all concepts that cut across the entire algorithmic creative process; yet, a descriptive distinction between its input and output phases can once again prove useful in clarifying the implications of their reassessment in this context.

Looking at the input side of the AI creative process, some of the areas where this narrative and normative shift toward an inclusive conception of copyright law could operate at the EU level are: (i) the interpretation of the dividing line between simple ideas and expression, starting from the consideration that the vast quantities of works AI ingests and elaborates for training purposes, are relevant primarily for their informational content rather than for any direct exploitation of their expressive form - even though this point is increasingly debated; (ii) the scope of the TDM exceptions under the CDSM Directive, with different possible interpretations of the conditions for their application (including lawful access to training materials), the concept of "right of reproduction" and the functioning of the opt-out mechanism; (iii) the restrictiveness/extensiveness of the three factors of the three-step test that shapes and limits the interpretation of copyright exceptions and limitations.

The interests around which an inclusive conception of copyright could revolve on this side of the AI process are manifold. Among private interests, authors of the works used to train an AI have both economic interests (such as the right to receive remuneration or compensation for the time and effort invested in creating such works, and to retain control over their exploitation) and moral interests, including the recognition of authorship and the protection of the integrity of their creations. Also among private interests, the AI industry holds a strong interest in accessing vast datasets, which are essential for effective training and continued innovation. At the same time, the public interests at stake include fostering research and innovation; ensuring diversity and representativeness in training datasets to prevent biased outcomes; and preserving a competitive market, rather than allowing data access to be consolidated in the hands of a few dominant actors.

On these premises, operationalizing the idea of copyright as an inclusive framework encompassing different operational regimes could involve envisioning a graduated scale of exclusivity, calibrated according to the conditions under which training data are accessed and whether the outputs of the process do – or do not – reproduce elements of the works used during training. For instance, the degree of exclusivity could vary depending on (i) whether the training data were accessed legitimately – taking into account factors such as the good faith of those who enabled the training (e.g., the AI provider, the dataset curator, or other intermediaries); (ii) whether the outputs of the generative process reproduce substantial parts of the works used in training or, conversely, consist of sufficiently transformed or non-identifiable material; (iii) whether such outputs are offensive, explicitly unwanted or carry inappropriate messages (racist, discriminatory, etc.).[927]

When the outputs of an AI system do not reproduce substantial or identifiable parts of the works used during training, and are not offensive, inappropriate, etc., and the training process has been conducted in good faith by the relevant actors, the public interest could be considered predominant. In such cases, a more flexible interpretation of both the requirements and operational scope of TDM exceptions could be enabled, as well as a less restrictive application of the three-step test.

This flexibility, however, should be grounded in clear and transparent criteria, ideally established *ex ante* by the legislator, to guide courts and regulatory bodies in conducting such assessments. The underlying rationale should be that, where AI outputs do not replicate identifiable portions of the training material, and where the training has been carried out in good faith, the general interest ought to prevail: (i) in virtue of the informational (and non-expressive) value of the data extracted and processed during training; (ii) in virtue of the

927 Geiger, 'Elaborating a Human Rights Friendly Copyright Framework' (n 321).

desirability of building inclusive and diverse datasets, which are essential to avoid systemic biases and allow less homogenized outputs; (iii) in virtue of the need to preserve a competitive market and freedom of research, since a rigid interpretation of "lawful access" and the reproduction right – combined with a strict application of the three-step test – would likely favor only the largest AI players at the detriment of smaller ones and research organizations.

From an operational perspective, AI systems could be allowed to process and rework the informational content of these works, provided that such use is carried out in good faith (for instance, they are not aware that training data come from unlawful sources, such as piracy websites), and possibly subject to the payment of a proportionate fee. This would allow training activities to proceed without incurring the prohibitive costs associated with extensive licensing regimes. At the same time, authors' private interests should not be entirely disregarded. However, such interests should be subject to certain limitations. In particular, authors should not have the right to exercise granular, preventive control over whether their works are used for training purposes – unless the opt-out mechanism provided by law is operational. Nonetheless, authors could still be entitled to an economic reward, ensuring that their creative effort and investment are duly recognized. They may also retain moral rights, such as the right to oppose inappropriate uses of their work or to claim authorship, especially where the output replicates even non-substantial parts of their original expression.[928]

This would align with the idea that, in most cases, authors whose works are already published – particularly those circulating online – tend to assert claims primarily grounded in economic prerogatives (such as the right to receive compensation or remuneration) and moral entitlements. These include, for instance, the right to be acknowledged as the author, especially in light of the reputational value associated with social sharing, engagement metrics, and online visibility in today's digital landscape.[929] Many authors, particularly in the online environment, are in fact generally supportive of the circulation of their works[930] – provided that such use does not entail misuse or inappropriate modification, which again relates to the protection of moral interests. This is why a proposal to grant authors such prerogatives, rather than the full spectrum of exclusionary powers, could constitute a reasonable approach even in the private interests of the authors.

---

928 Geiger, 'Elaborating a Human Rights Friendly Copyright Framework' (n 321).

929 Borghi M, 'Rewarding Creativity in Law, Economics and Literature', in ANCILLA IURIS, 54–63 (2006); Ginsburg, 'Fair Use in the United States' (n 499) 35.

930 It is the very nature of intellectual works, as immaterial goods, that makes them inherently inclined toward circulation (see Dusollier, 'Propriétées Inclusives' (n 835) 85).

However, this presupposes an assessment of whether a flexible application of copyright's exceptions and limitations – supported by a more nuanced interpretation of the three-step test – and a broader reading of "lawful access" are viable approaches.

1.1.1 Toward a More Flexible Interpretation of the Three-Step Test and Exceptions and Limitations

A more flexible interpretation of exceptions, limitations and the three-step test is both possible and increasingly advocated in recent EU scholarship,[931] especially in light of the ongoing restyling of intellectual property framework.

The premise for such flexibilization lies in the growing recognition of the unsustainability of the current system which sees the EU exceptions and limitations mechanism narrowly defined within a closed catalogue, which, except for minor deviations, does not allow the creation of additional "free spaces" not explicitly envisaged by the legislator.[932]

It is a system where exclusive rights are defined in broad terms (see the 2001 InfoSoc Directive), while exceptions are drafted as optional, exhaustive, and, as seen, additionally subjected to strict interpretation of the "three-step test".[933]

Indeed, based on the idea that exceptions, limitations and the three-step test are intended to secure sufficient breathing space within copyright law for

931 For arguments in favor of a more flexible framework, see, *inter alia*, Priora G and Sganga C, 'Interim Report on EU and National Sources and Private Practices on Legitimate Uses and Flexibilities, Rethinking Digital Copyright Law for a Culturally Diverse, Accessible, Creative Europe' (Grant Agreement No 870626 2020); Sganga C, 'A New Era for EU Copyright Exceptions and Limitations? Judicial Flexibility and Legislative Discretion in the Aftermath of the CDSM Directive and the Trio of the Grand Chamber of the CJEU' (2020) 21 ERA Forum 311 <https://ssrn.com/abstract=3804228> accessed 9 August 2025, 311–339; Sganga C and others, 'Copyright Flexibilities: Mapping and Comparative Assessment of EU and National Sources' (2023) <https://ssrn.com/abstract=4325376> accessed 9 August 2025; Geiger C, 'Flexibilising Copyright – Remedies to the Privatisation of Information by Copyright Law' (2008) 39(2) IIC 178. On the pitfalls of the narrative of flexibilities, see Rosati E, 'Copyright Reformed: The Narrative of Flexibility and Its Pitfalls in Policy and Legislative Initiatives (2011–2021)' (2023) 31(1) Asia Pacific Law Review 33–54.

932 Geiger C and Izyumenko E, 'Towards a European "Fair Use" Grounded in Freedom of Expression' [2019] SSRN Electronic Journal <https://www.ssrn.com/abstract=3379531> accessed 9 August 2025.

933 Ibid, 3 ff.

future creativity, innovation, and cultural exchange,[934] a growing body of scholarship supports the idea that they should not be interpreted restrictively by default. Instead, they ought to be understood in light of their underlying normative objectives, particularly promoting access to knowledge, supporting educational uses, and safeguarding the public interest, through a balanced and purposive approach.[935]

Accordingly, with reference to the three-step test, while its traditional application in international copyright law tends to treat its three criteria as distinct and cumulative conditions, some scholars in EU advocate now that the test – rather than being applied in a rigid or sequential manner – should be understood as a unified and coherent framework capable of accommodating the full spectrum of interests at stake in copyright law.[936]

This interpretive shift appears to find support in recent case law from the Court of Justice of the European Union,[937] which, contrary to its earlier approach,[938] has increasingly stressed the importance of achieving a "fair balance" of rights and interests under Article 5(5) of the InfoSoc Directive. Moreover, the 2019 CDSM Directive seems to build upon this evolution, when, in Recital 6, explicitly stresses the idea that the exceptions and limitations introduced therein must aim to maintain a "fair balance" between the interests of rightsholders and those of users.[939] In this sense, a flexible interpretation of the three-step test could be seen as essential.

However, it is not only the three-step test that could, and should be indeed, subject to a more flexible interpretation in the light of all the interests at stake.

934 Geiger C, 'Promoting Creativity through Copyright Limitations: Reflections on the Concept of Exclusivity in Copyright Law, 12 Vanderbilt Journal of Entertainment and Technology Law 515 (2020).

935 Geiger C and others, 'Declaration. A Balanced Interpretation of the "Three-Step Test" in Copyright Law' (2010) 1 JIPITEC 119.

936 These include the interests of authors and rightsholders and those of third parties, including users and the general public (Wymeersch (n 545)). See also Geiger and others (n 935) 122.

937 Wymeersch (n 545).

938 For a long time, the European legislator's restrictive approach to exceptions and limitations has been reinforced by the jurisprudence of the CJEU, which has consistently held since Infopaq that copyright exceptions must be interpreted strictly; see Geiger and Izyumenko, 'Towards a European "Fair Use"' (n 932) 3 ff.

939 Recital 6 of CDSM Directive (n 116): "The exceptions and limitations provided for in this Directive seek to achieve a fair balance between the rights and interests of authors and other rightholders, on the one hand, and of users on the other. They can be applied only in certain special cases that do not conflict with the normal exploitation of the works or other subject matter and do not unreasonably prejudice the legitimate interests of the rightholders".

Some EU scholars have even called for the introduction of an "exceptions and limitations" open-ended clause akin to the US fair use doctrine. This position is grounded in the observation that, in certain respects, the European system is already evolving in that direction, and that some form of "fair use" may already be considered a reality in Europe.[940]

In any case, even in the absence of (legislative reform introducing such) an open-ended clause, some scholars argue that the already existing exceptions and limitations should be interpreted in a more teleological manner. Accordingly, as interpreted by some strands of the doctrine, despite their name, exceptions and limitations should not be treated merely as derogations from copyright protection, but rather as a positive expression of an "entitlement"[941] to access intellectual works. They should not be understood as simply negative spaces within intellectual property law, but mechanisms that organize alternative and collective uses of such works.[942] Moreover, they could benefit from a horizontal application of fundamental rights (such as freedom of expression, education, and scientific research) that they are meant to safeguard.[943] In this light, exceptions and limitations should be seen as equal and opposing forces to exclusive rights,[944] albeit applicable in a gradual and scalable manner. Therefore, they would reflect a form of symmetry between users and rightsholders in line with the idea that within the cultural ecosystem, creation is a shared space in which authors and users coexist "*non de manière égale, mais de manière symétrique*".[945]

940 Indeed, the growing tendency of national courts within the EU to invoke fundamental rights (particularly freedom of expression and information) to resolve copyright disputes increasingly mirrors the practice in common law jurisdictions. The balancing of interests required by this approach resembles, in several respects, the multi-factor analysis typically employed in fair use assessments. See Geiger and Izyumenko, 'Towards a European "Fair Use"' (n 932).

941 A more generic expression such as "entitlement" is preferred here, as characterizing the "inclusive" entitlement of access as a right, power, or privilege is a complex issue (see Dusollier, 'The Commons as a Reverse Intellectual Property' (n 835) 262) and cannot be easily addressed at this stage of the analysis.

942 Rochfeld, Martin and Cornu (n 676) 57.

943 Sganga C, 'The Past, Present and Future of EU Copyright Flexibilities' (2024) 55 IIC – International Review of Intellectual Property and Competition Law 5, 15.

944 Dusollier, 'Propriétées Inclusives' (n 835) 84.

945 "*En droit d'auteur, une substitution d'une approche relationnelle et inclusive à l'approche exclusiviste organiserait les multiples usages de la création au sein d'un écosystème culturel, faisant de la création le lieu où les droits de l'auteur et les usages des oeuvres par les utilisateurs cohabiteraient, non de manière égale, mais de manière symétrique*"; see Dusollier, 'Propriétées Inclusives' (n 835) 92. In line with this idea of symmetry, it is worth recalling that, in general legal theory, exclusive rights themselves are conceived as

Within the scope of this analysis, and as a consequence of the interpretative shift toward a more flexible understanding of both exceptions and limitations and the three-step test, the interpretation and application of Articles 3 and 4 of the CDSM Directive should reflect the principle of symmetry between exclusive and inclusive entitlements. This means that the interpretation of these provisions should no longer be solely focused on safeguarding economic exclusivity (i.e., the commercial interests of authors and publishers) but should also take into account broader public interest objectives – such as the advancement of scientific research, technological development, and equitable access to knowledge.

In particular, in the scenarios discussed above – where the general interest carries the greatest weight in relation to competing interests (i.e., when situated at the end of the spectrum where the public interest is most expansive) – this shift would have concrete operational consequences: access would become the rule, not the exception.

1.1.2 Toward a More Flexible Interpretation of the Lawful Access Requirement

A less rigid interpretation of "lawful access" – as a requirement for the operation of the two TDM exceptions of the CDSM directive – could also be envisioned.

In contemporary copyright law, the concept of lawfulness has increasingly become a condition for the applicability of exceptions – appearing in various forms such as lawful use, lawful access, and lawful source. The terminology varies across EU directives: the "lawful acquirer of a computer program" or "a person having a right to use a computer program" (Directive 2009/24/EC), the "lawful user" of a database (Directive 96/9/EC), and "lawful use" as mentioned in Article 5(1) of the InfoSoc Directive.[946]

However, as some scholars have pointed out, the proliferation of the notion of lawfulness has been inconsistent and currently lacks a clear and coherent normative definition at the EU level.

---

exceptions to the principle of free circulation and access to intangible goods. It follows that both of these forces – exclusive rights and user rights – operate within the limits imposed by the principle of proportionality (Gliściński K, 'Intellectual Property Rights as Private Rights: Implications of the Theory of Internally Limited Rights and Incentive Theory for Reconstructing the Normative Content of Rights in Intangible Goods' (2025) 28 The Journal of World Intellectual Property 516).

946 Synodinou, 'Lawfulness for Users in European Copyright Law:' (n 316); Margoni, 'TDM Opt-Outs' (n 480), Synodinou TE, 'Navigating User Lawfulness in European Copyright Law: From Lawful Use to Lawful Access' (Kluwer Copyright Blog, 19 March 2025) <https://legalblogs.wolterskluwer.com/copyright-blog/navigating-user-lawfulness-in-european-copyright-law-from-lawful-use-to-lawful-access/> accessed 9 August 2025.

As Synodinou has noted, lawfulness is a circular concept: is it not the very function of an exception to transform an otherwise unlawful act – namely, an infringement of an exclusive right – into a lawful one that does not require authorization?[947]

This circularity and conceptual vagueness have indeed given rise to significant legal uncertainties and interpretative ambiguities.

Part of the confusion stems from the failure to clearly distinguish between the different concepts that have emerged thus far.

For instance, Recital 33 of the InfoSoc Directive refers to a "lawful use" and adopts in this regard a relatively flexible approach, defining it as any use authorized by the rightsholder or not restricted by law. Building on this, the Court of Justice of the European Union appears to have implicitly taken on the role of expanding and refining the meaning of lawfulness, particularly in relation to acts carried out by users. Still, ambiguity remains.[948]

In the context of the CDSM Directive, the term employed is "lawful access". Yet, it remains unclear whether this concept, as used in this context, also presupposes access to lawful sources, or whether the focus is solely on the legality of the act of access itself, regardless of the original source of the content.

To clarify its scope, Recital 14 of the CDSM Directive states that – albeit only with regard to Art. 3 – "Lawful access should be understood as covering access to content based on: an open access policy or through contractual arrangements between rightholders and research organisations or cultural heritage institutions, such as subscriptions or through other lawful means. Lawful access should also cover access to content that is freely available online".

As has been noted, this formulation presents three alternative definitions of lawful access:[949] first, a subjective definition, also partially reflected in Recital 33 of the InfoSoc Directive and in case law concerning "lawful source", where lawful access is linked to the will or consent of the rightsholder (by contract, for instance). Second, a general definition, that states lawful access can also be secured through "other lawful means". Third, a novel definition, whereby lawful access includes access to content that is freely available online, that is, content not subject to technical access restrictions. While the legal basis here remains the rightsholder's consent, one could argue for the emergence of an objectified consent – an implicit authorization inferred from the rightsholder's decision to make the work publicly accessible without restriction.[950]

947 Synodinou, 'Navigating User Lawfulness in European Copyright Law' (n 946).
948 Ibid.
949 Ibid.
950 Ibid.

Taken together, these formulations suggest that the legislator of the CDSM Directive has arguably adopted an expansive, liberal interpretation of lawful access, according to which TDM may be carried out lawfully, irrespective of any contractual restrictions or even the lawfulness of the source, whenever a copyright-protected work is freely available online (i.e., publicly accessible and not protected by technical measures).

Such an interpretation, however, may be contested in terms of its normative desirability, and it remains to be seen whether it will withstand the new challenges posed by generative AI training.

Indications on the scope of the concept are likewise absent from the copyright chapter of the General-Purpose AI Code of Practice adopted under the AI Act, whose only direct reference appears in Measure 1.2, establishing an obligation to "reproduce and extract only lawfully accessible copyright-protected content when crawling the World Wide Web".

Within the scope of this measure, signatories commit to ensuring lawful access by: (a) "not circumventing effective technological measures as defined in Article 6(3) of Directive 2001/29/EC that are designed to prevent or restrict unauthorised acts in respect of works and other protected subject matter, in particular by respecting any technological denial or restriction of access imposed by subscription models or paywalls"; (b) "excluding from their web-crawling websites that make available to the public content and which are, at the time of web-crawling, recognised as persistently and repeatedly infringing copyright and related rights on a commercial scale by courts or public authorities in the European Union and the European Economic Area. For the purpose of compliance with this measure, a dynamic list of hyperlinks to lists of these websites issued by the relevant bodies in the European Union and the European Economic Area will be made publicly available on an EU website." In essence, signatories are required not to circumvent technological protection measures (e.g., paywalls) and to refrain from crawling, or having others crawl on their behalf, websites listed in a public blacklist of persistently infringing sources maintained by EU bodies. This arguably implies that signatories are required to act in good faith when using – or commissioning the use of – web crawlers for text and data mining purposes.

Notably, this approach appears to align with a purpose-driven interpretation of lawful access advanced by some scholars, which holds that the lawful access requirement should focus on the user's conduct rather than the legal status of the source. What matters, in this framework, is whether the TDM beneficiary accessed the material under lawful conditions – for instance, not through hacking or breach of contract – rather than whether the source was itself authorized to disseminate the content.[951] These interpretations, however, will once again have to be tested against the realities of the near future.

That said, the blurred boundaries surrounding the notion of lawful access, though generally inconvenient, may in this context be seen as a feature rather than a flaw, allowing for a more flexible understanding of the requirement. Building on the idea of scalable protection, a liberal interpretation of lawful access – such as considering any content freely accessible online (i.e., not protected by technical measures) to be lawful – should not be accepted in all cases. However, where the public interest clearly predominates (i.e., at the end of the spectrum where it outweighs competing interests), such an interpretation may offer a reasonable and normatively sound solution.

1.1.3 A Few Reflections on Fair Remuneration

From what has been argued so far, when the internal balancing of interests – between authors, private rightsholders more broadly, and the general public – tips toward the end of the spectrum where the public interest prevails, private exclusive entitlements should proportionally recede.

However, in light of ongoing concerns over market dilution, the substitution of human creators, the displacement of creative work, and the concentration of power in the hands of a few actors in the AI industry, one issue that clearly warrants attention is the fair remuneration of authors whose works have been ingested by AI systems during the training process – although a full discussion lies beyond the scope of this analysis. Indeed, these economic prerogatives – despite the need for a more flexible interpretation of exceptions, limitations, the three-step test, and lawful access – may nonetheless need to be safeguarded to prevent disproportionate harm to authors' legitimate interests.

This is particularly relevant in cases where individual creators lack the support of powerful intermediaries within the cultural industries or the collective bargaining strength of collective management organizations (CMOs) capable of negotiating fair licensing terms with AI developers.

Accordingly, the focus of the debate should shift away from attempts to restrict exceptions and limitations, to interpret the three-step test and lawful

951 Margoni, 'TDM Opt-Outs' (n 480). This distinction between lawful access and lawful source is critical: it shifts the legal focus from the provenance of the data to the conduct of the data miner, aligning with a more open, innovation-friendly interpretation of copyright limitations. If, as it is argued by the author, this view is acceptable, then the lawful access requirements of Arts. 3 and 4 may lead to different outcomes than until now assumed. At least in the case of Art. 3 – TDM by research organizations for research purposes – it could be possible to have lawful access to unlawful sources.

access narrowly, or to legitimize full, ex ante control by authors over the use of their works. Instead, the emphasis should be placed (beyond the possible recognition of moral entitlements) on ensuring fair remuneration for authors.

In this respect, the ongoing debate around AI may provide a timely opportunity to reflect more broadly on the introduction of a specifically remunerated exception for creative reuse – one that could encompass transformative reuses of protected content. This would be particularly relevant in the digital environment (though also applicable in the analogue world), where creators increasingly incorporate protected elements into their creative processes. Sampling, for instance, stands as a clear example of this trend.[952]

A remuneration obligation for the use of protected materials in AI training may even be justified from a human rights perspective. As has been argued by some scholars, this obligation stems from the right to the protection of the creator's moral and material interests, as enshrined in international and European legal instruments (Articles 27(2) and 17 UDHR; Article 15(1)(c) ICESCR; Article 17(2) EUCFR; Protocol No. 1, Article 1 ECHR). Accordingly, authors should be adequately remunerated for the commercial use of their works, unless a strong and legitimate justification exists to override this entitlement.[953]

In response to this concern, it has been proposed that the use of copyright-protected works for AI training could give rise to a limitation-based remuneration right, or alternatively, be subject to other forms of remuneration schemes in favor of human creators.[954]

---

952 Geiger, 'Elaborating a Human Rights Friendly Copyright Framework' (n 321).

953 Geiger, 'Elaborating a Human Rights Friendly Copyright Framework' (n 321).

954 *Inter alia*, see Geiger C, Schonherr F and Jütte BJ, 'Limitation-Based Remuneration Rights as a Compromise Between Access and Remuneration Interests in Copyright Law: What Role for Collective Rights Management?' (2024) SSRN Electronic Journal <https://www.ssrn.com/abstract=4714080> accessed 11 August 2025; Grassmuck VR, 'Academic Studies on the Effect of File-Sharing on the Recorded Music Industry: A Literature Review' [2010] SSRN Electronic Journal <http://www.ssrn.com/abstract=1749579> accessed 11 August 2025; Handke C, Quintais JP and Balazs B, 'The Economics of Copyright Compensation Systems for Digital Use' (2013); Quintais JP, 'Alternative Compensation Models for Large-Scale Non-Commercial Online Uses' (ALAI International Congress – 50 Years of the German Copyright Act: Remuneration for the Use of Works – Exclusivity vs. Other Approaches, Bonn, 18–20 June 2015, forthcoming in ALAI Conference Proceedings, 1 July 2015) <https://ssrn.com/abstract=2625492> accessed 9 August 2025, Senftleben, 'Generative AI and Author Remuneration' (n 330), 'Generative AI and Author Remuneration' (n 330), Geiger and Iaia, 'The Forgotten Creator' (n 306); see also Lucchi N, 'ChatGPT: A Case Study on Copyright Challenges for Generative AI Systems' (European Journal of Risk Regulation, 12 June 2023) 1–23 <https://ssrn.com/abstract=4483390> or <http://dx.doi.org/10.2139/ssrn.4483390> accessed 9 August 2025; Strowel A, 'ChatGPT

The limitation-based remuneration solution, for example, would be consistent with the European Union's long-standing experience with "permitted-but-paid" models as conceptualized by Ginsburg in the US,[955] whereby certain uses are allowed under exceptions and limitations, but remain subject to equitable remuneration.

In any case, collective rights management by CMOs would be essential to the effective implementation of such remuneration schemes. Making collective management mandatory, at least for certain categories of uses, for instance, could ensure efficiency, fairness, and broad representativeness.[956] In this context, the role of the AI Office would be particularly important in coordinating policy efforts, setting remuneration benchmarks, and ensuring compliance.

The amount of remuneration to be paid would need to be monitored closely – and preferably by an independent body – to avoid creating excessive barriers for start-ups and smaller AI developers. Any such remuneration scheme should remain proportionate, taking into account both the economics of the sector and the potential losses that authors may incur.[957]

In conclusion, introducing a form of alternative remuneration scheme for machine learning purposes could represent a workable compromise, enabling the reimagining of an inclusive operational copyright regime that fosters an attractive environment for artificial creativity without marginalizing the role of human authors.

1.2 The Output Side

Looking at the output side of the AI creative process, some of the areas where this narrative and normative shift toward an inclusive conception of copyright law could operate are: (i) the interpretation of the scope of intellectual work, particularly the requirement of originality and its relationship with the public domain; (ii) as for the input side, the extension of exceptions and limitations (beyond those under Articles 3 and 4 of the CDSM Directive); (iii) the flexibility of the three-step test.

Just as on the input side of the process, the interests around which an inclusive conception of copyright could revolve on the output side are at least: (i) on the private side, the interests of authors (though it remains to be seen who

---

and Generative AI Tools: Theft of Intellectual Labor?' (2023) 54 IIC 491 <https://doi.org/10.1007/s40319-023-01321-y>.

955 Ginsburg, 'Fair Use for Free, or Permitted-but-Paid?' (n 496).

956 Geiger and Iaia, 'The Forgotten Creator' (n 306).

957 Ibid.

should be recognized as holding that status). These interests can be both economic, such as the right to fair remuneration/compensation for creative labor and time investment, and moral, including the right to be credited and to prevent distortion or misuse of one's work. The private interests also include those of the AI industry, which are closely tied to significant investments in AI development, data infrastructure, and innovation; (ii) on the public side, there are both collective and general interests in accessing the creative outputs generated by AI systems – especially if these are seen as part of newly created knowledge. More broadly, there is a public interest in promoting new forms of creative expression (particularly considering the cumulative nature of knowledge), and fostering a diverse and pluralistic cultural landscape

In this context, to operationalize the idea of a pluralistic and inclusive copyright framework, a graduated scale of exclusivity could be based on two different grounds: first, on what has already been discussed in the previous paragraphs regarding exceptions, limitations, the three-step test, and lawful access – all of which would remain applicable if, depending on the circumstances, a specific AI-based output were recognized as an original work; second, on the nature of the AI-based output itself: whether it reflects the personal touch of a human author (AI-assisted works); whether it does not (fully AI-generated works); or whether it lacks a personal touch but still results from some form of human input (hybrid works).

Particularly, outputs that do reflect an individual's personal imprint would qualify for full copyright protection. Outputs that do not express the author's "personal touch" should be considered part of the public domain, as they would not meet the originality threshold. For outputs that are in the grey area – which may not express personality of their author in the strict sense but nonetheless result from human input, effort, and/or investment – an alternative copyright operational regime could be envisioned.

In this third case, such works would occupy a point on the spectrum where the creators' private interests, while present, would not merit the highest level of protection. Since these outputs do not embody the creators' personal touch, they would not engage personality rights but would instead reflect only their economic interests (including compensation for time, effort, or financial investment). The level of protection should therefore be calibrated on this basis. At the same time, the public interest in accessing these works could be considered predominant – though not absolute – as the creators still hold legitimate interests worthy of protection, even if these do not amount to personality rights.

From an operational perspective, such hybrid creations could be subject to a more flexible regime than that applied to "classic" works (this latter including the category of AI-assisted outputs): (i) they could be subject to collective and open access models; (ii) the creator could be granted only moral rights[958] and a subset of economic entitlements; (iii) in cases where these outputs are used for commercial purposes, remuneration could still be envisaged; (iv) when exceptions and limitations apply, the balance of interests could shift more decisively in favor of the public, allowing for a more permissive interpretation of the three-step test (balancing from within[959]); (v) the fair balance with "external" fundamental rights could also lean more strongly toward the conflicting fundamental right, as opposed to the private interest of the rightsholder (balancing from outside).

In this case as well, however, the flexibility inherent in the concept of "intellectual work" should be anchored in clear and transparent criteria – ideally established *ex ante* by the legislator, at least at an EU level – to allow for the consistent classification of such outputs.

Nevertheless, as will be discussed shortly, given the current EU digital policy agenda, which makes further legislative intervention in copyright law unlikely, this distinction should instead be derived hermeneutically from the existing copyright acquis and further developed through case law.

One possible approach would be the formulation of a judicial test to guide courts in assessing cases where the application of such distinctions is required. This test should have at its core a renewed assessment of the entire creative process, which should take into account the quality (creative or otherwise) of the human contribution, the varying roles (technical or otherwise) of the individuals involved in creating the work, the external characteristics of the works (whether trivial or not), and – in the case of generative AI – the degree of automation of the algorithmic process in the specific instance.[960]

However, to ground such a breakdown of copyright into a set of scalable operational regimes based on the nature of the intellectual work – which is (i) the very essence of copyright law, i.e., its subject matter, (ii) the embodiment of the operation of the idea/expression dichotomy, and (iii) the mechanism which, *a contrario*, delineates the public domain – systematic reflections should be undertaken in a rigorous and highly technical manner.

958 To the extent that the link with the author weakens, an adapted moral rights regime could be justified; see Bensamoun and Farchy (n 4) 42.

959 Azzi T, 'La balance des intérêts en droit de la propriété littéraire et artistique' in V Barbes, C Guillerminet and S Mauclair (eds), La notion d'intérêt(s) en droit (Institut francophone pour la justice et la démocratie 2022).

960 In this regard, see the tests referred to by Militsyna, 'Human Creative Contribution to AI-Based Output' (n 407).

1.2.1 The Abstract Possibility of Differentiating between Types of Intellectual Works

The idea of differentiating between types of intellectual works has already been advanced in legal scholarship and is therefore far from unprecedented.

First, there is a strand of French doctrine that differentiates between "copyright" in the strict sense – *rectius*, authors' right, i.e. the right of the author – and the "*droit de l'œuvre*" ("right of the work"), "*plus objectif et où le lien à l'auteur-créateur personne physique est plus relâché*".[961] In particular, the latter would be a "more objective" right that, in line with some recent reflections on the concept of originality,[962] would presuppose a genetically weaker link between the creation and its author.

Furthermore, the distinction between the different regimes echoes the one already proposed in the proposal for a European Copyright Code (ECC) of the Wittem Project[963] between factual and functional works, on the one hand, and productions in the artistic field, on the other.[964]

It also recalls the distinction advanced by some authors between truly artistic creations and commonplace works,[965] as well as the notion of "*quasi-création*" that had been envisaged in relation to creations situated midway through the production process – i.e., between the idea and the final work.[966]

Similarly, in the United States, a distinction has been drawn between "low authorship" works, which are primarily concerned with labor and economic investment, and "high authorship" works, which reflect not only economic interests but also the person of the creator.[967]

In the same vein, other scholars distinguish between industrial products and creative works, emphasizing that this difference should not merely be envisaged for the future but is already present in the current reality of copyright. As noted, "despite the use of the notion of 'author's own intellectual

961 Bensamoun, 'Libre propos sur l'existence d'un droit de l'oeuvre' (n 919) 18 ff.

962 Bensamoun and Farchy (n 4) 41.

963 Wittem Project (n 369).

964 See footnote 7 of commentary to Art. 1.1 of the ECC.

965 If one distinguishes between truly artistic creations and commonplace works, only the former would attract copyright protection in the strict sense, subject, inter alia, to a relatively high standard of originality. The latter, by contrast, could receive a different form of protection (for example, through related rights); see Rahmatian (n 844).

966 Buydens M, La protection de la quasi-création (Larcier 1993). It should be noted that this proposal never translated into a legislative response.

967 Rahmatian (n 844).

creation' as the sole criterion of protection, copyright already includes more and more industrial products".[968]

According to this doctrine, failing to distinguish between these two types of works is not only systematically inconsistent but also has undesirable systemic consequences, including that it may further legitimize the "over-propertization of information, facts and data". More precisely: "the lack of distinction between works based on their object has consequences that go far beyond the difficult adaptability to technical or informational creations of provisions conceived for artistic creations. In fact, this commixture conceals the stronger impact that the exclusivity over informational works has on the public domain, and the monopoly it confers on objects that often do not differ much from ideas for their nature of 'raw', upstream materials".[969]

On this view, it is precisely the "constitutional propertization" of copyright that "offers the systematic basis to introduce a differentiated treatment between various works, particularly where their enforcement conflicts with others' rights and specific public policy goals".[970]

As further observed, "the differentiation of property regimes has to be taken into account to correctly reflect the characteristics of the object and the nature of the interests underlying them and the rights", and this requires adapting "the scope of exclusive rights and [the approach] when interpreting exceptions and the fair balance".[971]

To support the idea that this differentiation between industrial products and creative works already exists within copyright, this doctrine explicitly recalls the trajectory of the recognition of protection for software and databases as paradigmatic examples, later followed by attempts to secure protection before the courts for "television guides, football fixtures, sporting events, and the like".[972]

From a functional perspective too, however, grounding a breakdown of copyright into a set of scalable operational regimes based on the nature of the intellectual work could be imaginable. Indeed, such an approach could represent a step toward reconciling the growing economic demands surrounding current copyright law with the humanist dimension that underpins this body of law.

---

968 Sganga, 'Propertizing European Copyright' (n. 345) 239.
969 Ibid.
970 Ibid.
971 Ibid.
972 Ibid.

On the one hand, the personalistic conception of copyright law underpinning the reflections of the *droit d'auteur* tradition[973] would be saved for works that can be said to express the author's personal touch.

On the other hand, the patrimonial prerogatives of those who invest in economic activities for the production of intellectual works could be recognized and valued even when the results of such activities cannot, strictly speaking, be attributed to an act of free and creative intellectual creation.

At the same time, calibrating the protection of such products could serve the broader public interest in fostering a vibrant cultural environment and ensuring access to works, even when they do not fall entirely outside the scope of copyright protection.

On the basis of these reflections, and to summarize the discussion thus far, all creations that qualify as intellectual works would be subject to "classic" (full) copyright when they meet the traditional criteria, while hybrid works – possibly assimilated to "factual and functional works", industrial works, commonplace works, *quasi-créations*, and the like – could receive a differentiated treatment. Such works would indeed satisfy the "skill and labor" threshold but not the "free and creative choices" requirement and would therefore not be considered original.

As said, this differentiated, less exclusive, regime would merely give new form to what has already existed for some time, at least in part, in practice: a decomposition of copyright into distinct operational disciplines that can be applied in a modular and scalable manner. Although described by some as "utopian", given recent legislative developments at the European level that appear to move in the opposite direction,[974] such differentiation between categories of works could in fact prove a concrete response to the increasing diffusion of AI-based works – which, in turn, would merely serve as the occasion for reflections that are equally applicable beyond this specific context.

1.2.2 Operationalizing the Difference between Types of Intellectual Works

Given the abstract possibility of differentiating between different types of works, the challenge at this stage concerns both the policy desirability of such a solution and the practical operability.

From the first perspective, the policy desirability of recognizing economic entitlements over works that do not bear the author's personal blueprint should be carefully assessed, given the risks they may pose in terms of further

973 Bensamoun and Farchy (n 4).

974 Rahmatian (n 844) 52.

enclosure of knowledge. Nevertheless, the underlying assumption is that pursuing – through appropriate legal instruments – the economic interests of providers and users of AI systems generating intellectual works could help preserve both the operativity of the existing regulatory framework and its "breathing spaces" for access, despite its ongoing restyling as a form of "corporate copyright", and could enable the copyright regime to fulfil its social function.[975]

The central aim would be precisely to ensure that the law does not overlook – and thereby leave open to commodification and easy appropriation by powerful private actors[976] – the grey area between "classic" intellectual works (creative expressions of ideas) and free ideas.

Also, this renewed architecture of copyright law would arguably apply not only to works generated through the use of AI, but to any kind of works, even outside the AI context.

In this sense, this "variable-geometry" reinterpretation of the discipline would align with the need to ensure greater transparency across the entire legal framework[977] and would confer new and distinct legitimacy on the interests at stake in each specific case, with the advantage of introducing in a more systematic manner appropriate counterbalances to the trend toward exclusive appropriation currently prevailing in copyright law. Indeed, the idea is that if – and only if – it were agreed that such works deserve protection, this protection should not be accorded on the same terms as that granted to "classic" works.

From the second perspective, the task is to anchor this differentiation of regimes in criteria that are as objective as possible. That said, introducing a new requirement for protection would not be desirable.[978] At the same time, however, the *souplesse* of the requirements currently in force for accessing copyright protection could offer a certain margin for maneuver.

---

975 Drexl, Hilty et al. (n 228).

976 Dusollier, 'The Commons as a Reverse Intellectual Property' (n 835) 271.

977 Geiger, 'The Social Function of Intellectual Property Rights' (n 87).

978 The difference would not be one of degree, but of kind: a higher threshold of creativity or originality (in a quantitative sense) would not be required for works eligible for copyright compared to hybrid ones; rather, the focus would be on the nature of the human intervention involved in their creation (in qualitative terms). Indeed, fixing the distinction between creativity and originality in quantitative terms would risk leading to "downward solutions" detrimental to creative works – in a paradoxical outcome whereby only original works, more easily obtained than creative ones, would end up being protected; see Fabbio (n 360) 301.

1.2.2.1 A Possible Difference between Creativity and Originality

As noted, the AOIC standard, originality, and creativity are concepts whose lines of distinction are often blurred. Their inherent circularity – whereby, taken to its extreme, an intellectual creation can be considered the "author's own" because it is original, and original because it is the "author's own", as well as creative because it is original, and original because it is creative – lies at the root of this inconsistency.

While this circularity has persisted until now, the emergence of AI in the creative process has arguably begun to break it. Indeed, with the advent of AI systems – which merely simulate creativity[979] yet are nevertheless capable of producing works that, from an external, objective, standpoint,[980] are in every respect indistinguishable from those created by humans and may, in fact, be "original" – the recognition of hybrid outputs as intellectual works necessarily opens the door to questioning the very concept of originality and its biunivocal link with creativity.

It is precisely in these fissures that the differentiation between hybrid and classic works could be grounded – namely, in a reinterpreted understanding of the interrelation between all these concepts, and specifically in a clearer differentiation between creativity and originality.

This distinction is already apparent, for example, in the Italian legal system, where case law normally fails to provide an unambiguous definition of the terms "creativity" and "originality", yet often expressly acknowledges that they are not identical concepts. For example, in one emblematic judgment,[981] the Italian Court of Cassation appears to employ the terms "originality" and "creative character" interchangeably when addressing the first plea, which concerned precisely the concept of originality. Later in the judgment, however – following what now seems to be a consolidated orientation[982] – the Court specifies that "the legal concept of creativity, to which the provision of Law No. 633 of 1941 [Italian Copyright Act], Article 1, refers, does not coincide with the concept of creation, originality, or absolute novelty, but rather with the personal and individual expression of an objectivity belonging to the categories listed, by way of

---

979 Having defined creativity as an expression of the link between an author and their work, it is difficult to argue that the creations of AI systems are the result of their "creativity".

980 The AI, exactly « *comme la personne humaine* », is capable of producing « *effectivement une forme qui peut être objectivement appréhendée comme une œuvre* »; see Bensamoun and Farchy (n 4).

981 Italian Supreme Court, Section I, sent no 25173, 28 November 2011.

982 In addition to Italian Supreme Court, Section I, sent no 25173, 28 November 2011; see also Italian Supreme Court, no 5089, 12 March 2004; Italian Supreme Court, 13 November 2015, no 23292; and Italian Supreme Court 23 March 2017, no 7477.

example, in Article 1 of the aforementioned Law, so that an original work receives protection provided that a creative act, however minimal, is detectable in it and capable of manifesting itself in the external world".

According to some interpretations developed within this same legal system, creativity has been understood as encompassing originality – meaning that originality is merely one aspect of creativity which, alongside novelty, would be required for a work to qualify as an intellectual work and thus be eligible for copyright protection.[983] This contrasts with certain reflections within EU scholarship, which instead tend to identify creativity as a component of originality, rather than the other way around.[984]

Whatever the precise interrelation between these two concepts, one constant in *droit d'auteur* is that the requirement for copyright protection has always been linked to the creator's exercise – an "*acte de création consciente*"[985] – of "free", "creative" and "personal" choices, thereby reflecting their personality. Yet, as noted above, some observers suggest that this requirement has been undergoing a process of transformation, with "originality" increasingly understood as relating to the intrinsic characteristics of the work itself, akin to a "*nouveauté dans l'univers des formes*".[986]

Nevertheless, a significant strand of copyright scholarship continues to emphasize the importance, for the purposes of copyright protection, of valuing the connection between the work and its author, as evidenced by the general recognition of the requirement of a human author. This is precisely why the idea of differentiating these criteria has emerged: to preserve this value within the notion of creativity. In this vein, should originality be reinterpreted in objective terms, creativity could instead be understood as embedding the requirement of a link between a work and its author.

Building on this observation, a possible taxonomy of intellectual works could be imagined as follows: (i) "creative and original" works, to which full copyright protection applies; (ii) works that are "only original", to which a less exclusive regime would apply; and (iii) products lacking both originality and creativity, which therefore do not qualify as intellectual works and are to be regarded as "free ideas" or as another category of goods, for which no copyright protection is envisaged.

---

983 Qualifying originality and novelty as two components of creativity is Sirotti Gaudenzi A, Il nuovo diritto d'autore (Maggioli Editore 2016) 79.

984 "This definition of originality has embedded in it the notion of creativity" (see Ramalho, 'Ex Machina, Ex Auctore?' (n 684)).

985 Binctin (n 458) 41 ff.

986 As for the French law, see Vivant and Bruguiere, 'Droit d'auteur et droits voisins' (n 456) no 271., Larrieu, 'Le robot et le droit d'auteur' (n 456); Gautier (n 724) no 35.

More specifically, under this taxonomy, works lacking originality should receive no protection and should therefore fall into the public domain. A distinct legal framework should apply to works that are not only original but also creative, fully protected by copyright, compared to those that are merely original and eligible for protection under a regime akin to "*droit de l'oeuvre*".[987]

Accordingly, in the context of AI-based outputs, creativity could, and indeed should, be regarded as present in all AI-assisted outputs, given their capacity, in principle, to express the author's personality owing to the preeminence of human intellectual input, whereas in AI-generated and hybrid works it may be absent. Nevertheless, the latter – although not creative – could still result from a (qualitatively) considerable human input and labor, be indistinguishable from human-created works from an external perspective, and, above all, be neither trivial nor banal, thereby likely meeting the current low threshold for originality, even without expressing the author's personality.

In such a framework, the interests at stake would expand or contract depending on the nature of the work, according to the said graduated scale. In particular, where works are neither creative nor original, the public's right of access to free knowledge and the general interests in the free flow of ideas, and in the promotion of creativity and innovation, should prevail over all other interests: as free ideas, works that are neither original nor creative would necessarily be understood as incapable of appropriation. Where works are only original and lack a creative imprint, the essentially economic interests of the market and of intermediaries in the creative industries might receive greater protection, at the expense of an "absolute" right of access (for instance, through the recognition of remuneration rights, but not exclusive rights). Finally, where works are both creative and original, the author's interest in protecting their freedom of artistic expression should be considered paramount among all competing interests (for instance, through the recognition of the full set of economic and moral rights).

1.2.2.2 The Assessment of Originality and Creativity

Opting for a distinction between works subject to full copyright protection and those subject to a more limited regime would rest not on the introduction of a new criterion for access to protection, but rather on a clarified understanding of two core concepts of copyright.

In such a framework, at the risk of oversimplifying a distinction that would merit far more extensive treatment, if originality constitutes the criterion for discerning between free ideas and protected "expressed ideas", crea-

---

987 Bensamoun, 'Libre propos sur l'existence d'un droit de l'oeuvre' (n 919).

tivity would instead continue to be the repository of that "indefectible link" between the work and its creator that characterizes the traditional approach of *"droit d'auteur"* traditions.

The Wittem Project had already theorized a qualitative differentiation between factual and functional works and artistic works, drawing the distinction not on the basis of merely formal criteria but in light of a different assessment of the requirement of originality: "for factual and functional works, the focus will be more on a certain level of skill (judgement) and labour, whereas for productions in the artistic field the focus will be more on personal expression".[988]

The same reasoning could be applied to the distinction proposed here: the difference would not be in "the level of originality required, but the quality of originality resulting from the intellectual framework behind it".[989]

Accordingly, the (judicial) assessment of these two criteria should be differentiated.

Originality should be evaluated in reverse, in the negative (focusing on what is not trivial) as something "originating from the author" (own), whereas creativity should be assessed in the positive.

Indeed, this latter could be grounded on the same indicia and presumptions (style, choice of words, celebrity of the author, etc.) that have so far been developed by the doctrine and jurisprudence of continental European traditions in relation to the unitary requirement of originality/creativity, applying the principle that a work, in order to be (also) creative, must not only "originate from the author", but must also have been shaped by the author's individual and distinct personality; it must not be commonplace, a work that could be attributed to anyone.[990]

Originality, by contrast, would subsist whenever there were a "qualitative element of material alteration as a choice by the author's intellect (intellectual creation)".[991] A work would be considered original if it possessed a minimum degree of individuality.[992] Thus, an original work would be one that is "not trivial" or "not merely routine",[993] and is endowed with a minimum of expressive complexity, in line with the principle that simple ideas are excluded from

988 See footnote 7 of commentary to Art. 1.1 of the ECC.

989 This would be consistent with what has already been noted in the past in relation to the distinction between "copyright" and "author's right"; see Rahmatian (n 844) 17.

990 Rahmatian (n 844) 17.

991 Ibid, 15.

992 Ibid, 30.

993 Fabbio (n 360) 306.

protection and, above all, not dictated by mere technical or functional requirements in line with the so-called "technical exclusion".[994]

To determine whether such works fulfil the condition of originality, judges could rely – as they already do – on expert opinions in the relevant field, or make use of indicators such as "the institutional acceptance of the work", "its success", "the complexity of its creation", "the first impression it gives", "its social function", "the incentive to purchase", "its presentation", and "the author's intention", among others,[995] as well as on the concept of the "objective observer".[996]

In the context of AI-based works, the assessment of originality could draw on an adapted version of the so-called Alan Turing test, under which the output of an AI system should be considered original if it is able to "pleasantly surprise and cause the same enjoyment as if it had been generated by a human being".[997] Obviously, however, the Alan Turing test would represent only one step in a much more complex logical and argumentative pathway which would begin upstream with the assessment of the AI output's protectability *in abstracto*

994 Otherwise, "it would end up transforming copyright at best into absolute investment protection, and in many cases into a first-come-first-served award disconnected from any consideration not only of the result achieved but also of the investment possibly made", Fabbio (n 360).

995 Van Gompel S and Lavik E, 'Quality, Merit, Aesthetics and Purpose: An Inquiry into EU Copyright Law's Eschewal of Other Criteria than Originality' (2013) Amsterdam Law School Legal Studies Research Papers No 51.

996 Inguanez D, 'A Refined Approach to Originality in EU Copyright Law in Light of the ECJ's Recent Copyright/Design Cumulation Case Law' (2020) 51 IIC 797 <https://doi.org/10.1007/s40319-020-00962-7> accessed 9 August 2025, 808.

997 Papadopoulou A, 'Creativity in Crisis: Are the Creations of Artificial Intelligence Worth Protecting?' (2021) 3 Journal of Intellectual Property, Information Technology and E-Commerce Law 408. The Alan Turing test is grounded in the evaluation of the performativity of the computer program during the so-called imitation game (from the English The Imitation Game – which inspired the film of the same name), developed as part of the mathematician's reflections on the capacity of machines to think. This would be a test grounded in the evaluation of the performativity of the computer program during the so-called imitation game (from the English The Imitation Game – which inspired the film of the same name), developed as part of the mathematician's reflections on the capacity of machines to think. The game has three human participants and one machine. In the initial part of the game, there is a man, a woman and an examiner, who asks questions in writing to the first two players who, in turn, are placed in a different room. The official objective of the game for the examiner is to guess the sexual gender of the players, with the man having the task of confusing him while the woman has that of helping him. In the second part of the game, the man is replaced by software programmed to provide answers that make the examiner believe that the game is normally going on with humans. See also Turing A, 'Computing Machinery and Intelligence' (1950) LIX(36) Mind, 442: "Are there imaginable digital computers which would do well in the imitation game?".

under copyright law, and conclude with the possible determination of whether the requirements of originality and, where applicable, creativity are met.

2 Concluding Remarks

The need to systematically rethink copyright legislation in a more sustainable way is increasingly seen within legal scholarship as a priority and, with the advent of generative AI in the broader context of knowledge capitalism, perhaps even as indispensable. The aim of this analysis was to operationalize the idea of reconceiving copyright not as a form of unlimited ownership, but as an inclusive property right that no longer revolves solely around the paradigm of exclusivity, but also embraces that of inclusivity.[998]

Despite its nature as a property right, copyright should, in fact, be understood as a regulatory framework capable of safeguarding constitutionally relevant interests of actors beyond the creative industries and bigger rightsholders, thereby overcoming the "form of exclusivist appropriation, characterised by the tendentially unlimited power of private subjects over economic goods"[999] that underpins the modern concept of property.

(Re)thinking copyright in these terms entails viewing it not only as a right to protect works, but also as a "right to access".[1000]

Supporting such an approach first requires recovering the idea that copyright, in its dimension as a fundamental right, pursues a precise social function – one embodied in the promotion of cultural progress, the protection of freedom of (artistic) expression, and the safeguarding of the right of access to creative artifacts and information – and then imagining differentiated operational regimes to give effect to this function.

---

998 Quarta (n 33); Rochfeld, Martin and Cornu (n 676).

999 Salvi (n 906) 11.

1000 However, attention must be paid to the notion of "access right": "The term 'access right' in the context of this chapter needs to be clearly differentiated from its past, diametrically opposite understanding. In fact, the term 'access right' has been used in previous scholarly work to describe the right to control, even forbid, access to copyright works, which resulted from technical protection measures (TPM) and their legal protection by copyright law"; see Geiger, 'Copyright as an Access Right' (n 378) 5; Hoeren T, 'Access Right as a Postmodern Symbol of Copyright Deconstruction?' in J Ginsburg and J Besek (eds), Adjuncts and Alternatives to Copyright, Proceedings of the ALAI Congress June 13–17, 2001 (Kernochan Center for Law Media and the Arts 2002) 360; Heide T P, 'Copyright in the EU and the United States: What "Access Right"?' (2001) EIPR 476; Olswang S, 'Access Right: An Evolutionary Path for Copyright in the Digital Era?' (1995) EIPR 215.

In light of the above, adopting an inclusive copyright framework, in which flexibility manifests itself through a differentiated assessment of the weight of the three-step test and of exceptions and limitations (internal balancing), a redefined demarcation line between ideas and their expression, distinct categories of works, and a differentiated balancing of copyright with other fundamental rights (external balancing), emerges as a key option for operationalizing the social function of copyright and giving full effect to its constitutional foundation.

Far from being a mere theoretical exercise, such an approach would serve as the practical means to embed the fundamental rights both of access to creative artefacts and of freedom of artistic expression for human creators, in view of the collective interest in promoting culture.

Indeed, the value of such flexibility within copyright law lies in its potential to prevent a further enclosure of knowledge, restore legitimacy to this body of law, and enable the adoption of a new, normatively oriented narrative – in one sentence, ensure that "Caesar is given what is Caesar's."

These reflections are not entirely new: they build on issues already addressed, principles already stated, and operational solutions already proposed or embraced by scholarship and/or case law. Among those previously discussed is the French doctrine of the *échelle de communalité*, which holds that property should not be conceived as a monolithic institution-copyright being a paradigmatic example indeed – but rather as a scale, allowing for a plurality of "possible arrangements" among the interests at stake, depending on the varying pervasiveness, in different contexts, of the common interest of a given community.[1001]

For such a reconstruction to be meaningful, however, it must inevitably be brought back into a coherent system. This systematization is not only necessary but also, and precisely for that reason, the most delicate point.

The greatest risks of failing to achieve such systematization would include, among others, a significant aggravation of the already delicate situation of legal uncertainty in the sector and the instrumentalization of its concepts.

As regards legal uncertainty,[1002] this could be mitigated – though admittedly never entirely eliminated[1003] – through the appropriate development of tools (e.g., dedicated tests) for use by judges in the application phase.

1001 Rochfeld, Martin and Cornu (n 676).

1002 Notably, legal uncertainty facilitates the consolidation of power, with dominant players in the tech sector leveraging fair use in strategic litigation, both defensively and offensively to entrench their control over emerging technologies. See Frosio, 'Should We Ban Generative AI, Incentivise it or Make it a Medium for Inclusive Creativity?' (n 410) 5.

1003 See for all Karnell GWG, 'European Originality: A Copyright Chimera' [2002] Scandinavian Studies in Law 73 209.

The more serious risk, however, lies in the potential instrumentalization of a more flexible regime such as the one envisioned here, which could lead to new and unintended forms of knowledge enclosure – the very outcome it seeks to prevent. For instance, in the case of AI-based hybrid works, deciding whether to grant protection would require a context-based and policy assessment of the genuine necessity of recognizing a number of entitlements, rather than allowing such works to fall into the public domain. However, one possible justification for such recognition could be the acknowledgment that the public domain regime is weak and prone to commodification.[1004]

Ultimately, an inclusive reconstruction of copyright law would require revisiting and reassessing its dogmas and principles, at least at the EU level. Yet such a re-systematization will not be easy, as shown by the "copyright wars" that have been ongoing for decades – and not by coincidence.

The combination of the hallmarks of knowledge capitalism – the privatization of the public domain and of knowledge – with the sheer scale of the operators active in this field and the concentration of their power, makes it necessary to act on several fronts and through a multi-level approach.

On the one hand, legal scholarship, case law, and legislative initiatives must continue to address the governance of new technologies in a transversal way, building on the already extensive EU digital regulatory framework. The application of existing regimes – including, but not limited to, the AI Act, the Digital Services Act, the Digital Markets Act,[1005] and more broadly the frameworks on personal and non-personal data, competition, and consumer protection – to generative AI is to be welcomed and, in any case, unavoidable. Notable features of these frameworks include their risk-based approach, their focus on systemic risks posed by certain technologies, the proceduralization of rights-protection mechanisms, and the integration of public and private enforcement.[1006]

On the other hand, these pieces of legislation are not sufficient to address the broad range of transformations brought about by generative AI. The AI Act itself is illustrative in this regard: although it recognizes the need to address copyright issues in the context of general-purpose AI models, one of its main obligations in this respect is for providers to "put in place a policy to comply

---

1004 Dusollier, 'The Commons as a Reverse Intellectual Property' (n 835) 271.

1005 See AI Act (n 5), DMA (n 284), DSA (n 285).

1006 For an overview of the issues raised by the new technologies with respect to the protection of personal data, see Senigaglia R, Irti C and Bernes A (eds), Privacy and Data Protection in Software Services (Springer 2022); *amplius*, Irti C, Consenso "negoziato" e circolazione dei dati personali (Giappichelli 2021). For an analysis of the overlapping planes of copyright law and data protection law, see Pasa B, 'Copyright and Data Protection' (n 472).

with Union law on copyright and related rights". In doing so, it touches only briefly on the matter and ultimately defers the issue back to copyright law itself.

Therefore, if we wish to "aspire to usable results and continue to cultivate an idea of a legal system that reflects coherent and rational meanings – an order, to be precise", it becomes essential to "systematise this enormous mass of new norms through general categories and legal concepts that are reliable and suited to the times".[1007]

This would require a much-needed upstream intervention: not only on digital regulation, but also on the classical legal disciplines reshaped by these technologies. In this light, a specific *ex lege* reform of copyright could be necessary – for example, by introducing an open-ended exception regime, distinguishing between types of works, reinforcing extra-market considerations into the application of the three-step test, and clarifying the notion of lawful access.

However, such legislative intervention would not be easy. The greatest difficulty lies in the fact that, for any re-evaluation of copyright law to take place coherently, it would need to occur – at the very least – at the EU level. Yet, so far, EU institutions do not appear to consider a re-systematization of copyright law a priority.[1008] Indeed, the European Commission had long maintained that "there would be no obstacles to the functioning of the internal market in this area such as to make intervention by the European legislator a priority".[1009]

A further obstacle stems from the notoriously diverse approaches taken by European legal traditions: the Member States differ significantly on key issues such as the scope of the requirement of "originality" and the very concept of "intellectual creation",[1010] as well as on the provisions governing exceptions and limitations – differences that form the backdrop to much of the debate in this area. These divergences had already been documented in the early 2000s within the framework of the European Copyright Code project by the Wittem Project, which expressed concern that "the process of drafting copyright laws at the European level lacks transparency and that the voice of the academic world too often goes unheard".[1011]

1007 Orlando S, at https://www.dimt.it/news/intervista-al-prof-salvatore-orlando-diritto-privato-e-nuove-tecnologie-i-contenuti-degli-insegnamenti-sul-diritto-dei-dati/.

1008 Fabbio (n 360) 301–302.

1009 Fabbio (n 360) 285.

1010 See extensively Rahmatian (n 844).

1011 *"A concern that the process of copyright law making at the European level lacks transparency and that the voice of academia all too often remains unheard"*, cf. https://www.ivir.nl/copyrightcode/introduction/.

Nevertheless, notwithstanding these challenges, such a reform would be highly desirable.

In particular, such reform could allow for: (i) an *ex lege* (and *ex ante*) redefinition of the scope of application of copyright law, starting from a precise reconsideration of its subject matter, the concept of reproduction in relation to TDM activities, the range of exceptions and limitations, the introduction of statutory licenses, and the design of remuneration schemes based on limitations; and (ii) the recognition to courts (*ex post*) of greater room for maneuver in applying the reformed legislation, taking into account the calls from part of the scholarship for the entire system to respond with greater flexibility.

Not a bad starting point for a renewed conception of copyright law.

Conclusions

It is difficult to reach firm conclusions about generative AI, given its rapid evolution and its penetration into virtually every sphere of daily life – social, professional, and recreational alike.

This study has sought to map the key contours of the debate, where legal, sociological, and ethical considerations intersect, and where economic concerns are inseparably linked with systemic and societal ones.

In the face of the feeling – perhaps illusory, perhaps not – that everything is now beginning, the anxieties rooted in fear of the unknown coexist with the reassurance brought by scientific and technological progress, and with the exhilaration of new frontiers and the as-yet-unimaginable possibilities of the future.

The context in which discussions on generative AI have arisen is a complex one: the critical issues raised by this new set of technologies have penetrated deep into the interstices of copyright law, which today struggles to keep pace with the changes underway – just as it has, cyclically, at every stage of industrial development, from the printing press to photocopiers to the first computers.

With generative AI, however, the potential disruptions to copyright, already in the midst of an identity crisis, risk bringing it to a point of no return. The scale of the societal impact that artificial intelligence is likely to exert – including the systemic risks for cultural diversity and freedom of expression examined at the beginning of this work –, together with its transformative effect on the classic categories of copyright law, arguably makes the current landscape qualitatively different from any challenge that existing legislation has faced thus far.

The different solutions put forward so far by scholars, policymakers, and industry actors – both on the input and output sides of the creative process, as surveyed in the central part of this study – must be read in light of the exponential shift in power relations between the actors in the sector and the community as a whole.

Given the pervasiveness of this phenomenon, which constitutes nothing more than an occasion – the latest in terms of time, and the most significant in terms of impact – for a systematic rethinking of copyright law, developing a new narrative for intellectual property becomes desirable, if not indispensable in the era of knowledge capitalism.

In this context, what is required is a re-evaluation of copyright's value foundations: an analysis of its classic categories and underlying principles that is

 | HTTPS://DOI.ORG/10.1163/9789004730731-013

not an end in itself, but one oriented toward making a clear and deliberate choice about the nature and function of copyright and the essential justifications for granting its protection.

From the perspective adopted in this work, the starting point is the idea that copyright, even as (and, actually, insofar as it is) a specific manifestation of the right to property, must serve a precise social function: to guarantee cultural progress, the right to (artistic) expression and information, and, not least, access to knowledge.

Like the institution of property itself, copyright, in its constitutional dimension, is not a monolithic body of law. It can instead be reimagined as a variable-geometry framework, in which different regimes apply to different contexts, works, and uses of protected artifacts.

What is envisaged, therefore, is a legal discipline that, depending on the circumstances of each case, locates the balance between competing interests at different points along a spectrum of possible protections. Ideally introduced at the regulatory level, such a discipline should assist interpreters, and above all judges, in navigating the dense and multifaceted notions that characterize this field, such as lawful access, right of reproduction, originality, creativity, etc.

It should also support them in the complex task of disentangling the various stages of the algorithmic creative process, where input data cannot always be considered to carry expressive value, and the human intervention underlying a given output cannot always be regarded as qualitatively creative.

Expressly recognizing the flexibilities inherent in copyright should serve as a means to avoid further uncritical stretching of this legal framework and, conversely, to redesign the boundaries of "exclusivity" and "inclusivity" in a variable manner, depending on the relative weight of the underlying general interest.

In this context, it is essential to preserve the dialectic between the individual and collective dimensions of the discipline – acknowledging its potential transformation into a regulatory instrument that operates not only as a tool of private law but also of public law – and to respond to scholarly calls for a more sustainable framework.

As previously noted, even when envisaging a re-systematization of regulation that is not aimed at the extension *tout court of* the spaces of exclusivity, a prudential approach remains necessary: the potential social costs of such a restructuring must be carefully assessed.

That said, it is difficult to imagine the phenomenon of generative AI coming to a halt in the foreseeable future. On the contrary, it will likely continue to expand and enrich the existing landscape, further increasing the complexity of its governance – an area in which the often-fragmented interventions of legislators to date appear increasingly inadequate.

Along with the sense of astonishment it inspires, the practical applications of generative AI are likely to bring further uncertainty to the legal sphere – an uncertainty that must be addressed through clear concepts and shared definitions.

To this end, it may be necessary to return to the very roots of the legislation and, still upstream, revisit its dogmas and principles, at least at a European Union level, rethinking copyright as within — and against the drifts of — knowledge capitalism and as a tool for governing knowledge.

Within this framework, it would be preferable to make it an ally in fostering the democratic and sustainable development of AI, rather than yet another instrument concentrated in the hands of a few, thereby eroding its very promise to drive genuine innovation and support the circulation of knowledge. As has been aptly observed, "we must ensure that copyright law does not stifle AI's potential but rather guides it in a manner that amplifies the collective benefits of technological advancement".[1012]

1012 Frosio, 'Should We Ban Generative AI, Incentivise It or Make It a Medium for Inclusive Creativity?' (n 410) 7.

References

Abbott R and Rothman E, 'Disrupting Creativity: Copyright Law in the Age of Generative Artificial Intelligence' (2023) 75 Fla L Rev 1141 <https://ssrn.com/abstract=4185327> accessed 9 August 2025.

Abbott R, 'Intellectual Property and Artificial Intelligence, an Introduction' in R Abbott (ed), Research Handbook of Artificial Intelligence and Intellectual Property (Edward Elgar 2022).

Ajani G, '*E Pluribus Unum* (?): Illusioni dell'armonizzazione e utilità dell'ontologia' (2007) 36 Rivista di estetica 13.

Ajani G and Pasa B, Diritto comparato. Casi e materiali (Giappichelli 2013).

Ajani G, 'Contemporary Artificial Art and the Law. Searching for an Author' (2020) Brill Research Perspectives: Art and Law.

Amabile T, Creativity in Context (Westview Press 1996).

Angelopoulos C, 'The Myth of European Term Harmonisation: 27 Public Domains for the 27 Member States' [2012] SSRN Electronic Journal <http://www.ssrn.com/abstract=2145862> accessed 9 August 2025.

Angiolini C, 'La reconnaissance de l'intérêt commun en rapport avec les droits fondamentaux au sein des beni comuni en Italie' in J Rochfeld, GJ Martin and M Cornu (eds), L'échelle de communalité. Proposition de réformes pour intégrer les biens communs en droit (2021).

Annoni A, Benczur P, Bertoldi P and others, 'Artificial Intelligence: A European Perspective' in Craglia M (ed), EUR 29425 EN (Publications Office of the European Union 2018).

Alpa G, Bonell MJ, L Corapi, L Moccia, V Zeno-Zencovich and A Zoppini, Diritto privato comparato (Laterza 2012).

Ardizzone A, Benussi L, Blengino C, Glorioso A, Ramello GB, Ruffo G and Travostino M, Copyright digitale. L'impatto delle nuove tecnologie tra economia e diritto (Giappichelli 2009).

Ascarelli T, Teoria della concorrenza e dei beni immateriali (3rd edn, Giuffrè 1960).

Azzi T, 'La balance des intérêts en droit de la propriété littéraire et artistique' in V Barbes, C Guillerminet and S Mauclair (eds), La notion d'intérêt(s) en droit (Institut francophone pour la justice et la démocratie 2022).

Balduzzi R, 'La "liberalizzazione" dei diritti di proprietà intellettuale sui vaccini. Profili costituzionali e internazionali' (2022) 2 Quaderni costituzionali – Rivista italiana di diritto costituzionale 261.

Baldwin P, The Copyright Wars: Three Centuries of Transatlantic Battle (Princeton University Press 2014).

 | HTTPS://DOI.ORG/10.1163/9789004730731-014

Barcellona M, 'La metafora dei beni comuni: l'Impero, lo Stato e la democrazia nel tempo del capitale cognitivo' (2016) 3 Democrazia e Diritto.

Baškarada S and Koronios A, 'Data, Information, Knowledge, Wisdom (DIKW): A Semiotic Theoretical and Empirical Exploration of the Hierarchy and Its Quality Dimension' (2013) 18(1) Australasian Journal of Information Systems 5 <https://doi.org/10.3127/ajis.v18i1.748> accessed 10 June 2025.

Beckerman-Rodau A, 'The Problem with Intellectual Property Rights: Subject Matter Expansion' (2010) 13 Yale Journal of Law & Technology 35, also published as Suffolk University Law School Research Paper No 11-14 <https://ssrn.com/abstract=1754781> accessed 9 August 2025.

Bell D, The Coming of Post Industrial Society: A Venture in Social Forecasting (Basic Books 1973) xiii, 507 pp, ISBN 0-465-01281-7.

Benazeraf JA, *La qualification d'œuvre de l'esprit à l'épreuve du procès*: probatio diabolica? in Bensamoun A, Labarthe F and Tricoire A (eds), L'oeuvre de l'esprit en question(s). Un exercice de qualification (mare & martin 2015), 189.

Benazeraf JA and Barthez V, Rapport de mission. La preuve de l'originalité (Conseil Supérieur de la propriété littéraire et artistique (CSPLA) 2020).

Bensamoun A, Farchy J and Schira PF, Mission du CSPLA sur les enjeux juridiques et économiques de l'intelligence artificielle dans les secteurs de la création culturelle – Rapport final (Conseil Supérieur de la propriété littéraire et artistique (CSPLA) 2020).

Bensamoun A, 'Libre propos sur l'existence d'un droit de l'oeuvre applicable aux créations issues de l'intelligence artificielle' in Bruguiere JM and Geiger C (eds), Penser le droit de la pensée – Mélanges en l'honneur de Michel Vivant (1st edn, Dalloz 2020).

Bensamoun A, 'Intelligence artificielle et propriété intellectuelle' in Loiseau G and Bensamoun A (eds), Droit de l'intelligence artificielle (LGDJ 2022).

Bently L and Kretschmer M (eds), 'Le Chapelier's report (1791), Primary Sources on Copyright (1450–1900)' <http://www.copyrighthistory.org> accessed 9 August 2025.

Bently L, Sherman B, Gangjee D and Johnson P, Intellectual Property Law (5th edn, Oxford University Press 2018).

Berman PS, 'The Evolution of Global Legal Pluralism' in Cotterrell R and Del Mar M (eds), Authority in Transnational Legal Theory: Theorising Across Disciplines (Edward Elgar Publishing 2016).

Bernes A, 'Dati e ricerca genetica. Dalla tutela individuale alla gestione procedurale' (2022) BioLaw Journal – Rivista di BioDiritto Special Issue 1.

Bertani M, Diritto d'autore europeo (Giappichelli 2011).

Bertani M and Sarti D, Studi per Luigi Carlo Ubertazzi. Proprietà intellettuale e concorrenza (Giuffrè 2019).

Binctin N, 'L'influence de l'intelligence artificielle sur les mécanismes de la propriété intellectuelle' in Bruguiere JM and Geiger C (eds), Penser le droit de la pensée – Mélanges en l'honneur de Michel Vivant (1st edn, Dalloz 2020).

Blaszczyk M, 'Thaler v Perlmutter: Human Authors at the Center of Copyright?' (Legal Blogs, 8 April 2025) <https://legalblogs.wolterskluwer.com/copyright-blog/thaler-v-perlmutter-human-authors-at-the-center-of-copyright/#:~:text=On%20March%2018%2C%202025%2C%20the,be%20authored%20in%20the%20first>.

Bob BL, Sturm J and others, 'Music Transcription Modelling and Composition Using Deep Learning' (2016) arXiv:1604.08723 <https://arxiv.org/abs/1604.08723> accessed 9 August 2025.

Bonadio E and Lucchi N, 'How Far Can Copyright Be Stretched? Framing the Debate on Whether New and Different Forms of Creativity Can Be Protected' (2019) Intellectual Property Quarterly 115.

Bonadio E, 'Artificial Intelligence as Producer and Consumer of Copyright Works: Evaluating the Consequences of Algorithmic Creativity' (2020) 2 IPQ 112–137.

Borghi M, 'Hegel's Theory of Personality in Copyright Law: Questioning the Dominant (Anglo-American) Paradigm' [2024] SSRN Electronic Journal <https://www.ssrn.com/abstract=4771323> accessed 9 August 2025.

Borghi M, 'Rewarding Creativity in Law, Economics and Literature', in ANCILLA IURIS, 54–63 (2006).

Borji A, 'Generated Faces in the Wild: Quantitative Comparison of Stable Diffusion, Midjourney and DALL-E 2' (2022) arXiv:2210.00586 <https://arxiv.org/abs/2210.00586> accessed 9 August 2025.

Boyle J, 'The Second Enclosure Movement and the Construction of the Public Domain' (2003) 66 Law and Contemporary Problems 33.

Bradford A, 'The Brussels Effect' (2013) 107 *Northwestern University Law Review* 1.

Bradford A, Digital Empires: The Global Battle to Regulate Technology (1st edn, Oxford University PressNew York 2023) <https://academic.oup.com/book/46736> accessed 9 August 2025.

Brogden J and Erickson K, 'On the Process of Image Creation with Artificial Intelligence: Rephotography Using Midjourney AI', forthcoming.

Bruguiere JM and Geiger C (eds), Penser le droit de la pensée – Mélanges en l'honneur de Michel Vivant (1st edn, Dalloz 2020).

Bulayenko O, Quintais JP, Gervais D and Poort J, 'AI Music Outputs: Challenges to the Copyright Legal Framework' reCreating Europe Report (2022).

Buydens M, La protection de la quasi-création (Larcier 1993).

Burkholder JP, Grout DJ and Palisca CV, A History of Western Music (5th edn, W W Norton & Company 1996).

Burton-Jones A, 'The Transition to Knowledge Capitalism' in Alan Burton-Jones, *Knowledge Capitalism* (1st edn, Oxford University PressOxford 1999) <https://academic.oup.com/book/8553/chapter/154436851> accessed 9 August 2025.

Camardi C, 'Brevi riflessioni sull'argomentazione per principi nel diritto privato' (2017) 5 Rivista di Diritto Civile.

Camardi C, 'Contratti digitali e mercati delle piattaforme. Un promemoria per il civilista' (2021) 4 Jus Civile.

Camardi C (ed), La via Europea per l'intelligenza artificiale (CEDAM 2023).

Campus G, 'Artificial Intelligence, Machine Learning and Creativity in Visual Art: What Are the Protectability Requirements? Part 1: The Italian Supreme Court's "Floral Fractal" Case' (5 September 2023) Kluwer Copyright Blog <https://copyrightblog.kluweriplaw.com/2023/09/05/artificial-intelligence-machine-learning-and-creativity-in-visual-art-what-are-the-protectability-requirements-part-1-the-italian-supreme-courts-floral-fractal-case/> accessed 9 August 2025.

Campus G, 'Artificial Intelligence, Machine Learning and Creativity in Visual Art: What Are the Protectability Requirements? Part 2: The US Thaler v Perlmutter Case' (7 September 2023) Kluwer Copyright Blog <https://copyrightblog.kluweriplaw.com/2023/09/07/artificial-intelligence-machine-learning-and-creativity-in-visual-art-what-are-the-protectability-requirements-part-2-the-us-thaler-vs-perlmutter-case/> accessed 9 August 2025.

Caron C, 'Le droit d'auteur et les gens: petit abécédaire d'un divorce' in Bruguiere JM and Geiger C (eds), Penser le droit de la pensée – Mélanges en l'honneur de Michel Vivant (1st edn, Dalloz 2020).

Cascione C, Il diritto privato dei beni pubblici. Modelli di appartenenza e circolazione (Cacucci 2013).

Caso R, 'Assange e vaccini, ecco le contraddizioni etiche dell'Occidente' (2022) Agenda Digitale.

Caso R, 'Michelangelo's David and Cultural Heritage Images: The Italian Pseudo-Intellectual Property and the End of Public Domain' (Kluwer Copyright Blog, 2023) <https://legalblogs.wolterskluwer.com/copyright-blog/michelangelos-david-and-cultural-heritage-images-the-italian-pseudo-intellectual-property-and-the-end-of-public-domain/> accessed 9 August 2025.

Castells M, *The Rise of the Network Society* (The Information Age: Economy, Society and Culture, vol 1, Blackwell 1996); *The Power of Identity* (vol 2, Blackwell 1997); *End of Millennium* (vol 3, Blackwell 1998).

Chimienti L, Banche dati e diritto d'autore (Giuffrè 1999).

Chimienti L, Diritto di Autore 4.0. L'intelligenza artificiale crea? (Pacini 2020).

Ciani Sciolla J, Il pubblico dominio nella società della conoscenza. L'interesse generale al libero utilizzo del capitale intellettuale comune (Giappichelli 2021).

Clerico G and Rizzello S (eds), Diritto ed economia della proprietà intellettuale (CEDAM 1998).

Cohen JE, *Between Truth and Power: The Legal Constructions of Informational Capitalism* (Oxford University Press 2019).

Colangelo G, 'A Competition Policy Analysis of Copyright Protection in Generative AI' (Singapore Journal of Legal Studies, 2 April 2025) <https://ssrn.com/abstract=5201510> or http://dx.doi.org/10.2139/ssrn.5201510.

Council of the European Union, 'Commission Staff Working Paper on the Review of the EC Legal Framework in the Field of Copyright and Related Rights' (19 July 2004) SEC(2004) 995.

Crawford K, Atlas of AI: Power, Politics, and the Planetary Costs of Artificial Intelligence (Yale University Press 2021).

Craig C and Kerr I, 'The Death of the AI Author' (2021) 52(1) Ottawa Law Review 31 <https://ssrn.com/abstract=> accessed 9 August 2025.

Dalton A and Fauria K, 'Hollywood's Strikes Are Both Now Over as Actors Reach Deal with Studios and Return to Work with Writers' (AP News, 9 November 2023) <https://apnews.com/article/actors-strike-ends-hollywood-5769ab584bca99fe708c67d00d2ec241> accessed 10 June 2025.

Davies G, Copyright and the Public Interest (2nd edn, Sweet and Maxwell 2002).

De Cock Buning M, 'Artificial Intelligence and the Creative Industry: New Challenges for the EU Paradigm for Art and Technology by Autonomous Creation' in Barfield W and Pagallo U (eds), Research Handbook on the Law of Artificial Intelligence (Edward Elgar 2018).

De Franceschi A (ed), European Contract Law and the Digital Single Market (Intersentia 2016).

Degli Espositi M, Lagioia F and Sartor G, 'The Use of Copyrighted Works by AI Systems: Art Works in the Data Mill' (2018) 11 European Journal of Risk Management 51–69.

Délégué Y, 'Mallarmé, le sujet de la poésie' (2001) 101(5) Revue d'histoire littéraire de la France.

DeLong JV, Epstein RA, Lepage H and Palmer T, La proprietà (intellettuale) è un furto? (Rubbettino Editore 2006).

Deltorn JM and Macrez F, 'Authorship in the Age of Machine Learning and Artificial Intelligence' in O'Connor (ed), The Oxford Handbook of Music Law and Policy (Oxford University Press 2019) Centre for International Intellectual Property Studies (CEIPI) Research Paper No 2018-10.

De Sanctis V, La protezione delle opere dell'ingegno. Le opere letterarie e scientifiche, le opere musicali e le opere informatiche, vol II (Giuffrè 2003).

Dias Pereira AL, 'A Copyright Human-Centred Approach to AI?' (2021) 70(4) GRUR International 323.

Di Cataldo V, 'Banche-dati e diritto sui generis: la fattispecie costitutiva' (1997) I Annali italiani di diritto d'autore, della cultura e dello spettacolo 20.

Di Cataldo V, 'Proprietà intellettuale ed evoluzione del mondo' (2022) 2 Il Diritto Industriale.

Drexl J, Hilty R and others, 'Artificial Intelligence and Intellectual Property Law – Position Statement of the Max Planck Institute for Innovation and Competition of 9 April 2021 on the Current Debate' (2021) Max Planck Institute for Innovation & Competition Research Paper No 21-10 <https://ssrn.com/abstract=3822924> or http://dx.doi.org/10.2139/ssrn.3822924.

Drott E, 'Copyright, Compensation, and Commons in the Music AI Industry' (2021) 14(2) *Creative Industries Journal* 190, 191 https://doi.org/10.1080/17510694.2020.1839702 accessed 10 June 2025.

Dusollier S, 'Open Source and Copyleft: Authorship Reconsidered?' (2003) 26 Columbia Journal of Law and the Arts 281 <https://ssrn.com/abstract=2186190> accessed 22 May 2025.

Dusollier S, Dusollier S, 'Scoping Study on Copyright and Related Rights and the Public Domain' (WIPO 2010) CDIP/4/3/REV./STUDY/INF/1.

Dusollier S, 'The Commons as a Reverse Intellectual Property – from Exclusivity to Inclusivity' in Helena Howe and Jonathan Griffiths (eds), *Concepts of Property in Intellectual Property Law* (1st edn, Cambridge University Press 2013) <https://www.cambridge.org/core/product/identifier/9781107300880%23c04182-11-1/type/book_part> accessed 9 August 2025.

Dusollier S, 'Inclusive Properties' (2024) 29 Lex Electronica 81.

Ebers M, 'Standardizing AI – The Case of the European Commission's Proposal for an Artificial Intelligence Act' in The Cambridge Handbook of Artificial Intelligence: Global Perspectives on Law and Ethics (2021) <https://ssrn.com/abstract=3900378> accessed 9 August 2025.

Ebers M and others, 'The European Commission's Proposal for an Artificial Intelligence Act–A Critical Assessment by Members of the Robotics and AI Law Society (RAILS)' (2021) 4(4) J 589.

Edwards L, Szpotakowski I, Cifrodelli G, Sangaré J and Stewart J, 'Private Ordering and Generative AI: What Can We Learn From Model Terms and Conditions?' (2024) CREATe <https://doi.org/10.5281/zenodo.11276105>.

Engel C, 'Challenges in the Interdisciplinary Use of Comparative Law' (MPI Collective Goods Discussion Paper No 2020/29, 30 November 2020) <https://ssrn.com/abstract=3739754> accessed 22 May 2025.

Ercolani S, 'Computer Generated Works' (1998) Il Diritto di Autore 605.

Erickson K, 'AI and Work in the Creative Industries: Digital Continuity or Discontinuity?' (28 October 2024) Creative Industries Journal (online early version, forthcoming 2024) <https://ssrn.com/abstract=5006065> accessed 10 June 2025.

European Commission, 'Communication to the European Parliament, the Council, the European Economic and Social Committee and the Committee of the Regions

"A Single Market for Intellectual Property Rights. Boosting Creativity and Innovation to Provide Economic Growth, Jobs and First-Class Products and Services in Europe"' (24 May 2011) COM(2011) 287.

European Commission, 'Communication to the European Parliament, the Council, the European Economic and Social Committee and the Committee of the Regions "A Strategy for a Digital Single Market in Europe"' (6 May 2015) COM(2015) 192 final.

European Commission, 'Communication to the European Parliament, the Council, the European Economic and Social Committee and the Committee of the Regions "Towards a Modern and More European Copyright Framework"' (9 December 2015) COM(2015) 626 final.

European Commission, 'Communication to the European Parliament, the Council, the European Economic and Social Committee and the Committee of the Regions "Artificial Intelligence for Europe"' (25 April 2018) COM(2018) 237 final.

European Commission, 'Communication to the European Parliament, the Council, the European Economic and Social Committee and the Committee of the Regions "Coordinated Plan on Artificial Intelligence"' (7 December 2018) COM(2018) 795 final.

European Commission, 'Communication to the European Parliament, the Council, the European Economic and Social Committee and the Committee of the Regions "Building Trust in Anthropocentric Artificial Intelligence"' (8 April 2019) COM (2019) 168 final.

European Commission, 'White Paper on Artificial Intelligence – A European Approach to Excellence and Trust' (19 February 2020) COM(2020) 65 final.

European Commission, 'Communication to the European Parliament, the Council, the European Economic and Social Committee and the Committee of the Regions on "Unlocking the EU's Innovative Potential – An Action Plan on Intellectual Property to Support EU Recovery and Resilience"' (25 November 2020) COM (2020) 760 final.

European Commission, 'Establishing a European Declaration on Digital Rights and Principles for the Digital Decade' COM(2022) 27 final, 26 January 2022.

European Commission, 'Proposal for a Directive of the European Parliament and of the Council on the Adaptation of the Rules on Non-Contractual Liability to Artificial Intelligence (Artificial Intelligence Liability Directive)' COM(2022) 496 final, 28 September 2022.

European Commission, 'AI Continent Action Plan' (Communication to the European Parliament, the Council, the European Economic and Social Committee and the Committee of the Regions, 9 April 2025) COM(2025) 165 final <https://digital-strategy.ec.europa.eu/en/library/ai-continent-action-plan>.

European Commission, 'Commission Guidelines on the Definition of an Artificial Intelligence System Established by Regulation (EU) 2024/1689 (AI Act)' C(2025) 5053 final (Brussels, 29 July 2025).

European Commission, 'Commission Opinion on the Assessment of the General-Purpose AI Code of Practice within the Meaning of Article 56 of Regulation (EU) 2024/1689' C(2025) 5361 final (Brussels, 1 August 2025).

European Copyright Society, 'General Opinion on the EU Copyright Reform Package' (2017) <https://europeancopyrightsociety.org/wp-content/uploads/2015/12/ecs-opinion-on-eu-copyright-reform-def.pdf>.

Fabbio P, 'Opere protette e requisiti di tutela nel diritto d'autore UE' (2016) AIDA.

Fernandez A, 'Regulating Deep Fakes in the Proposed AI Act' (2022) MediaLaws.

Fishman LR, 'Comparing concepts of originality in EU, Lithuanian and US law: photographs, new clips, databases, plot lines, tv formats, and other new uses of copyright works' in Mira T Sundara Rajan (ed), Cambridge Handbook of Intellectual Property in Central and Eastern Europe (CUP 2019) 80–109.

Floridi L, The Fourth Revolution: On the Impact of Information and Communication Technologies (Oxford University Press 2014).

Floridi L, La quarta rivoluzione. Come l'infosfera sta trasformando il mondo (Milano 2017).

Floridi L and others, 'capAI – A Procedure for Conducting Conformity Assessment of AI Systems in Line with the EU Artificial Intelligence Act' (2022) <https:/s/ssrn.com/abstract=4064091> accessed 9 August 2025.

Foong C, 'GenAI Models and Copyright Infringement: Doctrinal Challenges and Regulatory Gap-Filling Using Unfair Competition Principles' (2025) 48(4) University of New South Wales Law Journal (forthcoming) <https://ssrn.com/abstract=5327096> or <http://dx.doi.org/10.2139/ssrn.5327096>.

Fritz J, 'The notion of "authorship" under EU law—who can be an author and what makes one an author? An analysis of the legislative framework and case law' (2024) 19(7) Journal of Intellectual Property Law & Practice 552 <https://doi.org/10.1093/jiplp/jpae022>.

Frosio G, 'Four Theories in Search of an A(I)uthor' in Abbott R (ed), Research Handbook of Artificial Intelligence and Intellectual Property (Edward Elgar 2022).

Frosio G, 'Should We Ban Generative AI, Incentivise it or Make it a Medium for Inclusive Creativity?' in Enrico Bonadio and Caterina Sganga (eds), A Research Agenda for EU Copyright Law (Edward Elgar) <https://ssrn.com/abstract=4527461> or <http://dx.doi.org/10.2139/ssrn.4527461>.

Frosio G, 'Generative AI in Court' in Koutras N and Selvadurai N (eds), Recreating Creativity, Reinventing Inventiveness – International Perspectives on AI and IP Governance (Routledge 2023) <https://ssrn.com/abstract=4558865> accessed 9 August 2025.

Fumagalli A, Bioeconomia e capitalismo cognitivo: verso un nuovo paradigma di accumulazione (4th reprint, 1st edn 2007, Carocci 2011).

Fumagalli A, Giuliani A, Lucarelli S and Vercellone C, Cognitive Capitalism, Welfare and Labour: The Commonfare Hypothesis (1st edn, Routledge 2019).

Gambaro A, 'Il diritto di proprietà' in Trattato Cicu-Messineo (1995).

Gambaro A, 'Consonanze e dissonanze nelle fonti dell'istituzione proprietaria' (2016) Jus Civile.

Gambino AM and Prosperetti E, 'Proprietà intellettuale nei sistemi di big data e nell'uso delle tecnologie di Intelligenza artificiale' in Giordano R, Panzarola A, Police A, Preziosi S and Proto M (eds), Il diritto nell'era digitale. Persona, Mercato, Amministrazione, Giustizia (Giuffrè 2022).

Gautier PY, Propriété littéraire et artistique (11th edn, PUF 2019).

Geiger C, Droit d'auteur et droit du public à l'information (Litec 2004).

Geiger C, "Constitutionalizing" Intellectual Property Law? The Influence of Fundamental Rights on Intellectual Property in Europe' (2006) 37(4) IIC 371.

Geiger C and others, 'Declaration. A Balanced Interpretation of the "Three-Step Test" in Copyright Law' (2010) 1 JIPITEC 119.

Geiger C, 'Flexibilising Copyright – Remedies to the Privatisation of Information by Copyright Law' (2008) 39(2) IIC 178.

Geiger C, 'Intellectual Property Shall Be Protected? – Article 17(2) of the Charter of Fundamental Rights of the European Union: A Mysterious Provision with an Unclear Scope' (2009) European Intellectual Property Review.

Geiger C, 'The Construction of Intellectual Property in the European Union: Searching for Coherence' in Geiger C (ed), Constructing European Intellectual Property: Achievements and New Perspectives, EIPIN Series Vol 1 (Edward Elgar 2013) 21.

Geiger C, 'The Social Function of Intellectual Property Rights, or How Ethics Can Influence the Shape and Use of IP Law' in Dinwoodie GB (ed), Intellectual Property Law: Methods and Perspectives (Edward Elgar 2013) 153, Max Planck Institute for Intellectual Property & Competition Law Research Paper No 13-06 <https://ssrn.com/abstract=2228067> accessed 9 August 2025.

Geiger C, 'Implementing Intellectual Property Provisions in Human Rights Instruments: Towards a New Social Contract for the Protection of Intangibles' in Geiger C (ed), Research Handbook on Human Rights and Intellectual Property (Edward Elgar 2015) 662.

Geiger C, 'Copyright as an Access Right: Securing Cultural Participation Through the Protection of Creators' Interests' in Giblin R and Weatherall K (eds), What If We Could Reimagine Copyright? (ANU Press 2017) 73, Max Planck Institute for Innovation & Competition Research Paper No 15-07 <https://ssrn.com/abstract=2643304> accessed 9 August 2025.

Geiger C, Frosio G and Bulayenko O, 'Text and Data Mining in the Proposed Copyright Reform: Making the EU Ready for an Age of Big Data?' (2018) 49 IIC 814 <https://doi.org/10.1007/s40319-018-0722-2>.

Geiger C, Frosio G and Bulayenko O, 'The Exception for Text and Data Mining (TDM) in the Proposed Directive on Copyright in the Digital Single Market – Legal Aspects' (Centre for International Intellectual Property Studies (CEIPI) Research Paper No 2018-02, 2 March 2018) <https://ssrn.com/abstract=3160586> or <http://dx.doi.org/10.2139/ssrn.3160586>.

Geiger C and Izyumenko E, 'Towards a European "Fair Use" Grounded in Freedom of Expression' [2019] SSRN Electronic Journal <https://www.ssrn.com/abstract=3379531> accessed 9 August 2025.

Geiger C, 'Promoting Creativity through Copyright Limitations: Reflections on the Concept of Exclusivity in Copyright Law, 12 Vanderbilt Journal of Entertainment and Technology Law 515 (2020).

Geiger C and Izyumenko E, 'The Constitutionalization of Intellectual Property Law in the EU and the Funke Medien, Pelham and Spiegel Online Decisions of the CJEU: Progress, But Still Some Way to Go!' (2020) 51(3) International Review of Intellectual Property and Competition Law 282, Centre for International Intellectual Property Studies (CEIPI) Research Paper No 2019-09 <https://ssrn.com/abstract=3472852> or <http://dx.doi.org/10.2139/ssrn.3472852> accessed 9 August 2025.

Geiger C, 'Elaborating a Human Rights-Friendly Copyright Framework for Generative AI' (2023) 55 IIC – International Review of Intellectual Property and Competition Law 1129.

Geiger C, Schonherr F and Jütte BJ, 'Limitation-Based Remuneration Rights as a Compromise Between Access and Remuneration Interests in Copyright Law: What Role for Collective Rights Management?' (2024) SSRN Electronic Journal <https://www.ssrn.com/abstract=4714080> accessed 11 August 2025.

Geiger C, 'Remuneration, Transparency and Copyright in the AI Act: A European Perspective' (International Association of Artificial Intelligence and Law (IAAIL), 2024).

Geiger C and Iaia V, 'The Forgotten Creator: Towards a Statutory Remuneration Right for Machine Learning of Generative AI' (2023) Computer Law & Security Review <https://papers.ssrn.com/sol3/papers.cfm?abstract_id=4594873> accessed 9 August 2025.

Geiger C and Iaia V, 'Towards an Independent EU Regulator for Copyright Issues of Generative AI: What Role for the AI Office (But More Importantly: What's Next)?' (2024) II Auteurs & Media 185 <https://ssrn.com/abstract=4914938> or <http://dx.doi.org/10.2139/ssrn.4914938>.

Gellert R, The Risk-Based Approach to Data Protection (Oxford University Press 2020).

Gervais D, 'The Machine as Author' (2020) 105 Iowa Law Review.

Gervais D, 'The Human Cause' in Abbott R (ed), Research Handbook of Artificial Intelligence and Intellectual Property (Edward Elgar 2022).

Ghidini G, Olivieri G and Falce V, 'Informazione e Big Data tra innovazione e concorrenza' in Quaderni Romani di Diritto Commerciale (Giuffrè 2018).

Ginsburg JC, 'How Copyright Got a Bad Name for Itself' (2002) 26(1) Columbia Journal of Law & the Arts 61.

Ginsburg JC, 'The Concept of Authorship in Comparative Copyright Law' [2003] SSRN Electronic Journal <http://www.ssrn.com/abstract=368481> accessed 9 August 2025.

Ginsburg JC, '"Une chose publique?" Author's Domain and the Public Domain in Early British, French and US Copyright Law' (2006) 65(3) The Cambridge Law Journal 636.

Ginsburg JC and Budiardjo LA, 'Authors and Machines' (2010) 34(2) Berkeley Technology Law Journal 343.

Ginsburg JC, 'Fair Use for Free, or Permitted-but-Paid?' (2014) 29 Berkeley Tech L J 1383 <https://scholarship.law.columbia.edu/faculty_scholarship/692>.

Ginsburg JC, 'People Not Machines: Authorship and What It Means in the Berne Convention' (2018) 49 IIC 131.

Ginsburg JC, 'Fair Use in the United States: Transformed, Deformed, Reformed?' (2020) 2020 Sing JLS 265 <https://scholarship.law.columbia.edu/faculty_scholarship/2676>.

Ginsburg JC, 'Humanist Copyright' [2025] SSRN Electronic Journal <https://www.ssrn.com/abstract=5170170> accessed 9 August 2025.

Gitelman L (ed), *"Raw Data" Is an Oxymoron* (MIT Press 2013).

Gliściński K, 'Intellectual Property Rights as Private Rights: Implications of the Theory of Internally Limited Rights and Incentive Theory for Reconstructing the Normative Content of Rights in Intangible Goods' (2025) 28 The Journal of World Intellectual Property 516.

Goasduff L, 'Is Synthetic Data the Future of AI?' (Gartner, 22 June 2022) <https://www.gartner.com/en/newsroom/press-releases/2022-06-22-is-synthetic-data-the-future-of-ai>.

Goldstein P, Stuetzle C and Bischoff S, 'Kneschke vs LAION – Landmark Ruling on TDM Exceptions for AI Training Data – Part 1' (Copyright Blog, 13 November 2024) <https://legalblogs.wolterskluwer.com/copyright-blog/kneschke-vs-laion-landmark-ruling-on-tdm-exceptions-for-ai-training-data-part-1/>.

Goldstein P, Stuetzle C and Bischoff S, 'Kneschke vs LAION – Landmark Ruling on TDM Exceptions for AI Training Data – Part 2' (Copyright Blog, 14 November 2024) <https://legalblogs.wolterskluwer.com/copyright-blog/kneschke-vs-laion-landmark-ruling-on-tdm-exceptions-for-ai-training-data-part-2/?output=pdf>.

Goold PR, 'The Curious Case of Computer-Generated Works under the Copyright, Designs and Patents Act 1988' [2021] 2 IPQ 120–129 <https://ssrn.com/abstract=4072004>.

Grassmuck VR, 'Academic Studies on the Effect of File-Sharing on the Recorded Music Industry: A Literature Review' [2010] SSRN Electronic Journal <http://www.ssrn.com/abstract=1749579> accessed 11 August 2025.

Greco P and Vercellone P, I diritti sulle opere dell'ingegno (Torino 1974)

Grewal DS, 'The Legal Constitution of Capitalism' in Boushey H, DeLong JB and Steinbaum M (eds), After Piketty: The Agenda for Economics and Inequality (Harvard University Press 2017).

Grossi P, An Alternative to Private Property: Collective Property in the Juridical Consciousness of the Nineteenth Century (Lydia G Cochran tr, University of Chicago Press 1981).

Guadamuz A, 'Do Androids Dream of Electric Copyright? Comparative Analysis of Originality in Artificial Intelligence Generated Works' in Hilty RM, Lee JA and Liu KC (eds), Artificial Intelligence and Intellectual Property (Oxford University Press 2021).

Guadamuz A, 'A Scanner Darkly: Copyright Liability and Exceptions in Artificial Intelligence Inputs and Outputs' (2024) 73(2) GRUR Int 111.

Guizzardi S, 'La protezione d'autore dell'opera dell'ingegno creata dall'Intelligenza Artificiale' (2019) AIDA XXVII.

Haggart B and Tusikov N, The New Knowledge: Information, Data and the Remaking of Global Power, vol 1 (Rowman & Littlefield Publishers 2023).

Haller S, Karnouskos S and Schroth C, 'The Internet of Things in an Enterprise Context' in John Domingue, Dieter Fensel and Paolo Traverso (eds), *First Future Internet Symposium – FIS 2008* (LNCS 5468, Springer 2009), 14–28.

Handke C, Quintais JP and Balazs B, 'The Economics of Copyright Compensation Systems for Digital Use' (2013).

Hao S, Han W, Jiang T, Li Y, Wu H, Zhong C, Zhou Z and Tang H, 'Synthetic Data in AI: Challenges, Applications, and Ethical Implications' (arXiv preprint, 3 January 2024) arXiv:2401.01629v1 [cs.LG].

Harari YN, 21 lezioni per il XXI secolo (Bompiani 2019).

Hartmann C, Allan JEM, Hugenholtz PB, Quintais JP and Gervais D, Trends and Developments in Artificial Intelligence: Challenges to Copyright (Institute for Information Law (IViR) and The Joint Institute for Innovation Policy (JIIP) 2020) <https://www.ivir.nl/publicaties/download/Trends_and_Developments_in_Artificial_Intelligence-1.pdf> accessed 9 August 2025.

Heeks R and Spiesberger P, 'Constructing an AI Value Chain and Ecosystem Model' [2024] SSRN Electronic Journal <https://www.ssrn.com/abstract=4960510> accessed 9 August 2025.

Heide T P, 'Copyright in the EU and the United States: What "Access Right"?' (2001) EIPR 476.

Hiller L and Isaacson L, Experimental Music: Composition With an Electronic Computer (McGraw-Hill 1959).

Hilty RM, Hoffmann J and Scheuerer S, 'Intellectual Property Justification for Artificial Intelligence' in Jyh-An Lee, Reto Hilty and Kung-Chung Liu (eds), *Artificial Intelligence and Intellectual Property* (1st edn, Oxford University PressOxford 2021) <https://academic.oup.com/book/39560/chapter/339430008> accessed 9 August 2025.

Hoeren T, 'Access Right as a Postmodern Symbol of Copyright Deconstruction?' in J Ginsburg and J Besek (eds), Adjuncts and Alternatives to Copyright, Proceedings of the ALAI Congress June 13–17, 2001 (Kernochan Center for Law Media and the Arts 2002) 360.

Hristov K, 'Artificial Intelligence and the Copyright Dilemma' (2017) 57(3) IDEA: The IP Law Review 453.

Hugenholtz PB (ed), The Future of Copyright in a Digital Environment (Kluwer Law International 1996).

Hugenholtz PB and Okediji R, 'Conceiving an International Instrument on Limitations and Exceptions to Copyright' (Amsterdam Law School Research Paper No 2012-43, Institute for Information Law Research Paper No 2012-37, 7 March 2012) <https://ssrn.com/abstract=2017629> or <http://dx.doi.org/10.2139/ssrn.2017629>.

Hugenholtz PB and Quintais JP, 'Copyright and Artificial Creation: Does EU Copyright Law Protect AI-Assisted Output?' (2021) 52 IIC – International Review of Intellectual Property and Competition Law 1190.

Hughes J, 'The Philosophy of Intellectual Property' (1988-1989) 77 Georgetown Law Journal.

Husa J, *Advanced Introduction to Law and Globalisation* (Edward Elgar Publishing 2018), 37.

Iaia V, 'Le derive della creatività nel diritto d'autore. Originalità, interessi finanziari, concorrenza' (26 September 2022) <https://doi.org/10.13119/11385_222500>.

Iaia V, 'To Be, or Not to Be … Original Under Copyright Law, That Is (One of) the Main Questions Concerning AI-Produced Works' (2022) 71(9) GRUR International 793.

Iaia V, Klein A and De Gaspari A, 'Stretching Copyright to AI-Generated Outputs: Case Law and Upcoming Regulations' (2025) ECTA Articles.

Iannarelli A, '"Proprietà", "immateriali", "atipicità": i nuovi scenari di tutela' in Resta G (ed), Diritti esclusivi e nuovi beni immateriali (Utet Giuridica 2010).

Ignatow G, 'Information Capitalism' in George Ritzer (ed), *The Wiley-Blackwell Encyclopedia of Globalization* (1st edn, Wiley 2017) <https://onlinelibrary.wiley.com/doi/10.1002/9780470670590.wbeog299.pub2> accessed 9 August 2025.

Inguanez D, 'A Refined Approach to Originality in EU Copyright Law in Light of the ECJ's Recent Copyright/Design Cumulation Case Law' (2020) 51 IIC 797 <https://doi.org/10.1007/s40319-020-00962-7> accessed 9 August 2025.

Irti C, Consenso "negoziato" e circolazione dei dati personali (Giappichelli 2021)

Izyumenko E, 'Freedom of Expression as a Rationale for IP Protection' (2023) 72(9) GRUR International 840–852 <https://doi.org/10.1093/grurint/ikad071>.

Jongsma D, 'The Nature and Content of the Three-Step Test in EU Copyright Law: A Reappraisal' in E Rosati (ed), Handbook of European Copyright Law (Routledge 2020) <https://ssrn.com/abstract=3665934> or <http://dx.doi.org/10.2139/ssrn.3665934>.

Josserand L, De l'esprit des droits et de leur relativité (2nd edn, Dalloz 1939, reissued 2006).

Kapczynski A, 'The Law of Informational Capitalism' (2020) 129 Yale Law Journal

Karnell GWG, 'European Originality: A Copyright Chimera' [2002] Scandinavian Studies in Law 73.

Keller P, 'Generative AI and Copyright: The Convergence of Opt-Outs' (Kluwer Copyright Blog, 23 November 2023) <https://copyrightblog.kluweriplaw.com/2023/11/23/generative-ai-and-copyright-convergence-of-opt-outs/>.

Klein PG, 'New Institutional Economics' (July 1998) <https://ssrn.com/abstract=115811> accessed 9 August 2025.

Kop M, 'AI & Intellectual Property: Towards an Articulated Public Domain' (2020) 28(1) Texas Intellectual Property Law Journal.

Kretschmer M, Margoni T and Oruç P, 'Copyright Law and the Lifecycle of Machine Learning Models' (2024) 55 IIC – International Review of Intellectual Property and Competition Law 110.

Kwet M, 'US Empire and the New Imperialism in the Global South' (2019) 60(4) *Race & Class* 3.

Laizure SC, 'Caution: ChatGPT Doesn't Know What You Are Asking and Doesn't Know What It Is Saying' (2024) 29(5) Journal of Pediatric Pharmacology and Therapeutics 558 <https://doi.org/10.5863/1551-6776-29.5.558>.

Landes WM and Posner RA, 'An Economic Analysis of Copyright Law' (1989) 18(2) The Journal of Legal Studies 325.

Larrieu J, 'Le robot et le droit d'auteur' in Mélanges A Lucas (LexisNexis 2014).

Lavagnini S, 'New York Times contro ChatGpt: ecco tutti i diritti in gioco' (Agenda Digitale, 29 December 2023) <http://agendadigitale.eu/mercati-digitali/new-york-times-contro-chatgpt-ecco-tutti-i-diritti-in-gioco/>.

Lauber-Rönsberg A and Hetmank S, 'The Concept of Authorship and Inventorship Under Pressure: Does Artificial Intelligence Shift Paradigms?' (2019) 14(7) Journal of Intellectual Property Law & Practice 576.

Lee E, 'Prompting Progress: Authorship in the Age of AI' (2024) 76 Florida Law Review <https://papers.ssrn.com/sol3/papers.cfm?abstract_id=4609687>.

Levinson J, 'Extending Art Historically' in J Levinson, The Pleasures of Aesthetics (OUP).

Libertini M, 'Tutela e promozione delle creazioni intellettuali e limiti funzionali della proprietà intellettuale' (2014) AIDA 1.

Livingston P, 'Intentionalism in Aesthetics' (1998) 29(4) New Literary History 831 <https://www.jstor.org/stable/20057514>.

Loi M, Making sense of the Digital Services Act. How to define platforms' systemic risks to democracy, AlgorithmWatch, 2023.

Lombardi EM, 'Innovazione digitale e incidenza sul paradigma proprietario: notazioni sul fenomeno "copyleft"' in Diritto privato. Nuovi orizzonti (Edizioni Scientifiche Italiane 2020).

Lorenz P, Perset K and Berryhill J, 'Initial Policy Considerations for Generative Artificial Intelligence' (2023) 1 OECD Artificial Intelligence Papers.

Lucas A and Sirinelli P, 'L'originalité en droit d'auteur' (1993) JCP G.

Lucas A, Lucas-Schloetter A and Bernault C, Traité de la propriété littéraire et artistique (5th edn, LexisNexis 2017).

Lucchi N, 'ChatGPT: A Case Study on Copyright Challenges for Generative AI Systems' (European Journal of Risk Regulation, 12 June 2023) 1–23 <https://ssrn.com/abstract=4483390> or <http://dx.doi.org/10.2139/ssrn.4483390> accessed 9 August 2025.

Lucchi N and Hunter S, 'Generative AI and Copyright – Training, Creation, Regulation' (2025) <https://www.europarl.europa.eu/RegData/etudes/STUD/2025/774095/IUST_STU(2025)774095_EN.pdf> accessed 9 August 2025.

Macario F, 'Commento all'art. 42 della Costituzione Italiana' in R Bifulco, A Celotto and M Olivetti (eds), Costituzione commentata (UTET giuridica, Torino 2006).

Macario F and Miletti MN, La funzione sociale nel diritto privato tra XX e XXI secolo. Atti dell'incontro di studio, Roma 9 ottobre 2015 (RomaTre Press 2017).

Macmillan F, 'Il diritto d'autore nell'era digitale: verso il declino dell'originalità dell'opera?' in Resta G (ed), L'Armonia del Diritto: Contributi ad una riflessione su diritto e musica (Roma TreEpress 2020) 109.

Macmillan F, '"Speaking Truth to Power": Copyright and the Control of Speech' in Pollicino O, Riccio GM and Bassini M (eds), Copyright and Fundamental Rights in the Digital Age. A Comparative Analysis in Search of a Common Constitutional Ground (Edward Elgar 2020).

Macmillan F, *Intellectual and Cultural Property: Between Market and Community* (1st edn, Routledge 2020).

Marella MR (ed), Oltre il pubblico e il privato. Per un diritto dei beni comuni (Ombre corte 2012).

Margoni T, 'The Harmonisation of EU Copyright Law: The Originality Standard' in Mark Perry (ed), *Global Governance of Intellectual Property in the 21st Century*

(Springer International Publishing 2016) <http://link.springer.com/10.1007/978-3-319-31177-7_6> accessed 9 August 2025.

Margoni T, 'Artificial Intelligence, Machine Learning and EU Copyright Law: Who Owns AI?' (2018) 1(XXVII) AIDA.

Margoni T, 'TDM Opt-Outs: Legal and Technical Considerations' in R Dreyfuss and others (eds), The Regulation of AI through IP (2025).

Marini G, 'Diritto e politica. La costruzione delle tradizioni giuridiche nell'epoca della globalizzazione' in Eppur si muove: The Age of Uniform Law. Essays in Honour of Michael Joachim Bonell to Celebrate His 70th Birthday (Unidroit 2016).

Mattei U and Pes LG, 'Civil Law and Common Law: Toward Convergence?' in Whittington KE, Kelemen RD and Caldeira GA (eds), The Oxford Handbook of Law and Politics (Oxford University Press 2008) 267.

Mattei U, Beni comuni. Un manifesto (Laterza 2011).

Mattei U, Quarta A, Valguarnera F and Fisher RJ, Property Meeting the Challenge of the Commons (Springer 2023).

Menell P, 'Intellectual Property: General Theories' in Menell P, Bouckaert B and De Geest G (eds), Encyclopedia of Law and Economics (Edward Elgar 2000).

Menell PS and others, 'Intellectual Property in the New Technological Age: 2023' [2023] SSRN Electronic Journal <https://www.ssrn.com/abstract=4507044> accessed 9 August 2025.

Messinetti D, 'Circolazione dei dati personali e dispositivi di regolazione dei poteri individuali' (1998) 16(3) Rivista critica del diritto privato 339 ff.

Mezei P, Copyright Exhaustion: Law and Policy in the United States and the European Union (Cambridge Intellectual Property and Information Law, CUP 2018).

Mezei P, 'From Leonardo to the Next Rembrandt: The Need for AI-Pessimism in the Age of Algorithms' (2020) 2 Institute of Comparative Law and Legal Theory 390–429.

Michaux B, 'Singularité technologique, singularité humaine et droit d'auteur' in Mélanges Poullet, Droit, normes et libertés dans le cybermonde (Larcier 2018).

Militsyna K, 'Human Creative Contribution to AI-Based Output – One Just Can('t) Get Enough' (2023) XX GRUR International 1.

Militsyna K, 'On the Carrot and the Stick That Unfair Competition Law Can Offer to AI-Based Work-Like Output' [2025] GRUR International ikaf098.

Miller AR, 'Copyright Protection for Computer Programs, Databases, and Computer-Generated Works: Is Anything New Since CONTU?' (1993) 106 Harv L Rev 977, 1060–1065.

Mischitelli M, 'I dati sintetici nuova frontiera dell'intelligenza artificiale: opportunità e limiti' (Agenda Digitale, 14 July 2021) <https://www.agendadigitale.eu/sicurezza/privacy/i-dati-sintetici-nuova-frontiera-dellintelligenza-artificiale-opportunita-e-limiti/>.

Moccia L, 'La comparaison juridique comme « global compass » pour l'étude du droit' (2024) 76(2) *Revue internationale de droit comparé* 7.

Mongillo R, Opere dell'ingegno, idee ispiratrici e diritto d'autore (Edizioni Scientifiche Italiane 2015).

Murray MD, 'Copyright, Originality, and the End of the Scénes à Faire and Merger Doctrines for Visual Works' (2006) Illinois Public Law and Legal Theory Research Papers Series No 06-09.

Musoni M, Karkare P, Teevan C and Domingo E, Global Approaches to Digital Sovereignty: Competing Definitions and Contrasting Policy (ECDPM Discussion Paper No 344, May 2023) <https://ecdpm.org/work/global-approaches-digital-sovereignty-competing-definitions-and-contrasting-policy> accessed 22 May 2025.

Nake F, Data, Information, and Knowledge (Science Direct Working Paper No S1574034X(04)70128 3, July 2002) (University of Bremen.

Negri A and Vercellone C, 'Il rapporto capitale/lavoro nel capitalismo cognitivo' (2007) Posse 46.

Newman CM, 'Transformation in Property and Copyright' [2010] SSRN Electronic Journal <http://www.ssrn.com/abstract=1688585> accessed 9 August 2025.

Nishijima M and Watanabe K, 'Interactive Music Composer Based on Neural Networks' (1993) 29(2) Fujitsu Scientific and Technical Journal 189.

Nivarra, 'Artificial Intelligence and Infringement of Intellectual Property: Intelligenza Artificiale e Violazione Della Proprietà Intellettuale' [2024] European Journal of Privacy Law & Technologies 84.

Nordemann JB, 'AIPPI: No Copyright Protection for AI Works Without Human Input, But Related Rights Remain' (2019) <http://copyrightblog.kluweriplaw.com/2019/11/21/aippi-no-copyright-protection-for-ai-works-without-human-input-but-related-rights-remain/> accessed 9 August 2025.

Nöth W, *Handbook of Semiotics* (First paperback ed, [4 Dr], Indiana Univ Press 1998).

Olswang S, 'Access Right: An Evolutionary Path for Copyright in the Digital Era?' (1995) EIPR 215.

Onyeagbako V, 'Justifications for Copyright and Patents Protection' (2020) <https://ssrn.com/abstract=3596193> accessed 9 August 2025.

Orlando S, 'Linguaggi di programmazione e responsabilità' (2022) Annuario OGID/Yearbook JODI.

Orlando S, 'Il diritto di Text and Data Mining (TDM) non esiste' (2023) 1 Rivista italiana di informatica e diritto.

Ostrom E, The Governing of Commons: The Evolution of Institutions for Collective Action (Cambridge University Press 1990).

Otero C, 'La protección constitucional del derecho de autor: Análisis del artículo 20.1 b/ de la Constitución española de 1978' (1986) 2 La Ley 370.

Othman A, 'Democratizing Creativity: The Rise of Generative AI in Digital Art and Storytelling' (November 2024) <https://www.researchgate.net/publication/385710773_Democratizing_Creativity_The_Rise_of_Generative_AI_in_Digital_Art_and_Storytelling> doi:10.13140/RG.2.2.11126.10563 accessed 10 June 2025.

Ottolia A, Big Data e innovazione computazionale (Giappichelli 2017).

Papadopoulou A, 'Creativity in Crisis: Are the Creations of Artificial Intelligence Worth Protecting?' (2021) 3 Journal of Intellectual Property, Information Technology and E-Commerce Law 408.

Pardolesi R and Romano R, Attuazione e tutela dei diritti, I – La concorrenza e la tutela dell'innovazione (Giuffrè 2009).

Pasa B, Industrial Design and Artistic Expression. The Challenge of Legal Protection (Brill 2020).

Pasa B, 'Copyright and Data Protection' in Senigaglia R, Irti C and Bernes A (eds), Privacy and Data Protection in Software Services (Springer 2022).

Parayil G (ed), *Political Economy and Information Capitalism in India* (Palgrave Macmillan UK 2005) <http://link.springer.com/10.1057/9780230595613> accessed 9 August 2025.

Patti S, Saggi di diritto privato comparato (Giappichelli 1986), 61, recalling Wolfgang Fikentscher, Methoden des Rechts in vergleichender Darstellung, vols I–V (JCB Mohr [Paul Siebeck] 1975–1977).

Patti S, 'La funzione sociale nella "civilistica italiana" dell'ultimo secolo' (2016) 2 Rivista critica del diritto privato.

Pentland A, 'The Data-Driven Society' (2013) 309 *Scientific American* 78, doi:10.1038/scientificamerican1013-78.; Henke N et al, *The Age of Analytics: Competing in a Data-Driven World* (McKinsey & Company 2016) https://www.mckinsey.com/business-functions/mckinsey-analytics/our-insights/the-age-of-analytics-competing-in-a-data-driven-world accessed 22 May 2025; Amanda Lee, 'Towards Informatic Personhood: Understanding Contemporary Subjects in a Data-Driven Society' (2019) *Information, Communication & Society* 1, doi:10.1080/1369118X.2019.1637446.

Peukert A, "Regulating IP Exclusion/Inclusion on a Global Scale: The Example of Copyright vs. AI Training" (Faculty of Law of Goethe University Frankfurt/M 2024) Research Paper of the Faculty of Law of Goethe University Frankfurt/M 3/2024 <https://papers.ssrn.com/abstract=4905400> accessed January 27, 2025.

Peukert A, 'Copyright in the Artificial Intelligence Act – A Primer' (2024) 73(6) GRUR International <https://ssrn.com/abstract=4771976> or <http://dx.doi.org/10.2139/ssrn.4771976> accessed 9 August 2025.

Piketty T, *Capitale e ideologia* (trad Federico Ferrone, La nave di Teseo 2020)

Pino G, 'Teorie e dottrine dei diritti della personalità. Uno studio di meta-giurisprudenza analitica' (2003) 1 Materiali per una storia della cultura giuridica 237.

Piola Caselli E, Commentario della nuova Legge 29 aprile 1941-XIX, n 633. Corredato dei lavori preparatori e di un indice delle leggi interessanti la materia (UTET 1943).

Pollicino O, Riccio GM and Bassini M, Copyright and Fundamental Rights in the Digital Age. A Comparative Analysis in Search of a Common Constitutional Ground (Edward Elgar 2020).

Pouillet E, Traité théorique et pratique des dessins et modèles de fabrique (2nd edn, Marchal et Billard 1884).

Priora G and Sganga C, 'Interim Report on EU and National Sources and Private Practices on Legitimate Uses and Flexibilities, Rethinking Digital Copyright Law for a Culturally Diverse, Accessible, Creative Europe' (Grant Agreement No 870626 2020).

Price M and Pollack M, 'The Author in Copyright: Notes for the Literary Critic' (1992) 5 Cardozo Arts & Entertainment Law Journal 703.

Pukas J and Nordemann JB, 'German Regional Court (Landgericht) of Hamburg paves the way to treat the reproduction of works as AI training data under the EU text and data mining exceptions' (Kluwer Copyright Blog, 25 October 2024) <https://legalblogs.wolterskluwer.com/copyright-blog/german-regional-court-landgericht-of-hamburg-paves-the-way-to-treat-the-reproduction-of-works-as-ai-training-data-under-the-eu-text-and-data-mining-exceptions/>.

Pugliatti S, Gli istituti del diritto civile (Milan 1943).

Pugliatti S, La proprietà nel nuovo diritto (Giuffrè, Milano 1954) 278.

Pugliatti S, La proprietà e le proprietà con riguardo particolare alla proprietà terriera (Giuffrè 1964).

Quarta A, Non-proprietà. Teoria e prassi dell'accesso ai beni (Edizioni Scientifiche Italiane 2016).

Quarta A and Smorto G, Diritto privato dei mercati digitali (Le Monnier 2020).

Quintais JP, 'Alternative Compensation Models for Large-Scale Non-Commercial Online Uses' (ALAI International Congress – 50 Years of the German Copyright Act: Remuneration for the Use of Works – Exclusivity vs. Other Approaches, Bonn, 18–20 June 2015, forthcoming in ALAI Conference Proceedings, 1 July 2015) <https://ssrn.com/abstract=2625492> accessed 9 August 2025.

Quintais JP, 'Generative AI, Copyright and the AI Act' (2025) 56 Computer Law & Security Review 106107 <https://doi.org/10.1016/j.clsr.2025.106107> or <https://ssrn.com/abstract=4912701>.

Rahmatian A, 'Originality in UK Copyright Law: The Old "Skill and Labour" Doctrine Under Pressure' (2013) 44 IIC – International Review of Intellectual Property and Competition Law 4.

Ramalho A, 'Ex Machina, Ex Auctore? Machines That Create and How EU Copyright Law Views Them' (2018) <http://copyrightblog.kluweriplaw.com/2018/11/12/ex-machina-ex-auctore-machines-that-create-and-how-eu-copyright-law-views-them/> accessed 9 August 2025.

Ramalho A, 'Originality Redux: An Analysis of the Originality Requirement in AI-Generated Works' [2019] AIDA 2–18.

Rauh Ortega AA, '"Under-the-Radar" Electronic Dance Musicians: Opportunities and Challenges with Digital Communication Technologies' (PhD thesis, University of Leeds 2018) <https://etheses.whiterose.ac.uk/21375/> accessed 9 August 2025.

Resta G (ed), 'Diritti esclusivi e nuovi beni immateriali' (Utet Giuridica 2010).

Resta G, 'Nuovi beni immateriali e numerus clausus dei diritti esclusivi' in Resta G (ed), Diritti esclusivi e 'nuovi' beni immateriali, Nuova giurisprudenza sistematica civile e commerciale (Utet Giuridica 2010).

Resta G, 'The New Frontiers of Personality Rights and the Problem of Commodification: European and Comparative Perspectives' (2011) 26 Tulane European and Civil Law Forum 33.

Resta G, 'La privatizzazione della conoscenza e la promessa dei beni comuni: riflessioni sul caso "Myriad Genetics"' (2011) Rivista critica del diritto privato 281.

Resta G, 'La privatizzazione del patrimonio culturale nell'era digitale' (2013) 1 Parolechiave.

Resta G, 'Le tassonomie e la precomprensione del comparatista' (2017) 4 Diritto pubblico comparato ed europeo.

Resta G, 'La comparazione tra diritto e storia economica: rileggendo Karl Polanyi' in Brutti M and Somma A (eds), Diritto: storia e comparazione. Nuovi propositi per un binomio antico (Max Planck Institute for European Legal History 2018) 463.

Resta G, 'Governare l'innovazione tecnologica: decisioni algoritmiche, diritti digitali e principio di uguaglianza' (2019) 2 Politica del diritto.

Resta G (ed), L'Armonia del Diritto: Contributi ad una riflessione su diritto e musica (Roma TreEpress 2020).

Riccio GM, Copyright collecting societies e regole di concorrenza (Giappichelli 2012).

Riccio GM, 'The Influence of the Court of Justice of the European Union on National Courts in Copyright Cases' in Pollicino O, Riccio GM and Bassini M (eds), Copyright and Fundamental Rights in the Digital Age. A Comparative Analysis in Search of a Common Constitutional Ground (Edward Elgar 2020).

Riccio GM and Rotolo F, 'La tutela in Italia delle opere dell'ingegno create dall'intelligenza artificiale: la necessità di un'analisi in chiave prospettica' in Pasa B (ed), Design e innovazione digitale. Dialogo interdisciplinare per un ripensamento delle tutele, Comparative Art Law – Diritto comparato dell'arte (Edizioni Scientifiche Italiane 2021).

Ricketson S, 'People or Machines: The Berne Convention and the Changing Concept of Authorship' (1991) 16 Columbia-VLA Journal of Law & the Arts 1.

Ricolfi M, 'Regulating de facto powers: shifting the focus' in *Law 2022* (Elgar 2022) ch 12, 174–84, DOI: 10.4337/9781803922256.00017.

Ricolfi M, 'Il diritto della proprietà intellettuale nella società algoritmica: fra metamorfosi e continuità' (2022) AIDA.

Rochfeld J, 'Penser autrement la propriété: la propriété s'oppose-t-elle aux "communs" ?' (2014) 3(XXVIII) Revue internationale de droit économique 351.

Rochfeld J, Martin GJ and Cornu M, L'échelle de communalité. Proposition de réformes pour intégrer les biens communs en droit, Rapport finale della «Mission de Recherche. Droit & Justice» (2021).

Rodotà S, Il terribile diritto. Studi sulla proprietà privata e i beni comuni (3rd edn, il Mulino 2013).

Romainville C, 'Cultural Diversity as a Multilevel and Multifaceted Legal Notion Operating in the Law on Cultural Policies' (2016) 22 International Journal of Cultural Policy 273.

Romano R, L'opera e l'esemplare nel diritto della proprietà intellettuale (CEDAM 2001).

Rosati E, 'Copyright Exceptions and Fair Use Defences for AI Training Done for "Research" and "Learning," or the Inescapable Licensing Horizon' [2025] European Journal of Risk Regulation 1.

Rosati E, 'Originality in US and UK Copyright Experiences as a Springboard for an EU-Wide Reform Debate' (2010) 41(5) IIC – International Review of Intellectual Property and Competition Law 524.

Rosati E, 'Closed Subject-Matter Systems Are No Longer Compatible with EU Copyright' (2014) <http://papers.ssrn.com/sol3/.papers.cfr?abstract_id=2468104> accessed 9 August 2025.

Rosati E, 'Why originality in copyright is not and should not be a meaningless requirement' (2018) 13 JIPLP 597–98.

Rosati E, 'Copyright Reformed: The Narrative of Flexibility and Its Pitfalls in Policy and Legislative Initiatives (2011–2021)' (2023) 31(1) Asia Pacific Law Review 33.

Ross P and Maynard K, 'Towards a 4th Industrial Revolution' (2021) 13(3) Intelligent Buildings International 159 <https://doi.org/10.1080/17508975.2021.1873625> accessed 22 May 2025.

Rossi G, 'L'intelligenza artificiale e la definizione di "opera dell'ingegno"' (2019) AIDA XXVII.

Rossi A, 'Opere in cerca d'autore: creatività, copyright e sistemi di Intelligenza Artificiale generativa di immagini' (2023) 4 Diritto di Internet.

Rotolo F, 'Creatività vs. originalità: la qualificazione di "opera dell'ingegno" nell'era dell'intelligenza artificiale' (2022) 2 Rassegna di Diritto della Moda e delle Arti.

Rotolo F, 'Diritto d'autore e Intelligenza Artificiale: il controllo dei contenuti online tramite sistemi di automatic filtering' in Camardi C (ed), La via Europea per l'intelligenza artificiale (CEDAM 2023).

Roveda L and others, 'A Human-Centric Framework for Robotic Task Learning and Optimization' (Social Science Research Network, 31 May 2022) <https://papers.ssrn.com/abstract=4124468> accessed 12 June 2025.

Rowley JE, 'The Wisdom Hierarchy: Representations of the DIKW Hierarchy' (2007) 33(2) Journal of Information Science 163 <https://doi.org/10.1177/0165551506070706>.

Sacco R, La proprietà (Giappichelli 1968).

Salvi C, 'Modelli di proprietà e principi costituzionali' (1986) Rivista critica del diritto privato 317.

Salvi C, L'invenzione della proprietà. La destinazione universale dei beni e i suoi nemici (Marsilio Editori 2021).

Samoili S, Lopez Cobo M, Gomez Gutierrez E, De Prato G, Martinez-Plumed F and Delipetrev B, AI Watch. Defining Artificial Intelligence, EUR 30117 EN (Publications Office of the European Union 2020).

Samuelson P, 'Allocating Ownership Rights in Computer-Generated Works' (1985) 47 U Pitt L Rev 1185, 1186–1187.

Samuelson P, 'Does Using In-Copyright Works as Training Data Infringe?' (Copyright Blog, 18 July 2025) <https://legalblogs.wolterskluwer.com/copyright-blog/does-using-in-copyright-works-as-training-data-infringe/>.

Sanseverino G, 'Ex machina. La novità e l'originalità dell'invenzione "prodotta" dall'AI' (2019) AIDA XXVII.

Sarti D, 'Il "giusto compenso" delle licenze dei gestori collettivi dei diritti d'autore nell'evoluzione della giurisprudenza statunitense' in Bertani M and Sarti D, Studi per Luigi Carlo Ubertazzi. Proprietà intellettuale e concorrenza (Giuffrè 2019) 719.

Scalzini S, 'Fattispecie costitutiva del diritto d'autore' in Genovese A and Olivieri G (eds), Proprietà intellettuale. Segni distintivi, brevetti, diritto d'autore (Wolters Kluwer 2021) 976.

Scarciglia R, Metodi e comparazione giuridica (3rd edn, Wolters Kluwer 2021).

Scarciglia R, *Methods and Legal Comparison: Challenges for Methodological Pluralism* (Edward Elgar Publishing 2023).

Screpanti E, 'Capitalist Forms and the Essence of Capitalism' (1999) 6 Review of International Political Economy 1.

Sejnowski TJ, *The Deep Learning Revolution* (MIT Press 2018).

Senftleben M, Copyright, Limitations and the Three-Step Test (Kluwer Law International 2004) 177, 198–201.

Senftleben M, 'Generative AI and Author Remuneration' (2023) 54 IIC 1535.

Senftleben M, 'TDM, GenAI and the Copyright Three-Step Test' (24 July 2025) <https://ssrn.com/abstract=5373903>.

Senigaglia R, 'La dimensione patrimoniale del diritto alla protezione dei dati personali' (2020) 2 Contratto e Impresa.

Senigaglia R, Irti C and Bernes A (eds), Privacy and Data Protection in Software Services (Springer 2022).

Sganga C, 'EU Copyright Law Between Property and Fundamental Rights: A Proposal to Connect the Dots' in Roberto Caso and Federica Giovanella (eds), *Balancing Copyright Law in the Digital Age* (Springer Berlin Heidelberg 2015) <http://link.springer.com/10.1007/978-3-662-44648-5_1> accessed 9 August 2025.

Sganga C, *Propertizing European Copyright* (Edward Elgar Publishing 2018) <https://www.elgaronline.com/view/9781786430403.xml> accessed 9 August 2025.

Sganga C, 'A New Era for EU Copyright Exceptions and Limitations? Judicial Flexibility and Legislative Discretion in the Aftermath of the CDSM Directive and the Trio of the Grand Chamber of the CJEU' (2020) 21 ERA Forum 311 <https://ssrn.com/abstract=3804228> accessed 9 August 2025.

Sganga C, 'Multilevel Constitutionalism and the Propertisation of EU Copyright: An Even Higher Protection or a New Structural Limitation?' in Jonathan Griffiths and Tuomas Mylly (eds), *Global Intellectual Property Protection and New Constitutionalism* (1st edn, Oxford University PressOxford 2021) <https://academic.oup.com/book/41133/chapter/350650490> accessed 9 August 2025.

Sganga C and others, 'Copyright Flexibilities: Mapping and Comparative Assessment of EU and National Sources' (2023) <https://ssrn.com/abstract=4325376> accessed 9 August 2025.

Sganga C, 'The Past, Present and Future of EU Copyright Flexibilities' (2024) 55 IIC – International Review of Intellectual Property and Competition Law 5.

Shakespeare D, Porcaro L, Gómez E and Castillo C, 'Exploring Artist Gender Bias in Music Recommendation' (25 September 2020) Proceedings of the 2nd Workshop on the Impact of Recommender Systems (ImpactRS, ACM RecSys 2020).

Shestak JJ, 'The Philosophical Foundations of Human Rights' in Symonides J (ed), Human Rights: Concepts and Standards (Unesco/Ashgate Publishing 2002).

Sica S and D'Antonio V, 'La commodification dei dati personali nella data driven society' in Stanzione P (ed), I "Poteri privati" delle piattaforme e le nuove frontiere della privacy (Giappichelli 2022) 129.

Sirotti Gaudenzi A, Il nuovo diritto d'autore (Maggioli Editore 2016).

Somma A, Diritto: storia e comparazione. Nuovi propositi per un binomio antico, vol 11 (Massimo Brutti ed, 1st edn, Max Planck Institute for European Legal History 2018) <http://www.rg.mpg.de/publikationen/gplh-11> accessed 9 August 2025.

Southerton C, 'Datafication' in Laurie A Schintler and Connie L McNeely (eds), *Encyclopedia of Big Data* (Springer, Cham 2022) https://doi.org/10.1007/978-3-319-32010-6_332 accessed 10 June 2025.

Synodinou TE, 'Lawfulness for Users in European Copyright Law: Acquis and Perspectives' (2019) 10 JIPITEC 20.

Synodinou TE and others (eds), EU Internet Law in the Digital Single Market (Springer International Publishing 2021) <https://link.springer.com/10.1007/978-3-030-69583-5> accessed 9 August 2025.

Synodinou TE, 'Navigating User Lawfulness in European Copyright Law: From Lawful Use to Lawful Access' (Kluwer Copyright Blog, 19 March 2025) <https://legalblogs.wolterskluwer.com/copyright-blog/navigating-user-lawfulness-in-european-copyright-law-from-lawful-use-to-lawful-access/> accessed 9 August 2025.

Spada P, 'Banche di dati e diritto d'autore (Il "genere" del diritto d'autore sulle banche di dati)' (1997) AIDA.

Spedicato G, Interesse pubblico e bilanciamento nel diritto d'autore (Giuffrè 2013).

Spedicato G, 'Creatività Artificiale, Mercato e Proprietà Intellettuale' (2019) 4 Rivista di diritto industriale 253.

Spedicato G, Principi di diritto d'autore (il Mulino 2020).

Spina Alì G, 'The Times They Are AI-Changin': Copyright and Computer Generated Works' [2019] AIDA 367–399.

Spina Alì G, 'Why Intellectual Property Does Not Belong in the Constitution(s): Four Considerations' (2020) 42(8) European Intellectual Property Review.

Stehr N, *Knowledge Capitalism* (1st edn, Routledge 2022) <https://www.taylorfrancis.com/books/9781003296157> accessed 9 August 2025.

Stieper M and Denga M, The International Reach of EU Copyright Through the AI Act (Institut für Wirtschaftsrecht, 2024).

Stokes S, 'Art and Copyright: Some Current Issues' (2006) 1(4) Journal of Intellectual Property Law & Practice.

Strowel A, 'ChatGPT and Generative AI Tools: Theft of Intellectual Labor?' (2023) 54 IIC 491 <https://doi.org/10.1007/s40319-023-01321-y>.

Takamura G, Nishide T, Kanazawa Y and Hayashi M, 'Bundle of Rights Reversed: Anticommons in a Japanese Common Property Forest Due to Legalization' (2021) 15(1) International Journal of the Commons 259 <https://doi.org/10.5334/ijc.1080>.

Toews R, 'Synthetic Data Is About To Transform Artificial Intelligence' (Forbes, 12 June 2022) <https://www.forbes.com/sites/robtoews/2022/06/12/synthetic-data-is-about-to-transform-artificial-intelligence/>.

Traina Chiarini R, 'Può essere protetta l'opera creata da A.I.? La questione arriva in Cassazione' (1 March 2023) Quotidiano Più <www.altalex.com>; accessed 9 August 2025.

Turing A, 'Computing Machinery and Intelligence' (1950) LIX(36) Mind.

Ubertazzi LC, Commentario breve alle leggi su proprietà intellettuale e concorrenza (6th edn, CEDAM 2016).

US Copyright Office, Sixty-Eighth Annual Report of the Register of Copyrights for the Fiscal Year Ending June 30, 1965 (1966) 5 https://www.copyright.gov/reports/annual/archive/ar-1965.pdf.

US Copyright Office, Compendium of US Copyright Office Practices § 101 (3rd edn 2021).

US Copyright Office, 'Copyright Registration Guidance, Works Containing Materials Generated by Artificial Intelligence' 88 FR 16190 (16 March 2023) https://copyright.gov/ai/ai_policy_guidance.pdf.

US Copyright Office, Copyright and Artificial Intelligence: Part 1 – Digital Replicas: A Report of the Register of Copyrights (July 2024) https://www.copyright.gov/ai/Copyright-and-Artificial-Intelligence-Part-1-Digital-Replicas-Report.pdf.

US Copyright Office, Copyright and Artificial Intelligence: Part 2 – Copyrightability: A Report of the Register of Copyrights (January 2025) <https://www.copyright.gov/ai/Copyright-and-Artificial-Intelligence-Part-2-Copyrightability-Report.pdf>.

US Copyright Office, Copyright and Artificial Intelligence: Part 3 – Generative AI Training pre-publication version: A Report of the Register of Copyrights (July 2024) <https://www.copyright.gov/ai/Copyright-and-Artificial-Intelligence-Part-3-Generative-AI-Training-Report-Pre-Publication-Version.pdf>.

Valk E and Toepoel I, 'DPG Media et al vs HowardsHome – A National Ruling on DSM's Press Publishers' Rights and TDM Exceptions' (Copyright Blog, 16 January 2025) <https://legalblogs.wolterskluwer.com/copyright-blog/dpg-media-et-al-vs-howardshome-a-national-ruling-on-dsms-press-publishers-rights-and-tdm-exceptions/>.

Van Gompel S and Lavik E, 'Quality, Merit, Aesthetics and Purpose: An Inquiry into EU Copyright Law's Eschewal of Other Criteria than Originality' (2013) Amsterdam Law School Legal Studies Research Papers No 51.

Varano V and Barsotti V, La tradizione giuridica occidentale: Testo e materiali per un confronto civil law common law (8th edn, Giappichelli 2024).

Vercellone C (ed), Capitalismo cognitivo: conoscenza e finanza nell'epoca postfordista (Manifestolibri 2006).

Vercellone C, The Hypothesis of Cognitive Capitalism (Birkbeck College and SOAS 2005) <https://halshs.archives-ouvertes.fr/halshs-00273641> accessed 10 June 2025.

Vivant M, 'Propriété intellectuelle et nouvelles technologies, À la recherche d'un nouveau paradigm' in Université de tous les savoirs, Qu'est-ce que les technologies?, vol 5 (Odile Jacob 2001).

Vivant M, 'Intelligence artificielle et propriété intellectuelle' (2018) 11 Communication – Commerce électronique 4.

Vivant M and Bruguiere JM, Droit d'auteur et droits voisins (4th edn, Dalloz 2019).

Wachowicz M, 'The Role of Artificial Intelligence on the Promotion of Cultural Diversity and Intellectual Property Rights' (2024) 55 IIC – International Review of Intellectual Property and Competition Law 1221.

Wang Y and Zhang J, 'Beijing Internet Court Grants Copyright to AI-Generated Image for the First Time' (Legal Blogs, 2 February 2024) <https://legalblogs.wolterskluwer.com/copyright-blog/beijing-internet-court-grants-copyright-to-ai-generated-image-for-the-first-time/>.

Webster F, *Theories of the Information Society* (2nd edn, Routledge 2002).

Wittem Project, European Copyright Code (2010) <https://www.ivir.nl/copyright code/>.

Wolff EN, *Top Heavy: The Increasing Inequality of Wealth in America and What Can Be Done About It* (The New Press 1995).
Wymeersch P, 'EU Copyright Exceptions and Limitations and the Three-Step Test: One Step Forward, Two Steps Back' (2023) 72(7) GRUR International 631 <https://doi.org/10.1093/grurint/ikad019>.
Zaccaria G, Postdiritto. Nuove fonti, nuove categorie (il Mulino 2022).
Zolynski C, 'L'œuvre de l'esprit: un original, des originaux' in Bensamoun A, Labarthe F and Tricoire A (eds), L'oeuvre de l'esprit en question(s). Un exercice de qualification (mare & martin 2015).
Zuboff S, 'Big Other: Surveillance Capitalism and the Prospects of an Information Civilization' (2015) 30 Journal of Information Technology 75 <https://ssrn.com/abstract=2594754> accessed 9 August 2025.
Zuboff S, Il capitalismo della sorveglianza. Il futuro dell'umanità nell'era dei nuovi poteri (LUISS University Press 2019).
Zuboff S, The Age of Surveillance Capitalism: The Fight for a Human Future at the New Frontier of Power (Profile Books 2019).

Essential CJEU Jurisprudence

Case C-5/08 Infopaq International A/S v Danske Dagblades Forening [2009] ECR I-6569.
Case C-393/09 Bezpečnostní softwarová asociace – Svaz softwarové ochrany v Ministerstvo kultury [2010] ECR I-13971 (BSA).
Joined Cases C-403/08 and C-429/08 Football Association Premier League Ltd and Others v QC Leisure and Others [2011] ECR I-9083 (FAPL).
Case C-145/10 Eva-Maria Painer v Standard VerlagsGmbH and Others [2011] ECR I-12533.
Case C-604/10 Football Dataco Ltd and Others v Yahoo! UK Ltd and Others EU:C:2012:115.
Case C-406/10 SAS Institute Inc v World Programming Ltd EU:C:2012:259.
Case C-310/17 Levola Hengelo BV v Smilde Foods BV EU:C:2018:899.
Case C-469/17 Funke Medien NRW GmbH v Bundesrepublik Deutschland EU:C:2019:623.
Case C-476/17 Pelham GmbH and Others v Ralf Hütter and Florian Schneider-Esleben EU:C:2019:624.
Case C-516/17 Spiegel Online GmbH v Volker Beck EU:C:2019:625.
Case C-683/17 Cofemel – Sociedade de Vestuário SA v G-Star Raw CV EU:C:2019:721.

Main EU regulatory references

Charter of Fundamental Rights of the European Union [2000] OJ C364/1.

Directive 96/9/EC of the European Parliament and of the Council of 11 March 1996 on the legal protection of databases [1996] OJ L77/20.

Directive 2001/29/EC of the European Parliament and of the Council of 22 May 2001 on the harmonisation of certain aspects of copyright and related rights in the information society [2001] OJ L167/10.

Directive 2004/48/EC of the European Parliament and of the Council of 29 April 2004 on the enforcement of intellectual property rights [2004] OJ L195/16.

Directive 2006/116/EC of the European Parliament and of the Council of 12 December 2006 on the term of protection of copyright and certain related rights (codified version) [2006] OJ L372/12.

Directive 2009/24/EC of the European Parliament and of the Council of 23 April 2009 on the legal protection of computer programs [2009] OJ L111/16.

Directive (EU) 2019/790 of the European Parliament and of the Council of 17 April 2019 on copyright and related rights in the Digital Single Market and amending Directives 96/9/EC and 2001/29/EC [2019] OJ L130/92.

Regulation (EU) 2022/1925 of the European Parliament and of the Council of 14 September 2022 on fair and contestable markets in the digital sector and amending Directives (EU) 2019/1937 and (EU) 2020/1828 (Digital Markets Act) [2022] OJ L265/1.

Regulation (EU) 2022/2065 of the European Parliament and of the Council of 19 October 2022 on a single market for digital services and amending Directive 2000/31/EC (Digital Services Act) [2022] OJ L277/1.

Regulation (EU) 2024/1689 of the European Parliament and of the Council of 13 June 2024 laying down harmonised rules on artificial intelligence and amending Regulations (EC) No 300/2008, (EU) No 167/2013, (EU) No 168/2013, (EU) 2018/858, (EU) 2018/1139 and (EU) 2019/2144 and Directives 2014/90/EU, (EU) 2016/797.

Main normative references in international law

Berne Convention for the Protection of Literary and Artistic Works (adopted 9 September 1886, last amended 28 September 1979).

UN General Assembly, Universal Declaration of Human Rights (adopted 10 December 1948 UNGA Res 217 A(III)).

Council of Europe, Convention for the Protection of Human Rights and Fundamental Freedoms (European Convention on Human Rights, as amended) (adopted 4 November 1950, entered into force 3 September 1953) ETS 5.

UN General Assembly, International Covenant on Economic, Social and Cultural Rights (adopted 16 December 1966, entered into force 3 January 1976) 993 UNTS 3.
Marrakesh Agreement Establishing the World Trade Organization, Annex 1C: Agreement on Trade-Related Aspects of Intellectual Property Rights (TRIPS Agreement) (signed 15 April 1994, entered into force 1 January 1995) 1869 UNTS 299.
WIPO, Convention Establishing the World Intellectual Property Organization (signed 14 July 1967, entered into force 26 April 1970) 828 UNTS 3.
WIPO Copyright Treaty (adopted 20 December 1996, entered into force 6 March 2002) 2186 UNTS 121.

Index

© 2026 KONINKLIJKE BRILL BV, LEIDEN | HTTPS://DOI.ORG/10.1163/9789004730731-015

www.ingramcontent.com/pod-product-compliance
Lightning Source LLC
LaVergne TN
LVHW081641161026
850117LV00052B/24